ONCE UPON [A TIME] AT THE END OF THE WORLD™

PRAISE FOR **ONCE UPON A TIME AT THE END OF THE WORLD**:

"*Once Upon a Time...* is both small and grand, a post-apocalyptic story at the beginning of love. It's lyrical and natural and beautiful, thanks to the lovely art by Alexandre Tefenkgi and Lee Loughridge, with support from the legendary Nick Dragotta and Rico Renzi. This is sweet and sad, fun and scary. A perfect issue one and you should let your retailer know to order one million of them."

—CHIP ZDARSKY (SEX CRIMINALS)

"Drew me in straight away, kept me reading to the end. A hearty recommendation for *Once Upon a Time at the End of the World.*"

—GARTH ENNIS (PREACHER)

"I haven't read a comic so overflowing with charm, sadness, violence, terror, and madness since Saga #1. I loved every single panel. This is your new favorite book, I promise."

—MATTHEW ROSENBERG (WHAT'S THE FURTHEST PLACE FROM HERE?)

"Jason is one of my favorite writers, and this is one of his most personal stories."

—ED BRUBAKER (FRIDAY)

Published by

BOOM! STUDIOS™

BOOK ONE

LOVE IN THE
WASTELAND

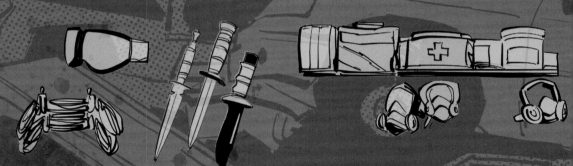

PON A TIME
HE END
HE WORLD™

WRITTEN BY.. JASON AARON

ILLUSTRATED BY...........ALEXANDRE TEFENKGI

COLORED BY .... LEE LOUGHRIDGE

FLASH-FORWARD SEQUENCES
ILLUSTRATED BY..NICK DRAGOTTA
COLORED BY ....RICO RENZI

LETTERED BY...................... ANDWORLD DESIGN

COVER BY..MIKE DEL MUNDO

LOGO DESIGNER.............................. **Jared K. Fletcher**
DESIGNER....................................... **Madison Goyette**

ASSISTANT EDITOR.......................... **Caroline Butler**
EDITOR.. **Allyson Gronowitz**
EXECUTIVE EDITOR............................ **Sierra Hahn**

BOOM! STUDIOS

ONCE UPON A TIME AT THE END OF THE WORLD Book One, June 2023. Published by BOOM! Studios, a division of Boom Entertainment, Inc., 6920 Melrose Ave, Los Angeles, CA 90038-3306. ONCE UPON A TIME AT THE END OF THE WORLD is ™ & © 2023 Golgonooza, Inc. Originally published in single magazine form as ONCE UPON A TIME AT THE END OF THE WORLD No. 1-5. ™ & © 2022, 2023 Golgonooza, Inc. All rights reserved. BOOM! Studios™ and the BOOM! Studios logo are trademarks of Boom Entertainment, Inc., registered in various countries and categories. All characters, events, and institutions depicted herein are fictional. Any similarity between any of the names, characters, persons, events, and/or institutions in this publication to actual names, characters, and persons, whether living or dead, events, and/or institutions is unintended and purely coincidental. BOOM! Studios does not read or accept unsolicited submissions of ideas, stories, or artwork.

BOOM! Studios, 6920 Melrose Ave, Los Angeles, CA 90038-3306. Printed in Canada. First Printing.

ISBN: 978-1-68415-907-9
eISBN: 978-1-64668-879-1

Ross Richie Chairman & Founder
Jen Harned CFO
Matt Gagnon Editor-in-Chief
Filip Sablik President, Publishing & Marketing
Stephen Christy President, Development
Adam Yoelin Senior Vice President, Film
Lance Kreiter Vice President, Licensing & Merchandising
Bryce Carlson Vice President, Editorial & Creative Strategy
Josh Hayes Vice President, Sales
Eric Harburn Executive Editor
Ryan Matsunaga Director, Marketing
Stephanie Lazarski Director, Operations
Mette Norkjaer Director, Development
Elyse Strandberg Manager, Finance
Michelle Ankley Manager, Production Design
Cheryl Parker Manager, Human Resources
Rosalind Morehead Manager, Retail Sales

Please be advised, this book contains sensitive subject matters related to suicide. If you or someone you know is having thoughts of suicide, you can call the National Suicide Prevention Lifeline at (800) 273-8255. A caller is connected to a certified crisis center near where the call is placed. The call is free and confidential.

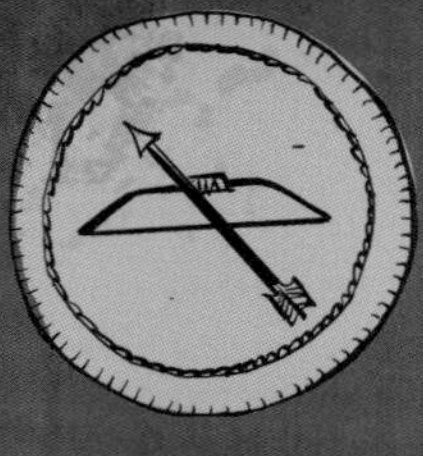
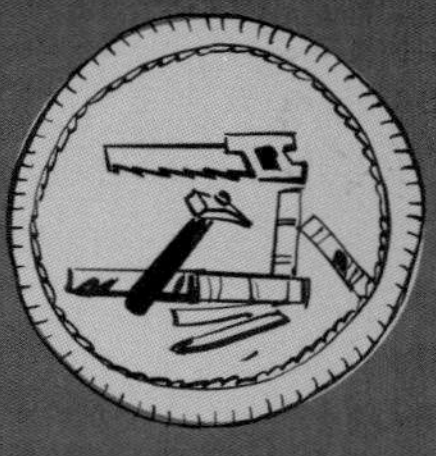
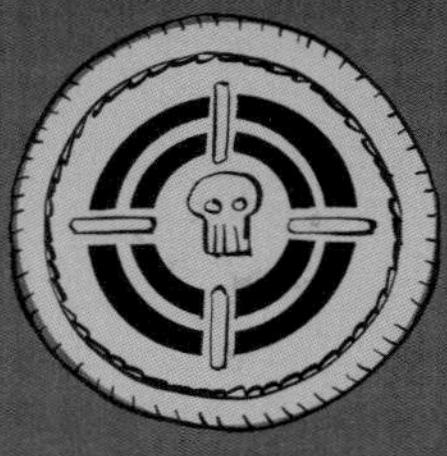
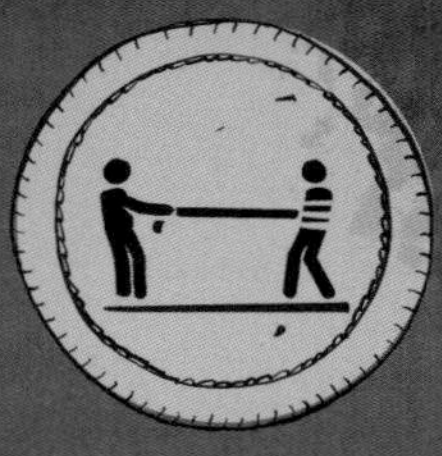

TABLE OF CONTENTS

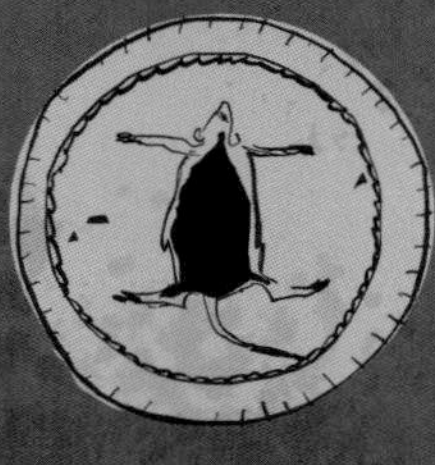
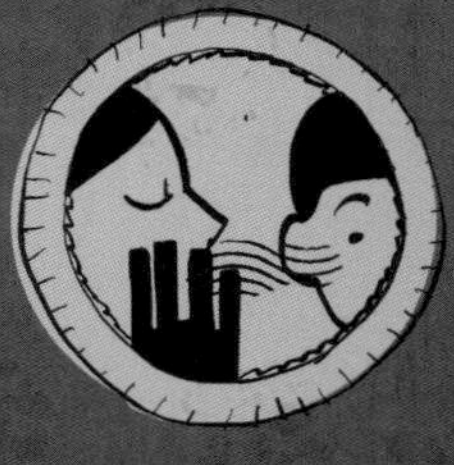
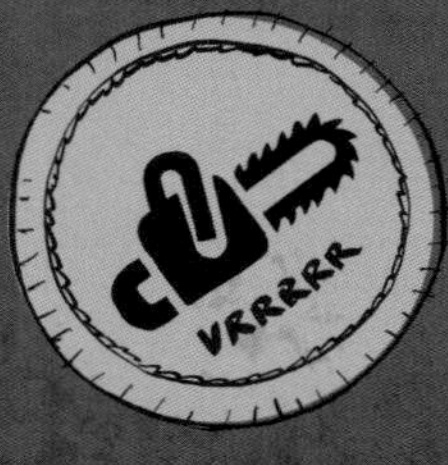
VRRRRR
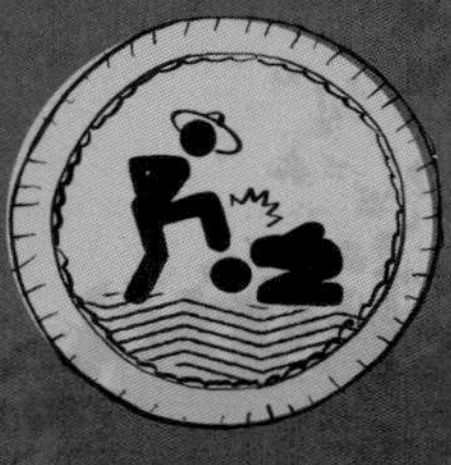

CHAPTER ONE

THE TOWER
IN THE SEA

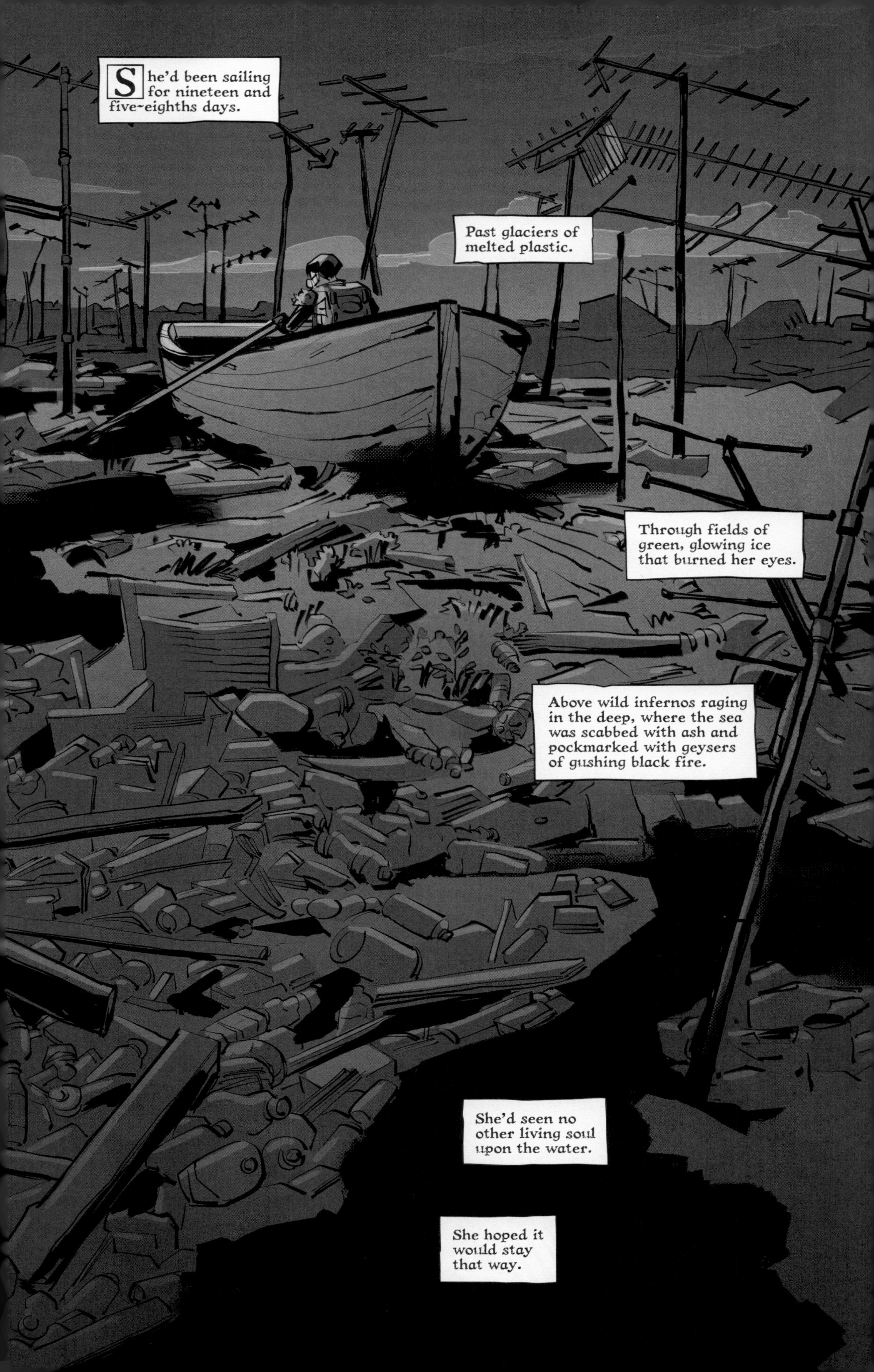
She'd been sailing for nineteen and five-eighths days.
Past glaciers of melted plastic.
Through fields of green, glowing ice that burned her eyes.
Above wild infernos raging in the deep, where the sea was scabbed with ash and pockmarked with geysers of gushing black fire.
She'd seen no other living soul upon the water.
She hoped it would stay that way.

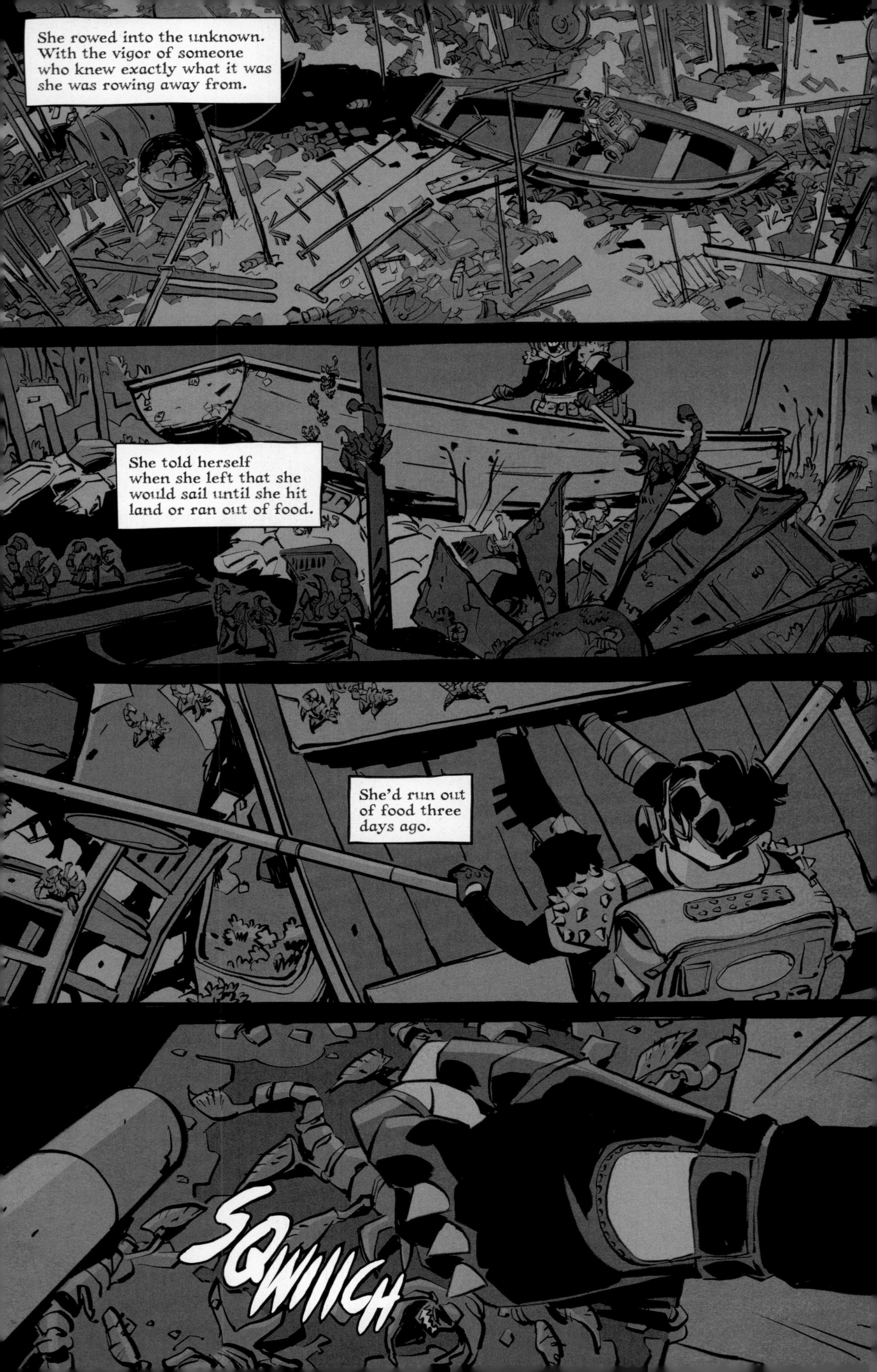
She rowed into the unknown. With the vigor of someone who knew exactly what it was she was rowing away from.
She told herself when she left that she would sail until she hit land or ran out of food.
She'd run out of food three days ago.
SQWIICH

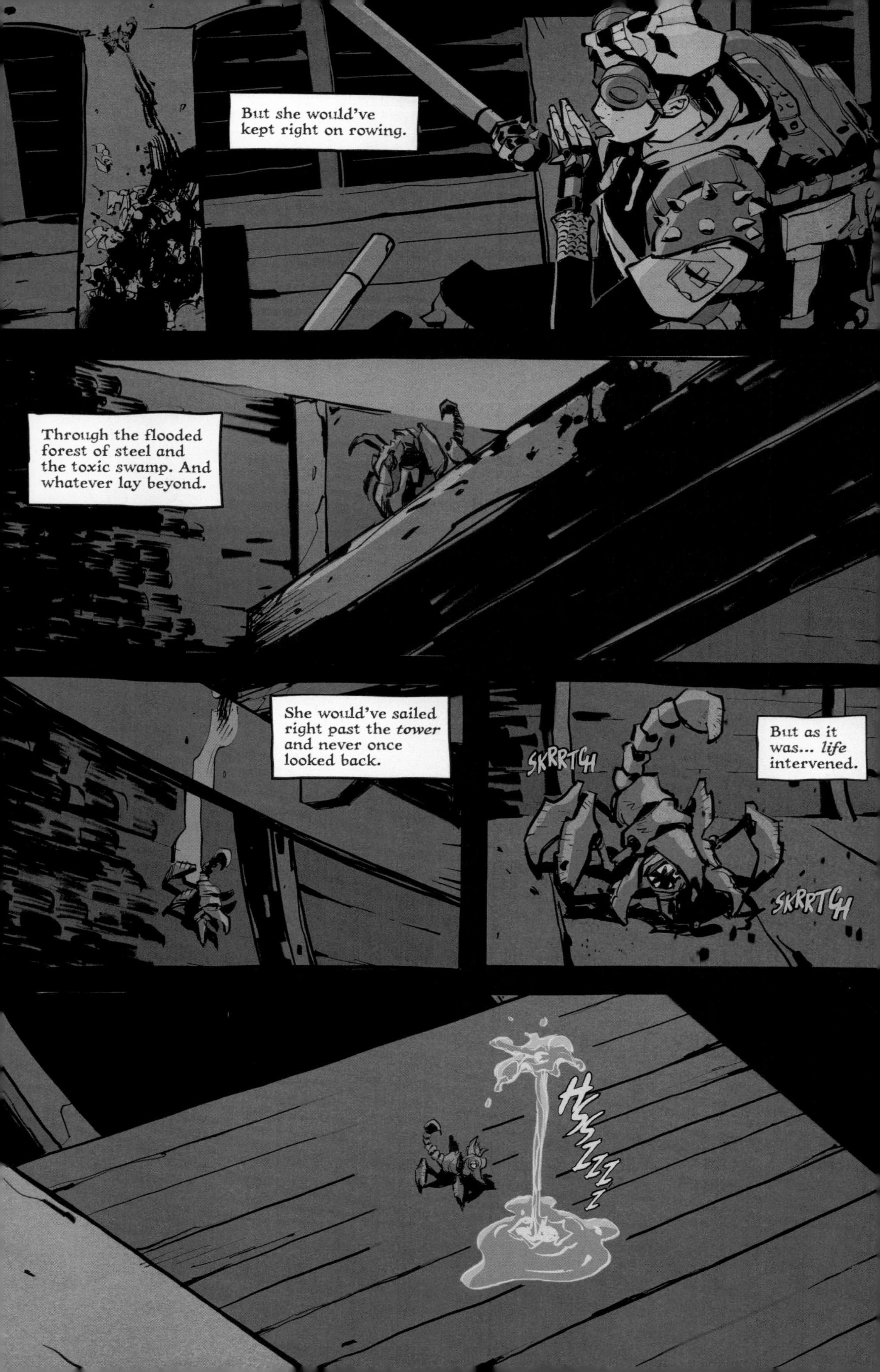
But she would've kept right on rowing.
Through the flooded forest of steel and the toxic swamp. And whatever lay beyond.
She would've sailed right past the *tower* and never once looked back.
But as it was... *life* intervened.
SKRRTCH
SKRRTCH
HSSZZZZ

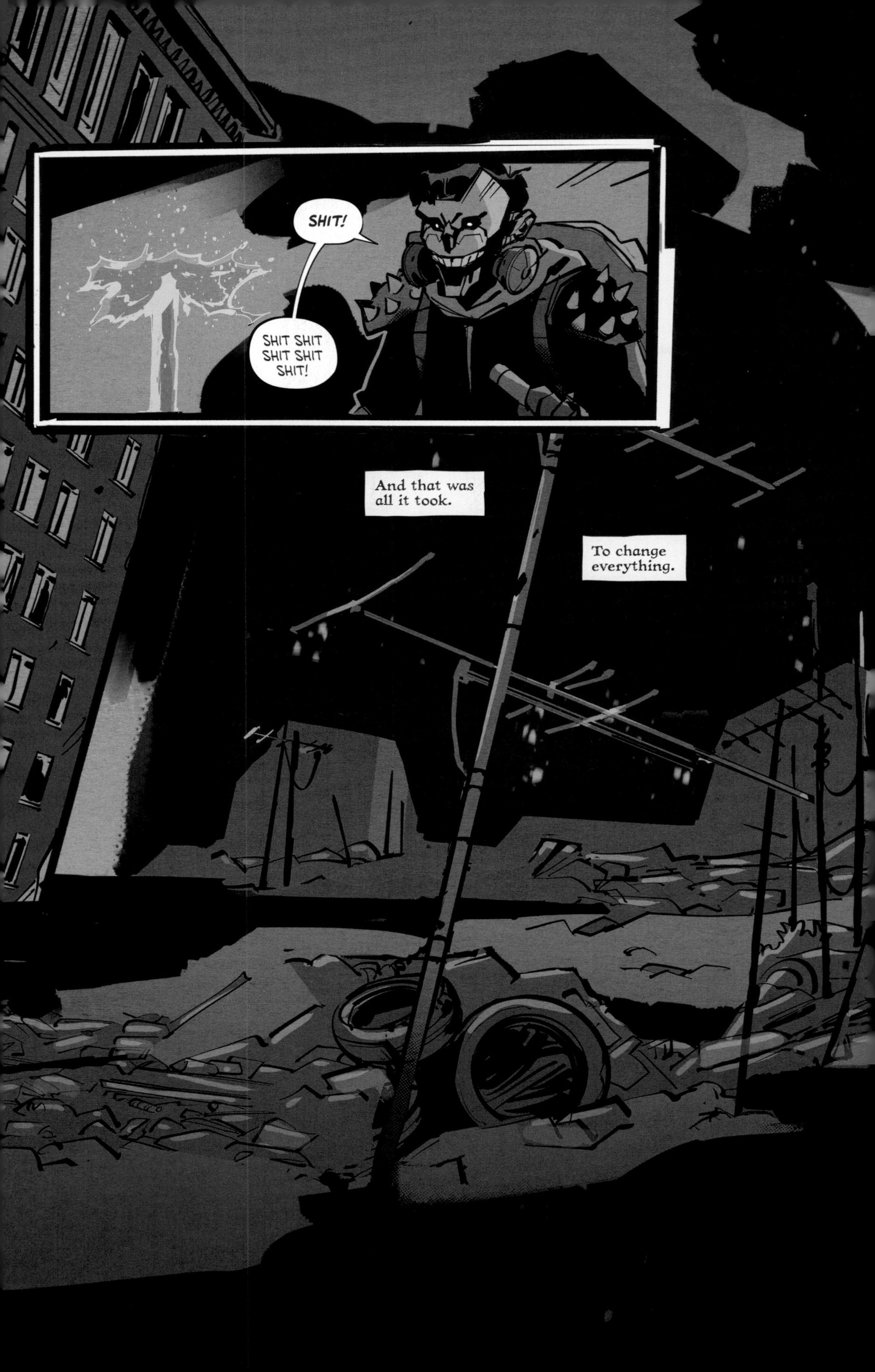
SHIT!
SHIT SHIT SHIT SHIT SHIT!
And that was all it took.
To change everything.

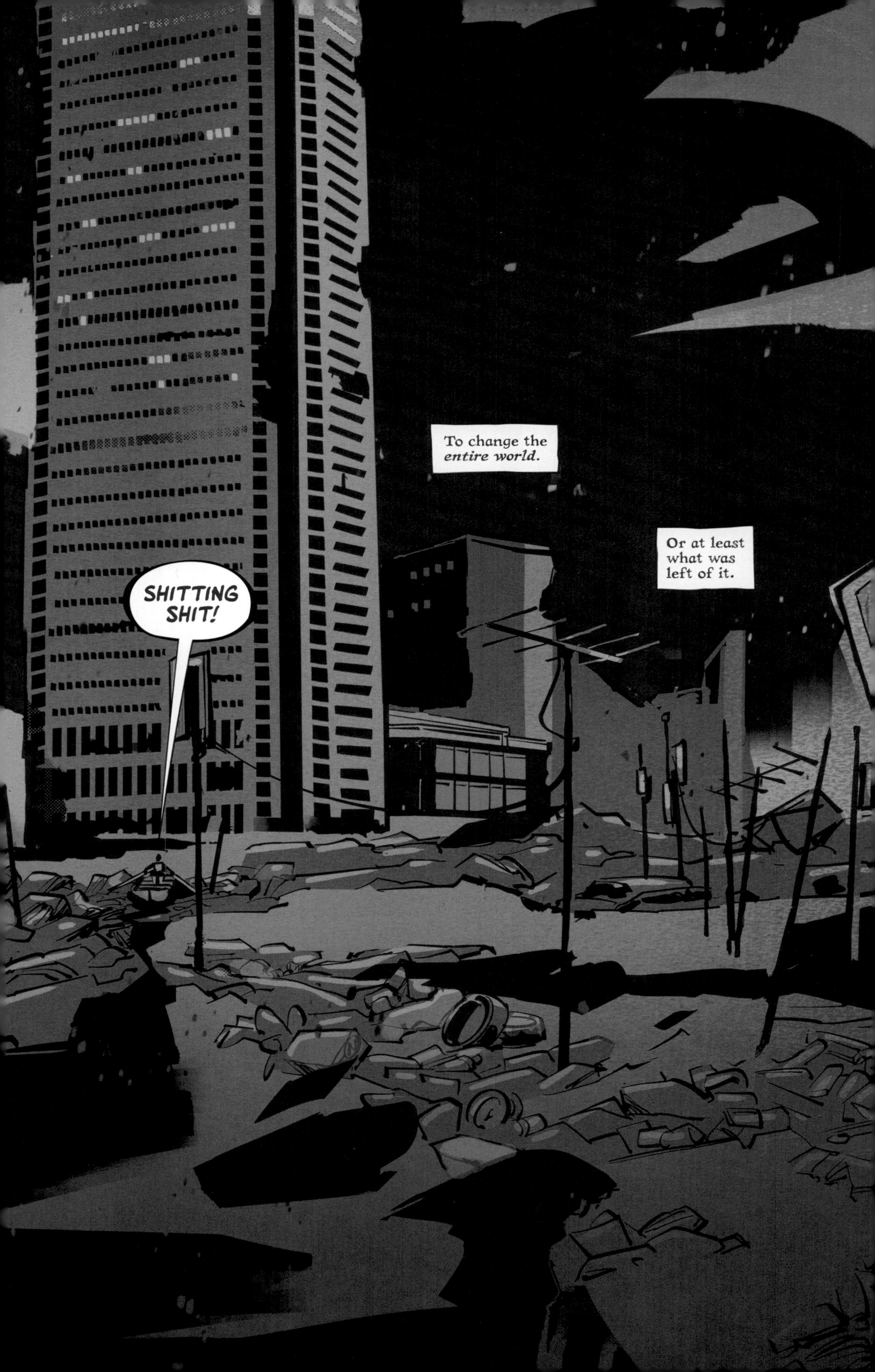
To change the *entire world*.
Or at least what was left of it.
SHITTING SHIT!

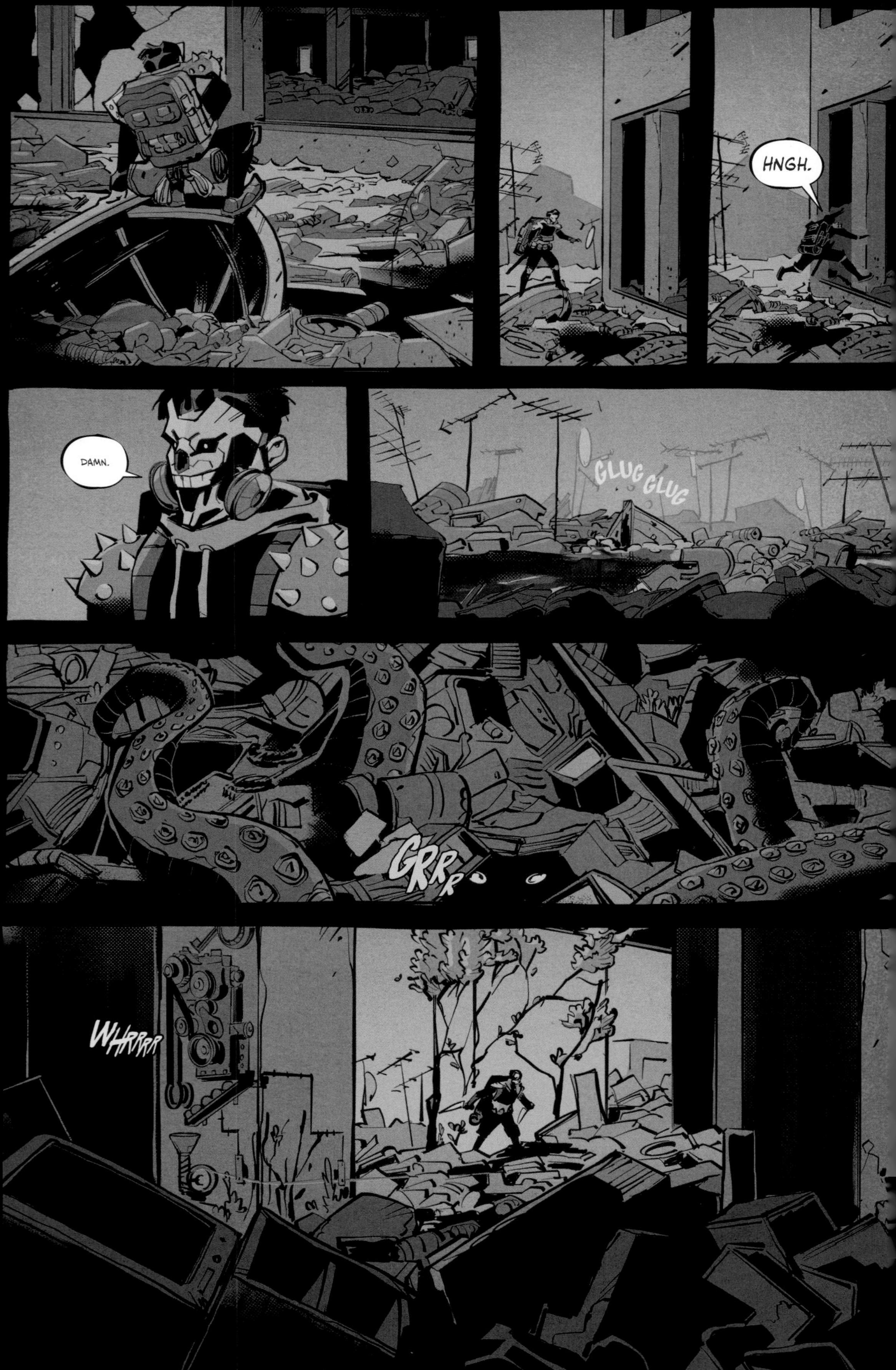
HNGH.
DAMN.
GLUG GLUG
GRRR
WHRRRR

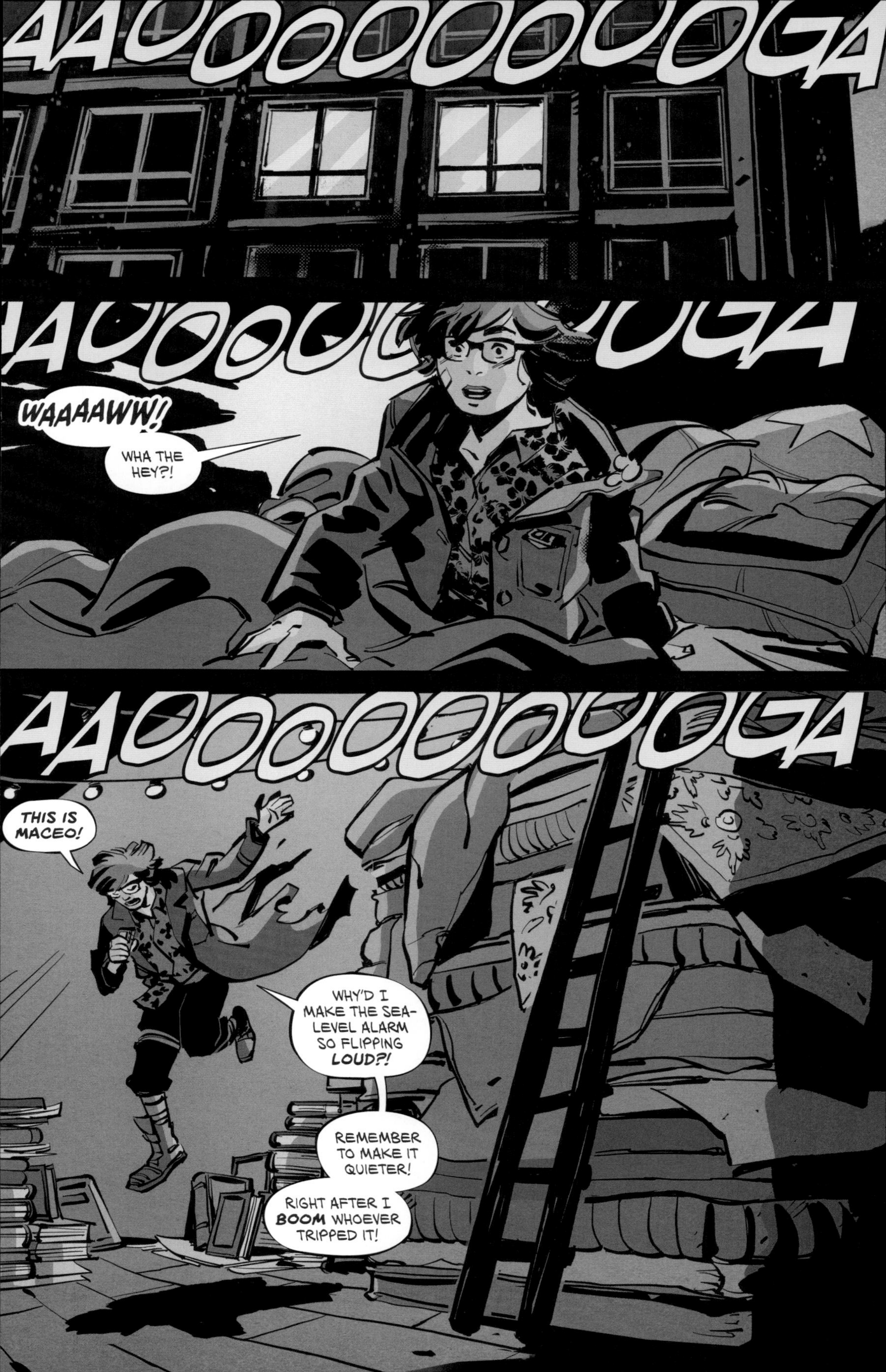
AAOOOOOOOOOGA
AAOOOOOOOOOGA
WAAAAWW!
WHA THE HEY?!
AAOOOOOOOOOGA
THIS IS MACEO!
WHY'D I MAKE THE SEA-LEVEL ALARM SO FLIPPING LOUD?!
REMEMBER TO MAKE IT QUIETER!
RIGHT AFTER I BOOM WHOEVER TRIPPED IT!

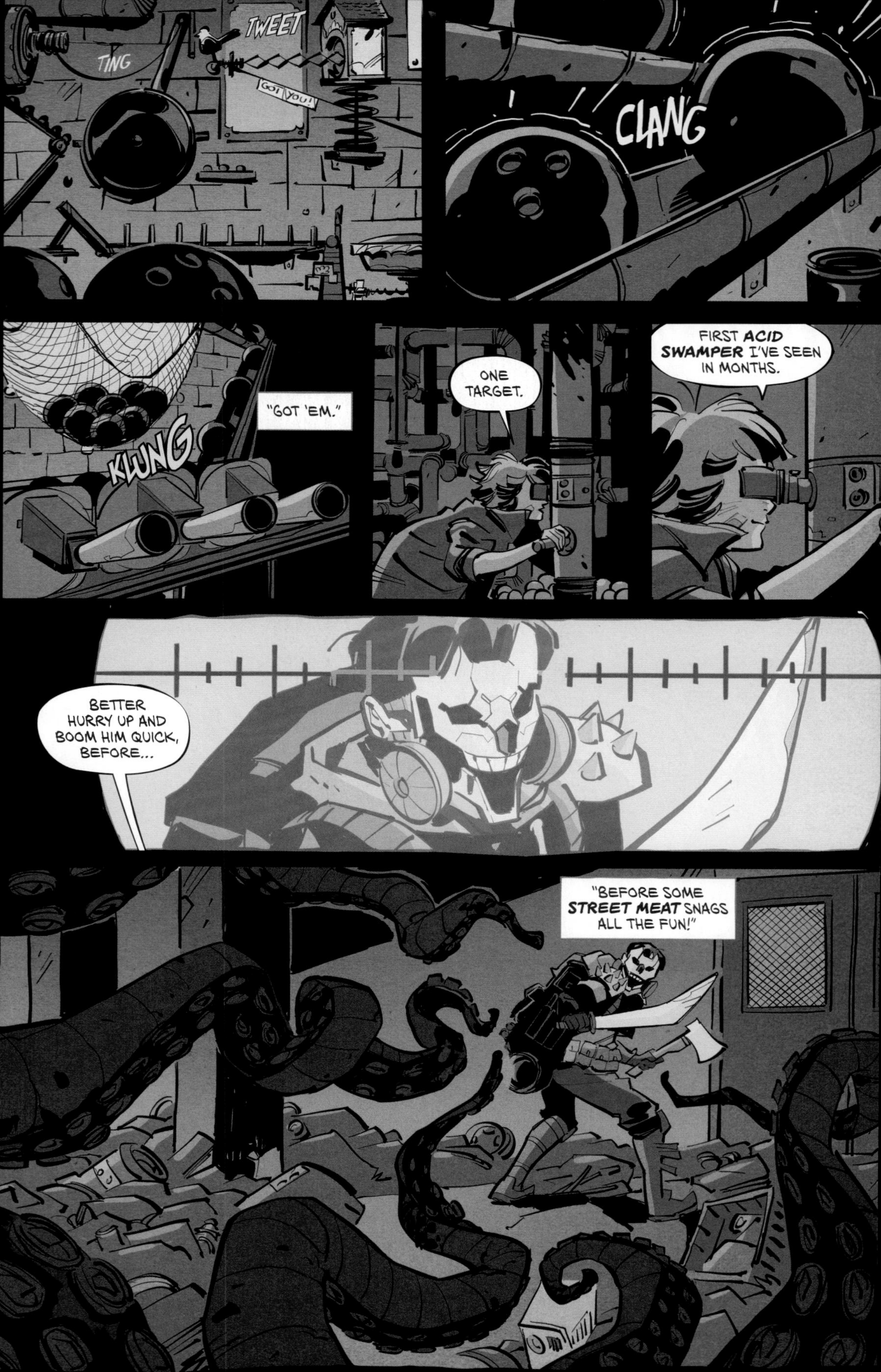
TING
TWEET
GOT YOU!
CLANG
"GOT 'EM."
KLUNG
ONE TARGET.
FIRST ACID SWAMPER I'VE SEEN IN MONTHS.
BETTER HURRY UP AND BOOM HIM QUICK, BEFORE...
"BEFORE SOME STREET MEAT SNAGS ALL THE FUN!"

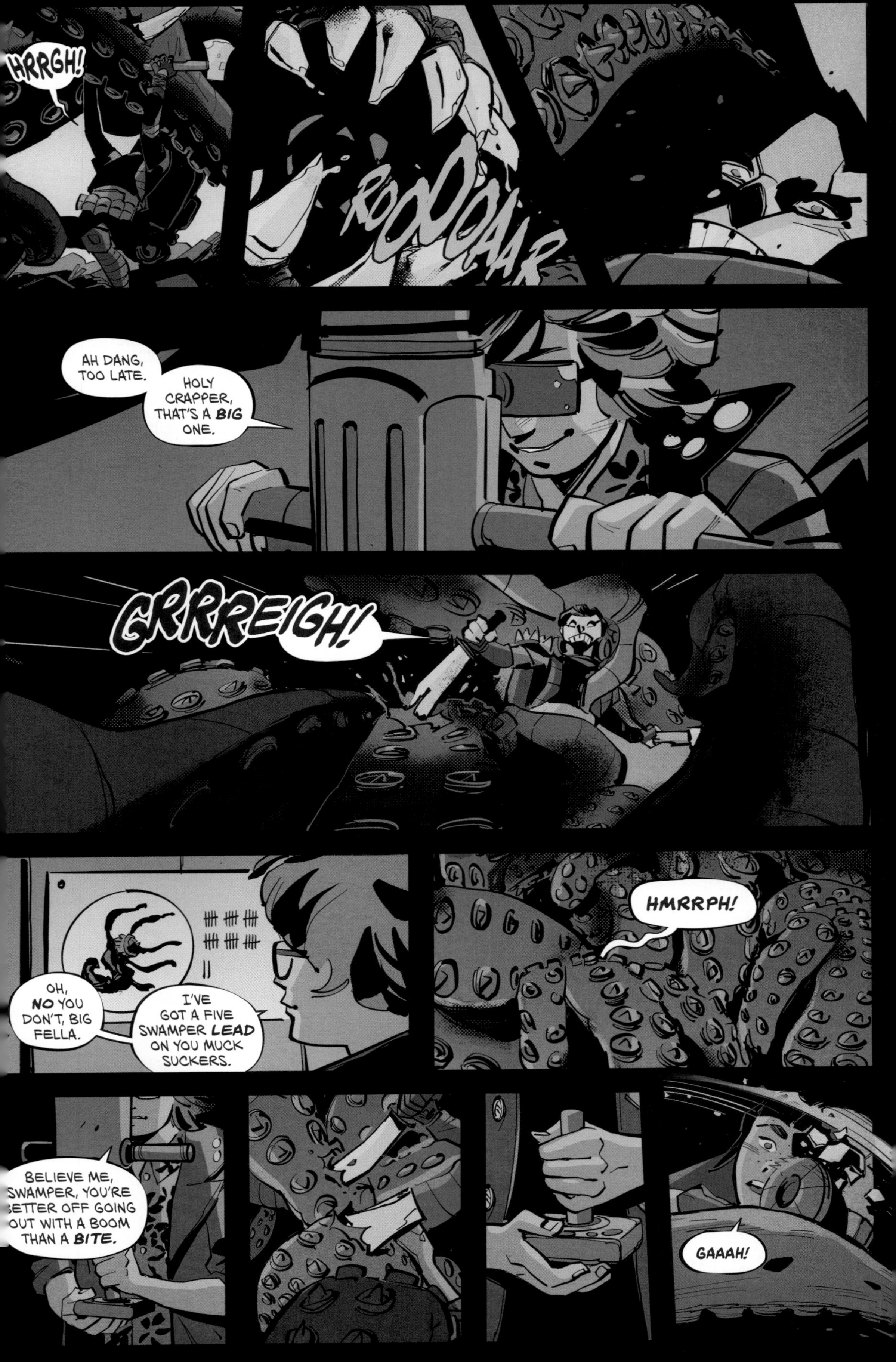
HRRGH!
ROOOOAAR
AH DANG, TOO LATE.
HOLY CRAPPER, THAT'S A BIG ONE.
GRRREIGH!
OH, NO YOU DON'T, BIG FELLA.
I'VE GOT A FIVE SWAMPER LEAD ON YOU MUCK SUCKERS.
HMRRPH!
BELIEVE ME, SWAMPER, YOU'RE BETTER OFF GOING OUT WITH A BOOM THAN A BITE.
GAAAH!

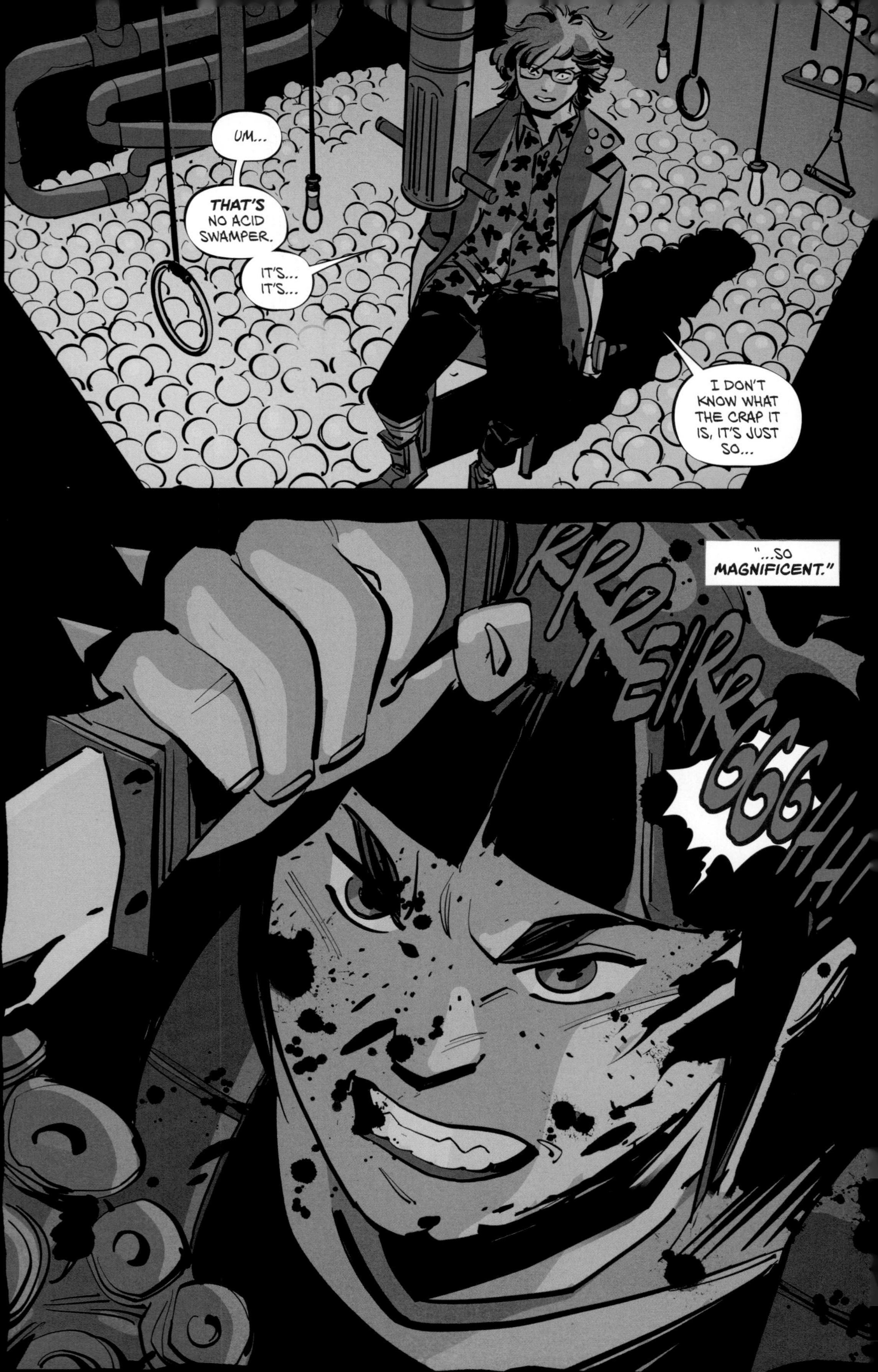
UM...
THAT'S NO ACID SWAMPER.
IT'S... IT'S...
I DON'T KNOW WHAT THE CRAP IT IS, IT'S JUST SO...
"...SO MAGNIFICENT."

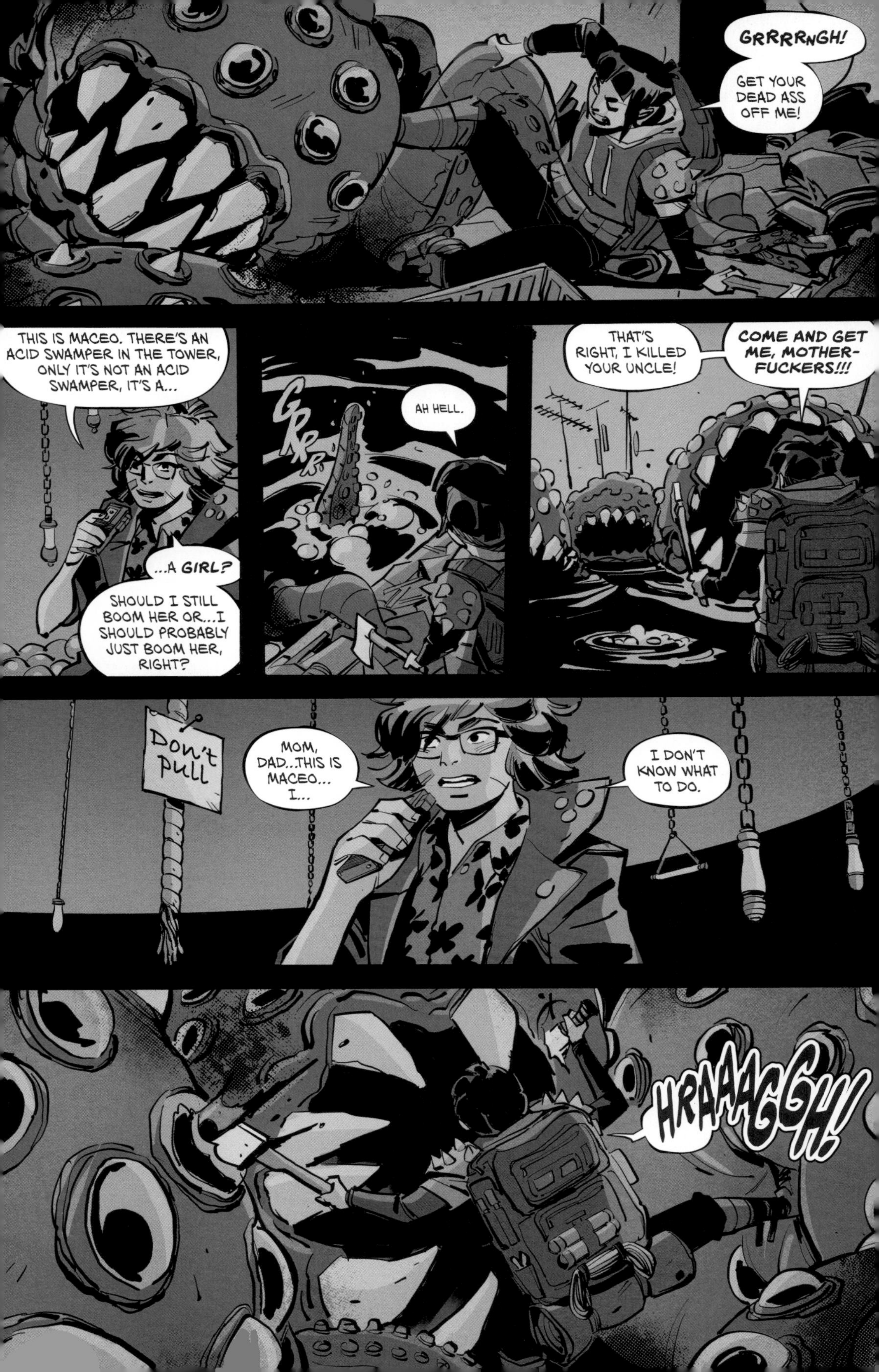
GRRRRNGH!
GET YOUR DEAD ASS OFF ME!
THIS IS MACEO. THERE'S AN ACID SWAMPER IN THE TOWER, ONLY IT'S NOT AN ACID SWAMPER, IT'S A...
...A GIRL?
SHOULD I STILL BOOM HER OR...I SHOULD PROBABLY JUST BOOM HER, RIGHT?
GRRR
AH HELL.
THAT'S RIGHT, I KILLED YOUR UNCLE!
COME AND GET ME, MOTHER-FUCKERS!!!
Don't pull
MOM, DAD...THIS IS MACEO... I...
I DON'T KNOW WHAT TO DO.
HRAAAGGH!

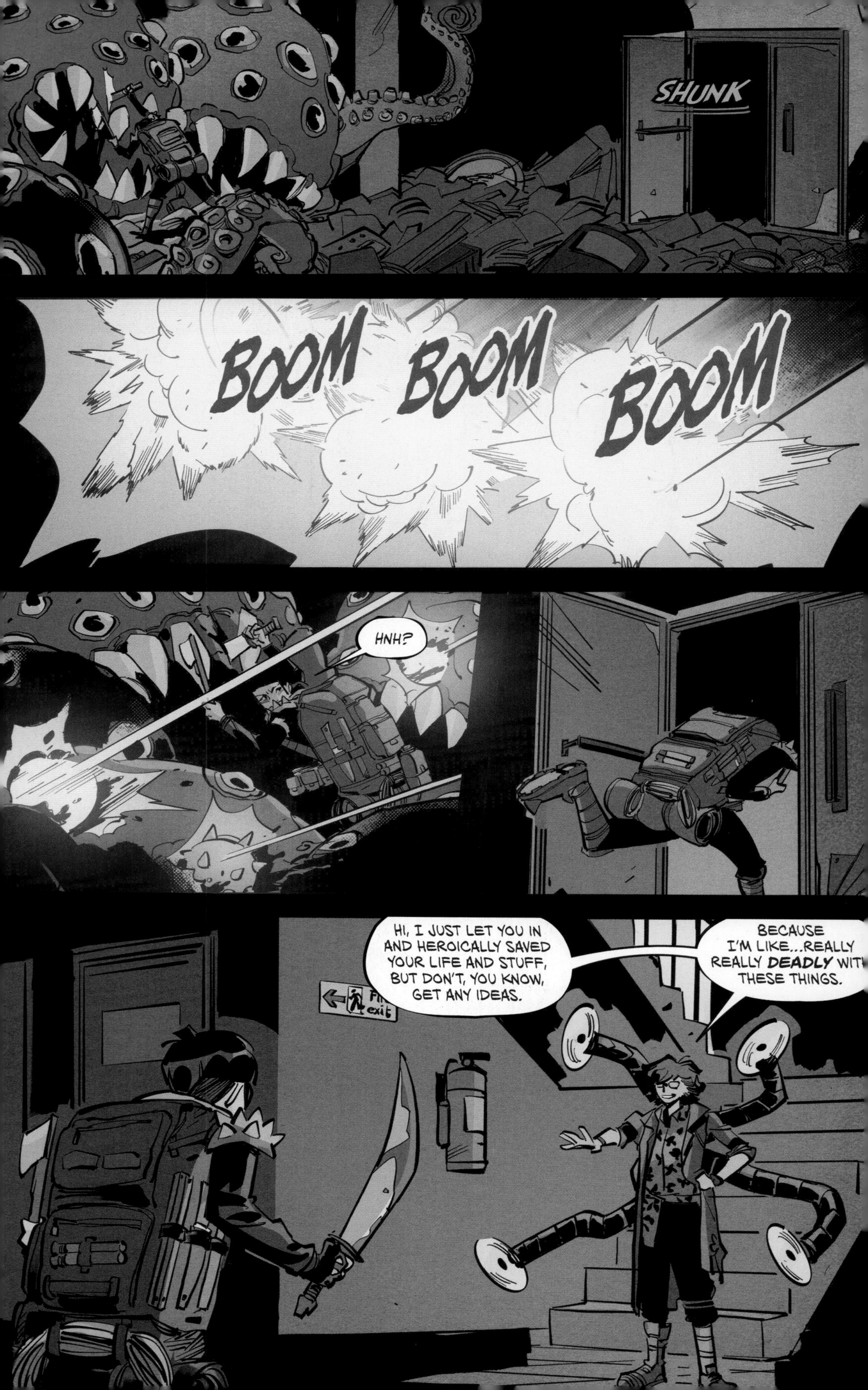
SHUNK
BOOM BOOM BOOM
HNH?
HI, I JUST LET YOU IN AND HEROICALLY SAVED YOUR LIFE AND STUFF, BUT DON'T, YOU KNOW, GET ANY IDEAS.
BECAUSE I'M LIKE...REALLY REALLY DEADLY WIT THESE THINGS.
exit

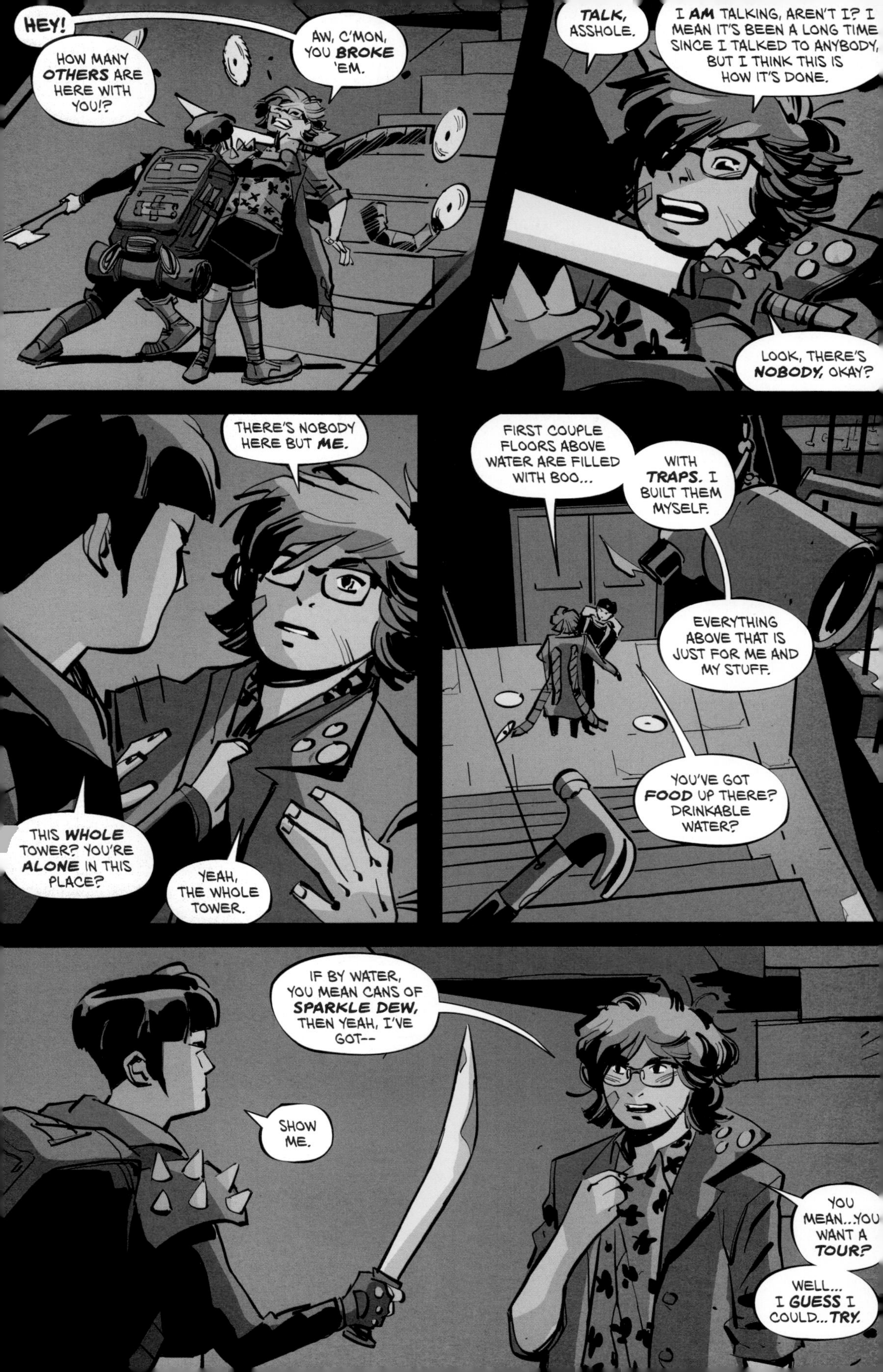
HEY!
HOW MANY OTHERS ARE HERE WITH YOU!?
AW, C'MON, YOU BROKE 'EM.
TALK, ASSHOLE.
I AM TALKING, AREN'T I? I MEAN IT'S BEEN A LONG TIME SINCE I TALKED TO ANYBODY, BUT I THINK THIS IS HOW IT'S DONE.
LOOK, THERE'S NOBODY, OKAY?
THERE'S NOBODY HERE BUT ME.
THIS WHOLE TOWER? YOU'RE ALONE IN THIS PLACE?
YEAH, THE WHOLE TOWER.
FIRST COUPLE FLOORS ABOVE WATER ARE FILLED WITH BOO...
WITH TRAPS. I BUILT THEM MYSELF.
EVERYTHING ABOVE THAT IS JUST FOR ME AND MY STUFF.
YOU'VE GOT FOOD UP THERE? DRINKABLE WATER?
IF BY WATER, YOU MEAN CANS OF SPARKLE DEW, THEN YEAH, I'VE GOT--
SHOW ME.
YOU MEAN...YOU WANT A TOUR?
WELL... I GUESS I COULD...TRY.

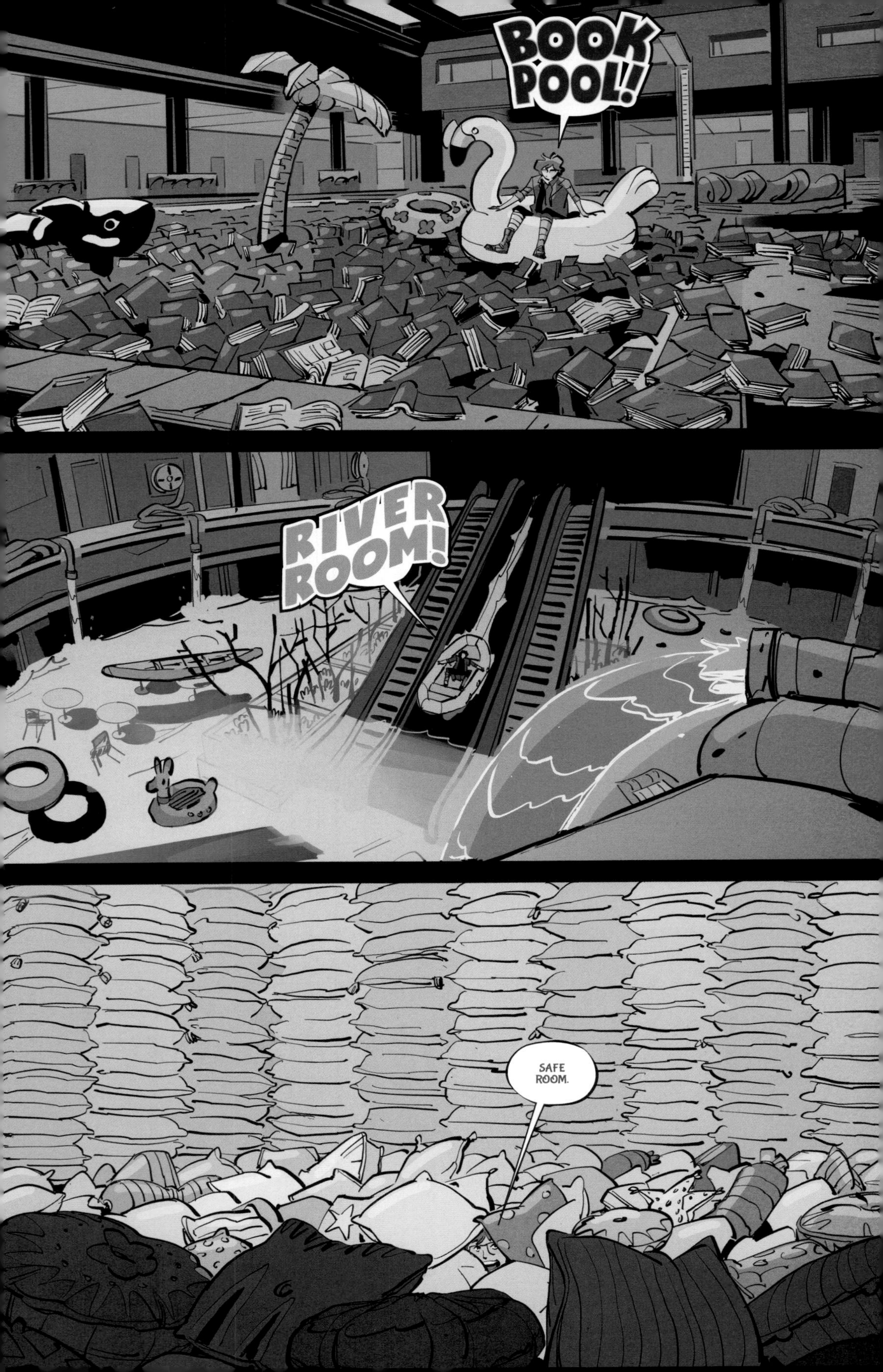
BOOK POOL!
RIVER ROOM!
SAFE ROOM.

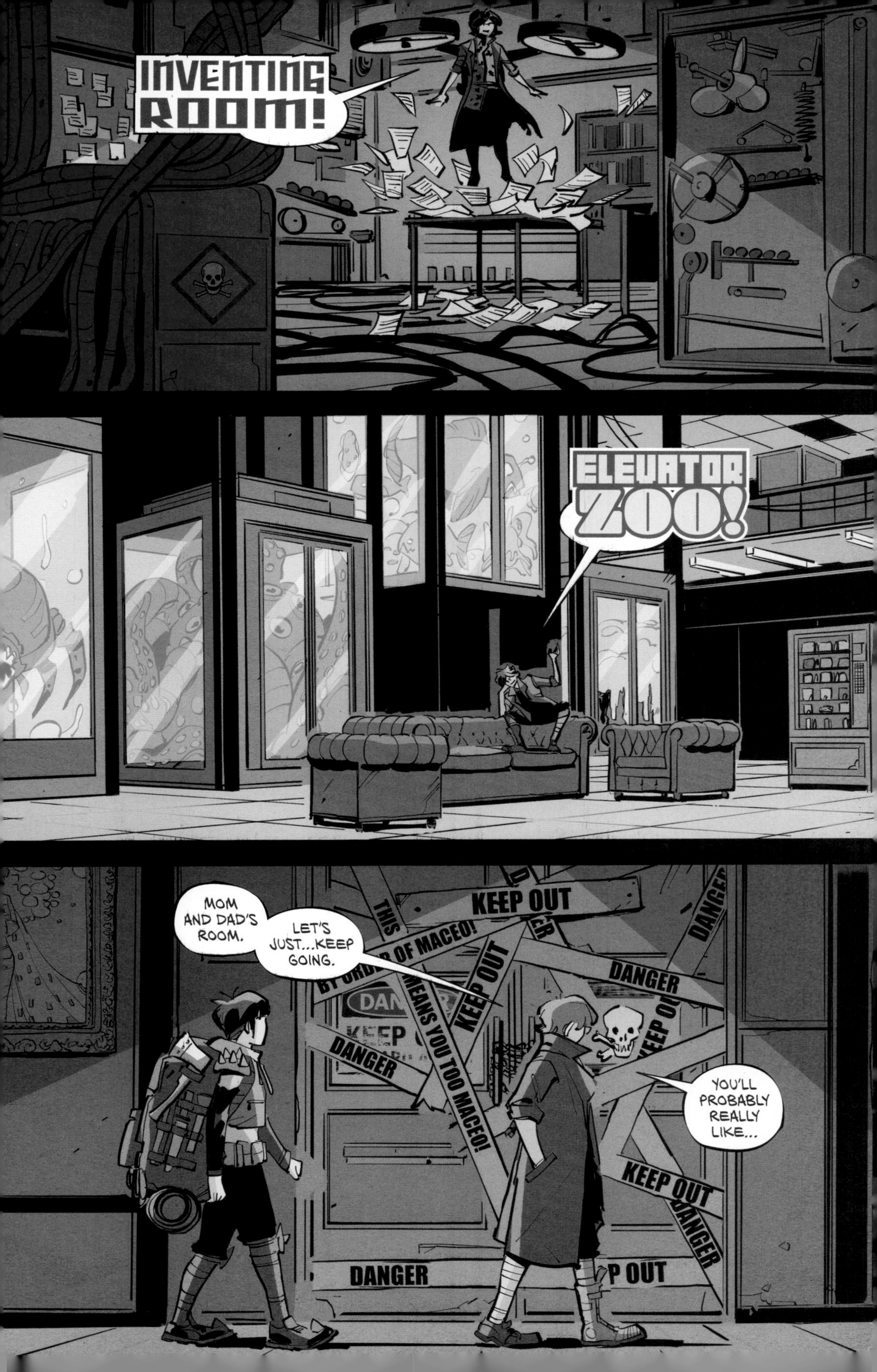
INVENTING ROOM!
ELEVATOR ZOO!
MOM AND DAD'S ROOM.
LET'S JUST...KEEP GOING.
KEEP OUT
THIS MEANS YOU TOO MACEO!
BY ORDER OF MACEO!
KEEP OUT
DANGER
DANGER
DANGER
YOU'LL PROBABLY REALLY LIKE...
KEEP OUT
DANGER
DANGER
P OUT

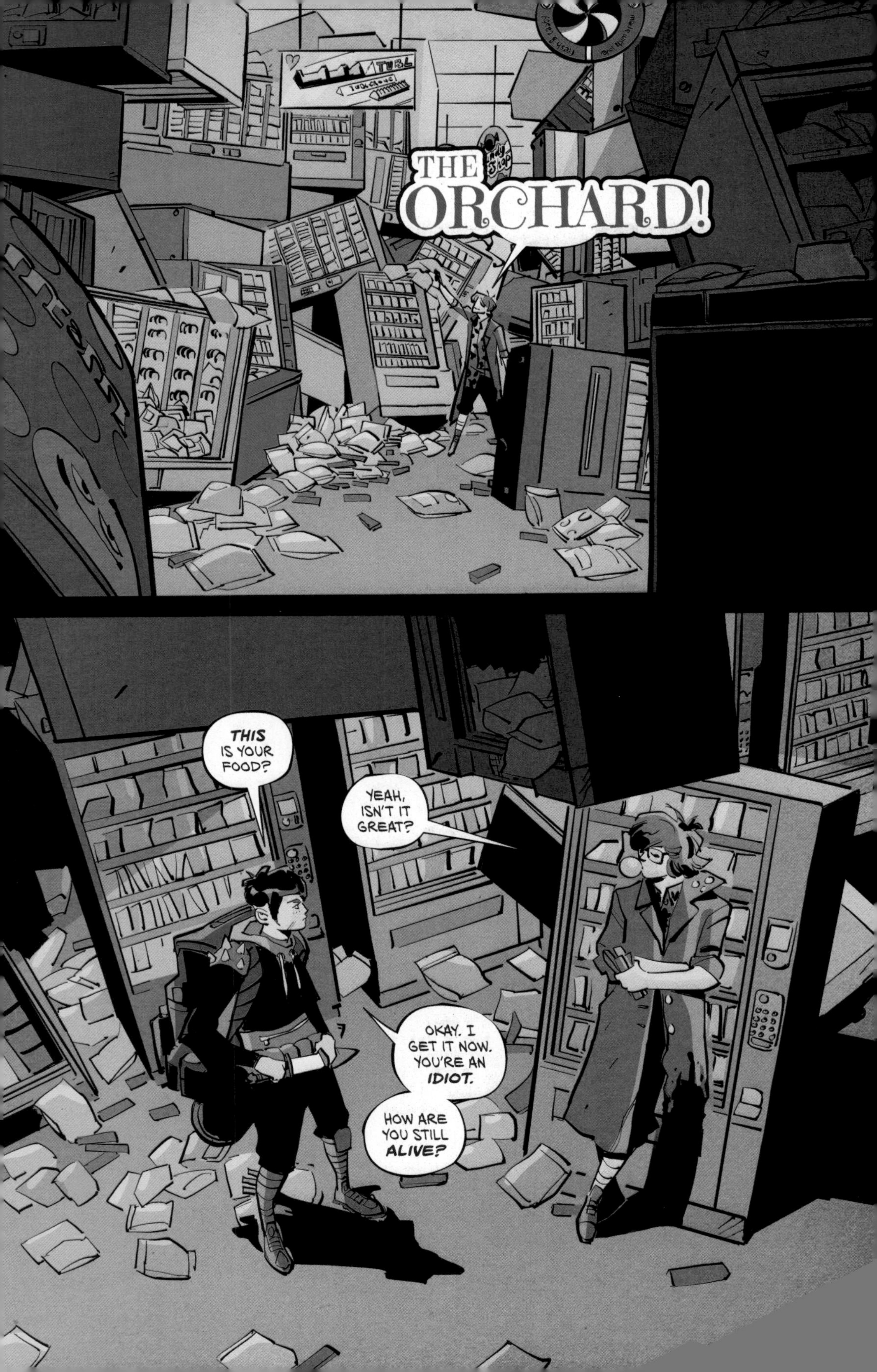
THE ORCHARD!
THIS IS YOUR FOOD?
YEAH, ISN'T IT GREAT?
OKAY. I GET IT NOW. YOU'RE AN IDIOT.
HOW ARE YOU STILL ALIVE?

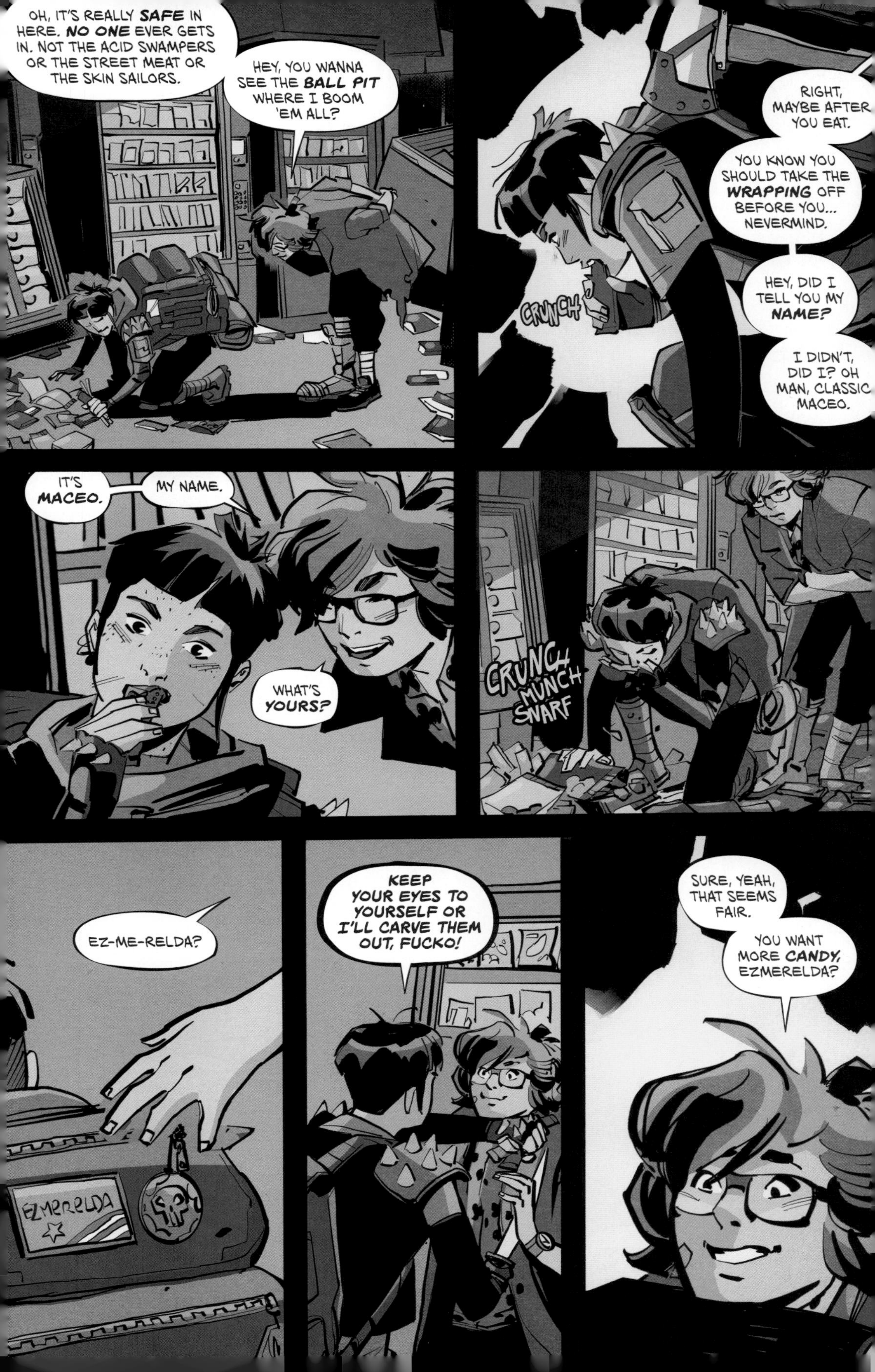
OH, IT'S REALLY SAFE IN HERE. NO ONE EVER GETS IN. NOT THE ACID SWAMPERS OR THE STREET MEAT OR THE SKIN SAILORS.
HEY, YOU WANNA SEE THE BALL PIT WHERE I BOOM 'EM ALL?
RIGHT, MAYBE AFTER YOU EAT.
YOU KNOW YOU SHOULD TAKE THE WRAPPING OFF BEFORE YOU... NEVERMIND.
CRUNCH
HEY, DID I TELL YOU MY NAME?
I DIDN'T, DID I? OH MAN, CLASSIC MACEO.
IT'S MACEO.
MY NAME.
WHAT'S YOURS?
CRUNCH
MUNCH
SNARF
EZ-ME-RELDA?
EZMERELDA
KEEP YOUR EYES TO YOURSELF OR I'LL CARVE THEM OUT, FUCKO!
SURE, YEAH, THAT SEEMS FAIR.
YOU WANT MORE CANDY, EZMERELDA?

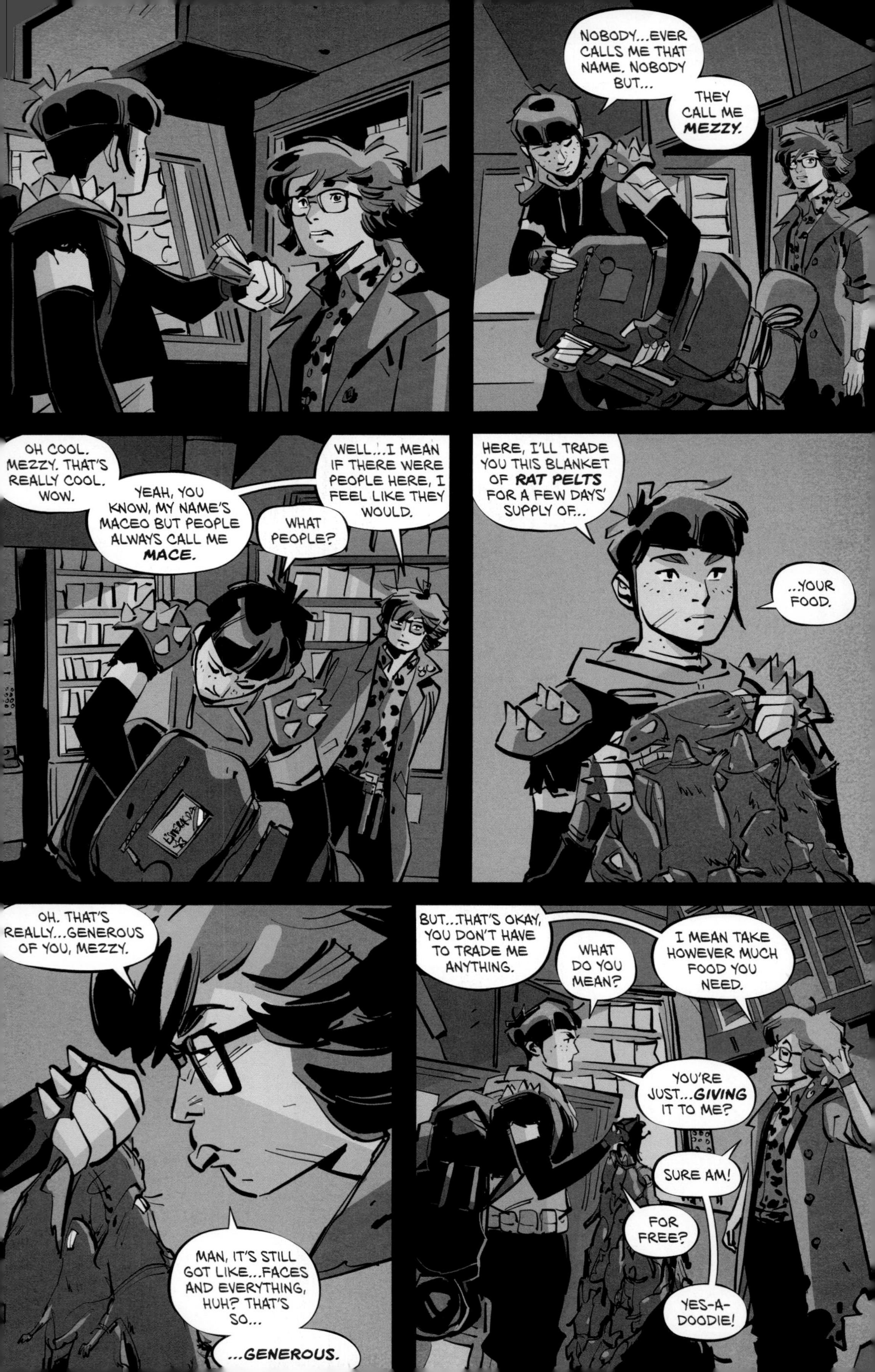
NOBODY...EVER CALLS ME THAT NAME. NOBODY BUT...
THEY CALL ME MEZZY.
OH COOL. MEZZY. THAT'S REALLY COOL. WOW.
YEAH, YOU KNOW, MY NAME'S MACEO BUT PEOPLE ALWAYS CALL ME MACE.
WELL...I MEAN IF THERE WERE PEOPLE HERE, I FEEL LIKE THEY WOULD.
WHAT PEOPLE?
HERE, I'LL TRADE YOU THIS BLANKET OF RAT PELTS FOR A FEW DAYS' SUPPLY OF...
...YOUR FOOD.
OH. THAT'S REALLY...GENEROUS OF YOU, MEZZY.
MAN, IT'S STILL GOT LIKE...FACES AND EVERYTHING, HUH? THAT'S SO...
...GENEROUS.
BUT...THAT'S OKAY, YOU DON'T HAVE TO TRADE ME ANYTHING.
WHAT DO YOU MEAN?
I MEAN TAKE HOWEVER MUCH FOOD YOU NEED.
YOU'RE JUST...GIVING IT TO ME?
SURE AM!
FOR FREE?
YES-A-DOODIE!

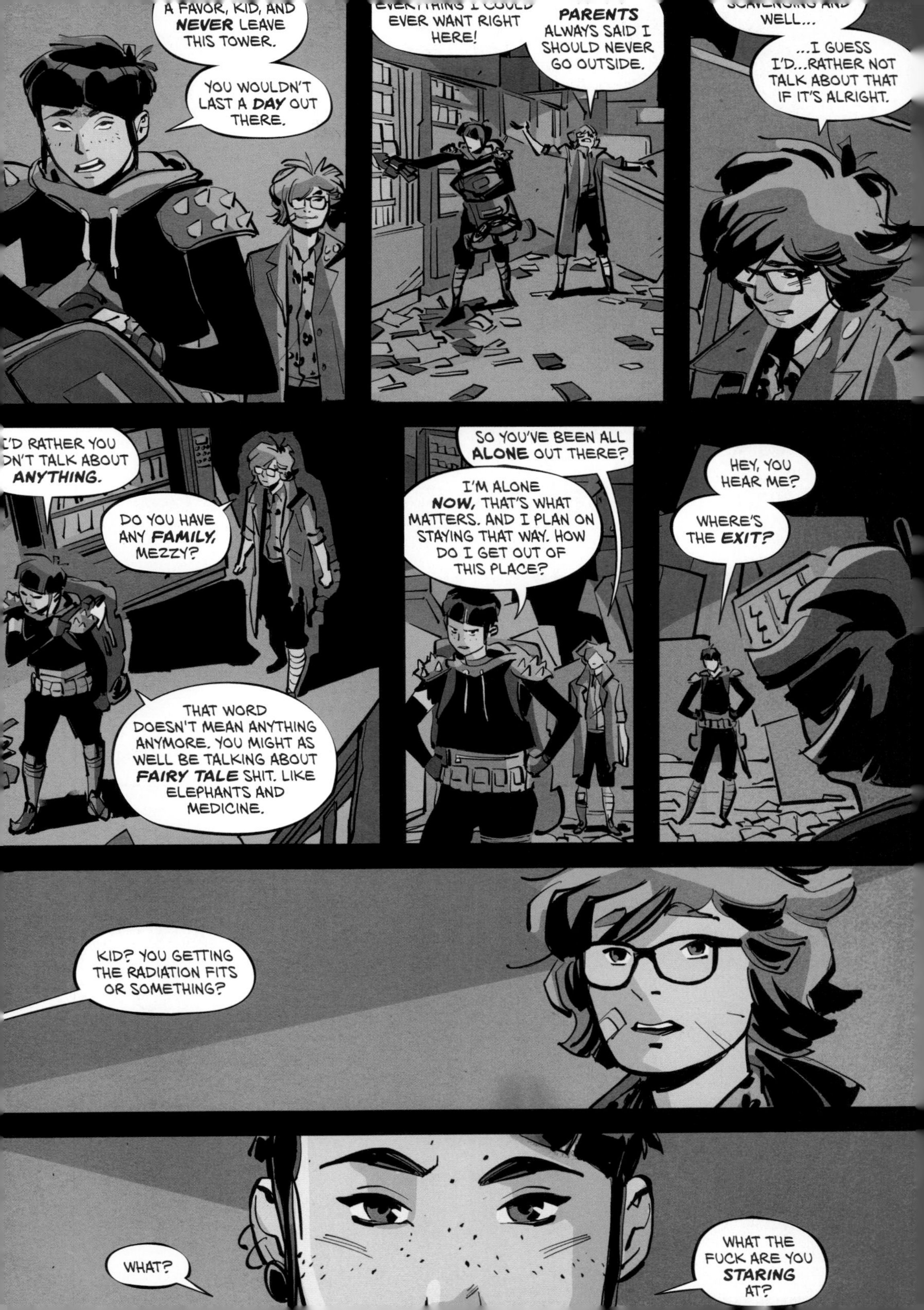
A FAVOR, KID, AND NEVER LEAVE THIS TOWER.
YOU WOULDN'T LAST A DAY OUT THERE.
EVERYTHING I COULD EVER WANT RIGHT HERE!
PARENTS ALWAYS SAID I SHOULD NEVER GO OUTSIDE.
WELL...
...I GUESS I'D...RATHER NOT TALK ABOUT THAT IF IT'S ALRIGHT.
I'D RATHER YOU DN'T TALK ABOUT ANYTHING.
DO YOU HAVE ANY FAMILY, MEZZY?
THAT WORD DOESN'T MEAN ANYTHING ANYMORE. YOU MIGHT AS WELL BE TALKING ABOUT FAIRY TALE SHIT. LIKE ELEPHANTS AND MEDICINE.
SO YOU'VE BEEN ALL ALONE OUT THERE?
I'M ALONE NOW, THAT'S WHAT MATTERS. AND I PLAN ON STAYING THAT WAY. HOW DO I GET OUT OF THIS PLACE?
HEY, YOU HEAR ME?
WHERE'S THE EXIT?
KID? YOU GETTING THE RADIATION FITS OR SOMETHING?
WHAT?
WHAT THE FUCK ARE YOU STARING AT?

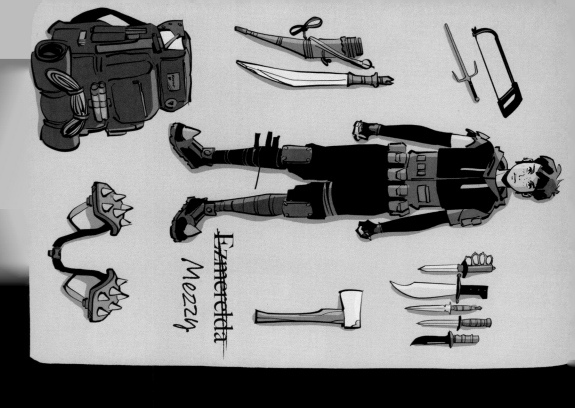

Ezmerelda
Mezzy

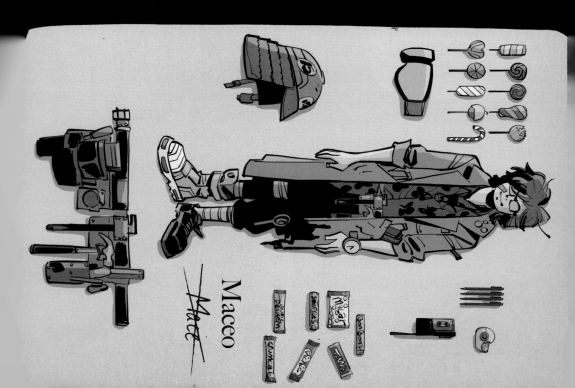

Maceo
Mace

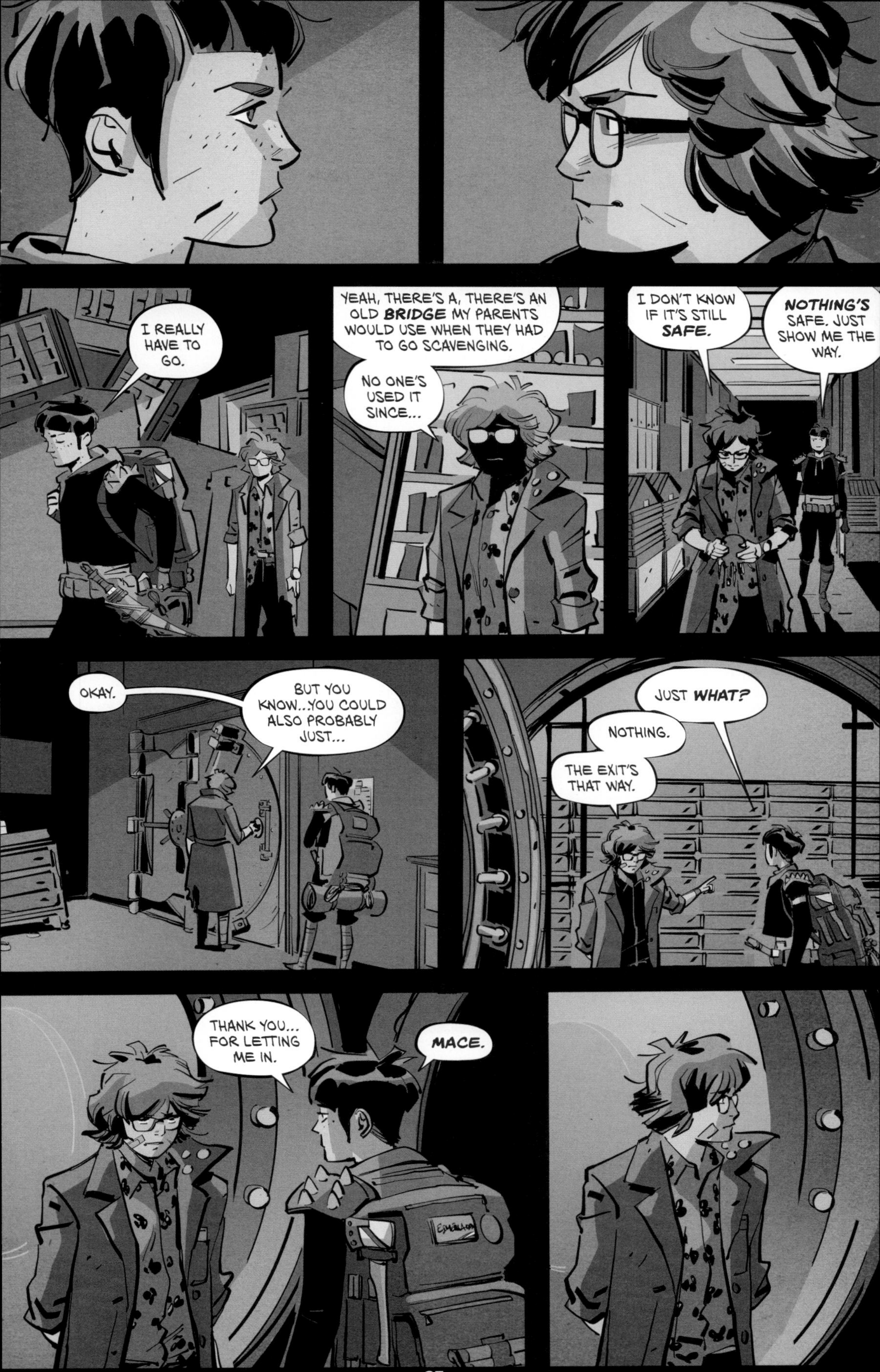
I REALLY HAVE TO GO.
YEAH, THERE'S A, THERE'S AN OLD BRIDGE MY PARENTS WOULD USE WHEN THEY HAD TO GO SCAVENGING.
NO ONE'S USED IT SINCE...
I DON'T KNOW IF IT'S STILL SAFE.
NOTHING'S SAFE. JUST SHOW ME THE WAY.
OKAY.
BUT YOU KNOW...YOU COULD ALSO PROBABLY JUST...
JUST WHAT?
NOTHING.
THE EXIT'S THAT WAY.
THANK YOU... FOR LETTING ME IN.
MACE.

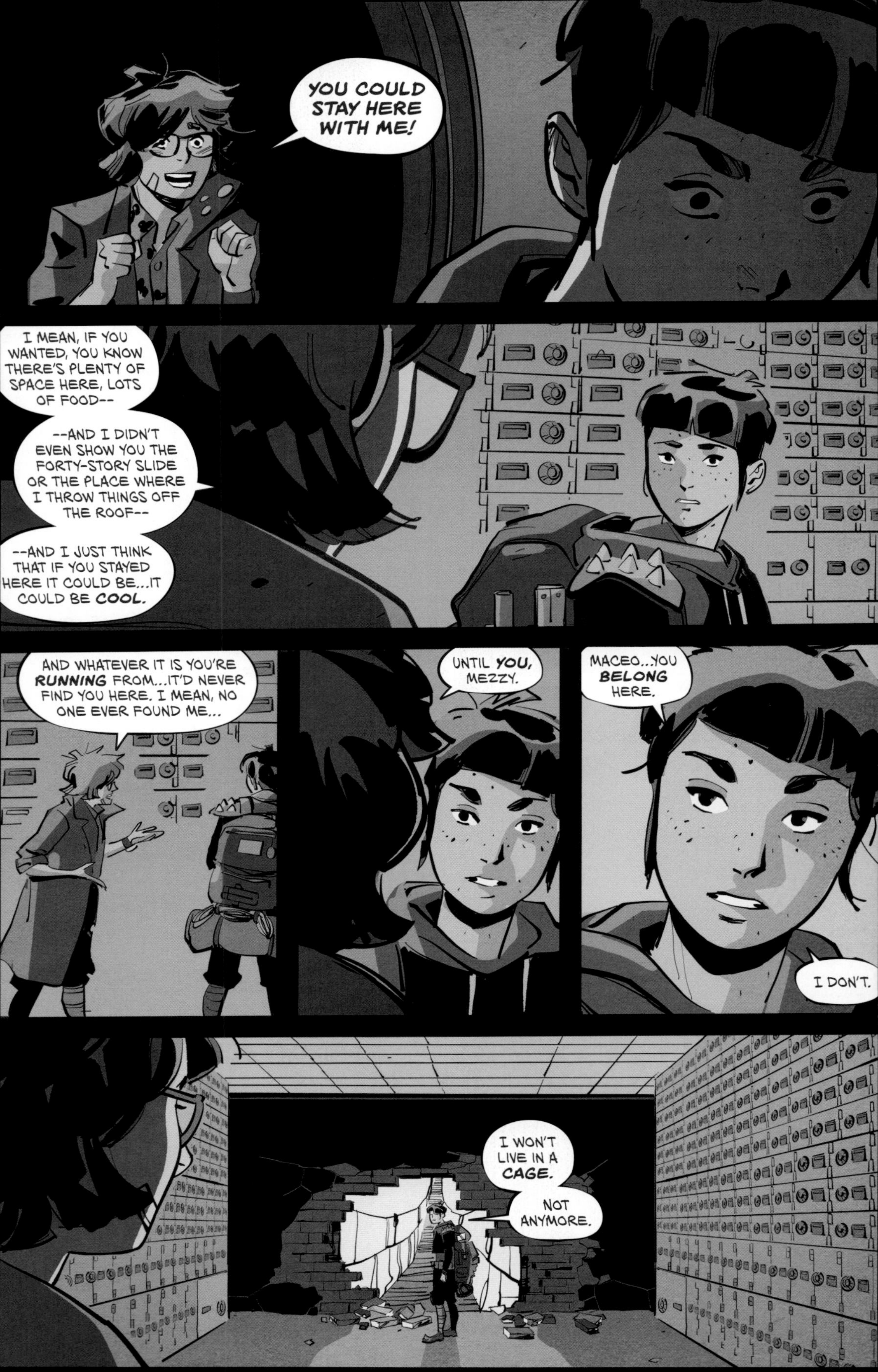
YOU COULD STAY HERE WITH ME!
I MEAN, IF YOU WANTED, YOU KNOW THERE'S PLENTY OF SPACE HERE, LOTS OF FOOD--
--AND I DIDN'T EVEN SHOW YOU THE FORTY-STORY SLIDE OR THE PLACE WHERE I THROW THINGS OFF THE ROOF--
--AND I JUST THINK THAT IF YOU STAYED HERE IT COULD BE...IT COULD BE **COOL.**
AND WHATEVER IT IS YOU'RE **RUNNING** FROM...IT'D NEVER FIND YOU HERE. I MEAN, NO ONE EVER FOUND ME...
UNTIL **YOU,** MEZZY.
MACEO...YOU **BELONG** HERE.
I DON'T.
I WON'T LIVE IN A **CAGE.**
NOT ANYMORE.

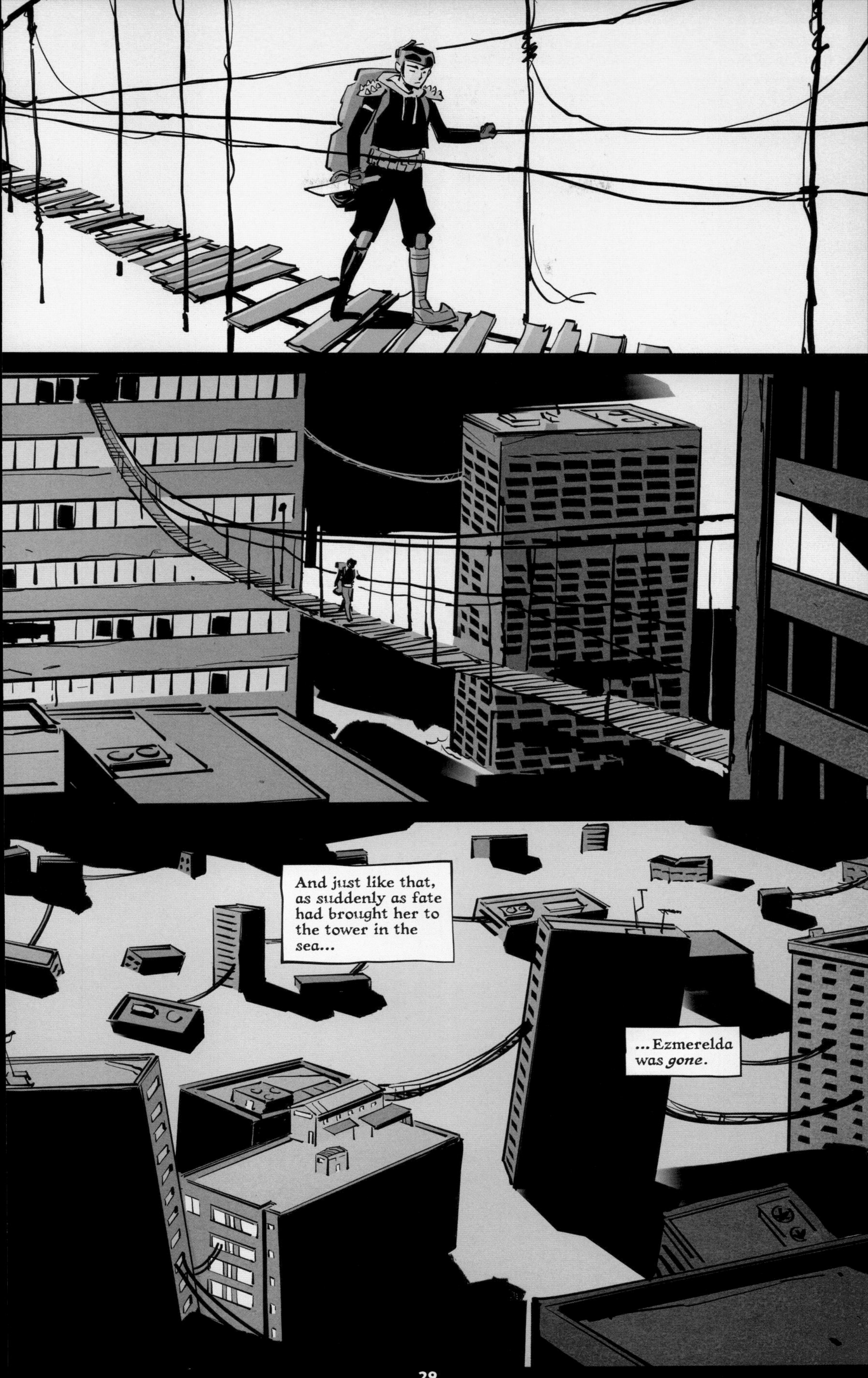
And just like that, as suddenly as fate had brought her to the tower in the sea...
...Ezmerelda was *gone*.

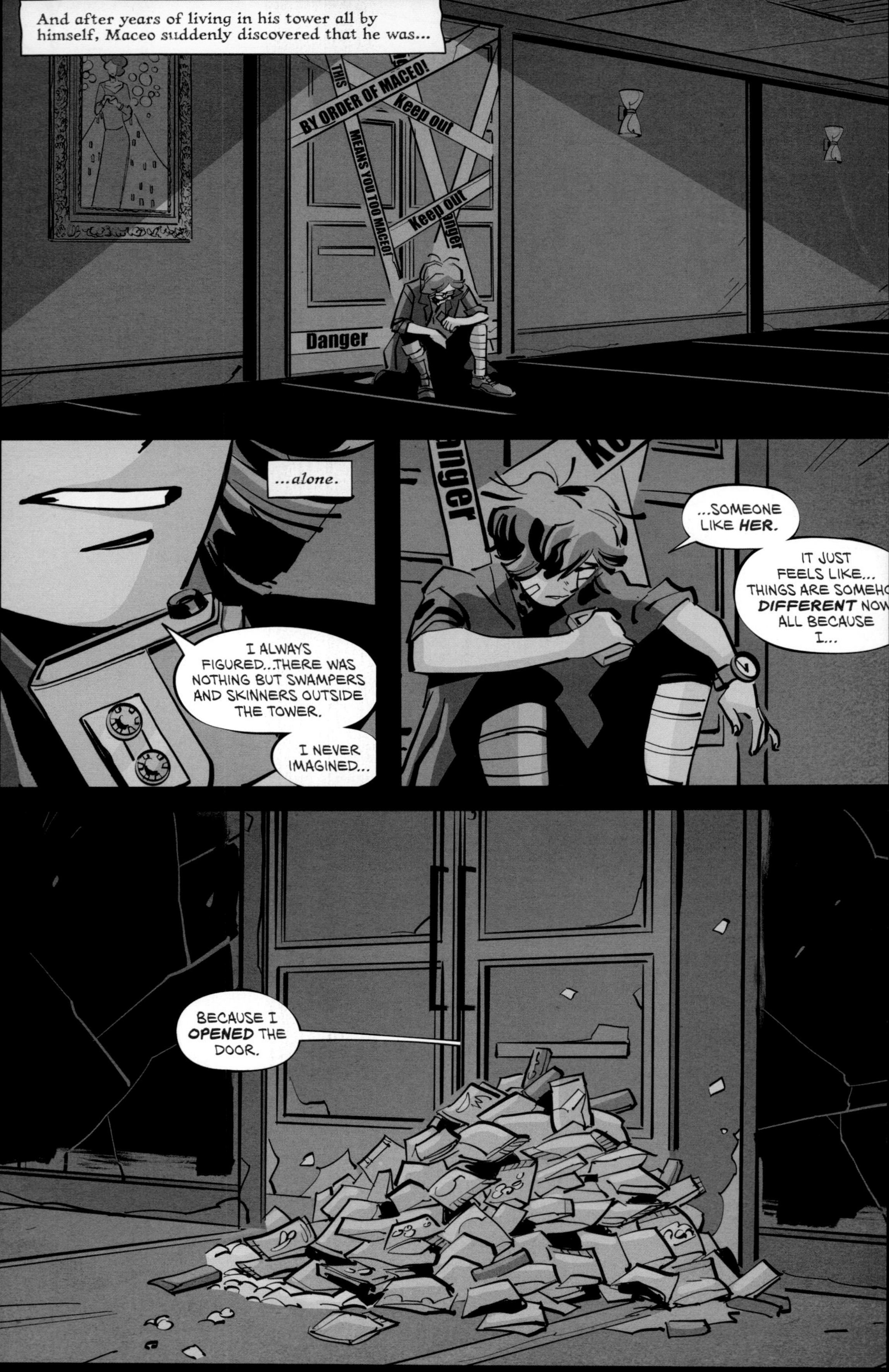

And after years of living in his tower all by himself, Maceo suddenly discovered that he was...
THIS
BY ORDER OF MACEO!
MEANS YOU TOO MACEO!
Keep out
Keep out
Danger
...alone.
I ALWAYS FIGURED...THERE WAS NOTHING BUT SWAMPERS AND SKINNERS OUTSIDE THE TOWER.
I NEVER IMAGINED...
...SOMEONE LIKE HER.
IT JUST FEELS LIKE... THINGS ARE SOMEHO DIFFERENT NOW ALL BECAUSE I...
BECAUSE I OPENED THE DOOR.

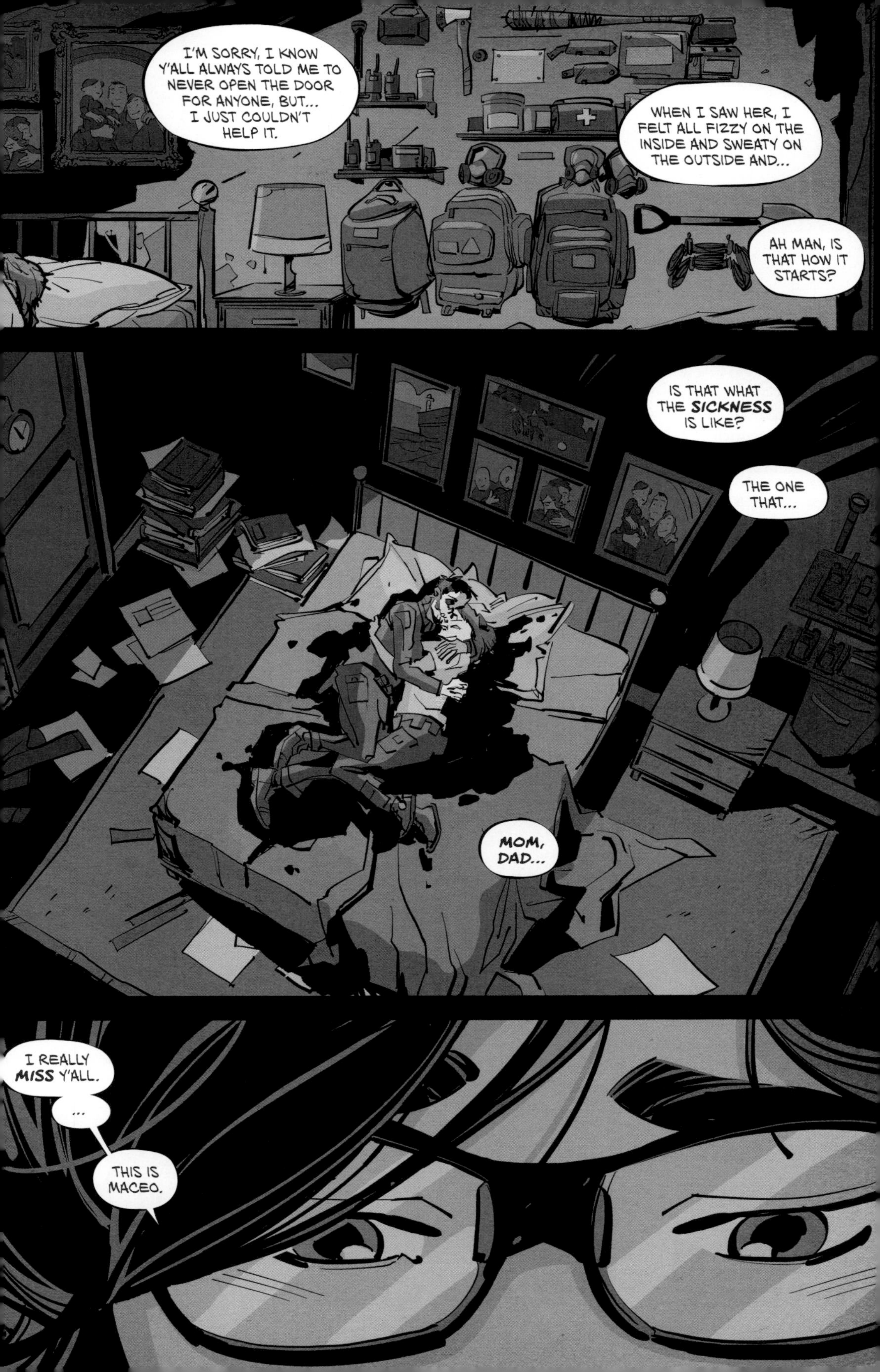
I'M SORRY, I KNOW Y'ALL ALWAYS TOLD ME TO NEVER OPEN THE DOOR FOR ANYONE, BUT... I JUST COULDN'T HELP IT.
WHEN I SAW HER, I FELT ALL FIZZY ON THE INSIDE AND SWEATY ON THE OUTSIDE AND...
AH MAN, IS THAT HOW IT STARTS?
IS THAT WHAT THE SICKNESS IS LIKE?
THE ONE THAT...
MOM, DAD...
I REALLY MISS Y'ALL.
...
THIS IS MACEO.

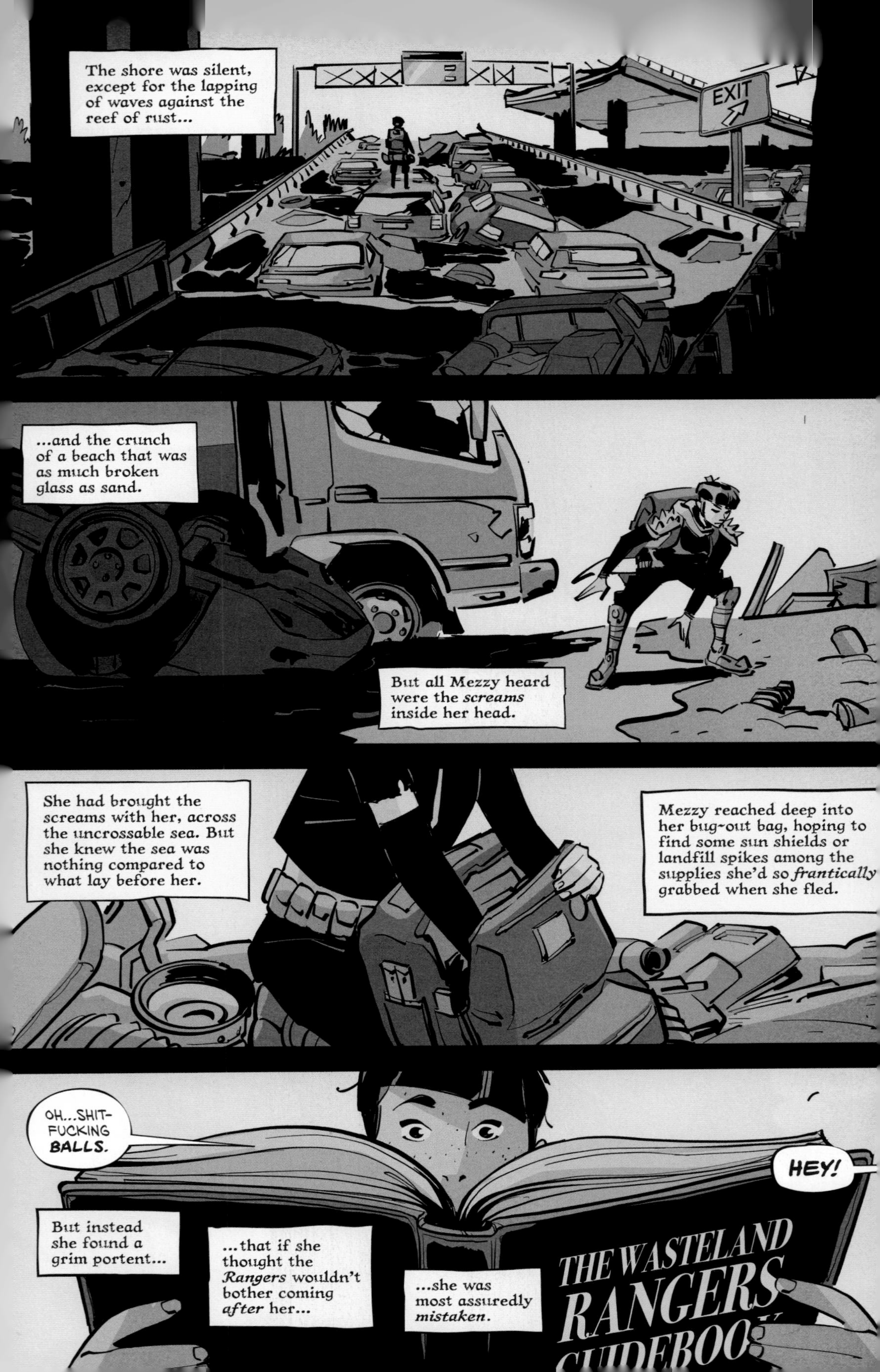
The shore was silent, except for the lapping of waves against the reef of rust...
EXIT
...and the crunch of a beach that was as much broken glass as sand.
But all Mezzy heard were the *screams* inside her head.
She had brought the screams with her, across the uncrossable sea. But she knew the sea was nothing compared to what lay before her.
Mezzy reached deep into her bug-out bag, hoping to find some sun shields or landfill spikes among the supplies she'd so *frantically* grabbed when she fled.
OH...SHIT-FUCKING **BALLS.**
HEY!
But instead she found a grim portent...
...that if she thought the *Rangers* wouldn't bother coming *after* her...
...she was most assuredly *mistaken*.
THE WASTELAND RANGERS

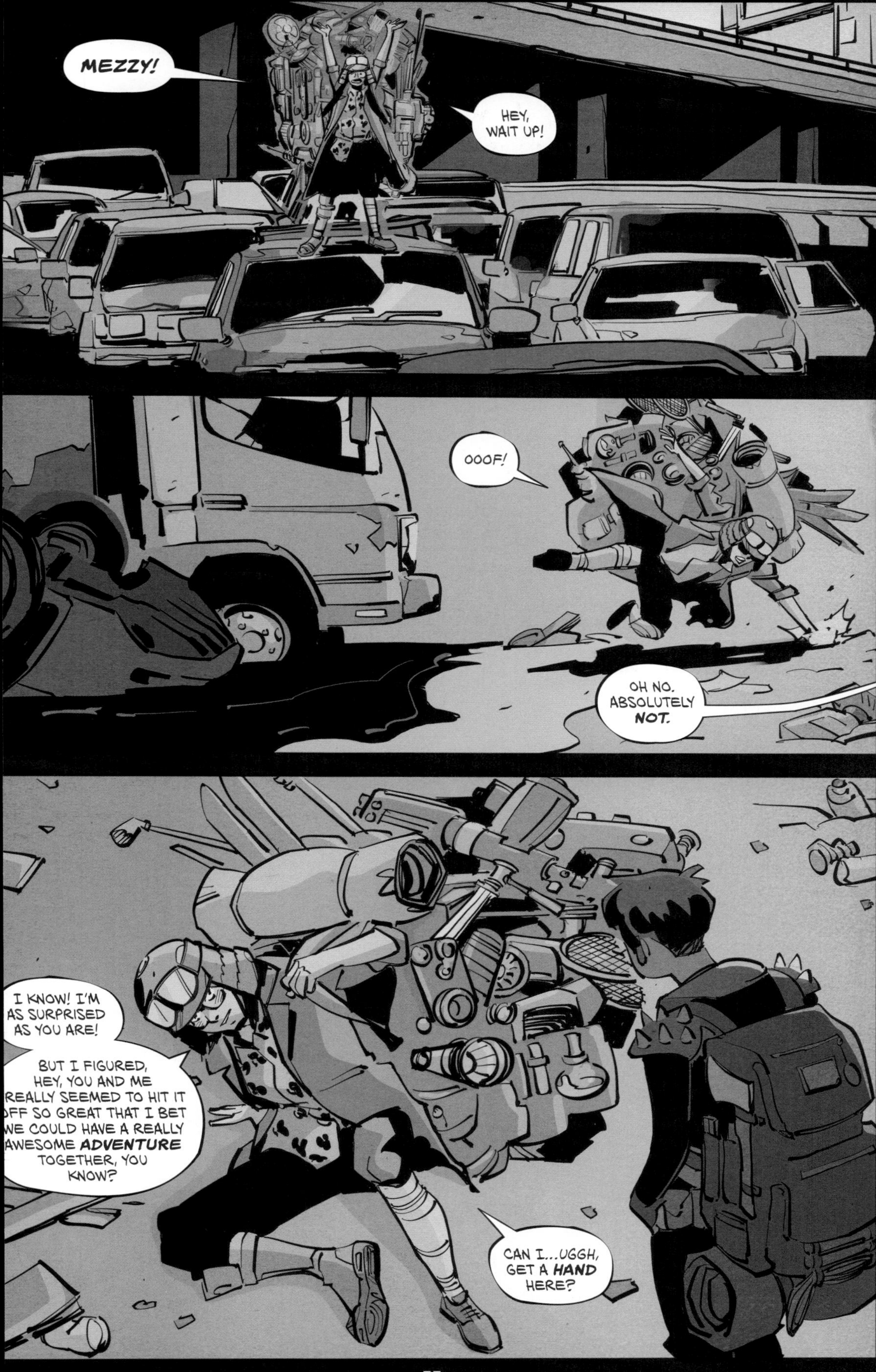
MEZZY!
HEY, WAIT UP!
OOOF!
OH NO. ABSOLUTELY NOT.
I KNOW! I'M AS SURPRISED AS YOU ARE!
BUT I FIGURED, HEY, YOU AND ME REALLY SEEMED TO HIT IT OFF SO GREAT THAT I BET WE COULD HAVE A REALLY AWESOME ADVENTURE TOGETHER, YOU KNOW?
CAN I...UGGH, GET A HAND HERE?

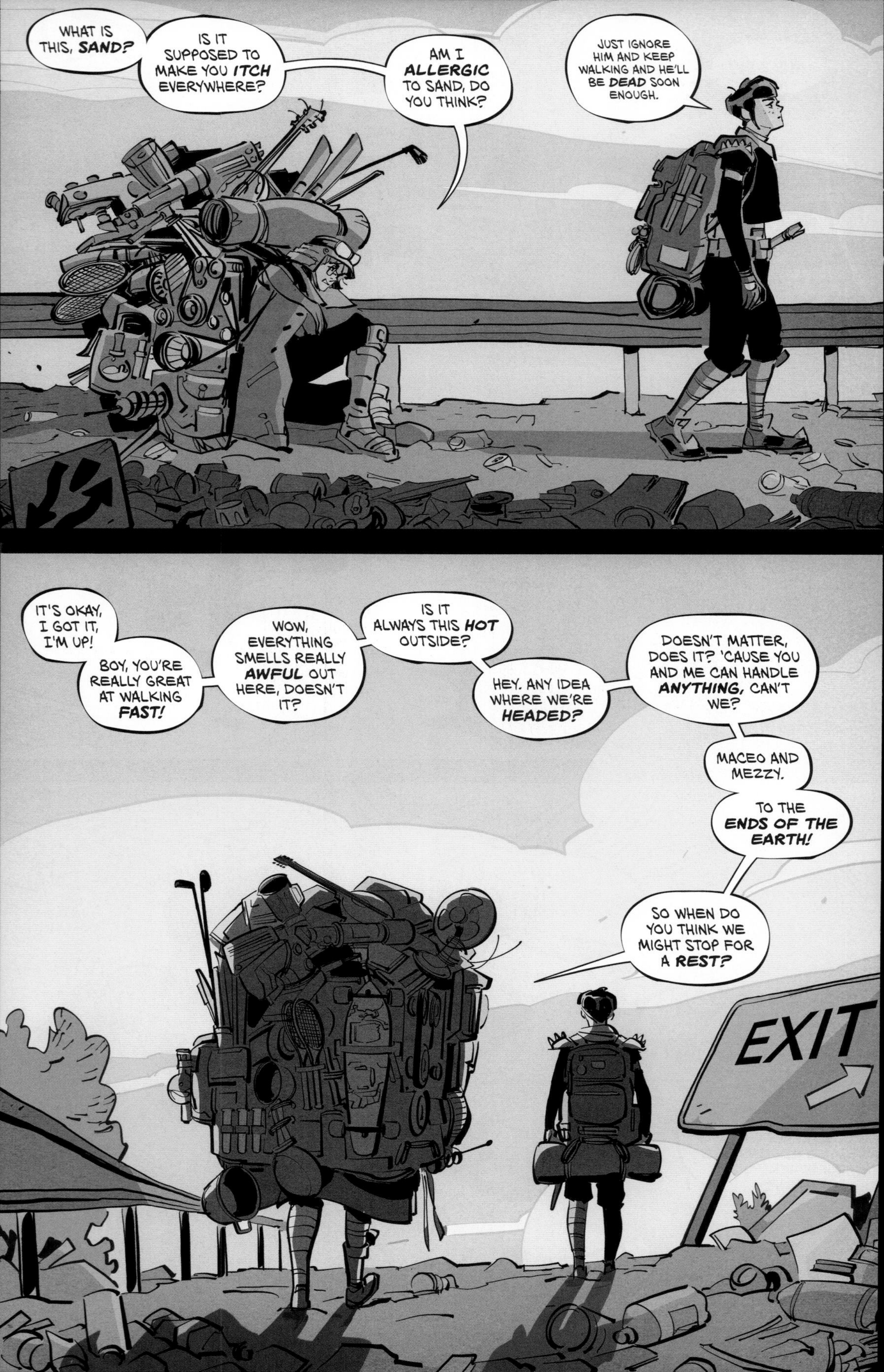
WHAT IS THIS, SAND?
IS IT SUPPOSED TO MAKE YOU ITCH EVERYWHERE?
AM I ALLERGIC TO SAND, DO YOU THINK?
JUST IGNORE HIM AND KEEP WALKING AND HE'LL BE DEAD SOON ENOUGH.
IT'S OKAY, I GOT IT, I'M UP!
BOY, YOU'RE REALLY GREAT AT WALKING FAST!
WOW, EVERYTHING SMELLS REALLY AWFUL OUT HERE, DOESN'T IT?
IS IT ALWAYS THIS HOT OUTSIDE?
HEY. ANY IDEA WHERE WE'RE HEADED?
DOESN'T MATTER, DOES IT? 'CAUSE YOU AND ME CAN HANDLE ANYTHING, CAN'T WE?
MACEO AND MEZZY.
TO THE ENDS OF THE EARTH!
SO WHEN DO YOU THINK WE MIGHT STOP FOR A REST?
EXIT

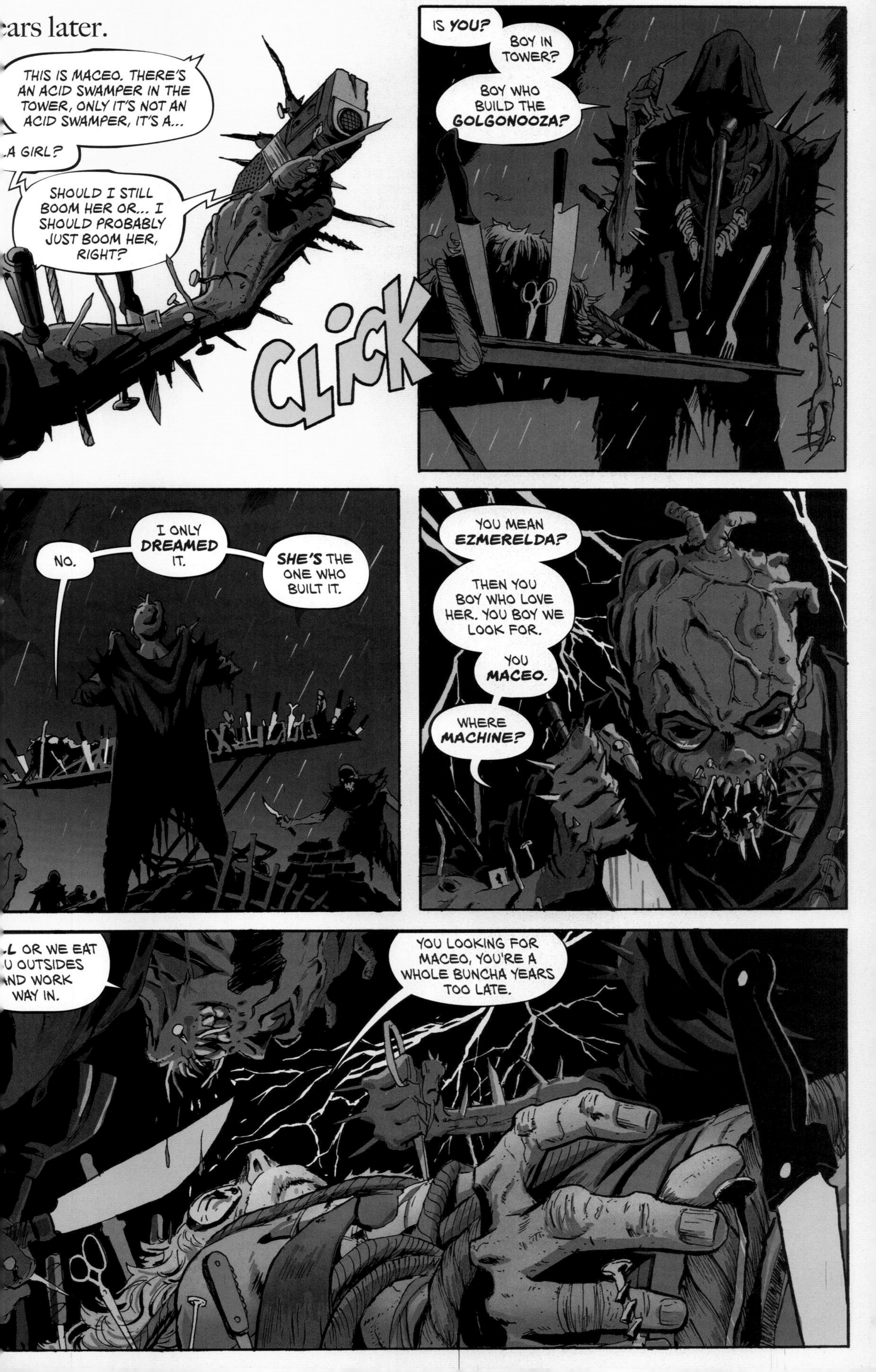
ears later.
THIS IS MACEO. THERE'S AN ACID SWAMPER IN THE TOWER, ONLY IT'S NOT AN ACID SWAMPER, IT'S A...
A GIRL?
SHOULD I STILL BOOM HER OR... I SHOULD PROBABLY JUST BOOM HER, RIGHT?
CLICK
IS YOU?
BOY IN TOWER?
BOY WHO BUILD THE GOLGONOOZA?
NO.
I ONLY DREAMED IT.
SHE'S THE ONE WHO BUILT IT.
YOU MEAN EZMERELDA?
THEN YOU BOY WHO LOVE HER. YOU BOY WE LOOK FOR.
YOU MACEO.
WHERE MACHINE?
L OR WE EAT U OUTSIDES AND WORK WAY IN.
YOU LOOKING FOR MACEO, YOU'RE A WHOLE BUNCHA YEARS TOO LATE.

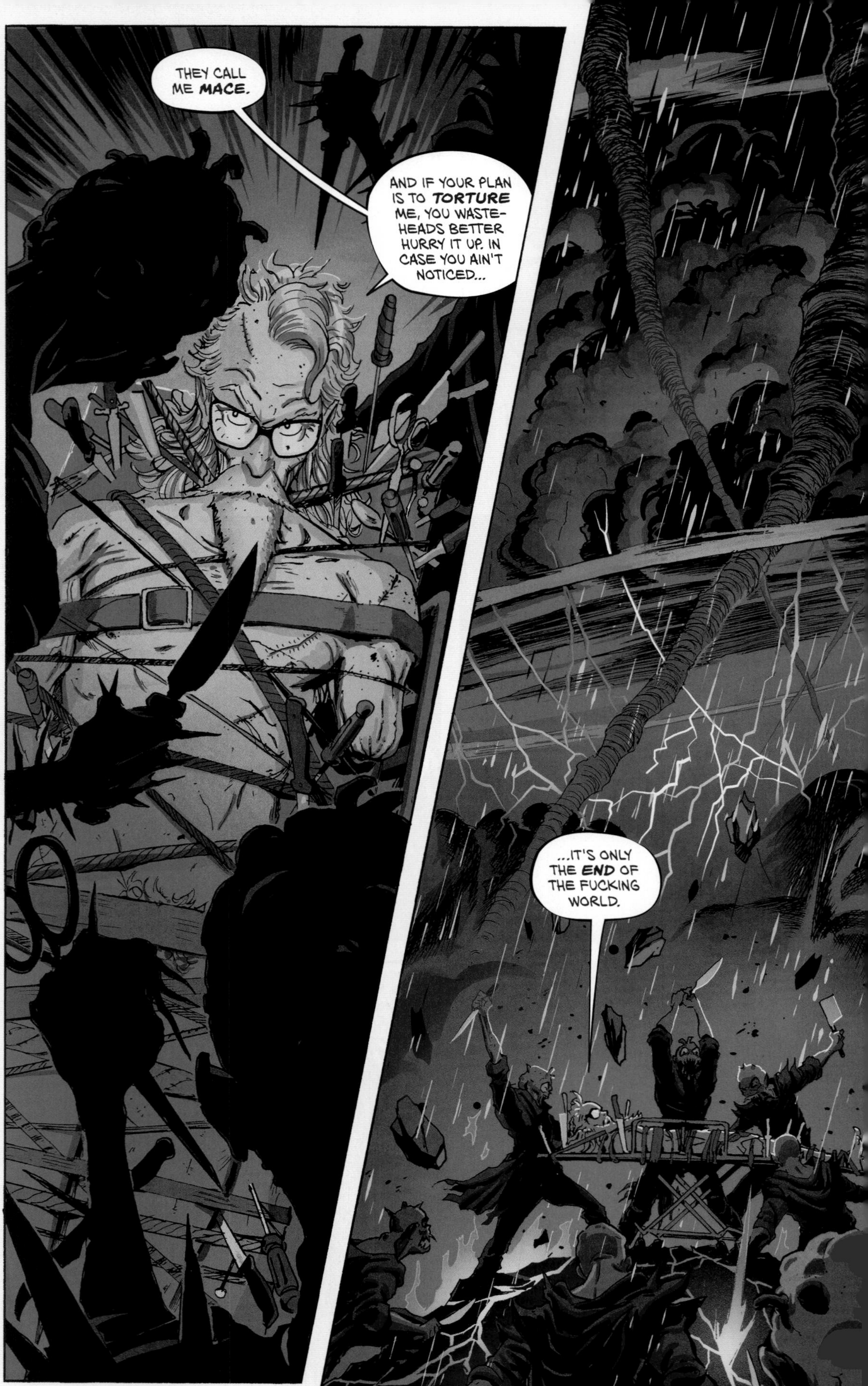
THEY CALL ME **MACE.**
AND IF YOUR PLAN IS TO ***TORTURE*** ME, YOU WASTE-HEADS BETTER HURRY IT UP. IN CASE YOU AIN'T NOTICED...
...IT'S ONLY THE ***END*** OF THE FUCKING WORLD.

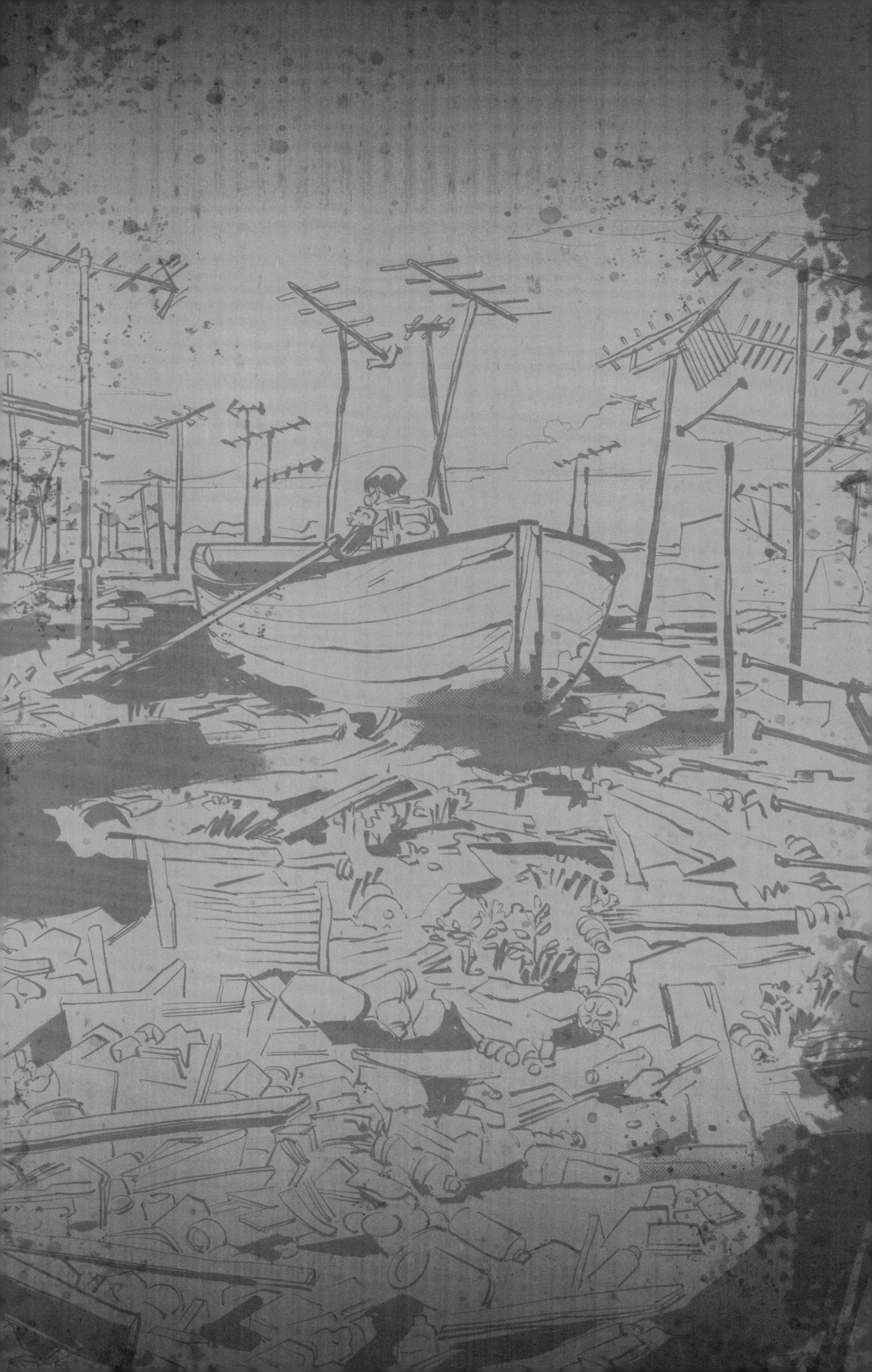

CHAPTER TWO

THE PROVERBS OF SURVIVAL

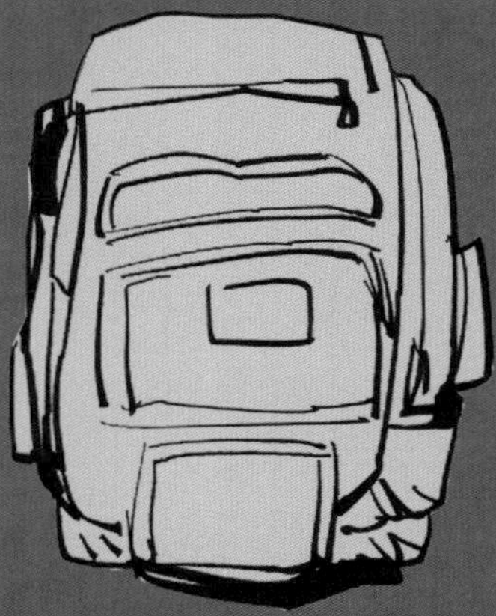

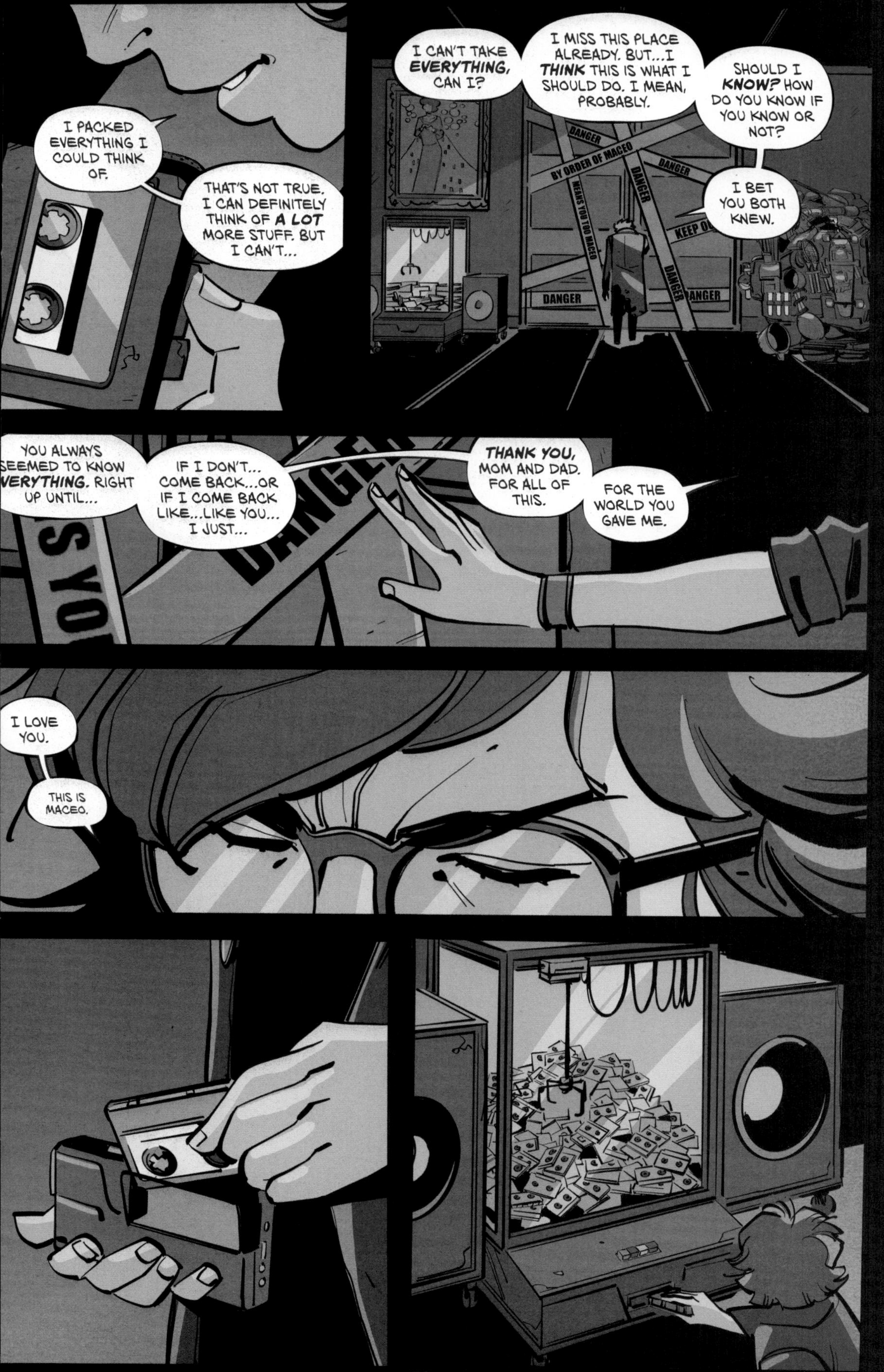
I PACKED EVERYTHING I COULD THINK OF.
THAT'S NOT TRUE. I CAN DEFINITELY THINK OF A LOT MORE STUFF. BUT I CAN'T...
I CAN'T TAKE EVERYTHING, CAN I?
I MISS THIS PLACE ALREADY. BUT...I THINK THIS IS WHAT I SHOULD DO. I MEAN, PROBABLY.
SHOULD I KNOW? HOW DO YOU KNOW IF YOU KNOW OR NOT?
I BET YOU BOTH KNEW.
DANGER
BY ORDER OF MACEO
MEANS YOU TOO MACEO
KEEP OU
YOU ALWAYS SEEMED TO KNOW EVERYTHING. RIGHT UP UNTIL...
IF I DON'T... COME BACK...OR IF I COME BACK LIKE...LIKE YOU... I JUST...
THANK YOU, MOM AND DAD. FOR ALL OF THIS.
FOR THE WORLD YOU GAVE ME.
I LOVE YOU.
THIS IS MACEO.

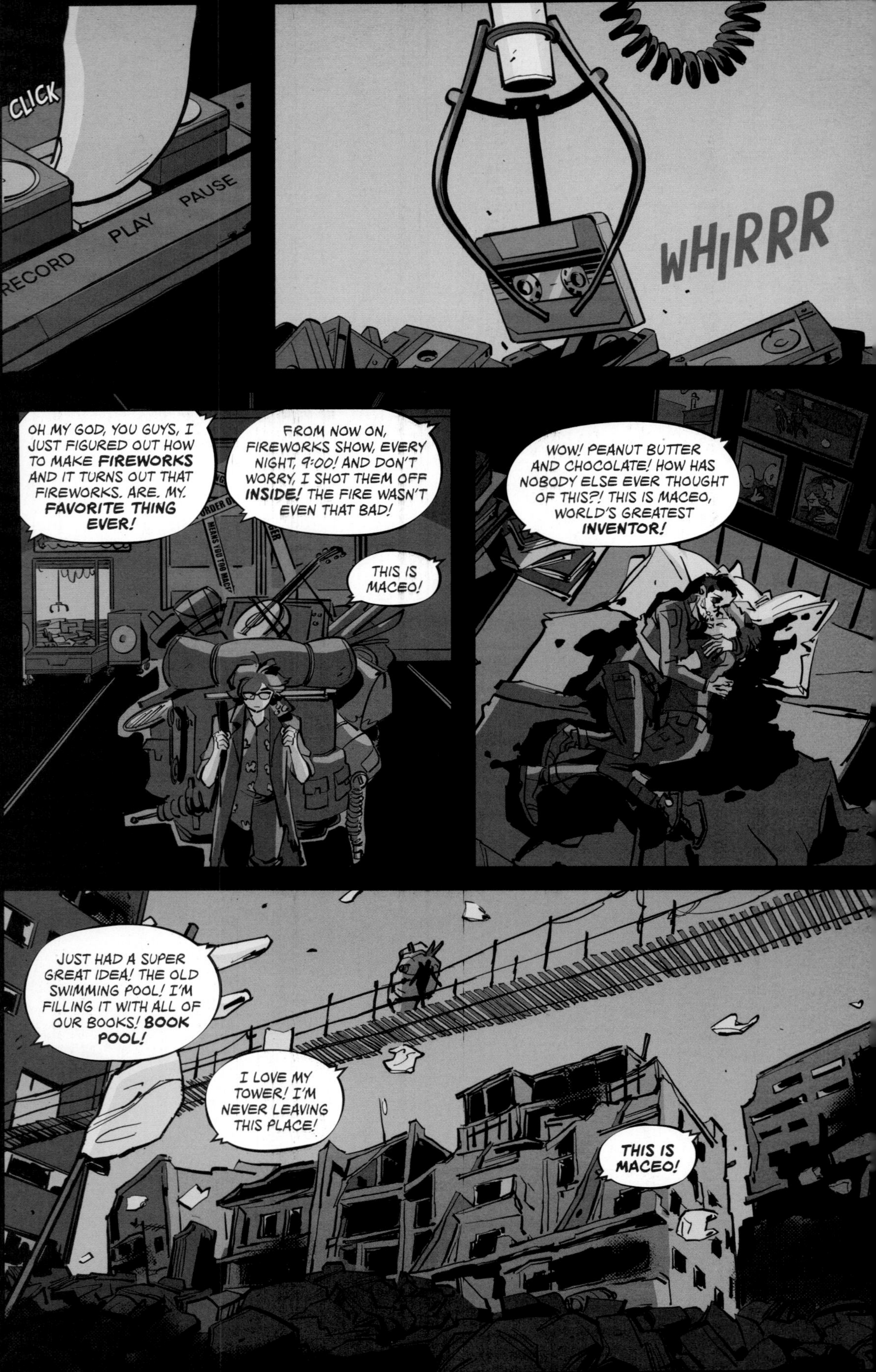
CLICK
RECORD
PLAY
PAUSE
WHIRRR
OH MY GOD, YOU GUYS, I JUST FIGURED OUT HOW TO MAKE **FIREWORKS** AND IT TURNS OUT THAT FIREWORKS. ARE. MY. **FAVORITE THING EVER!**
FROM NOW ON, FIREWORKS SHOW, EVERY NIGHT, 9:00! AND DON'T WORRY, I SHOT THEM OFF **INSIDE!** THE FIRE WASN'T EVEN THAT BAD!
THIS IS MACEO!
WOW! PEANUT BUTTER AND CHOCOLATE! HOW HAS NOBODY ELSE EVER THOUGHT OF THIS?! THIS IS MACEO, WORLD'S GREATEST **INVENTOR!**
JUST HAD A SUPER GREAT IDEA! THE OLD SWIMMING POOL! I'M FILLING IT WITH ALL OF OUR BOOKS! **BOOK POOL!**
I LOVE MY TOWER! I'M NEVER LEAVING THIS PLACE!
THIS IS MACEO!

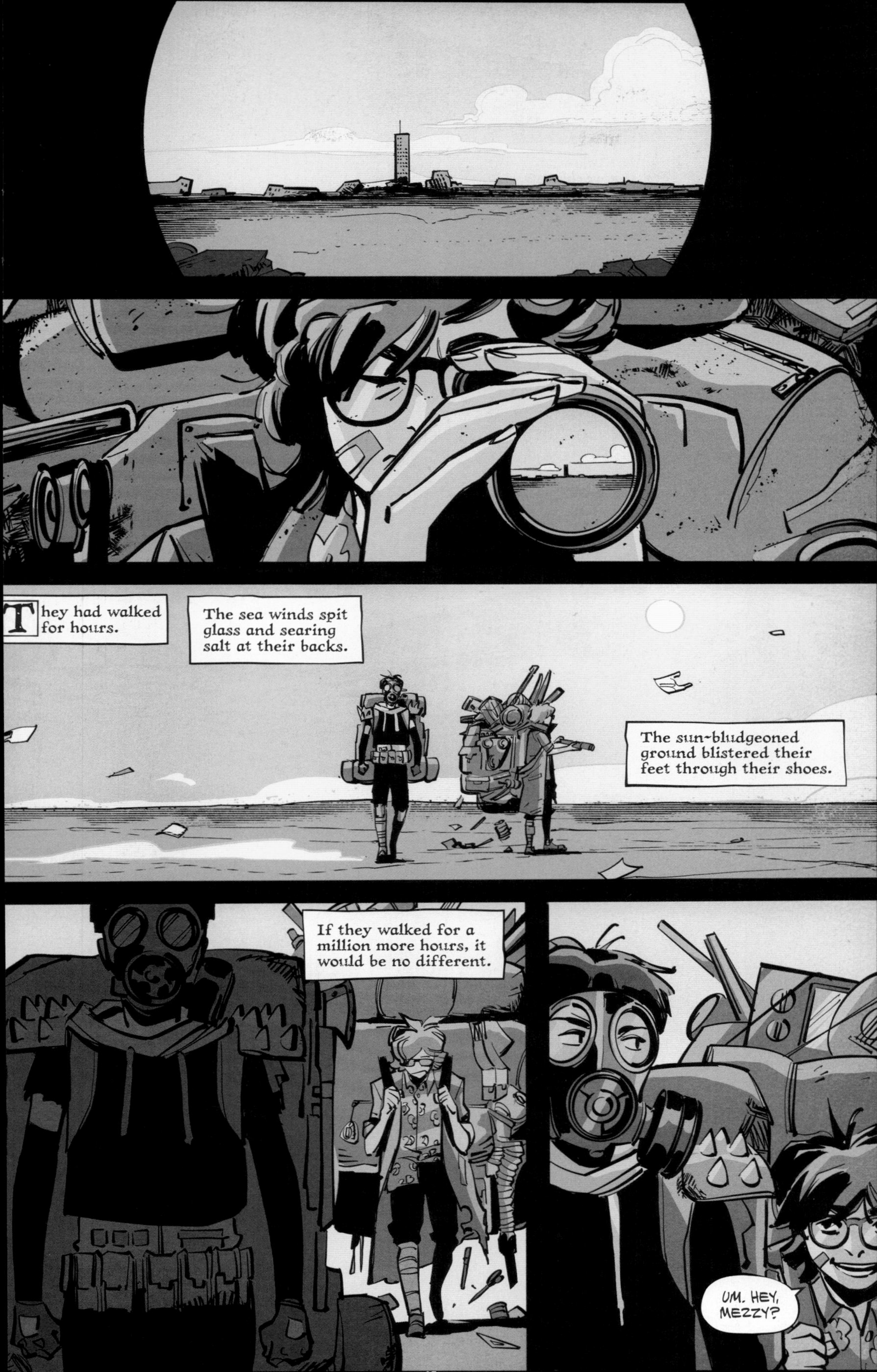
They had walked for hours.
The sea winds spit glass and searing salt at their backs.
The sun-bludgeoned ground blistered their feet through their shoes.
If they walked for a million more hours, it would be no different.
UM. HEY, MEZZY?

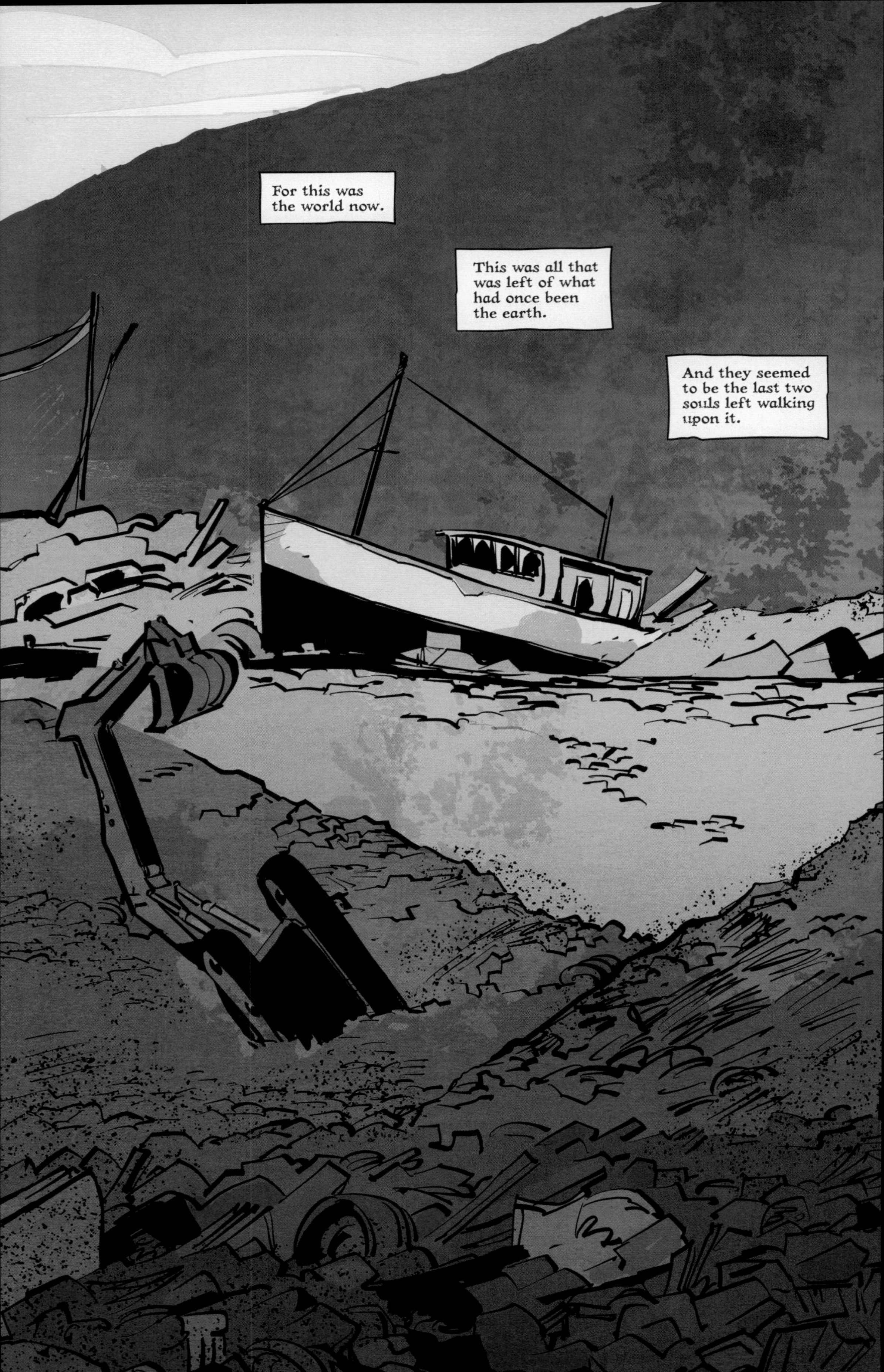
For this was the world now.
This was all that was left of what had once been the earth.
And they seemed to be the last two souls left walking upon it.

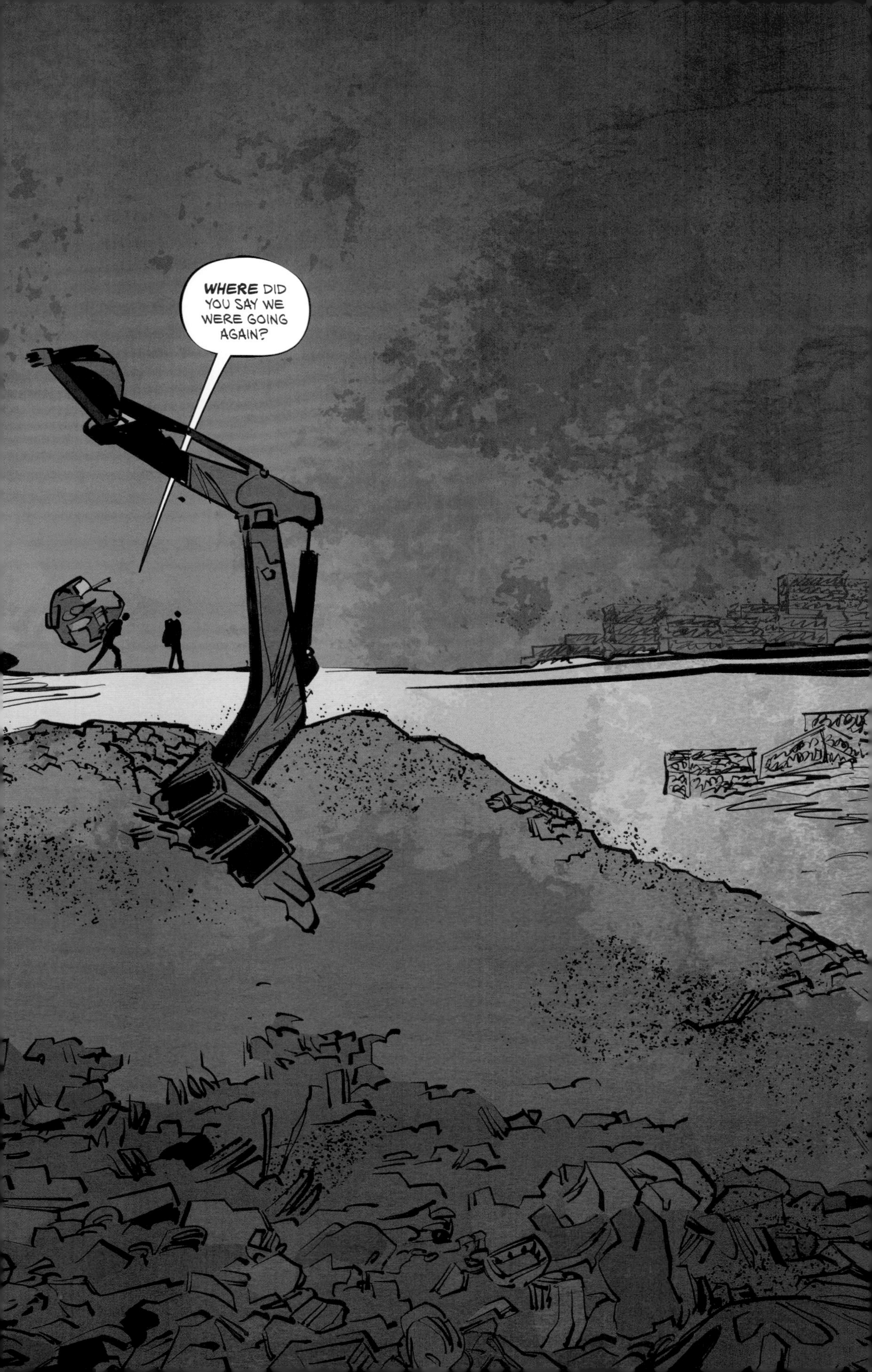
WHERE DID YOU SAY WE WERE GOING AGAIN?

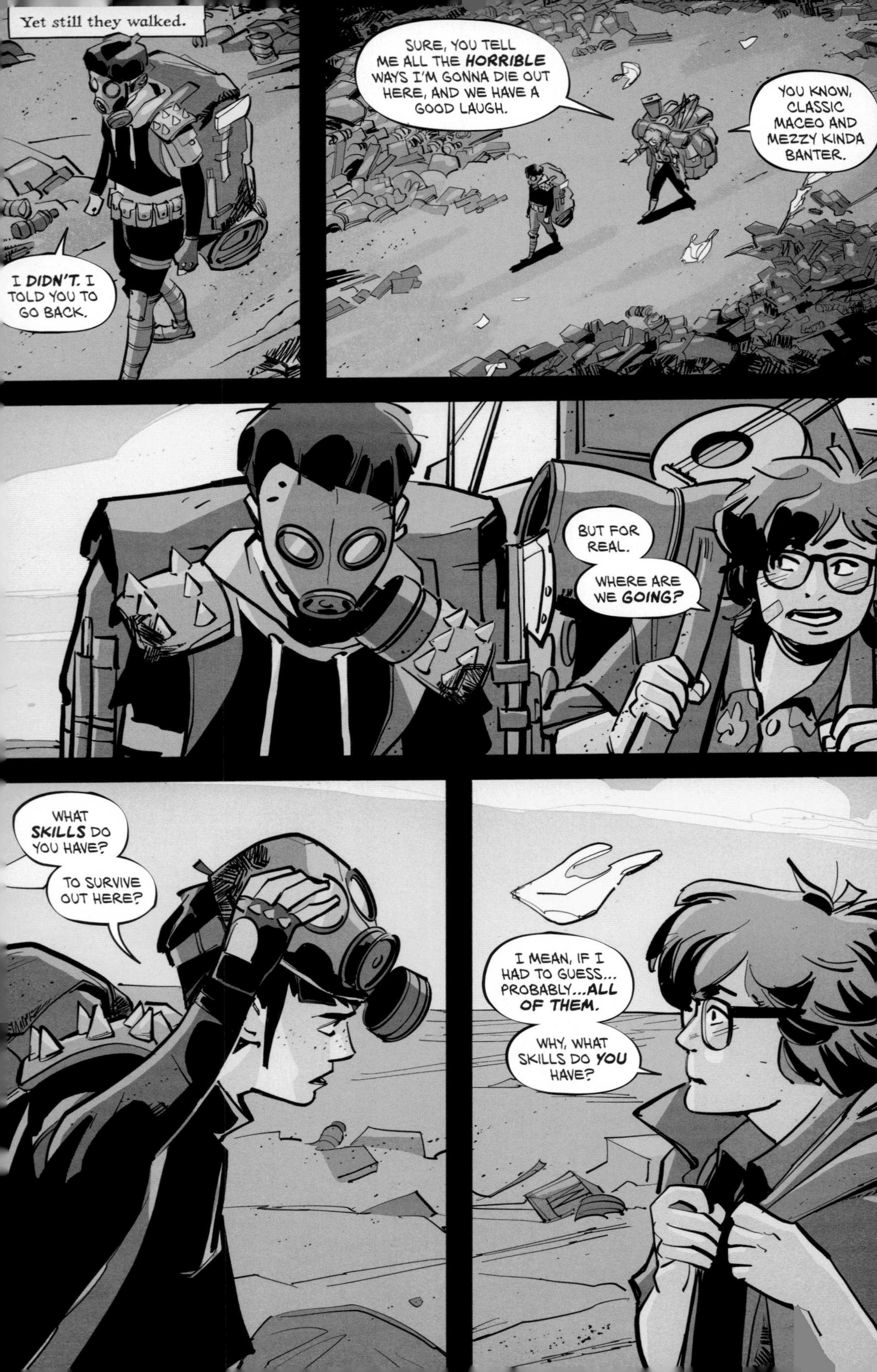
Yet still they walked.
I DIDN'T. I TOLD YOU TO GO BACK.
SURE, YOU TELL ME ALL THE HORRIBLE WAYS I'M GONNA DIE OUT HERE, AND WE HAVE A GOOD LAUGH.
YOU KNOW, CLASSIC MACEO AND MEZZY KINDA BANTER.
BUT FOR REAL.
WHERE ARE WE GOING?
WHAT SKILLS DO YOU HAVE?
TO SURVIVE OUT HERE?
I MEAN, IF I HAD TO GUESS... PROBABLY...ALL OF THEM.
WHY, WHAT SKILLS DO YOU HAVE?

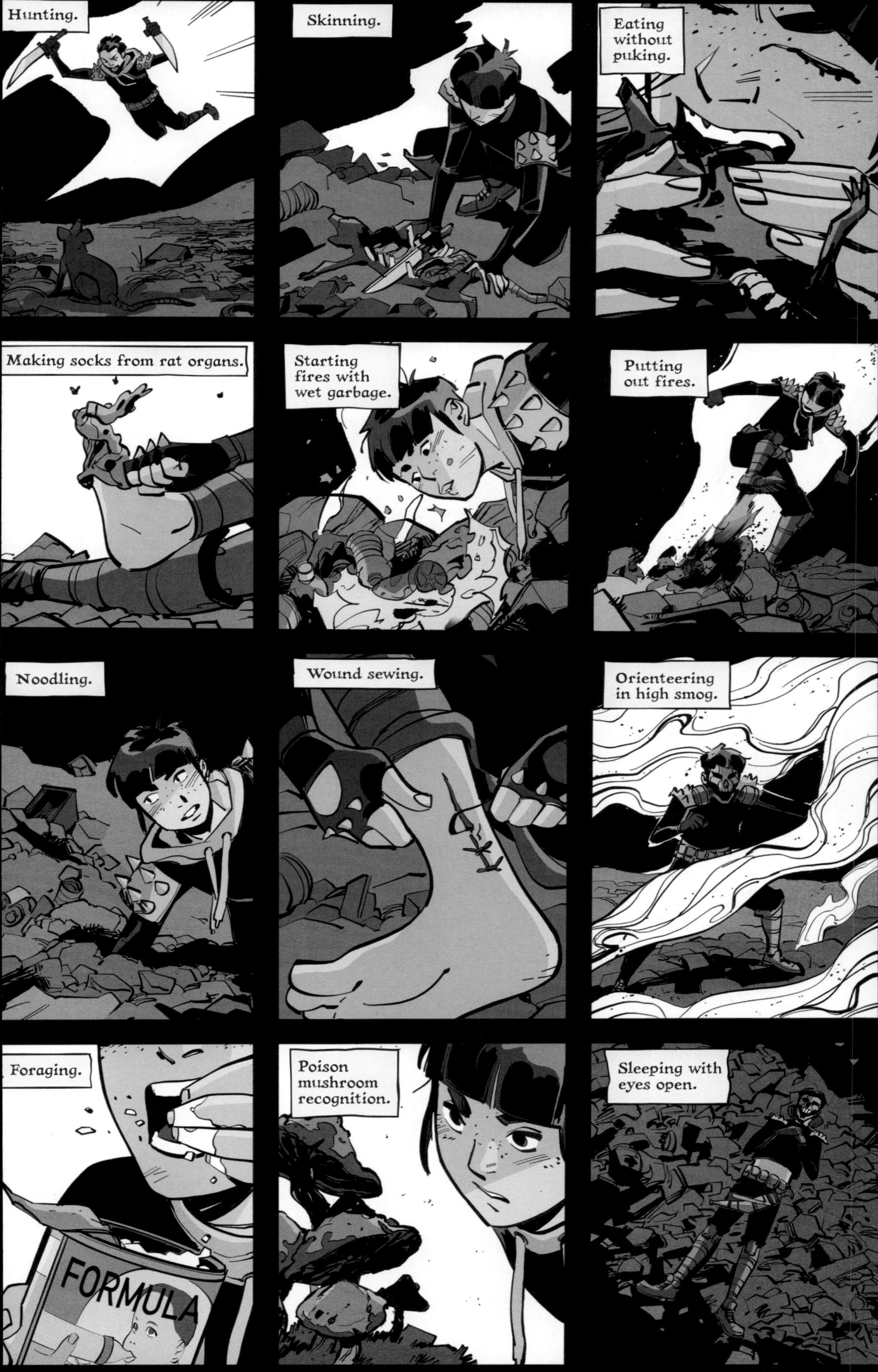
Hunting.
Skinning.
Eating without puking.
Making socks from rat organs.
Starting fires with wet garbage.
Putting out fires.
Noodling.
Wound sewing.
Orienteering in high smog.
Foraging.
FORMULA
Poison mushroom recognition.
Sleeping with eyes open.

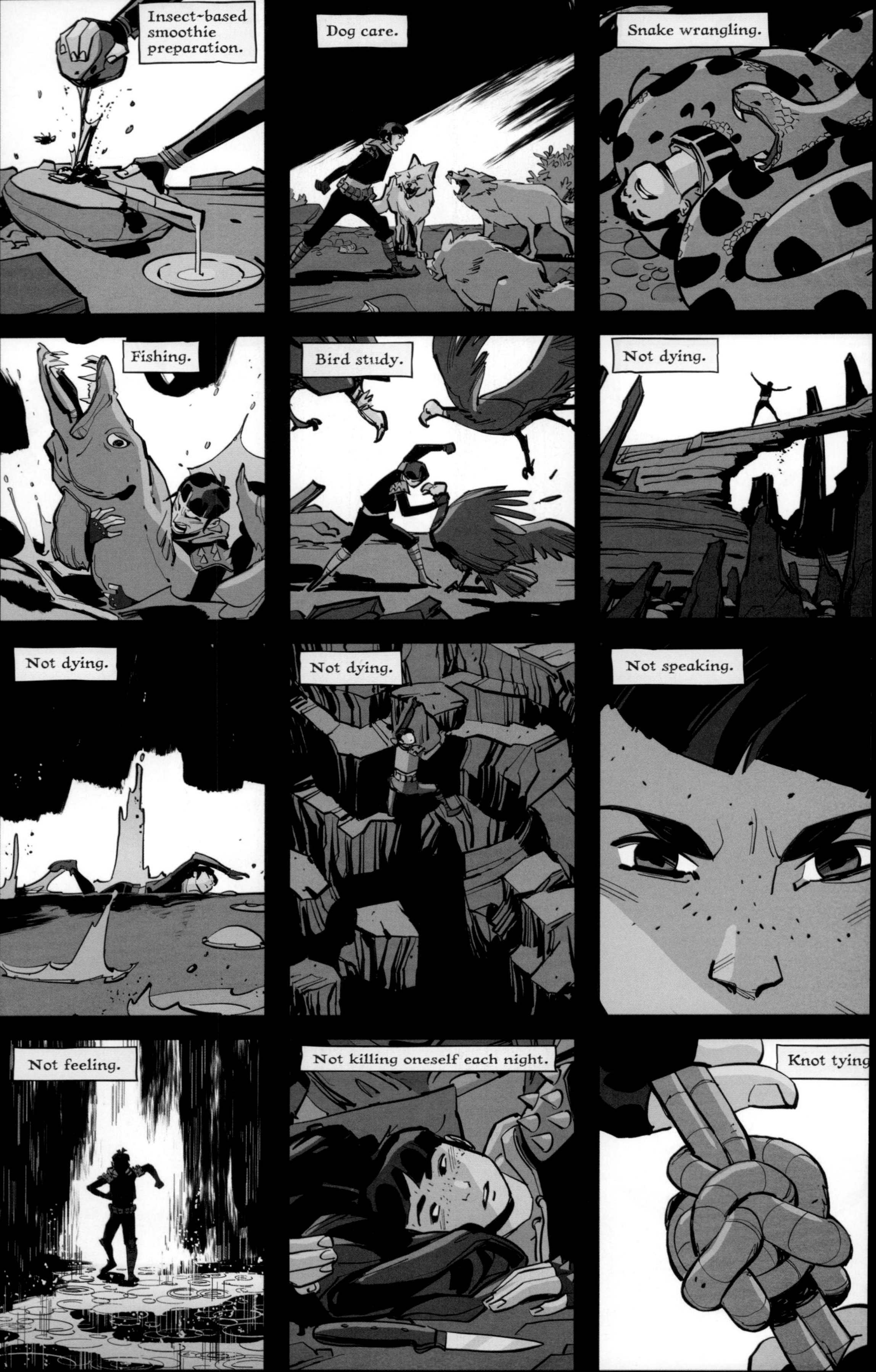
Insect-based smoothie preparation.
Dog care.
Snake wrangling.
Fishing.
Bird study.
Not dying.
Not dying.
Not dying.
Not speaking.
Not feeling.
Not killing oneself each night.
Knot tying

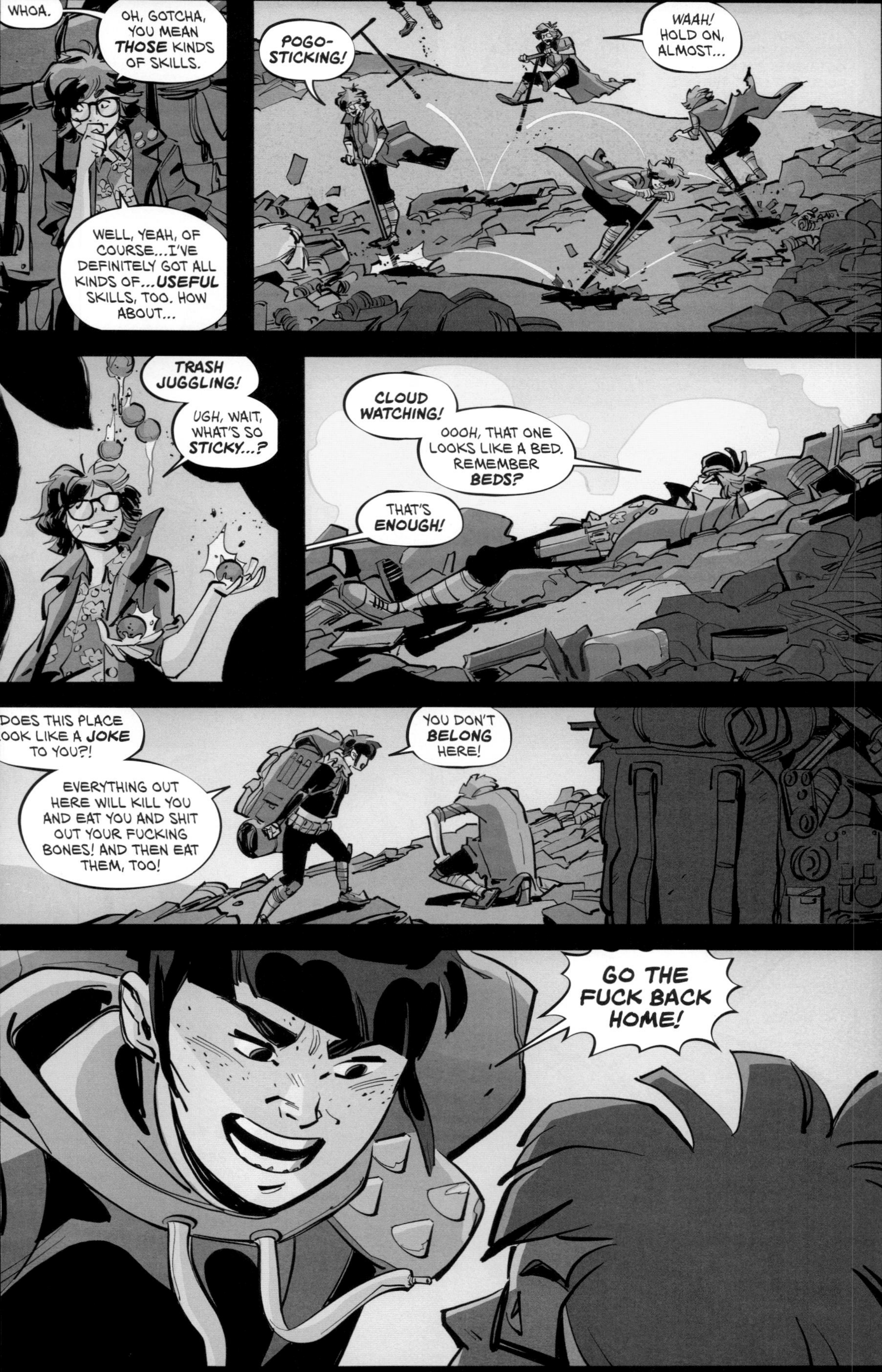
WHOA.
OH, GOTCHA, YOU MEAN THOSE KINDS OF SKILLS.
WELL, YEAH, OF COURSE...I'VE DEFINITELY GOT ALL KINDS OF...USEFUL SKILLS, TOO. HOW ABOUT...
POGO-STICKING!
WAAH! HOLD ON, ALMOST...
TRASH JUGGLING!
UGH, WAIT, WHAT'S SO STICKY...?
CLOUD WATCHING!
OOOH, THAT ONE LOOKS LIKE A BED. REMEMBER BEDS?
THAT'S ENOUGH!
DOES THIS PLACE LOOK LIKE A JOKE TO YOU?!
EVERYTHING OUT HERE WILL KILL YOU AND EAT YOU AND SHIT OUT YOUR FUCKING BONES! AND THEN EAT THEM, TOO!
YOU DON'T BELONG HERE!
GO THE FUCK BACK HOME!

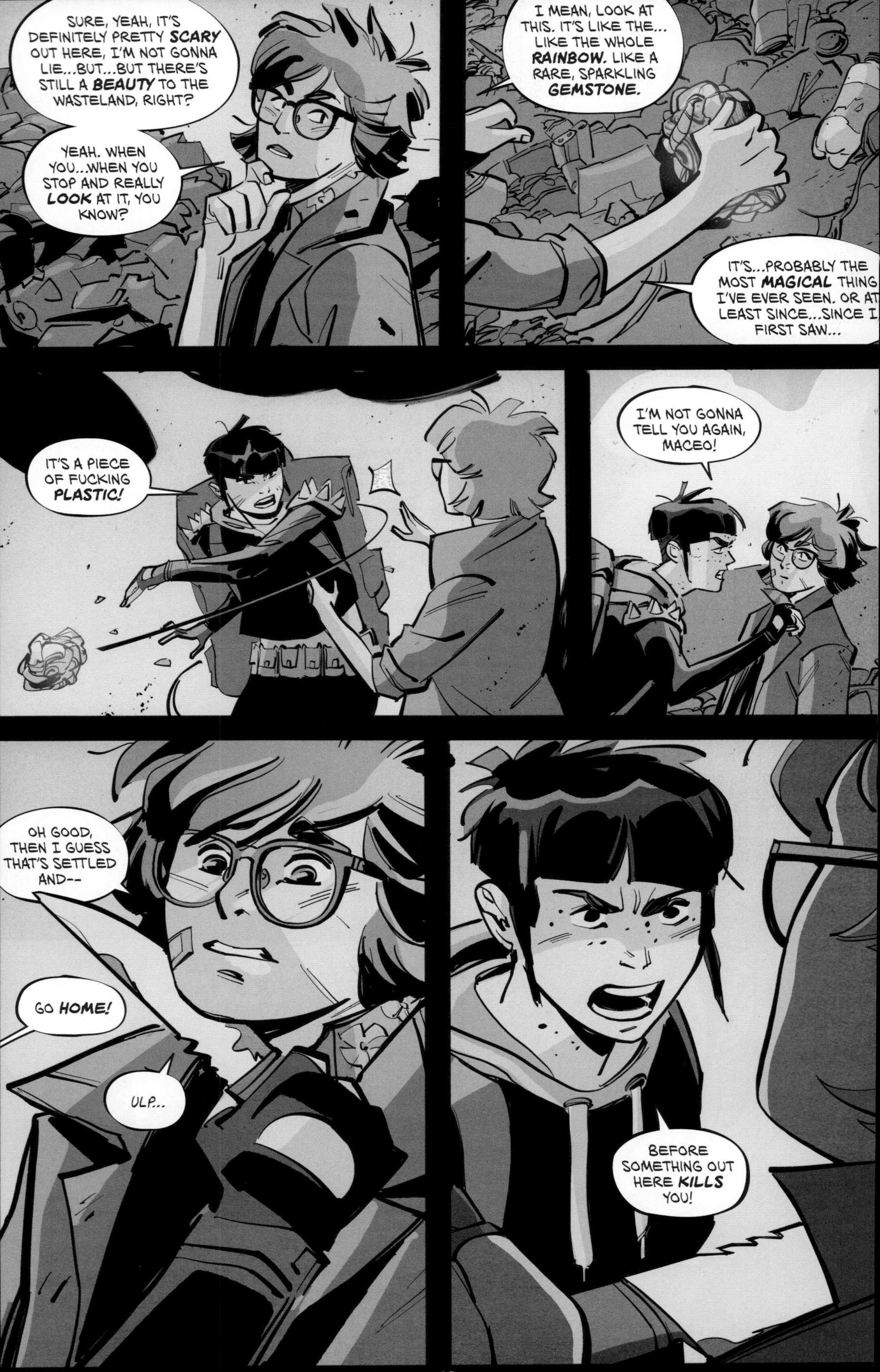
SURE, YEAH, IT'S DEFINITELY PRETTY **SCARY** OUT HERE, I'M NOT GONNA LIE...BUT...BUT THERE'S STILL A **BEAUTY** TO THE WASTELAND, RIGHT?
YEAH. WHEN YOU...WHEN YOU STOP AND REALLY **LOOK** AT IT, YOU KNOW?
I MEAN, LOOK AT THIS. IT'S LIKE THE... LIKE THE WHOLE **RAINBOW.** LIKE A RARE, SPARKLING **GEMSTONE.**
IT'S...PROBABLY THE MOST **MAGICAL** THING I'VE EVER SEEN. OR AT LEAST SINCE...SINCE I FIRST SAW...
IT'S A PIECE OF FUCKING **PLASTIC!**
I'M NOT GONNA TELL YOU AGAIN, MACEO!
OH GOOD, THEN I GUESS THAT'S SETTLED AND--
GO **HOME!**
ULP...
BEFORE SOMETHING OUT HERE **KILLS** YOU!

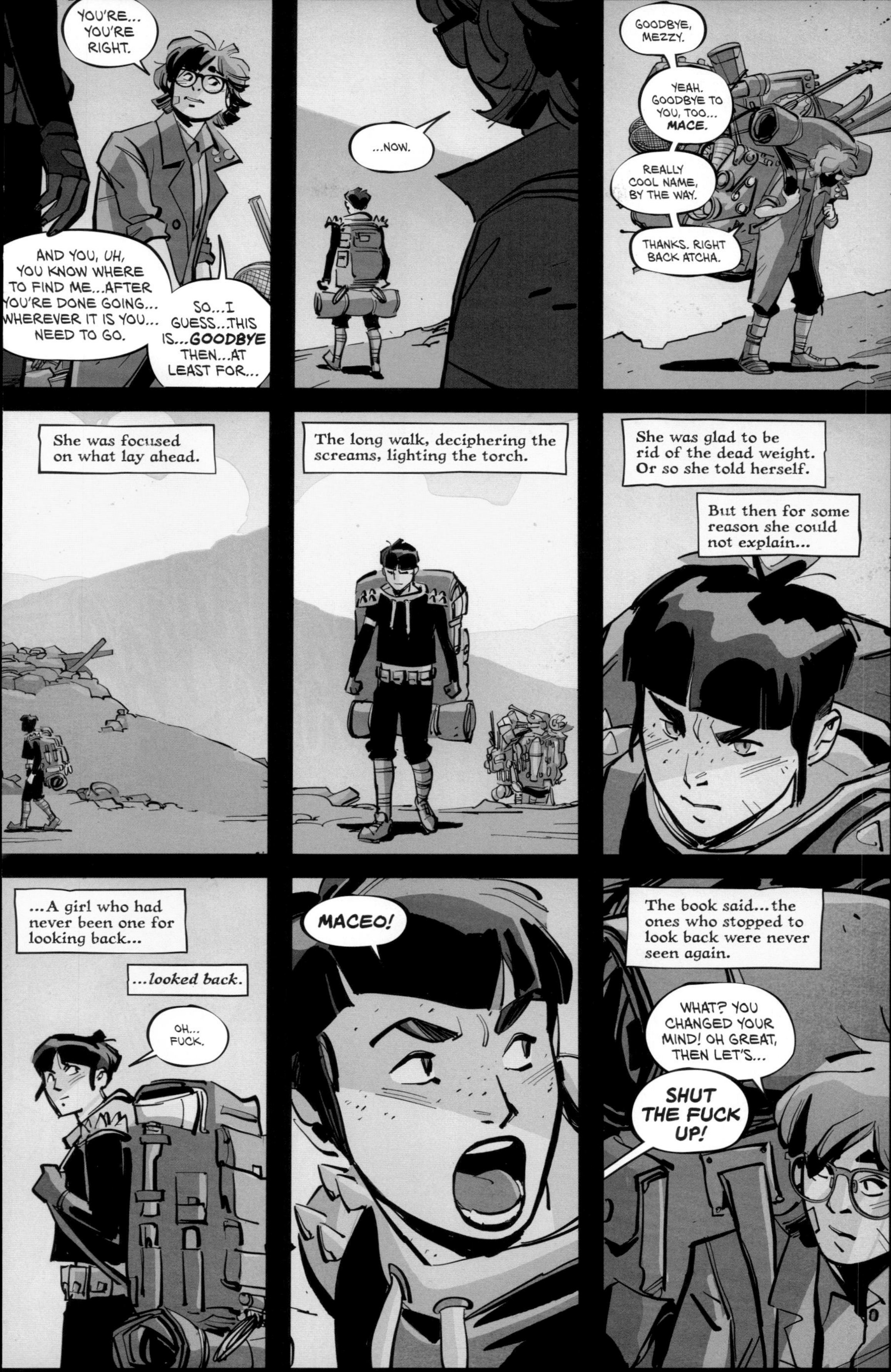
YOU'RE... YOU'RE RIGHT.
AND YOU, UH, YOU KNOW WHERE TO FIND ME...AFTER YOU'RE DONE GOING... WHEREVER IT IS YOU... NEED TO GO.
SO...I GUESS...THIS IS...GOODBYE THEN...AT LEAST FOR...
...NOW.
GOODBYE, MEZZY.
YEAH. GOODBYE TO YOU, TOO... MACE.
REALLY COOL NAME, BY THE WAY.
THANKS. RIGHT BACK ATCHA.
She was focused on what lay ahead.
The long walk, deciphering the screams, lighting the torch.
She was glad to be rid of the dead weight. Or so she told herself.
But then for some reason she could not explain...
...A girl who had never been one for looking back...
...looked back.
OH... FUCK.
MACEO!
The book said...the ones who stopped to look back were never seen again.
WHAT? YOU CHANGED YOUR MIND! OH GREAT, THEN LET'S...
SHUT THE FUCK UP!

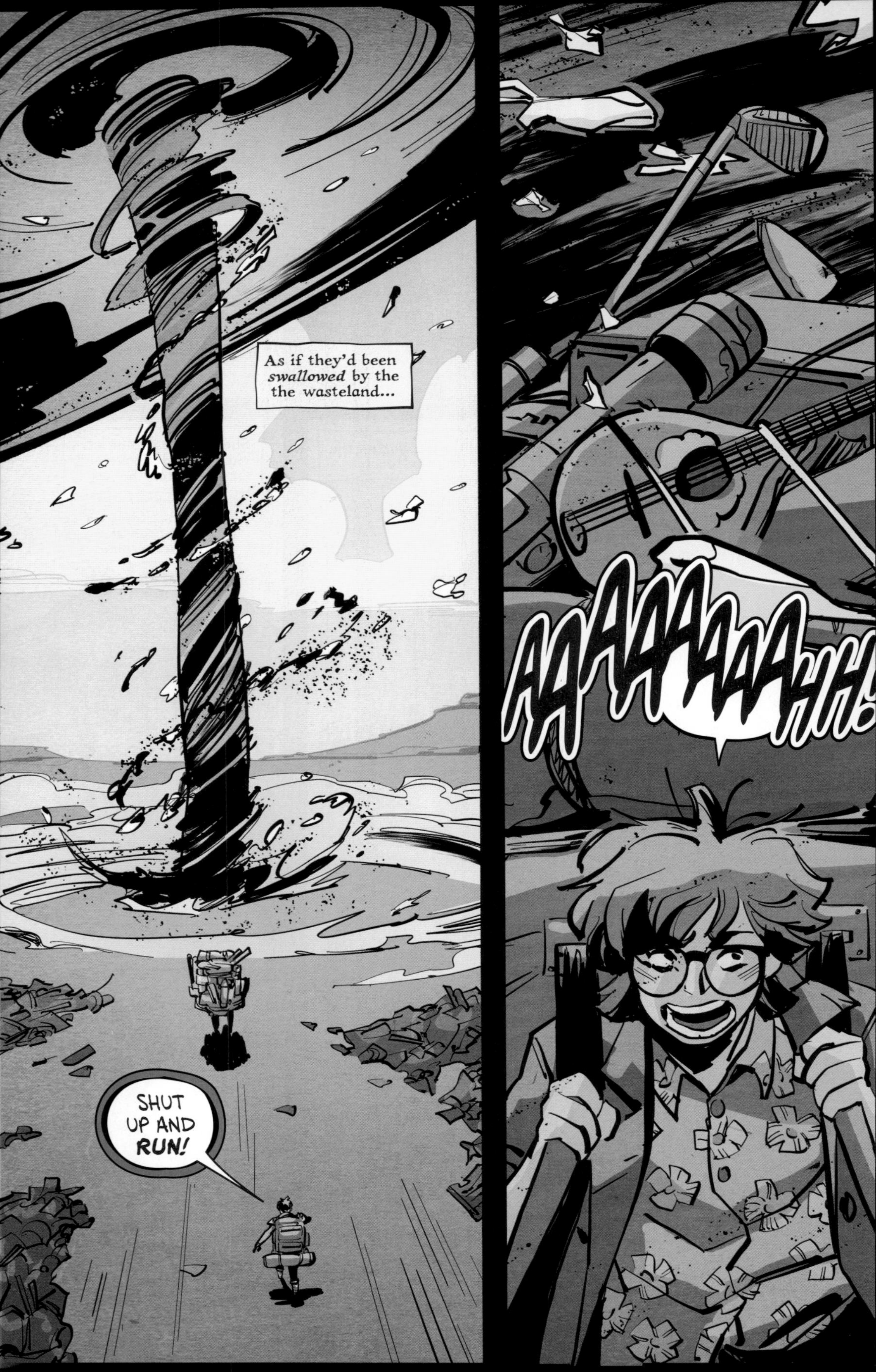
As if they'd been *swallowed* by the the wasteland...
SHUT UP AND **RUN!**
AAAAAAAAAHH!

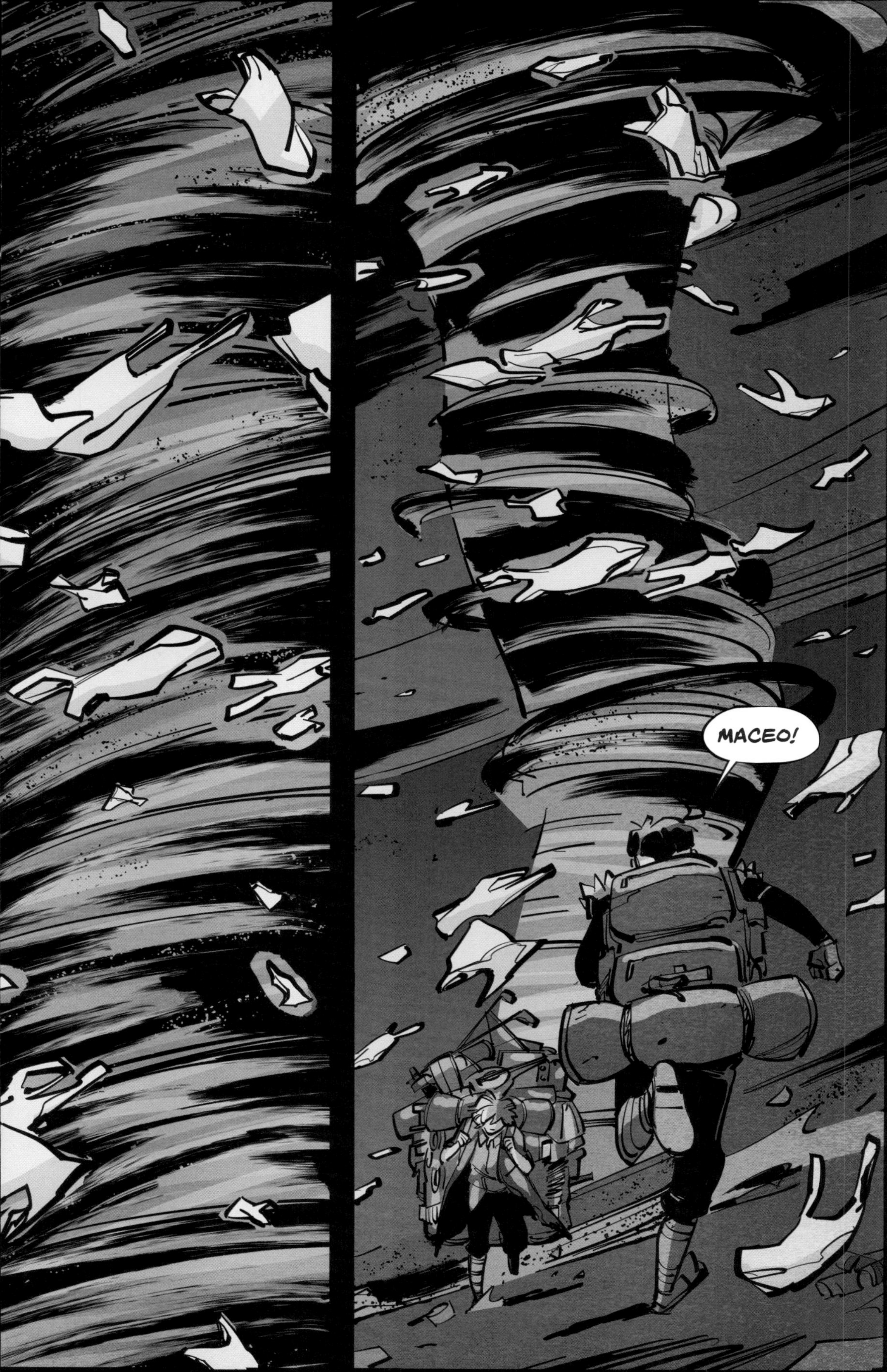
MACEO!

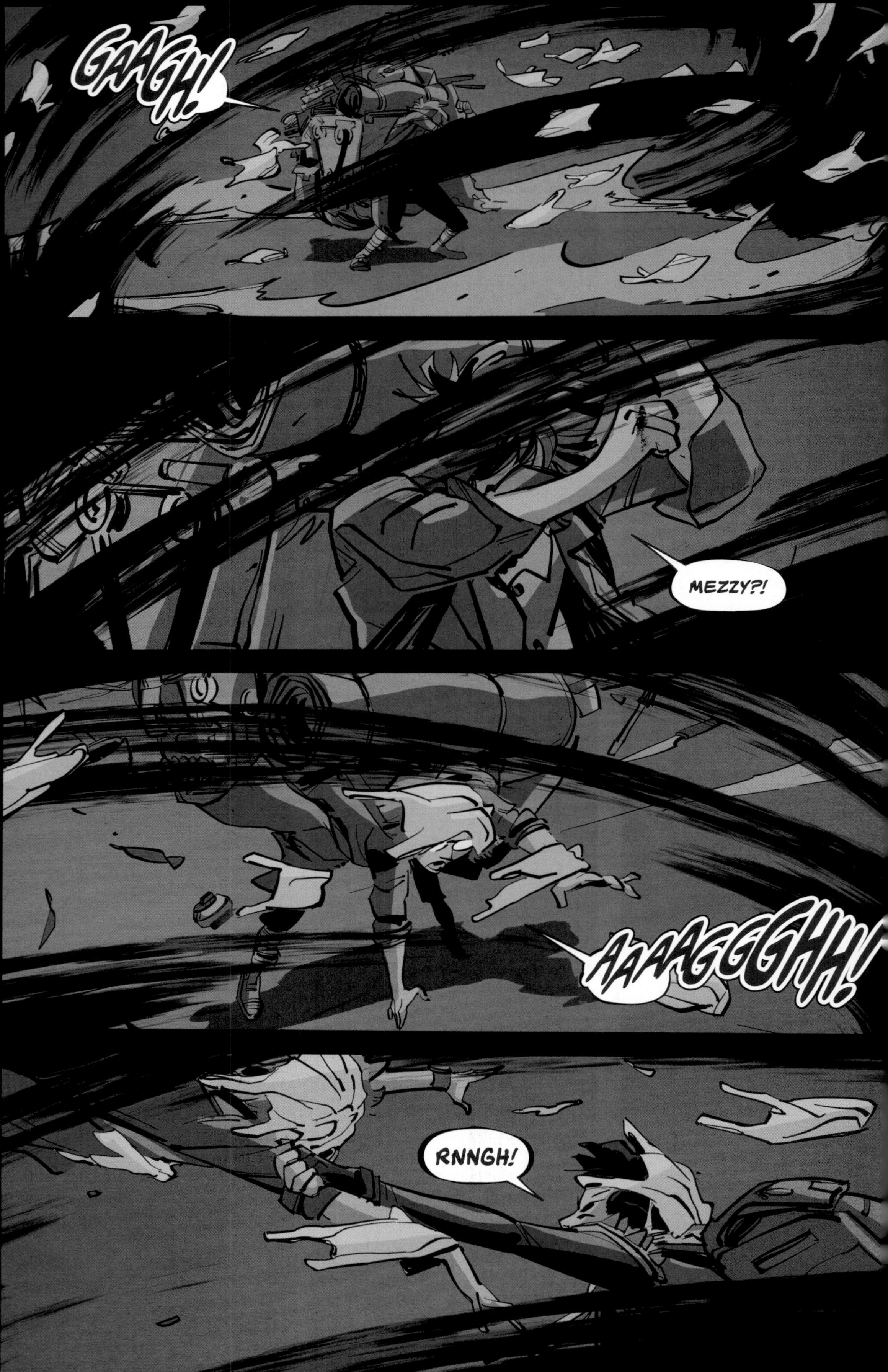
GAAGH!
MEZZY?!
AAAAGGGHH!
RNNGH!

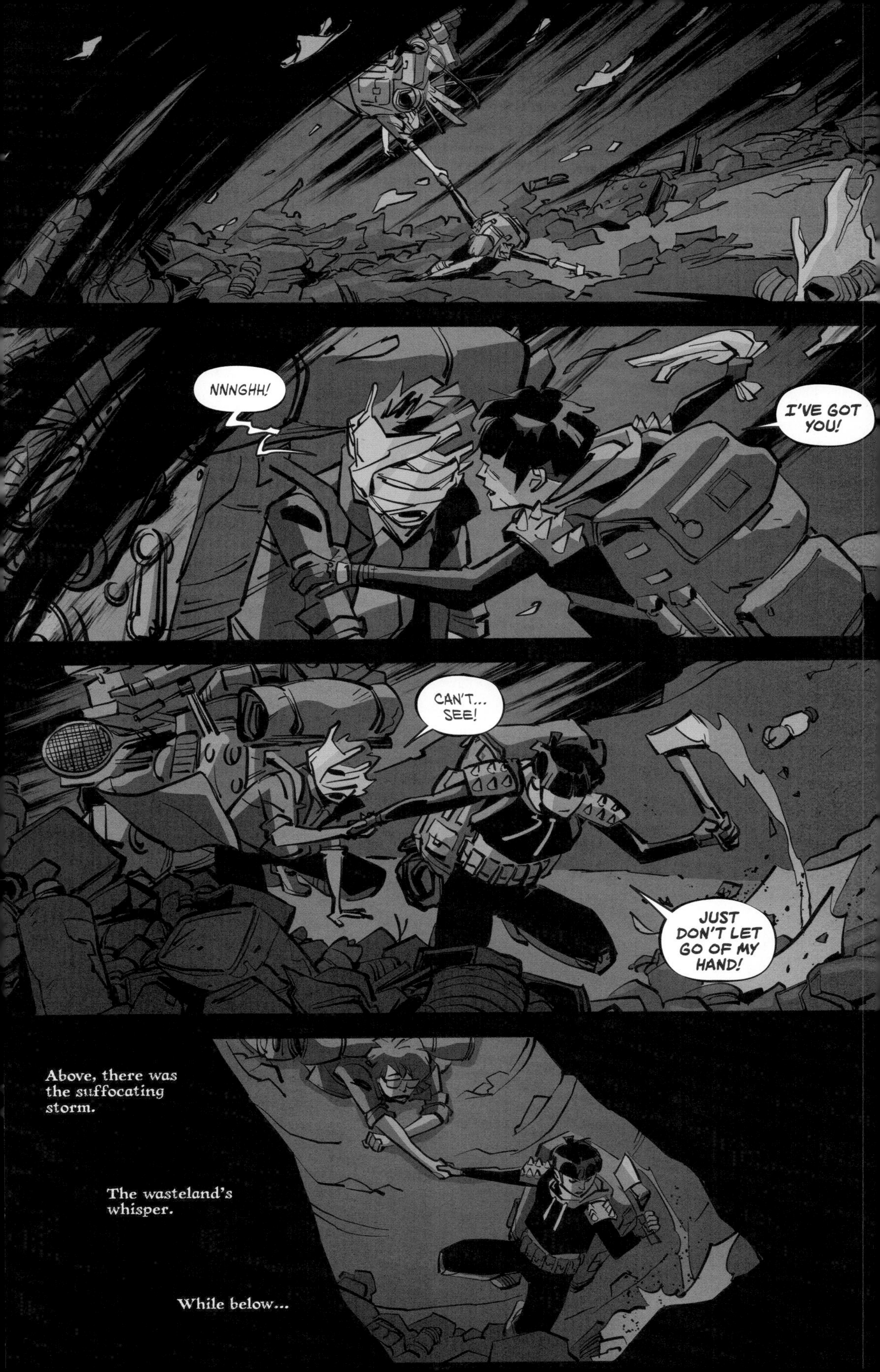
NNNGHH!
I'VE GOT YOU!
CAN'T... SEE!
JUST DON'T LET GO OF MY HAND!
Above, there was the suffocating storm.
The wasteland's whisper.
While below...

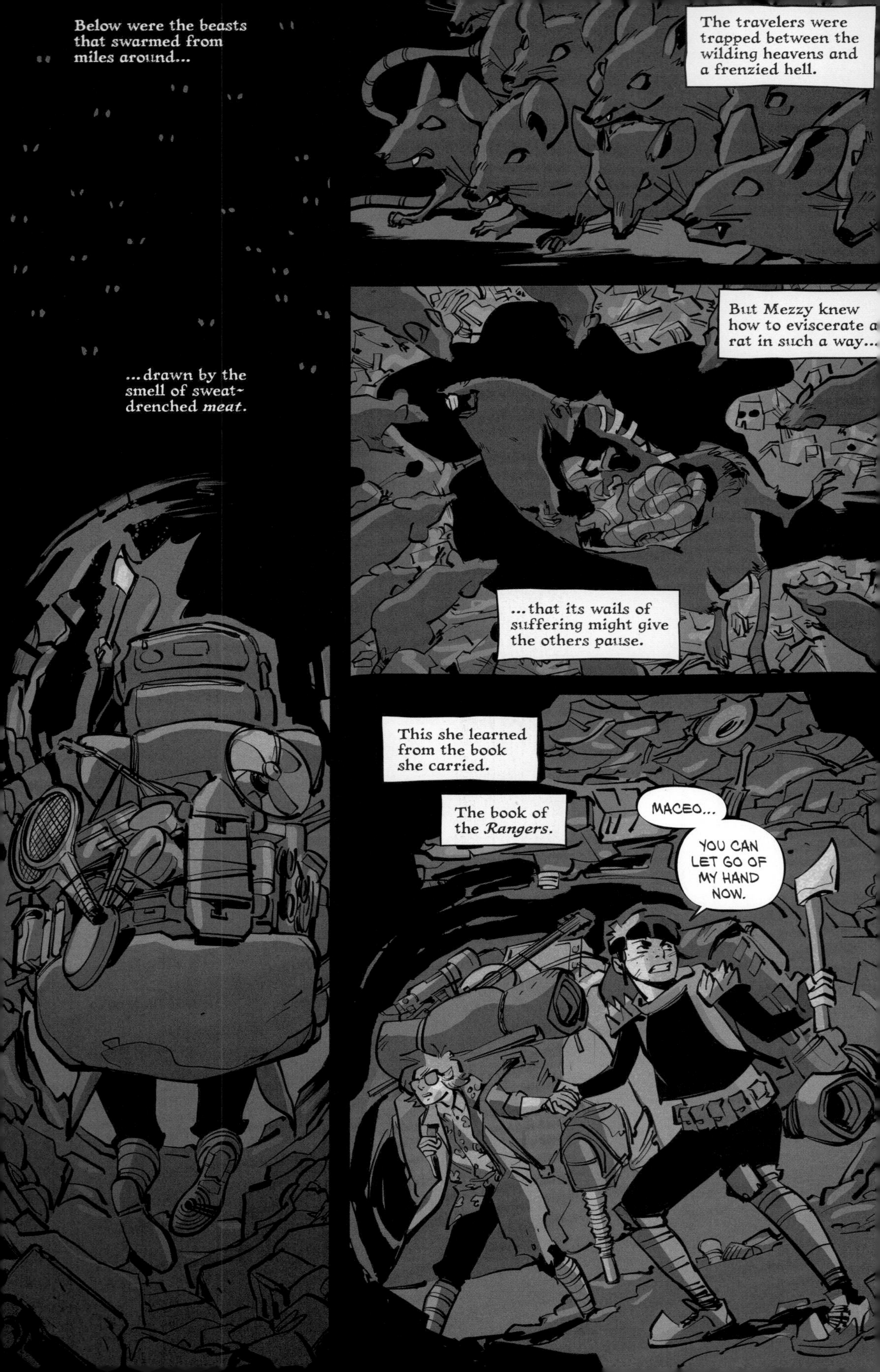
Below were the beasts that swarmed from miles around...
...drawn by the smell of sweat-drenched *meat*.
The travelers were trapped between the wilding heavens and a frenzied hell.
But Mezzy knew how to eviscerate a rat in such a way...
...that its wails of suffering might give the others pause.
This she learned from the book she carried.
The book of the *Rangers*.
MACEO...
YOU CAN LET GO OF MY HAND NOW.

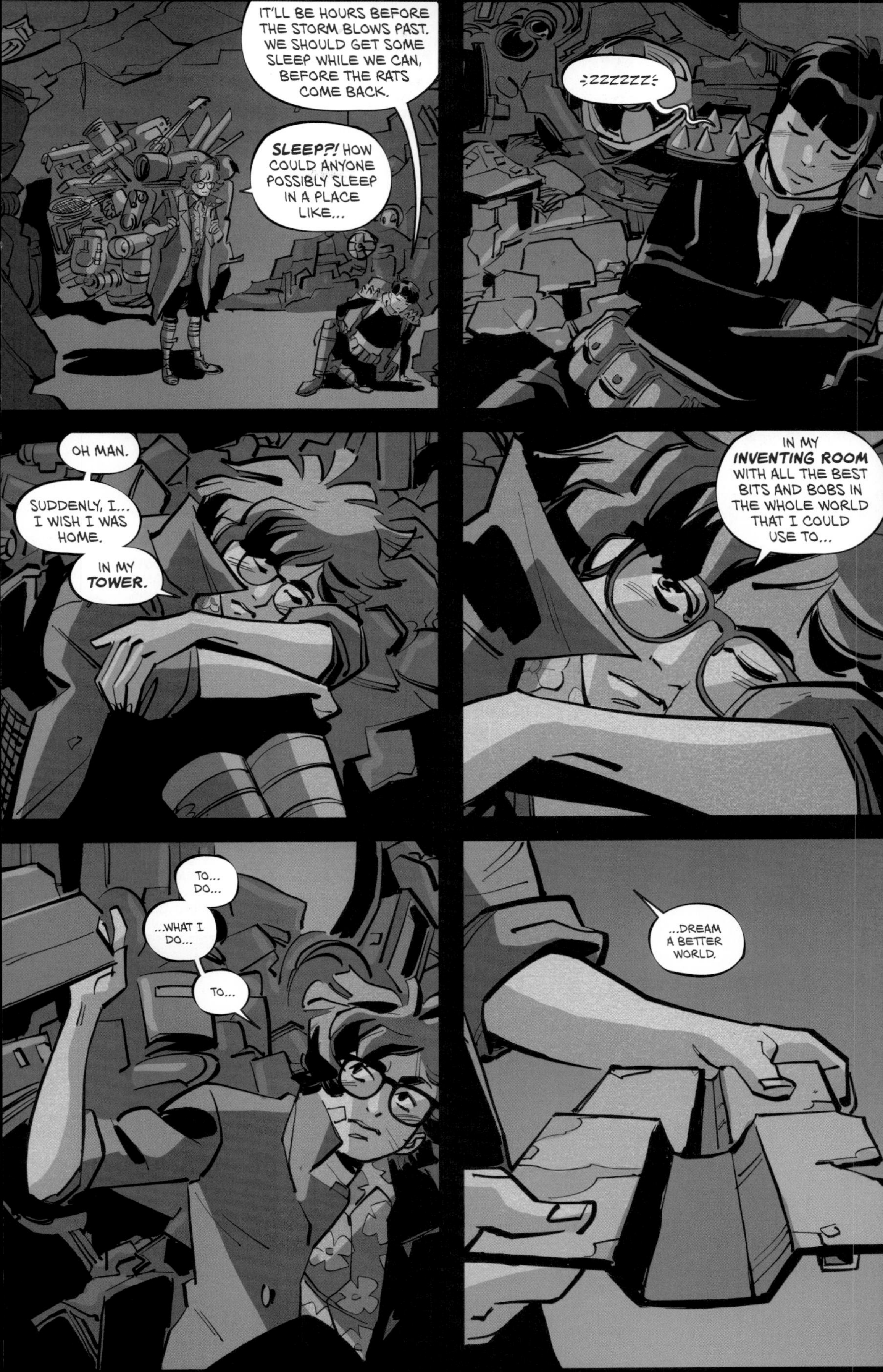
IT'LL BE HOURS BEFORE THE STORM BLOWS PAST. WE SHOULD GET SOME SLEEP WHILE WE CAN, BEFORE THE RATS COME BACK.
SLEEP?! HOW COULD ANYONE POSSIBLY SLEEP IN A PLACE LIKE...
ZZZZZZ
OH MAN.
SUDDENLY, I... I WISH I WAS HOME.
IN MY TOWER.
IN MY INVENTING ROOM WITH ALL THE BEST BITS AND BOBS IN THE WHOLE WORLD THAT I COULD USE TO...
TO... DO...
...WHAT I DO...
TO...
...DREAM A BETTER WORLD.

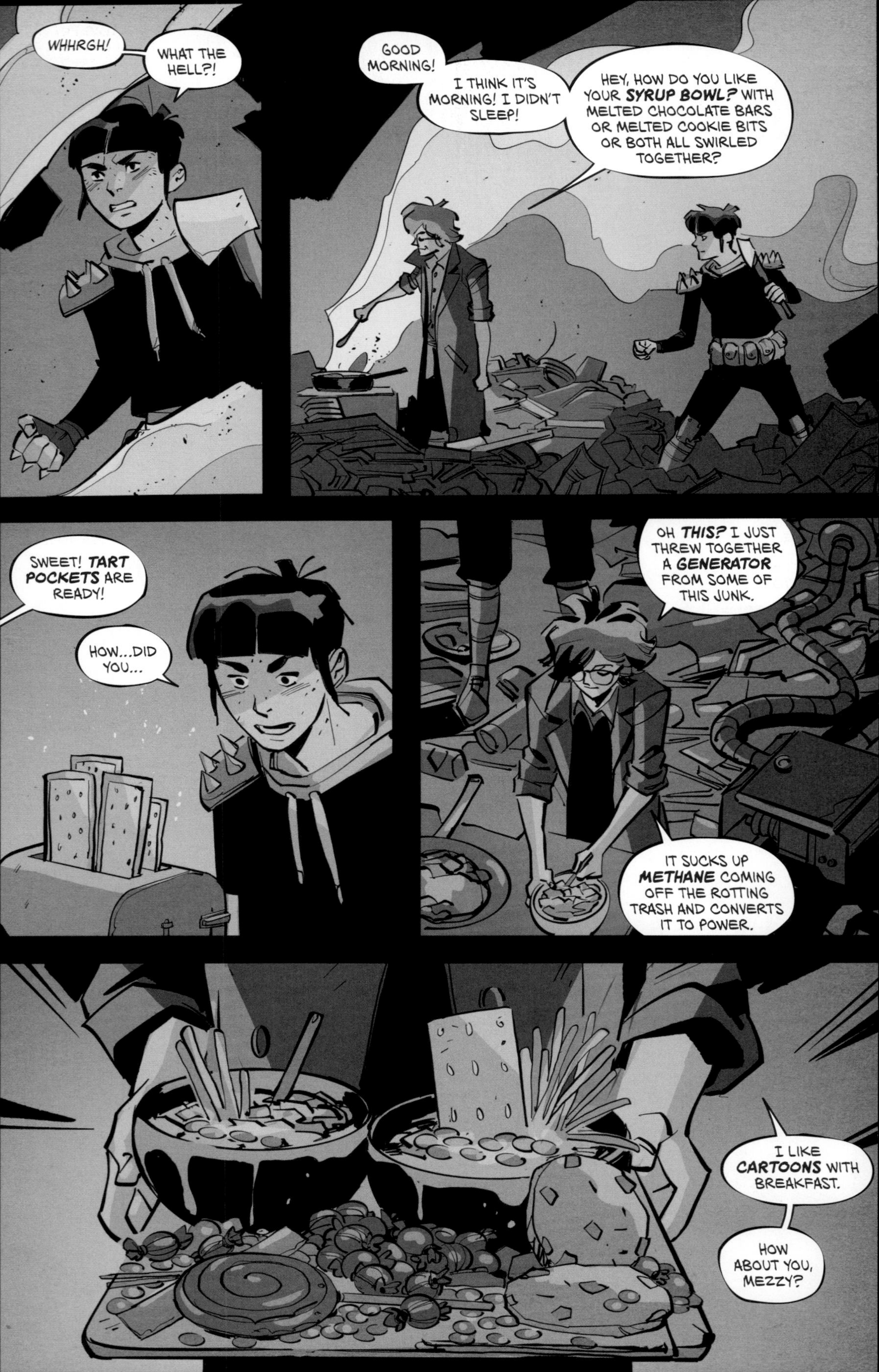
WHHRGH!
WHAT THE HELL?!
GOOD MORNING!
I THINK IT'S MORNING! I DIDN'T SLEEP!
HEY, HOW DO YOU LIKE YOUR **SYRUP BOWL?** WITH MELTED CHOCOLATE BARS OR MELTED COOKIE BITS OR BOTH ALL SWIRLED TOGETHER?
SWEET! **TART POCKETS** ARE READY!
HOW...DID YOU...
OH **THIS?** I JUST THREW TOGETHER A **GENERATOR** FROM SOME OF THIS JUNK.
IT SUCKS UP **METHANE** COMING OFF THE ROTTING TRASH AND CONVERTS IT TO POWER.
I LIKE **CARTOONS** WITH BREAKFAST.
HOW ABOUT YOU, MEZZY?

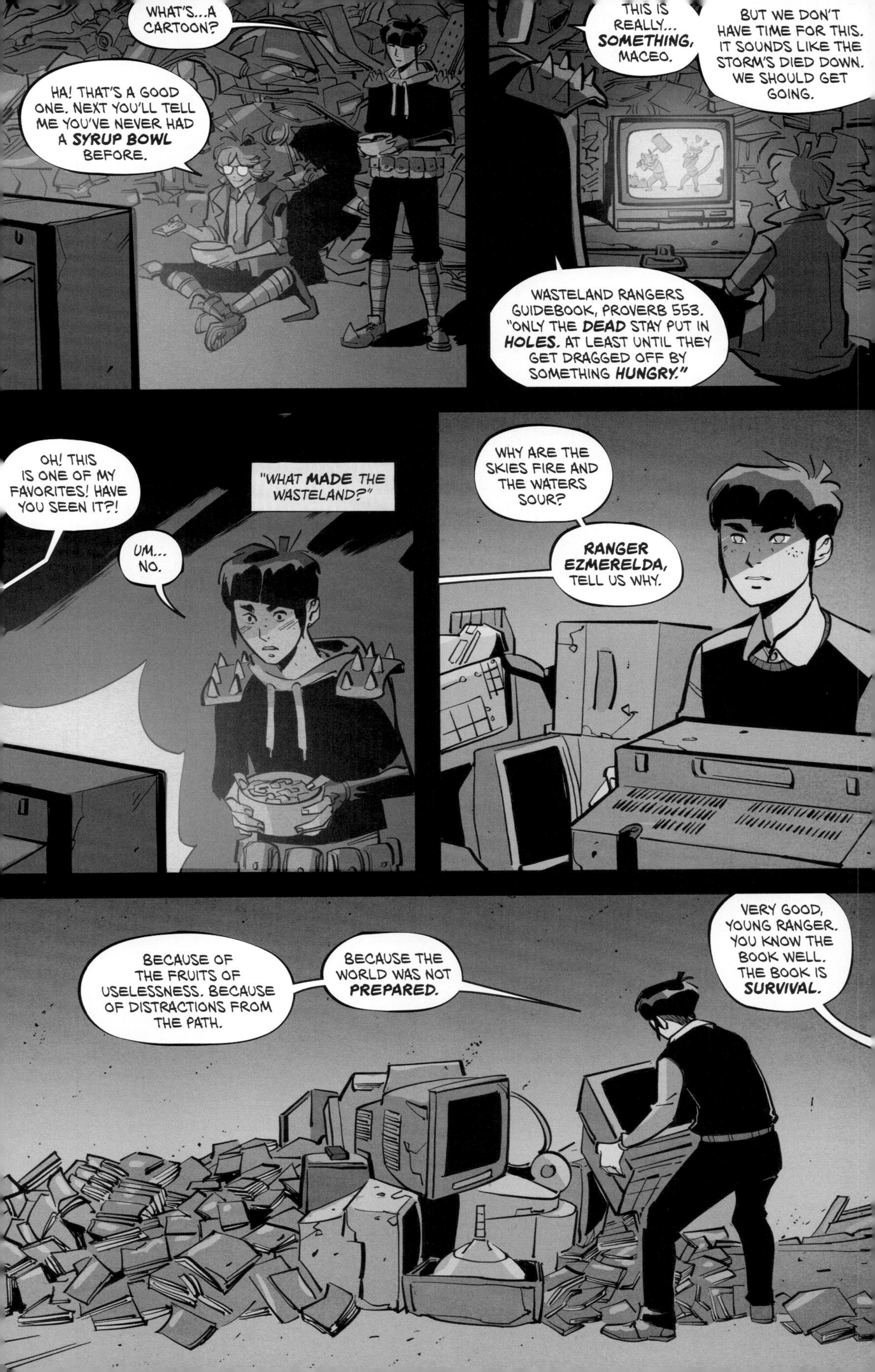
WHAT'S...A CARTOON?
HA! THAT'S A GOOD ONE. NEXT YOU'LL TELL ME YOU'VE NEVER HAD A SYRUP BOWL BEFORE.
THIS IS REALLY... SOMETHING, MACEO.
BUT WE DON'T HAVE TIME FOR THIS. IT SOUNDS LIKE THE STORM'S DIED DOWN. WE SHOULD GET GOING.
WASTELAND RANGERS GUIDEBOOK, PROVERB 553. "ONLY THE DEAD STAY PUT IN HOLES. AT LEAST UNTIL THEY GET DRAGGED OFF BY SOMETHING HUNGRY."
OH! THIS IS ONE OF MY FAVORITES! HAVE YOU SEEN IT?!
UM... NO.
"WHAT MADE THE WASTELAND?"
WHY ARE THE SKIES FIRE AND THE WATERS SOUR?
RANGER EZMERELDA, TELL US WHY.
BECAUSE OF THE FRUITS OF USELESSNESS. BECAUSE OF DISTRACTIONS FROM THE PATH.
BECAUSE THE WORLD WAS NOT PREPARED.
VERY GOOD, YOUNG RANGER. YOU KNOW THE BOOK WELL. THE BOOK IS SURVIVAL.

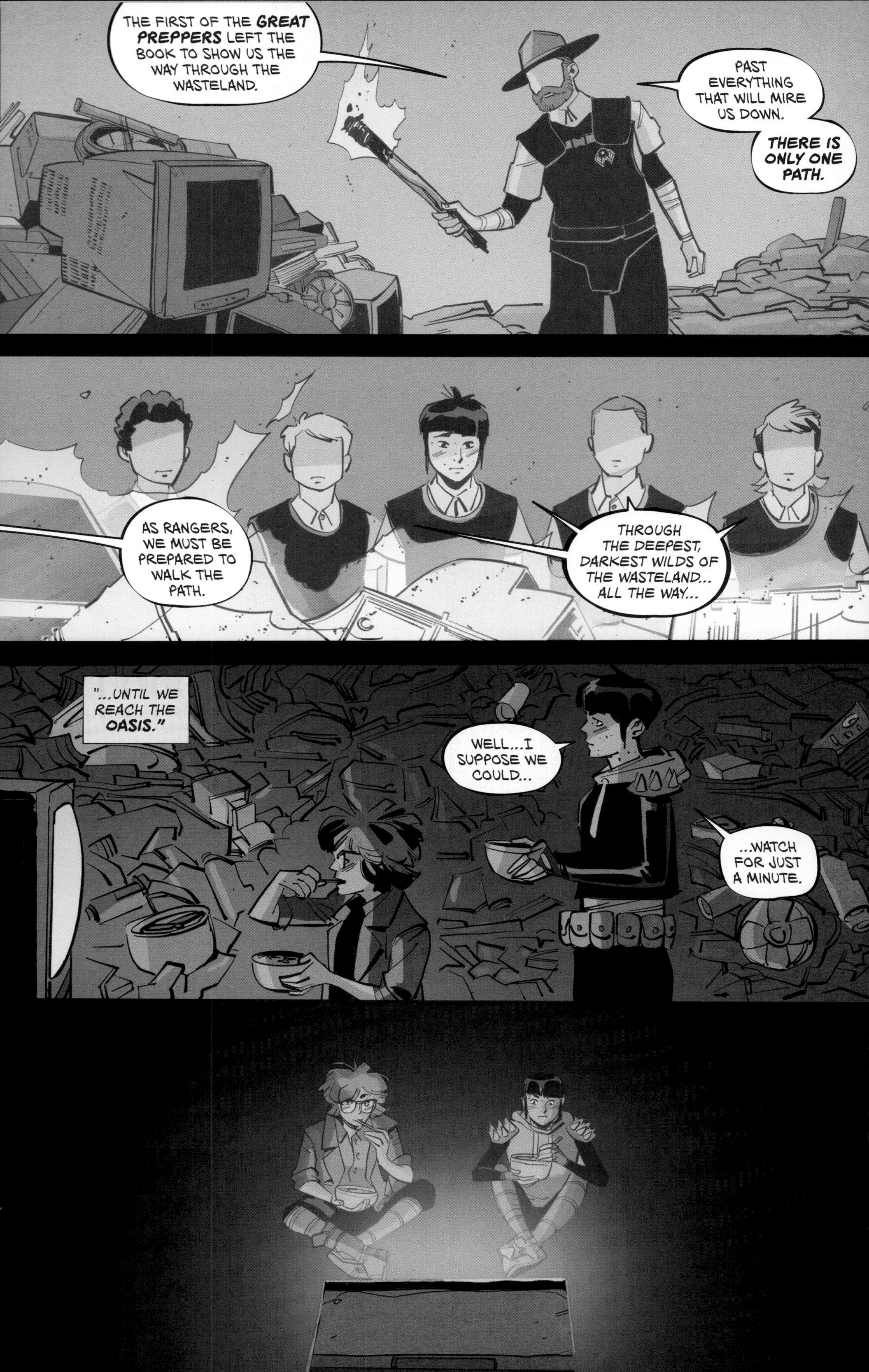
THE FIRST OF THE GREAT PREPPERS LEFT THE BOOK TO SHOW US THE WAY THROUGH THE WASTELAND.
PAST EVERYTHING THAT WILL MIRE US DOWN.
THERE IS ONLY ONE PATH.
AS RANGERS, WE MUST BE PREPARED TO WALK THE PATH.
THROUGH THE DEEPEST, DARKEST WILDS OF THE WASTELAND... ALL THE WAY...
"...UNTIL WE REACH THE OASIS."
WELL...I SUPPOSE WE COULD...
...WATCH FOR JUST A MINUTE.

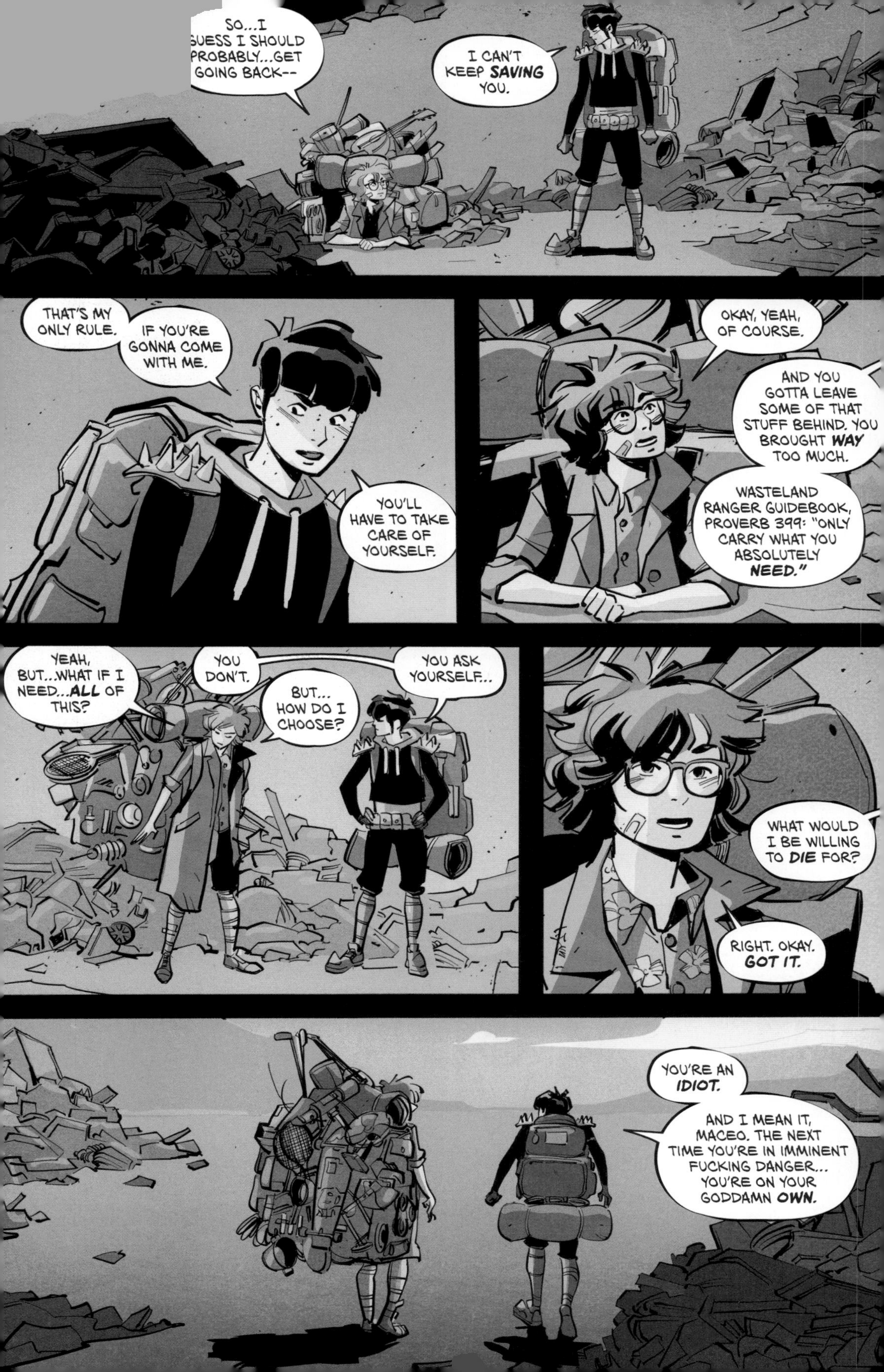
SO...I GUESS I SHOULD PROBABLY...GET GOING BACK--
I CAN'T KEEP **SAVING** YOU.
THAT'S MY ONLY RULE.
IF YOU'RE GONNA COME WITH ME.
YOU'LL HAVE TO TAKE CARE OF YOURSELF.
OKAY, YEAH, OF COURSE.
AND YOU GOTTA LEAVE SOME OF THAT STUFF BEHIND. YOU BROUGHT **WAY** TOO MUCH.
WASTELAND RANGER GUIDEBOOK, PROVERB 399: "ONLY CARRY WHAT YOU ABSOLUTELY **NEED.**"
YEAH, BUT...WHAT IF I NEED...**ALL** OF THIS?
YOU DON'T.
BUT... HOW DO I CHOOSE?
YOU ASK YOURSELF...
WHAT WOULD I BE WILLING TO **DIE** FOR?
RIGHT. OKAY. **GOT IT.**
YOU'RE AN **IDIOT.**
AND I MEAN IT, MACEO. THE NEXT TIME YOU'RE IN IMMINENT FUCKING DANGER... YOU'RE ON YOUR GODDAMN **OWN.**

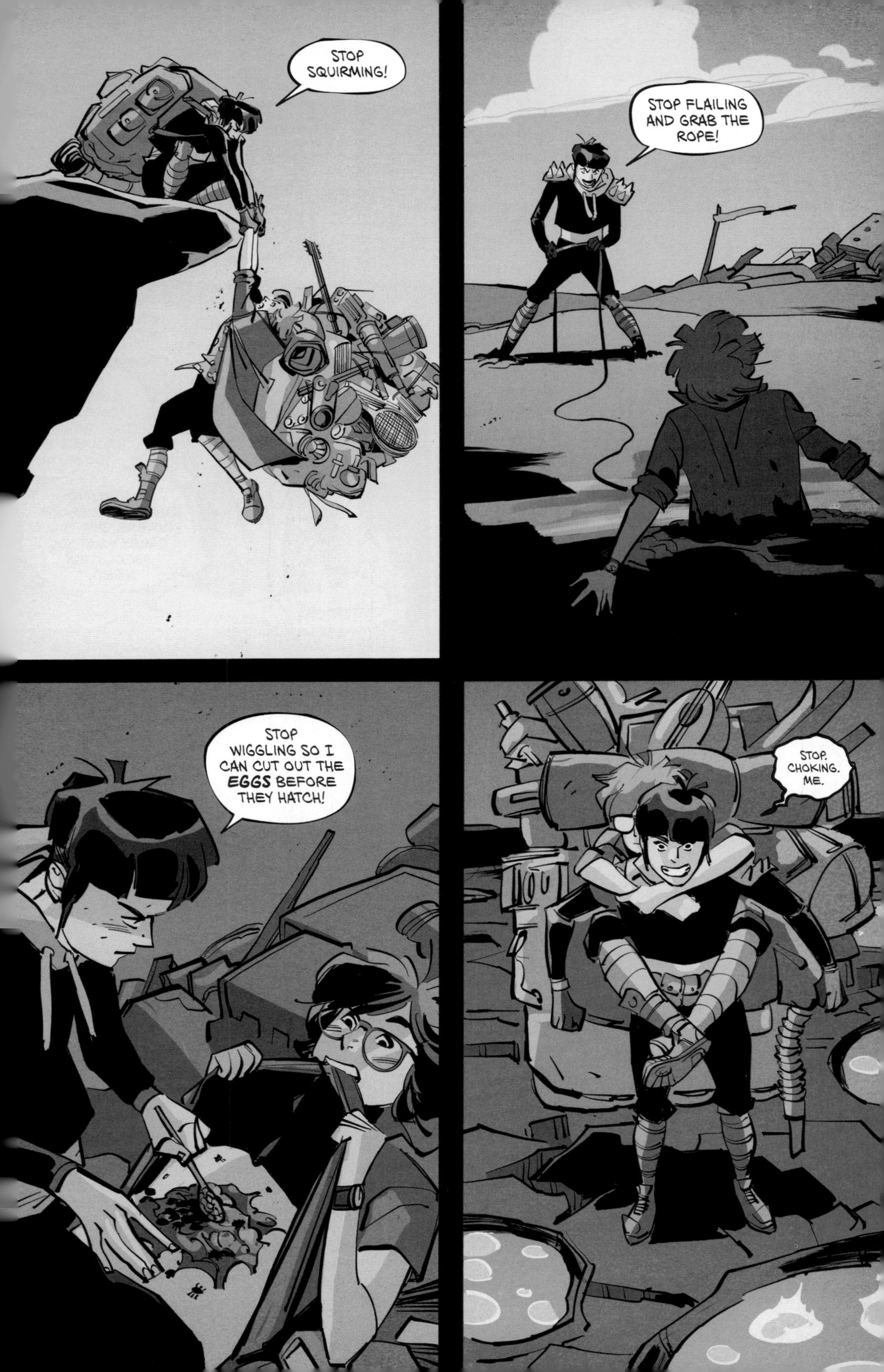
STOP SQUIRMING!
STOP FLAILING AND GRAB THE ROPE!
STOP WIGGLING SO I CAN CUT OUT THE *EGGS* BEFORE THEY HATCH!
STOP. CHOKING. ME.

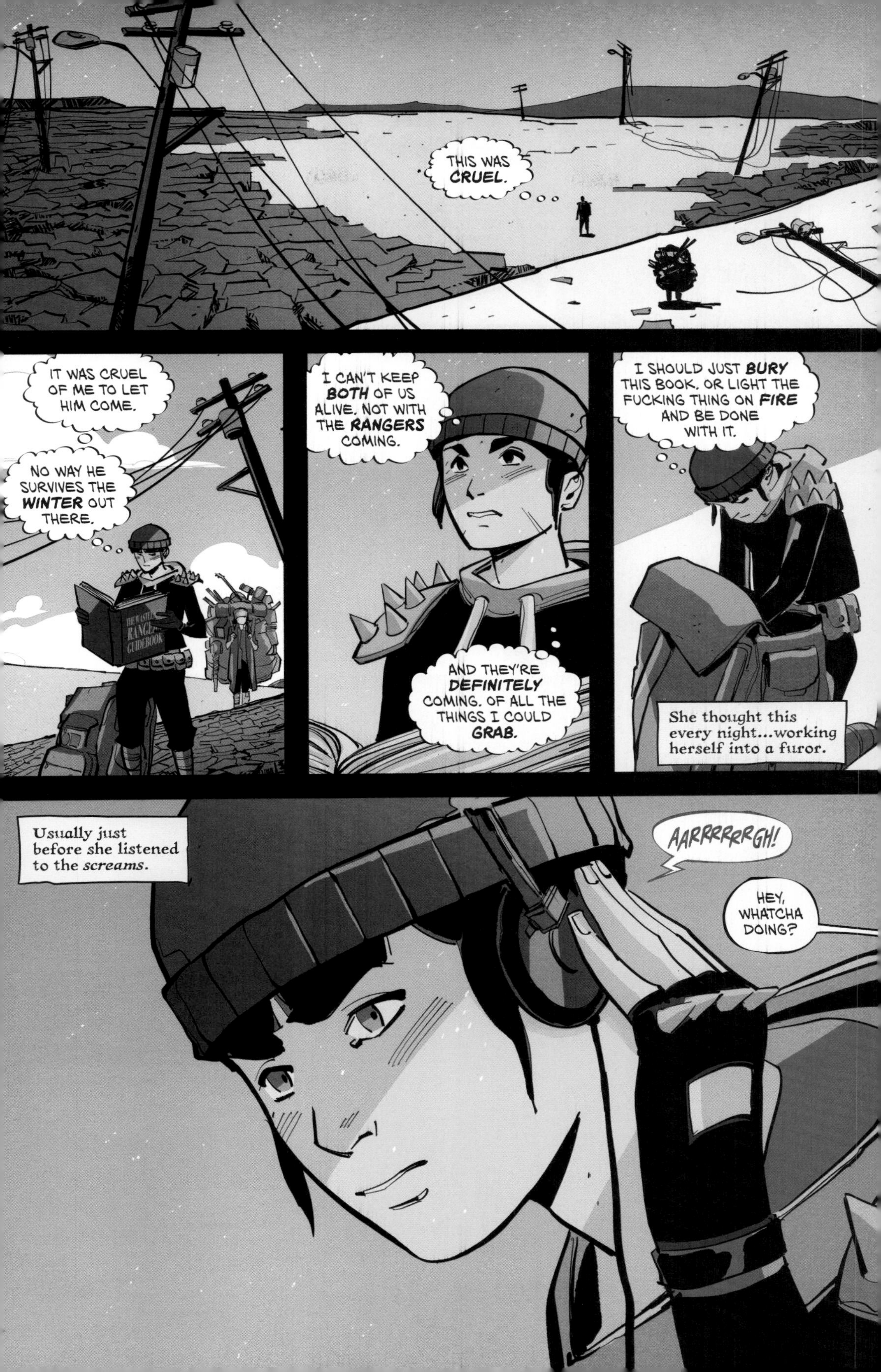
THIS WAS CRUEL.
IT WAS CRUEL OF ME TO LET HIM COME.
NO WAY HE SURVIVES THE WINTER OUT THERE.
THE WASTELAND RANGER GUIDEBOOK
I CAN'T KEEP BOTH OF US ALIVE. NOT WITH THE RANGERS COMING.
AND THEY'RE DEFINITELY COMING. OF ALL THE THINGS I COULD GRAB.
I SHOULD JUST BURY THIS BOOK. OR LIGHT THE FUCKING THING ON FIRE AND BE DONE WITH IT.
She thought this every night...working herself into a furor.
Usually just before she listened to the screams.
AARRRRRRGH!
HEY, WHATCHA DOING?

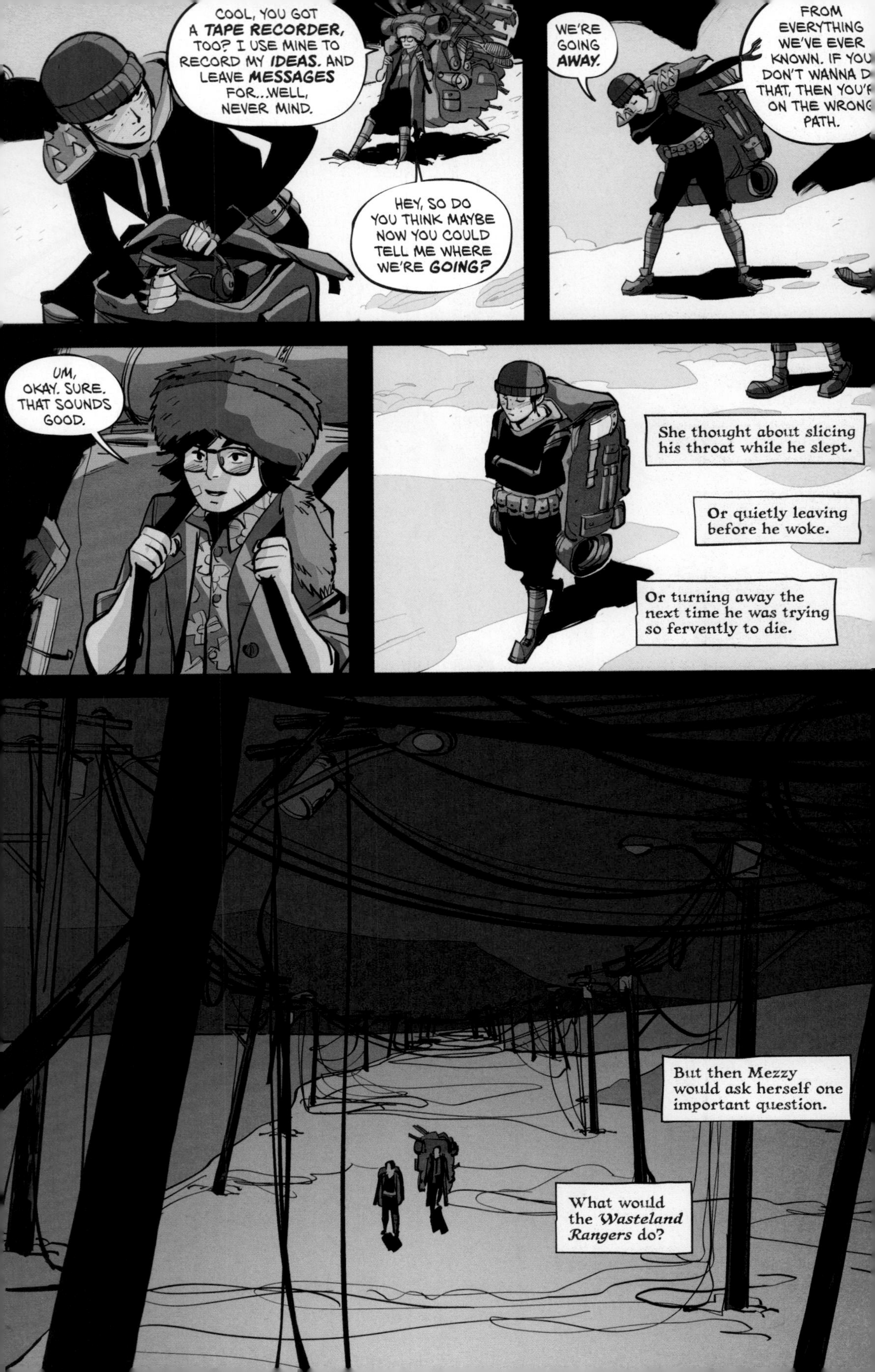
COOL, YOU GOT A TAPE RECORDER, TOO? I USE MINE TO RECORD MY IDEAS. AND LEAVE MESSAGES FOR...WELL, NEVER MIND.
HEY, SO DO YOU THINK MAYBE NOW YOU COULD TELL ME WHERE WE'RE GOING?
WE'RE GOING AWAY.
FROM EVERYTHING WE'VE EVER KNOWN. IF YOU DON'T WANNA DO THAT, THEN YOU'RE ON THE WRONG PATH.
UM, OKAY. SURE. THAT SOUNDS GOOD.
She thought about slicing his throat while he slept.
Or quietly leaving before he woke.
Or turning away the next time he was trying so fervently to die.
But then Mezzy would ask herself one important question.
What would the Wasteland Rangers do?

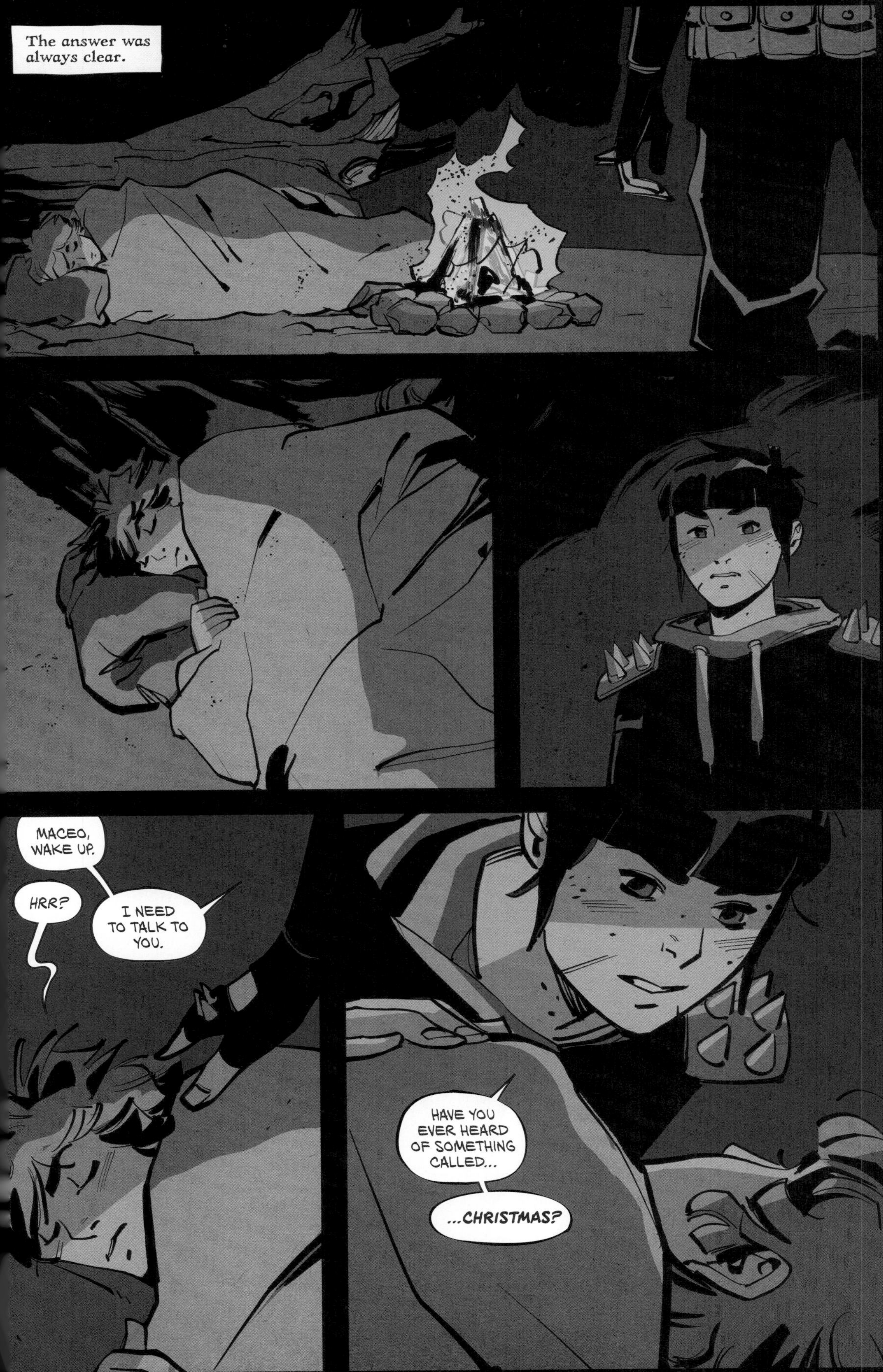

The answer was always clear.
MACEO, WAKE UP.
HRR?
I NEED TO TALK TO YOU.
HAVE YOU EVER HEARD OF SOMETHING CALLED...
...CHRISTMAS?

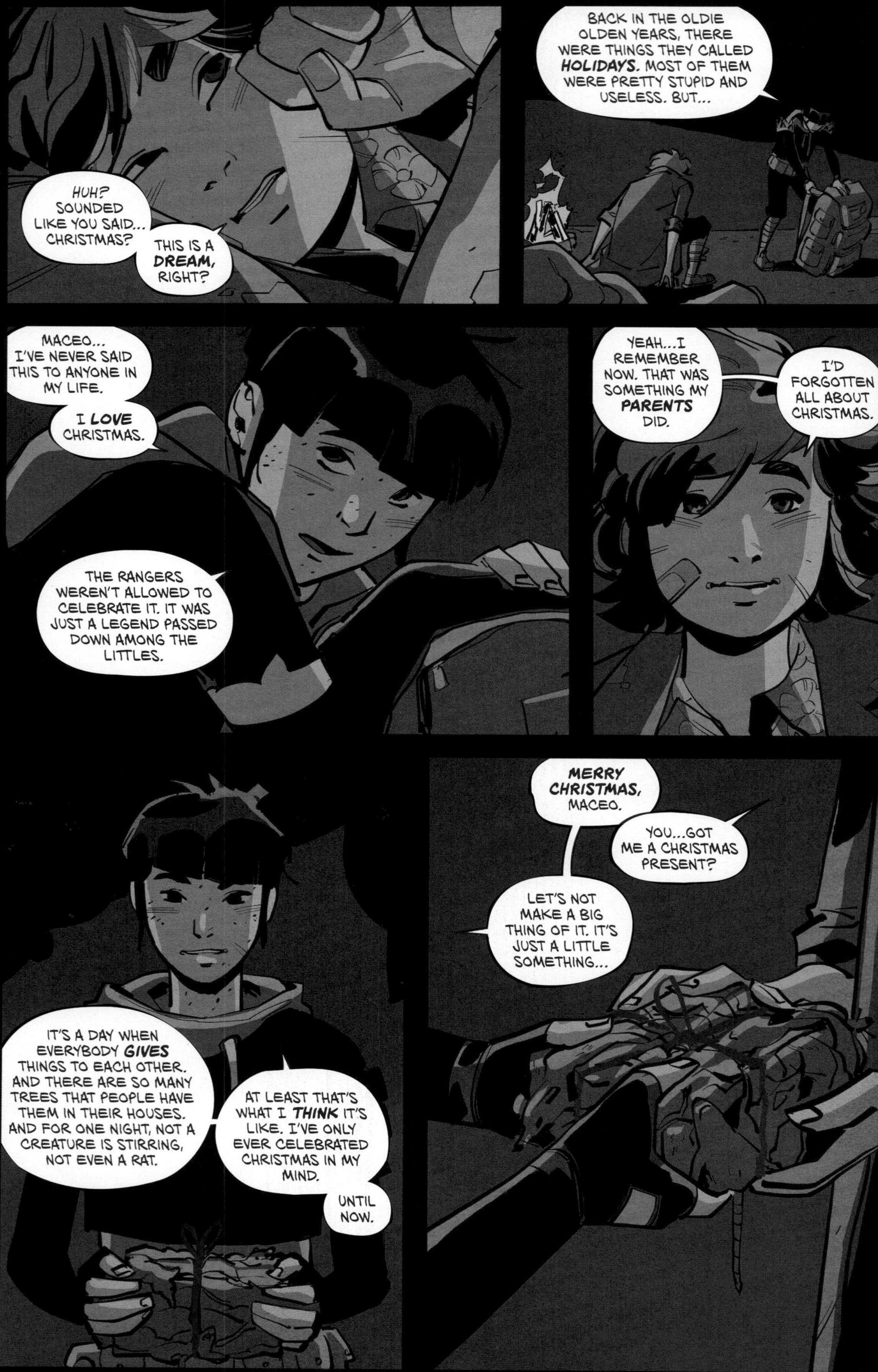
HUH? SOUNDED LIKE YOU SAID... CHRISTMAS?
THIS IS A **DREAM,** RIGHT?
BACK IN THE OLDIE OLDEN YEARS, THERE WERE THINGS THEY CALLED **HOLIDAYS.** MOST OF THEM WERE PRETTY STUPID AND USELESS. BUT...
MACEO... I'VE NEVER SAID THIS TO ANYONE IN MY LIFE.
I **LOVE** CHRISTMAS.
THE RANGERS WEREN'T ALLOWED TO CELEBRATE IT. IT WAS JUST A LEGEND PASSED DOWN AMONG THE LITTLES.
YEAH...I REMEMBER NOW. THAT WAS SOMETHING MY **PARENTS** DID.
I'D FORGOTTEN ALL ABOUT CHRISTMAS.
IT'S A DAY WHEN EVERYBODY **GIVES** THINGS TO EACH OTHER. AND THERE ARE SO MANY TREES THAT PEOPLE HAVE THEM IN THEIR HOUSES. AND FOR ONE NIGHT, NOT A CREATURE IS STIRRING, NOT EVEN A RAT.
AT LEAST THAT'S WHAT I **THINK** IT'S LIKE. I'VE ONLY EVER CELEBRATED CHRISTMAS IN MY MIND.
UNTIL NOW.
MERRY CHRISTMAS, MACEO.
YOU...GOT ME A CHRISTMAS PRESENT?
LET'S NOT MAKE A BIG THING OF IT. IT'S JUST A LITTLE SOMETHING...

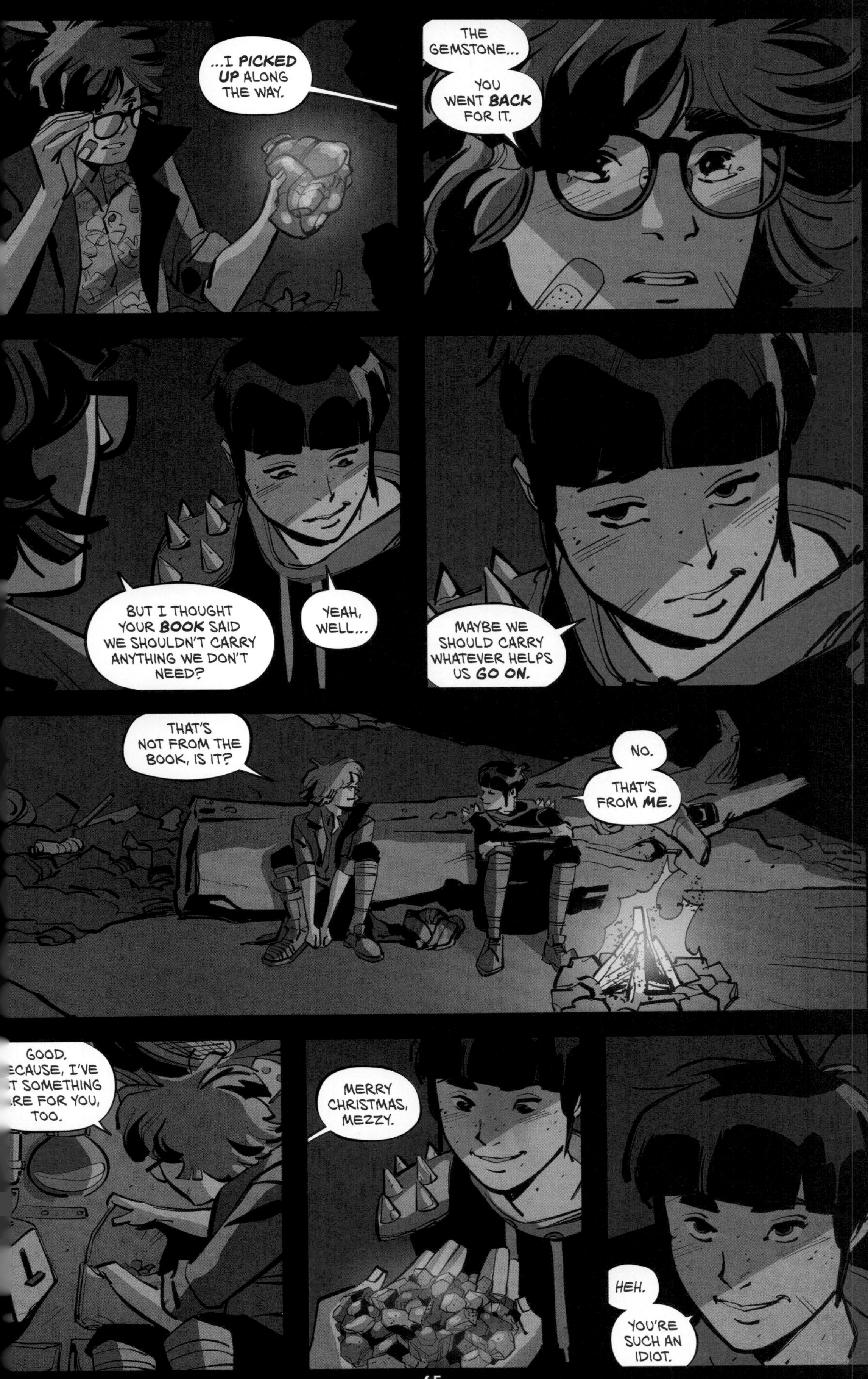
...I PICKED UP ALONG THE WAY.
THE GEMSTONE...
YOU WENT BACK FOR IT.
BUT I THOUGHT YOUR BOOK SAID WE SHOULDN'T CARRY ANYTHING WE DON'T NEED?
YEAH, WELL...
MAYBE WE SHOULD CARRY WHATEVER HELPS US GO ON.
THAT'S NOT FROM THE BOOK, IS IT?
NO.
THAT'S FROM ME.
GOOD. ECAUSE, I'VE T SOMETHING ERE FOR YOU, TOO.
MERRY CHRISTMAS, MEZZY.
HEH.
YOU'RE SUCH AN IDIOT.

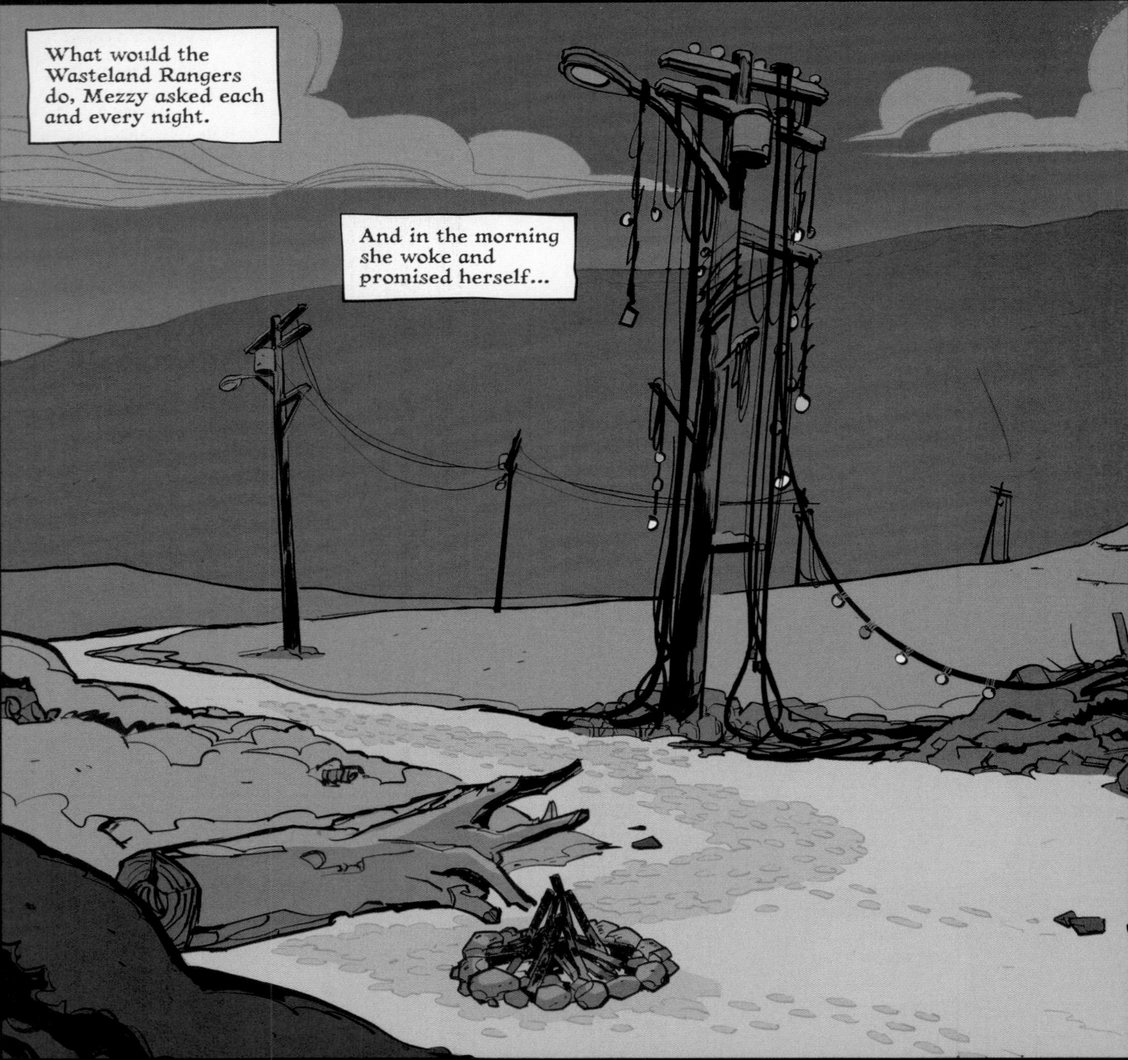
What would the Wasteland Rangers do, Mezzy asked each and every night.
And in the morning she woke and promised herself...

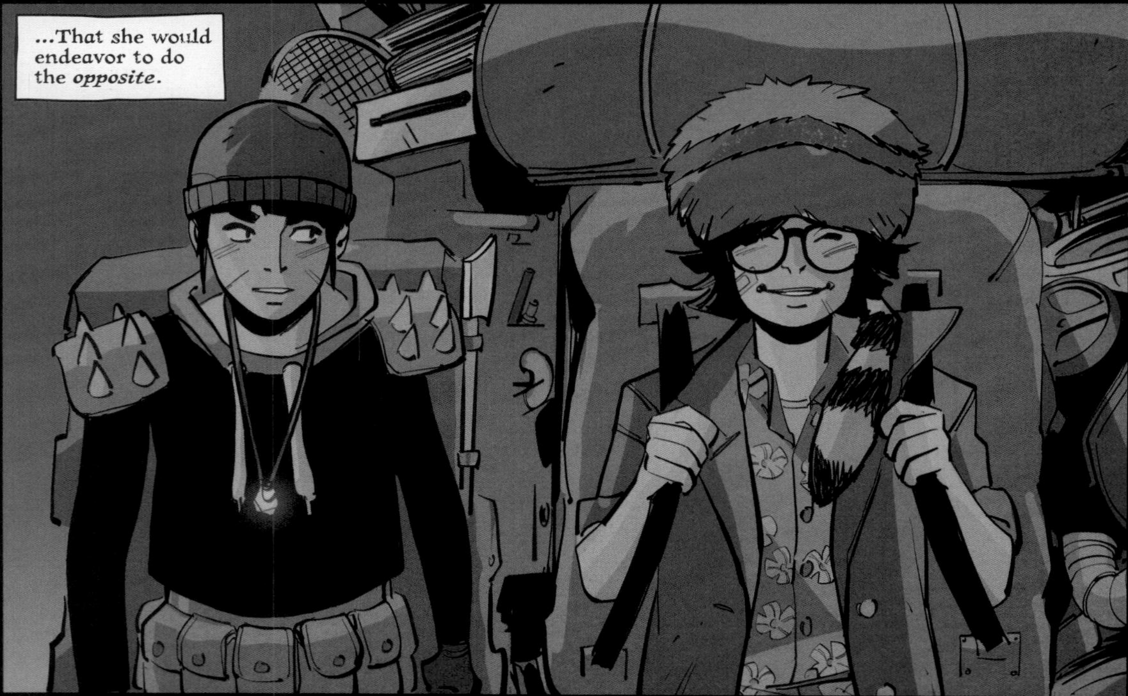
...That she would endeavor to do the *opposite*.

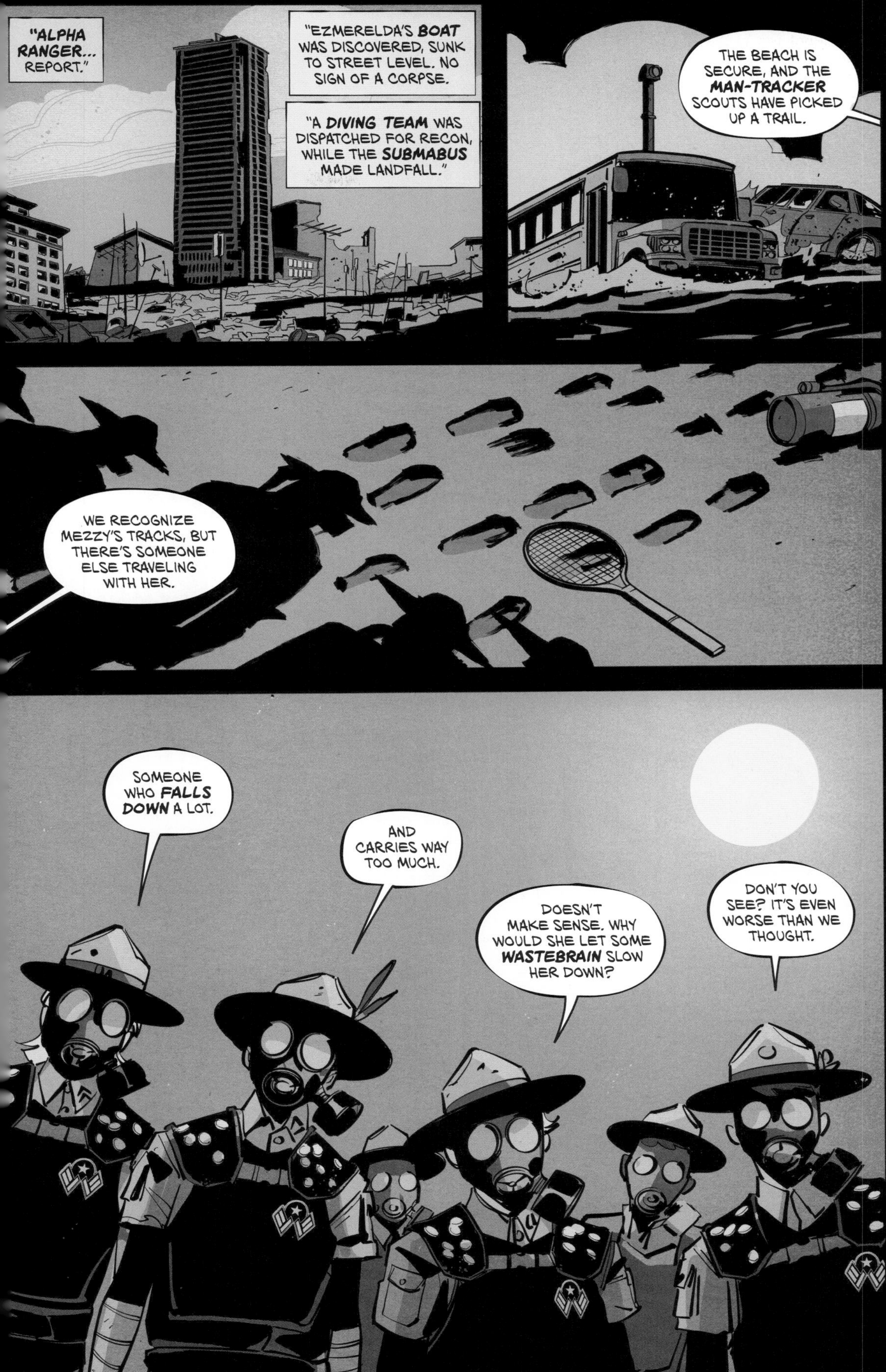
"ALPHA RANGER... REPORT."
"EZMERELDA'S BOAT WAS DISCOVERED, SUNK TO STREET LEVEL. NO SIGN OF A CORPSE.
"A DIVING TEAM WAS DISPATCHED FOR RECON, WHILE THE SUBMABUS MADE LANDFALL."
THE BEACH IS SECURE, AND THE MAN-TRACKER SCOUTS HAVE PICKED UP A TRAIL.
WE RECOGNIZE MEZZY'S TRACKS, BUT THERE'S SOMEONE ELSE TRAVELING WITH HER.
SOMEONE WHO FALLS DOWN A LOT.
AND CARRIES WAY TOO MUCH.
DOESN'T MAKE SENSE. WHY WOULD SHE LET SOME WASTEBRAIN SLOW HER DOWN?
DON'T YOU SEE? IT'S EVEN WORSE THAN WE THOUGHT.

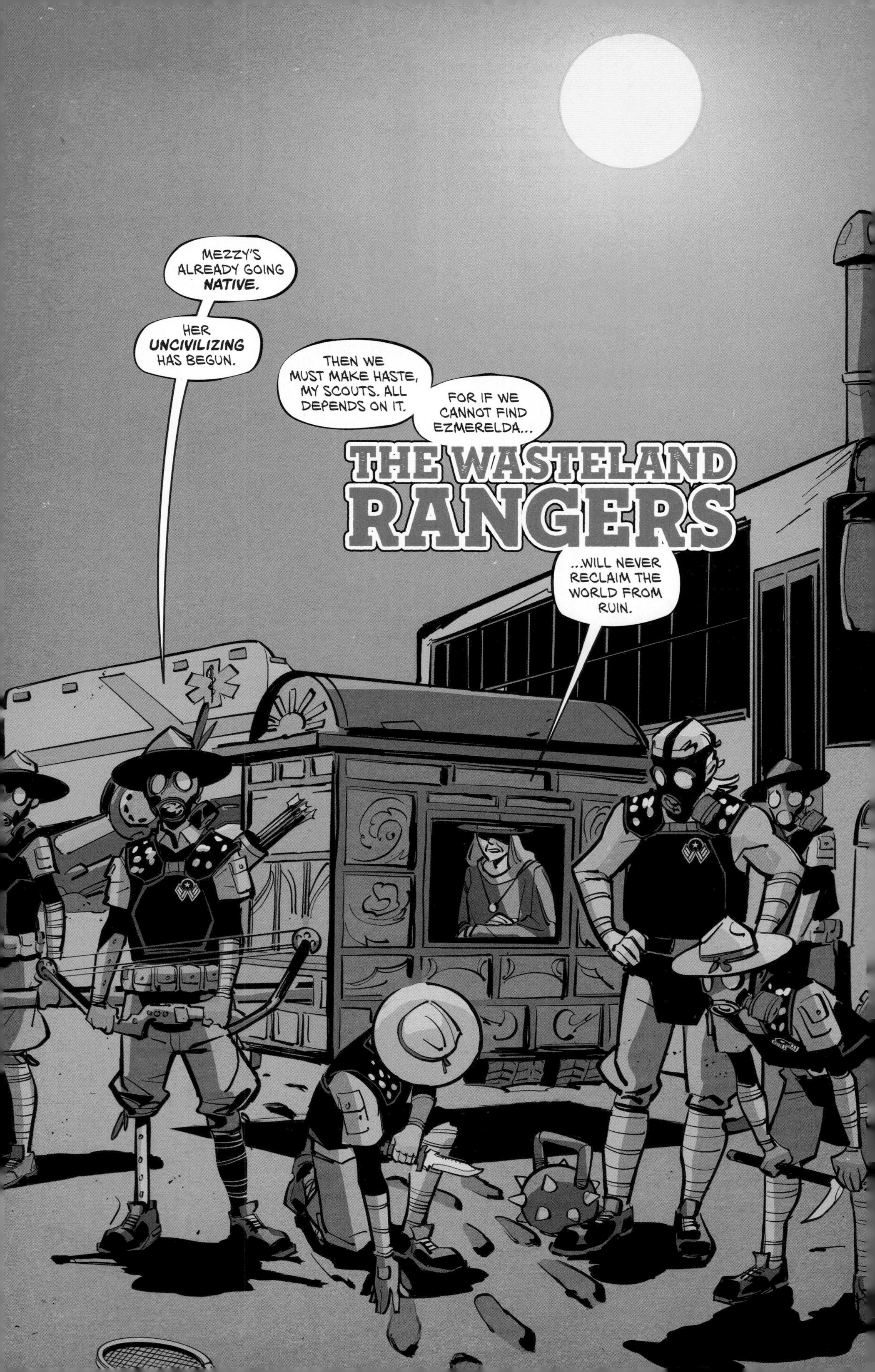
MEZZY'S ALREADY GOING NATIVE.
HER UNCIVILIZING HAS BEGUN.
THEN WE MUST MAKE HASTE, MY SCOUTS. ALL DEPENDS ON IT.
FOR IF WE CANNOT FIND EZMERELDA...
THE WASTELAND RANGERS
...WILL NEVER RECLAIM THE WORLD FROM RUIN.

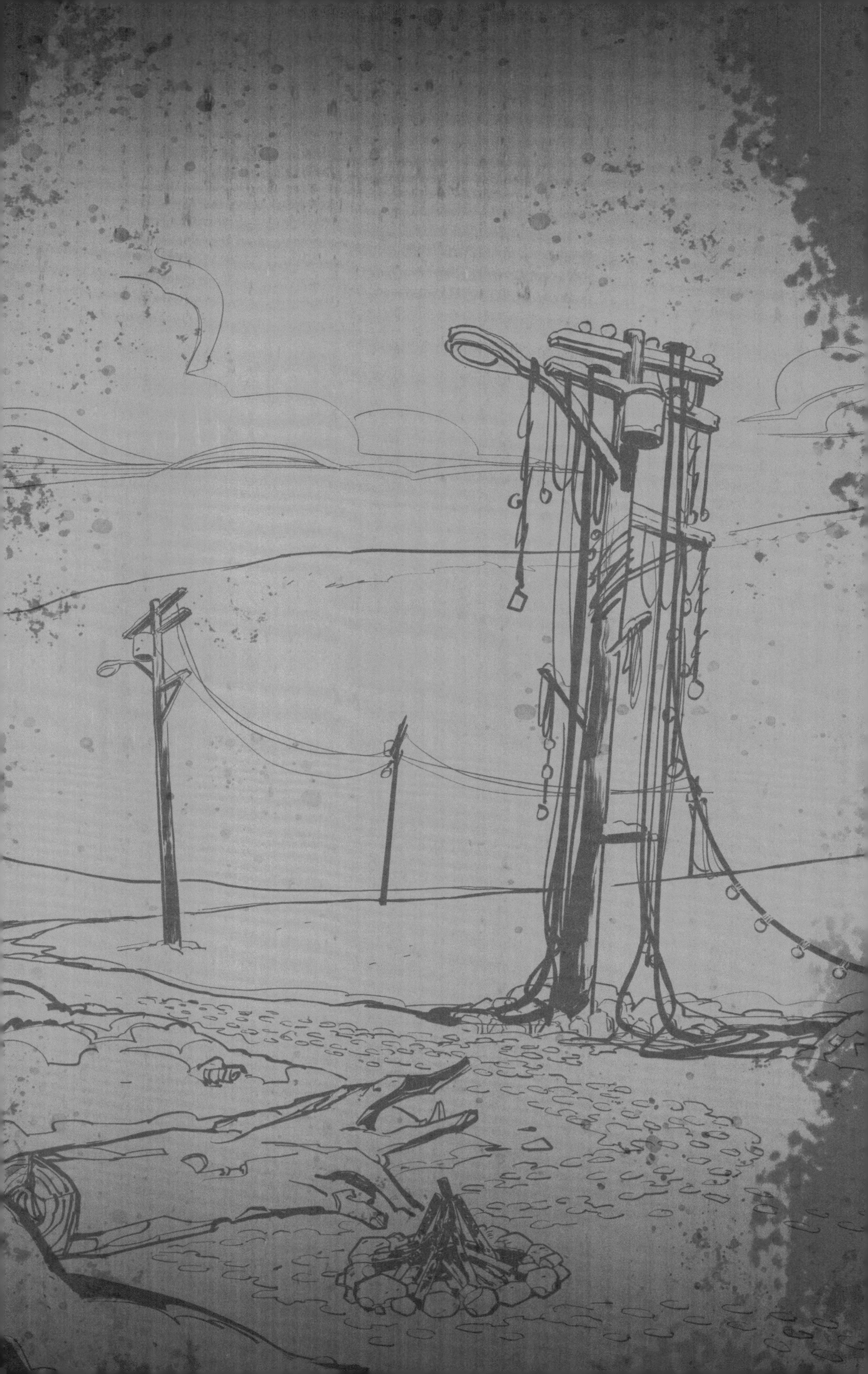

CHAPTER THREE

THE WAYS OF
THE STRAYED

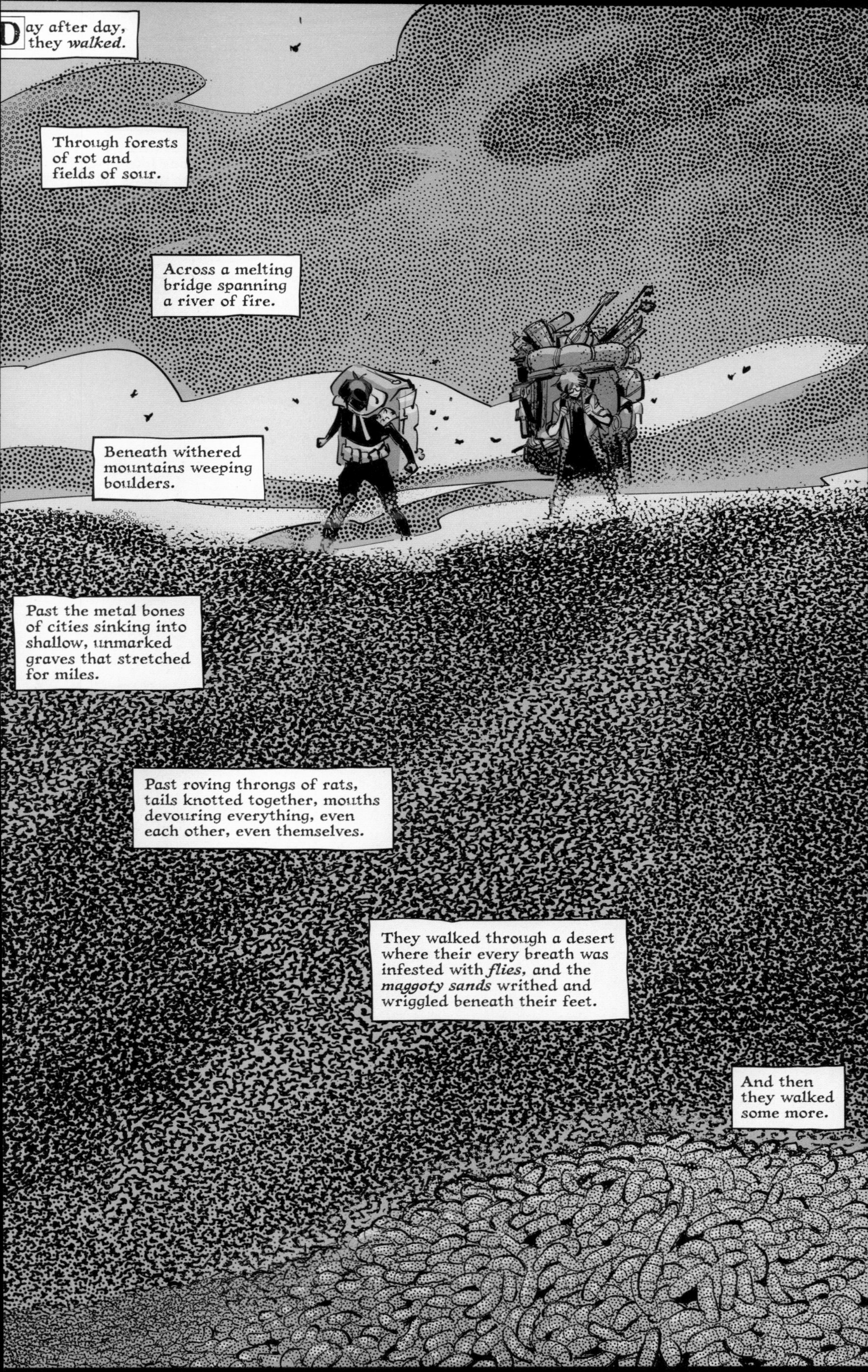
Day after day, they *walked*.
Through forests of rot and fields of sour.
Across a melting bridge spanning a river of fire.
Beneath withered mountains weeping boulders.
Past the metal bones of cities sinking into shallow, unmarked graves that stretched for miles.
Past roving throngs of rats, tails knotted together, mouths devouring everything, even each other, even themselves.
They walked through a desert where their every breath was infested with *flies*, and the *maggoty sands* writhed and wriggled beneath their feet.
And then they walked some more.

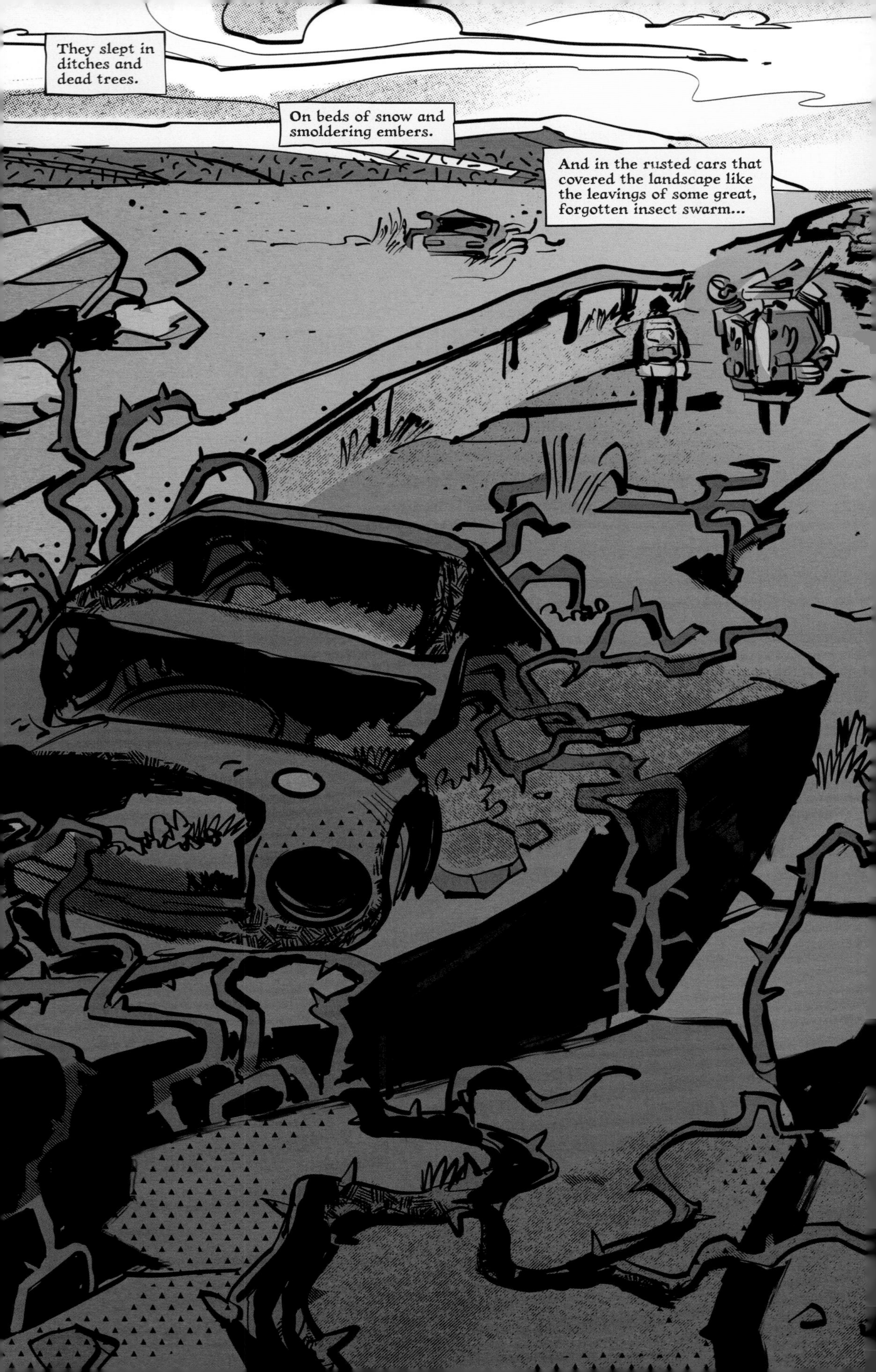
They slept in ditches and dead trees.
On beds of snow and smoldering embers.
And in the rusted cars that covered the landscape like the leavings of some great, forgotten insect swarm...

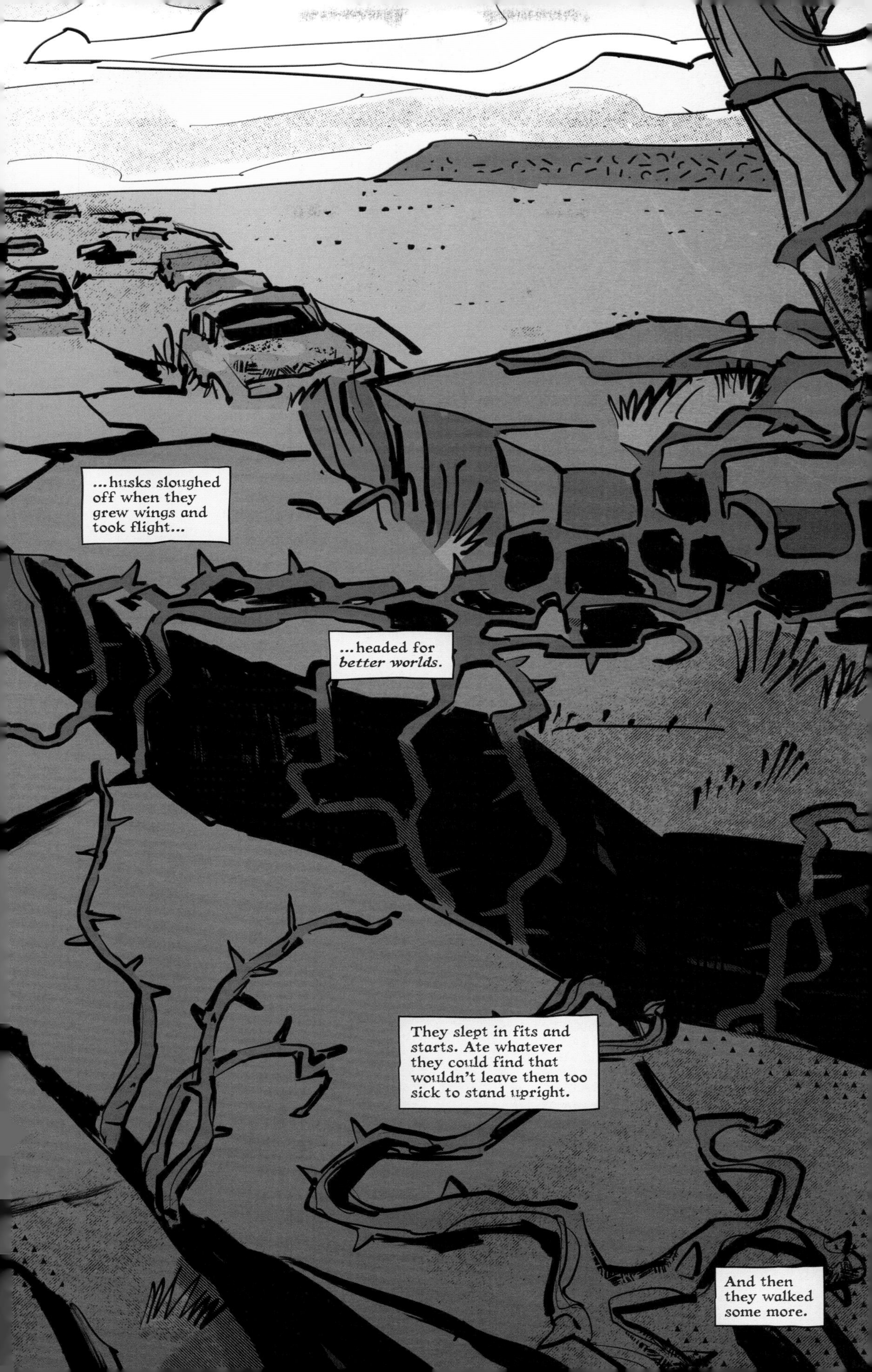
...husks sloughed off when they grew wings and took flight...
...headed for *better worlds*.
They slept in fits and starts. Ate whatever they could find that wouldn't leave them too sick to stand upright.
And then they walked some more.

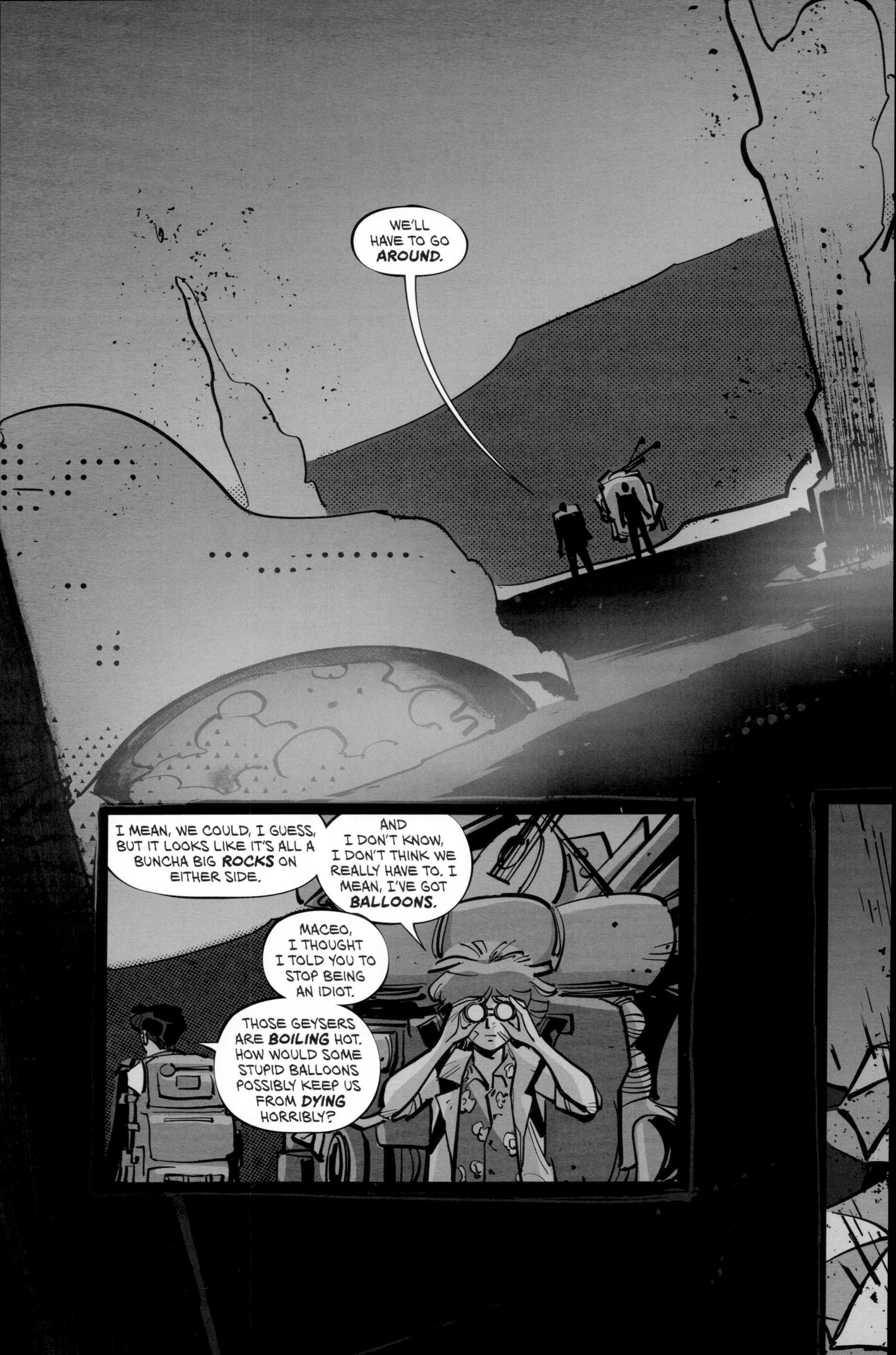
WE'LL HAVE TO GO AROUND.
I MEAN, WE COULD, I GUESS, BUT IT LOOKS LIKE IT'S ALL A BUNCHA BIG ROCKS ON EITHER SIDE.
AND I DON'T KNOW, I DON'T THINK WE REALLY HAVE TO. I MEAN, I'VE GOT BALLOONS.
MACEO, I THOUGHT I TOLD YOU TO STOP BEING AN IDIOT.
THOSE GEYSERS ARE BOILING HOT. HOW WOULD SOME STUPID BALLOONS POSSIBLY KEEP US FROM DYING HORRIBLY?

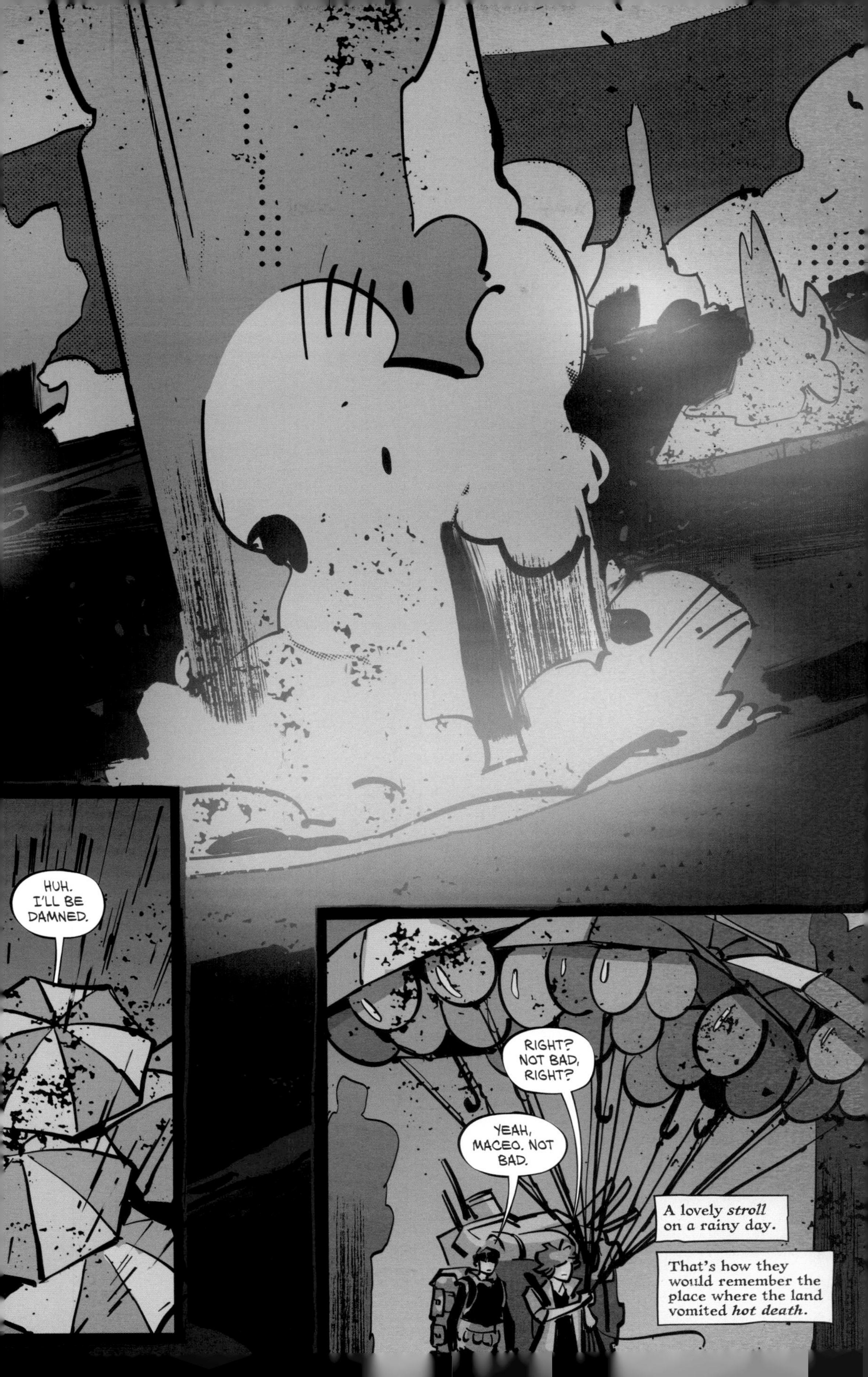
HUH. I'LL BE DAMNED.
RIGHT? NOT BAD, RIGHT?
YEAH, MACEO. NOT BAD.
A lovely *stroll* on a rainy day.
That's how they would remember the place where the land vomited *hot death*.

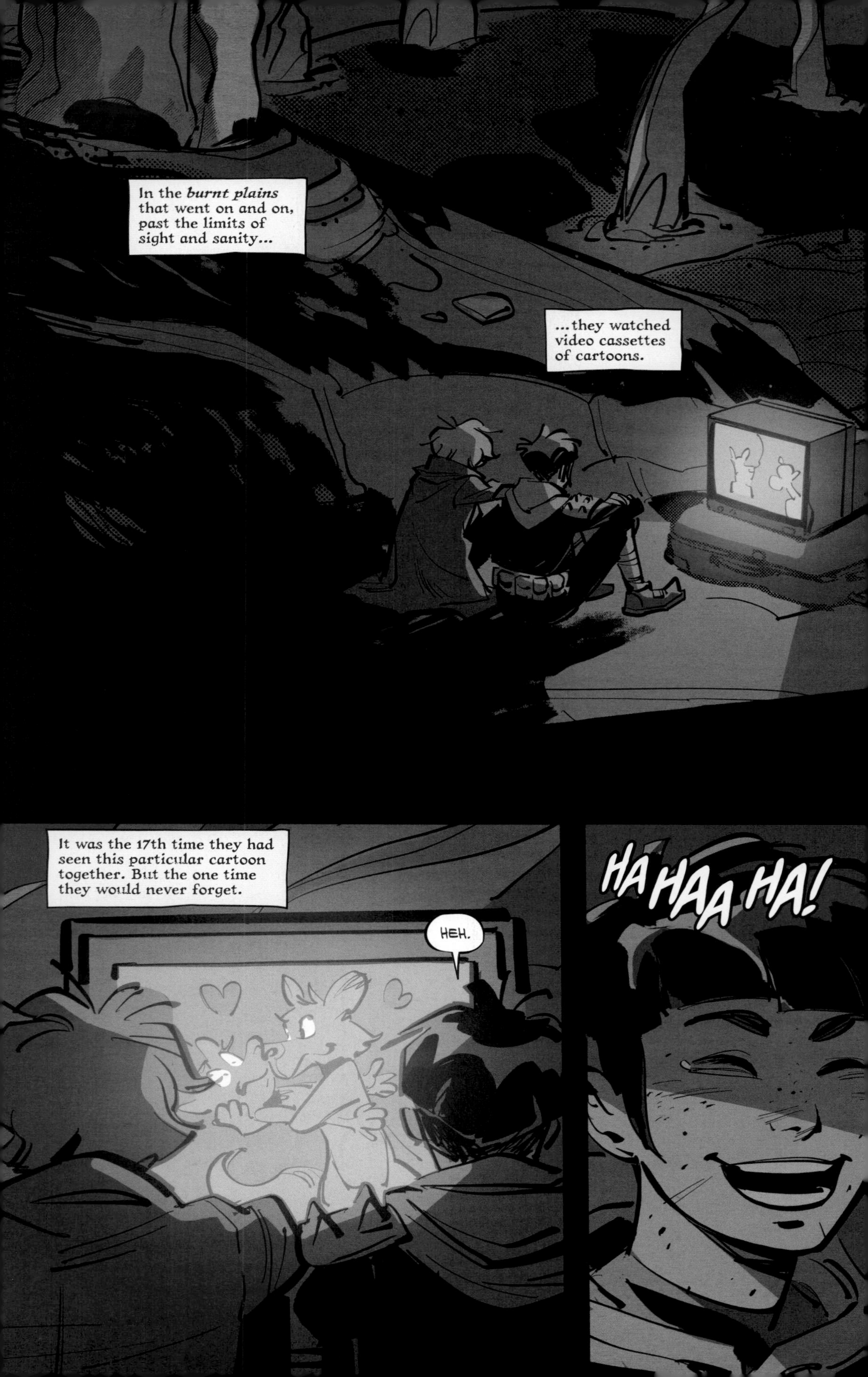
In the *burnt plains* that went on and on, past the limits of sight and sanity...
...they watched video cassettes of cartoons.
It was the 17th time they had seen this particular cartoon together. But the one time they would never forget.
HEH.
HA HAA HA!

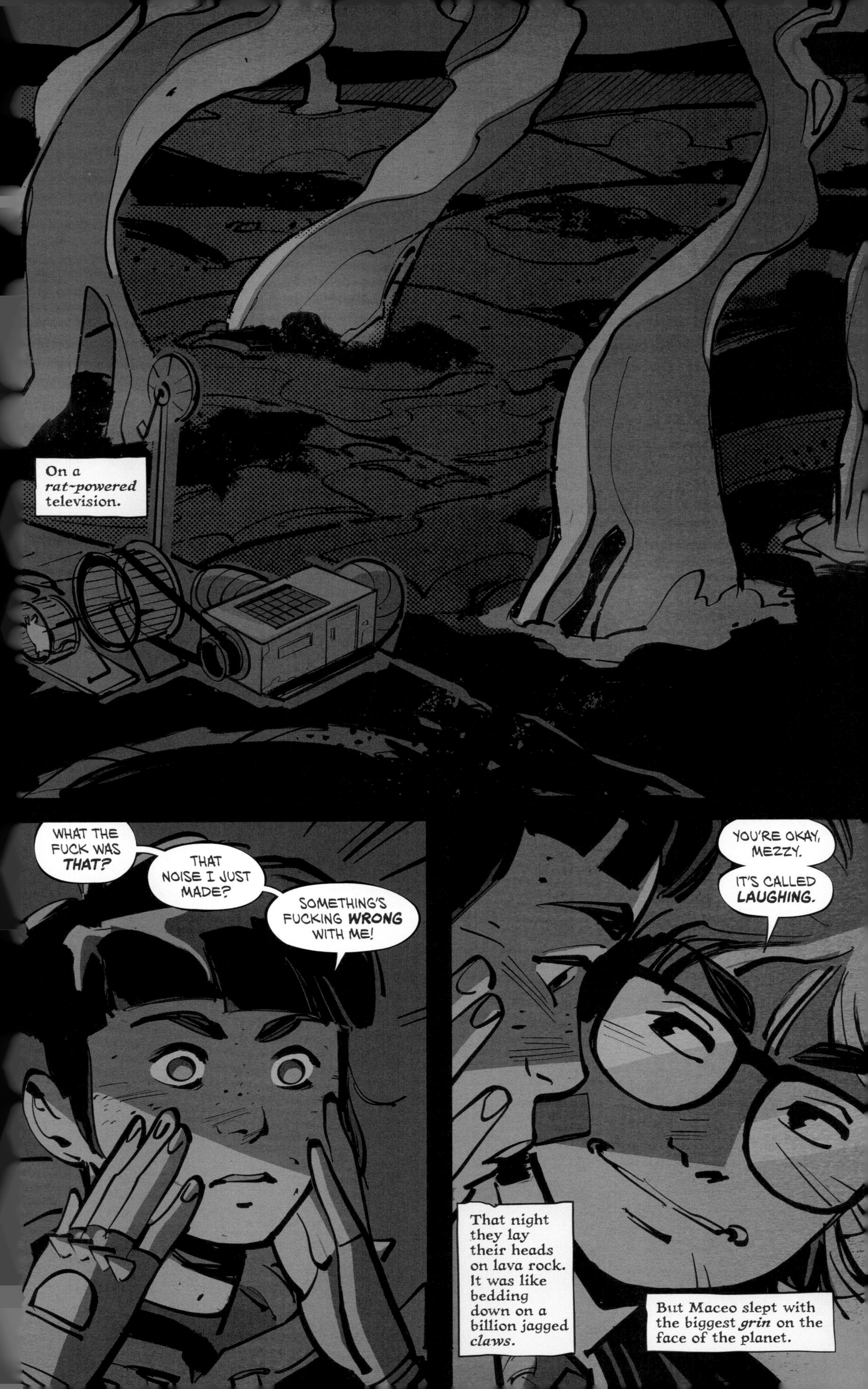
On a *rat-powered* television.
WHAT THE FUCK WAS **THAT?**
THAT NOISE I JUST MADE?
SOMETHING'S FUCKING **WRONG** WITH ME!
YOU'RE OKAY, MEZZY.
IT'S CALLED **LAUGHING.**
That night they lay their heads on lava rock. It was like bedding down on a billion jagged *claws.*
But Maceo slept with the biggest *grin* on the face of the planet.

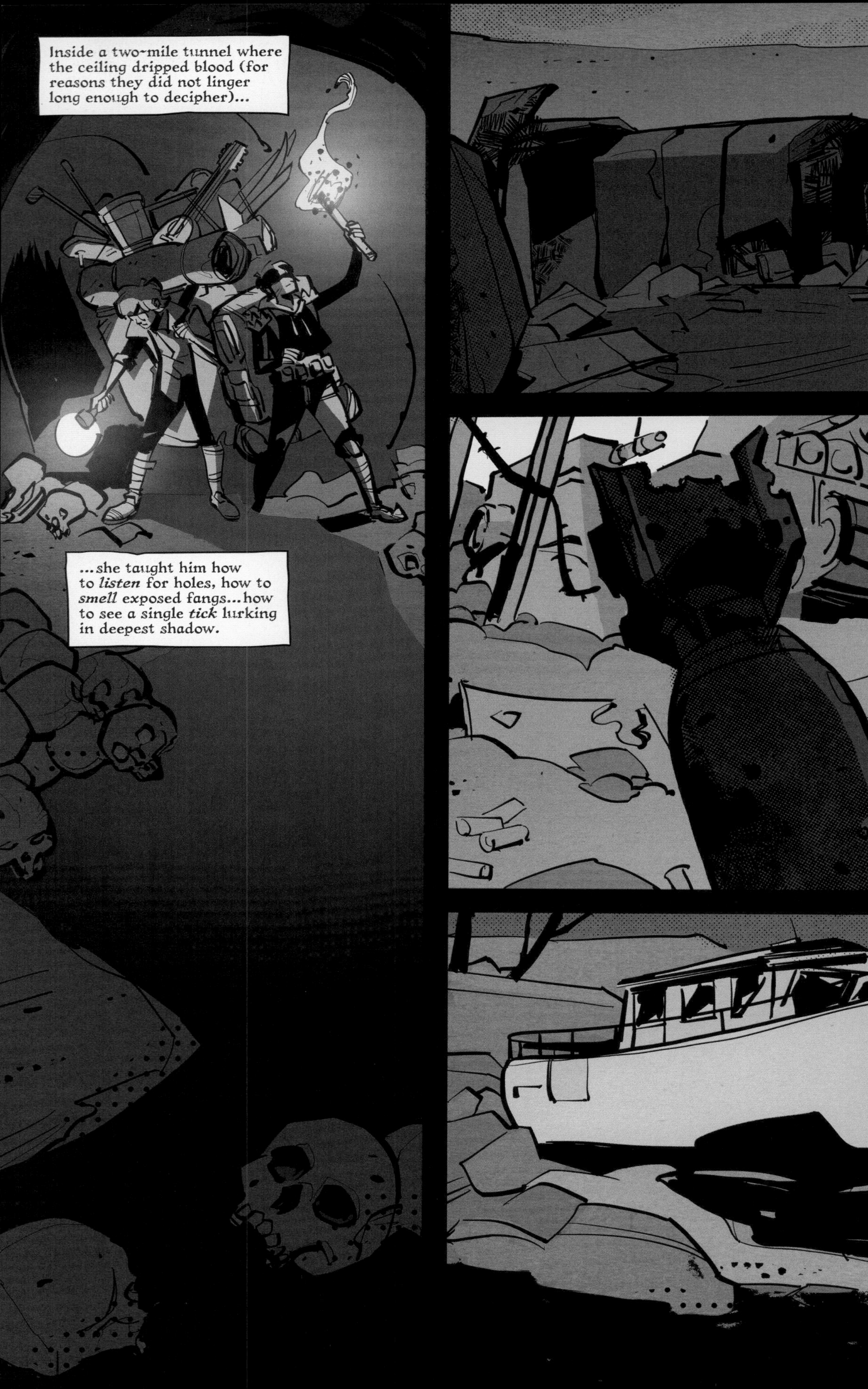
Inside a two-mile tunnel where the ceiling dripped blood (for reasons they did not linger long enough to decipher)...
...she taught him how to *listen* for holes, how to *smell* exposed fangs...how to see a single *tick* lurking in deepest shadow.

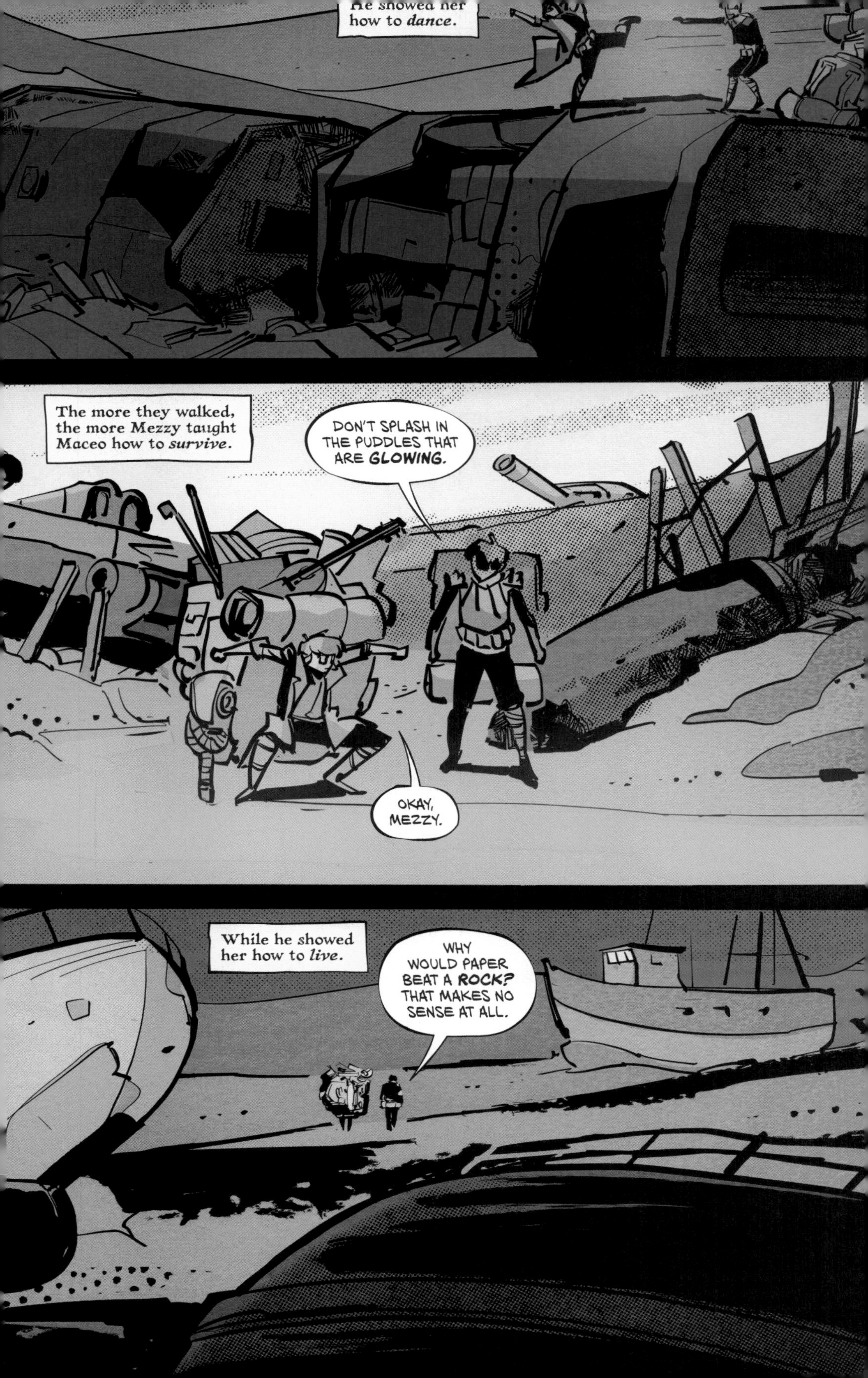
He showed her how to *dance*.
The more they walked, the more Mezzy taught Maceo how to *survive*.
DON'T SPLASH IN THE PUDDLES THAT ARE **GLOWING.**
OKAY, MEZZY.
While he showed her how to *live*.
WHY WOULD PAPER BEAT A **ROCK?** THAT MAKES NO SENSE AT ALL.

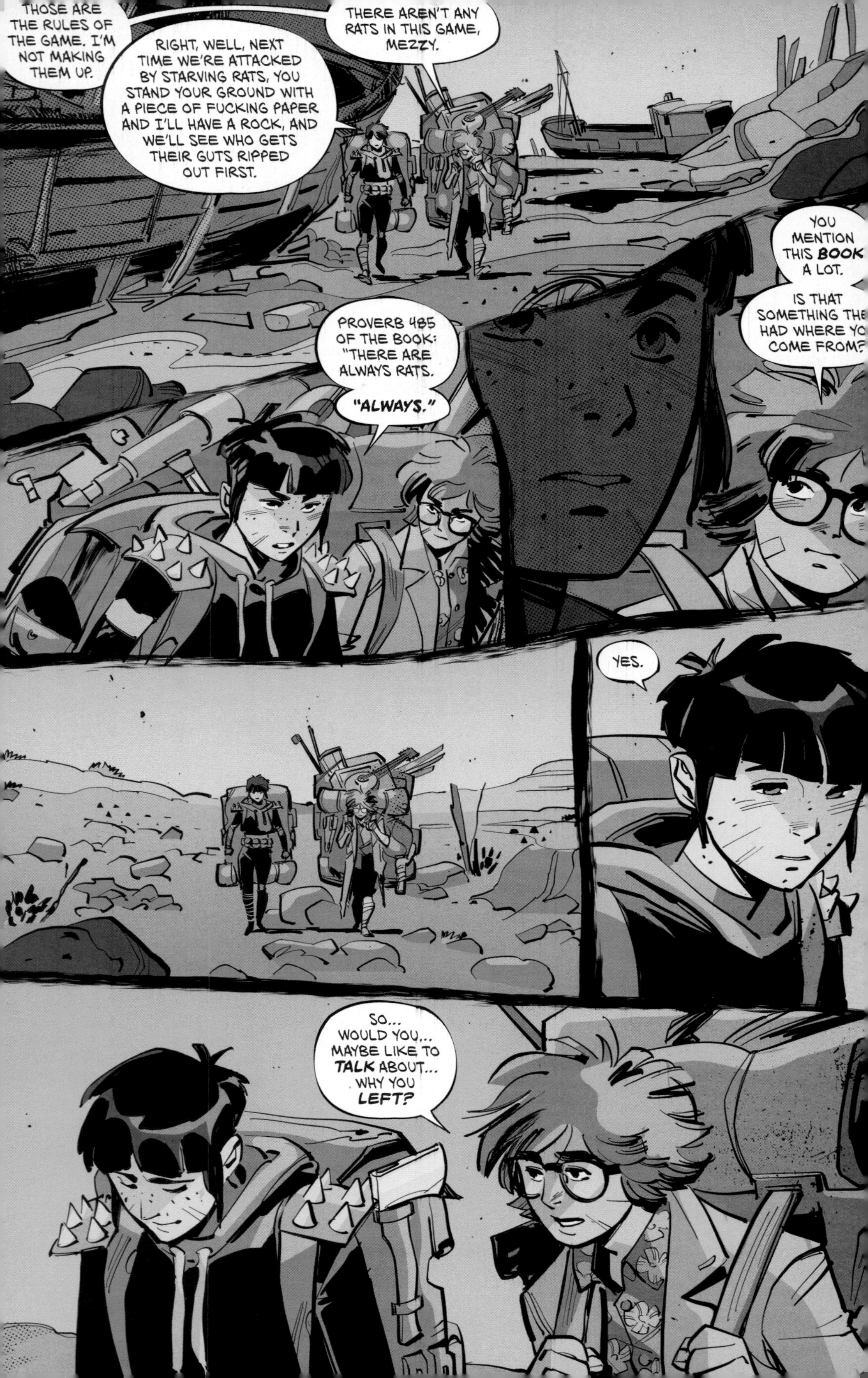

THOSE ARE THE RULES OF THE GAME. I'M NOT MAKING THEM UP.
THERE AREN'T ANY RATS IN THIS GAME, MEZZY.
RIGHT, WELL, NEXT TIME WE'RE ATTACKED BY STARVING RATS, YOU STAND YOUR GROUND WITH A PIECE OF FUCKING PAPER AND I'LL HAVE A ROCK, AND WE'LL SEE WHO GETS THEIR GUTS RIPPED OUT FIRST.
PROVERB 485 OF THE BOOK: "THERE ARE ALWAYS RATS.
"ALWAYS."
YOU MENTION THIS BOOK A LOT.
IS THAT SOMETHING THE HAD WHERE YO COME FROM?
YES.
SO... WOULD YOU... MAYBE LIKE TO TALK ABOUT... WHY YOU LEFT?

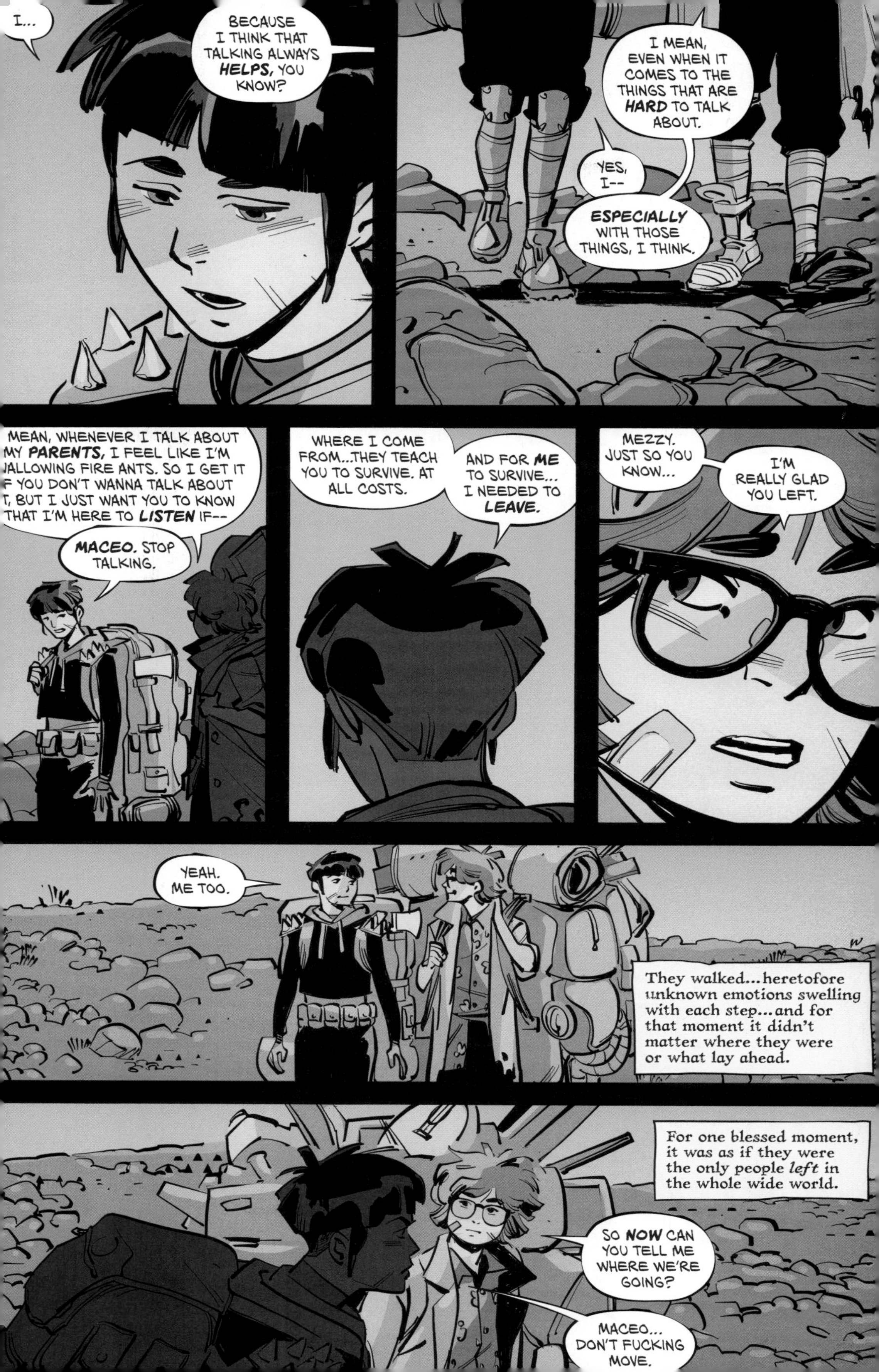
I...
BECAUSE I THINK THAT TALKING ALWAYS **HELPS,** YOU KNOW?
I MEAN, EVEN WHEN IT COMES TO THE THINGS THAT ARE **HARD** TO TALK ABOUT.
YES, I--
ESPECIALLY WITH THOSE THINGS, I THINK.
MEAN, WHENEVER I TALK ABOUT MY **PARENTS,** I FEEL LIKE I'M WALLOWING FIRE ANTS. SO I GET IT F YOU DON'T WANNA TALK ABOUT T, BUT I JUST WANT YOU TO KNOW THAT I'M HERE TO **LISTEN** IF--
MACEO. STOP TALKING.
WHERE I COME FROM...THEY TEACH YOU TO SURVIVE. AT ALL COSTS.
AND FOR **ME** TO SURVIVE... I NEEDED TO **LEAVE.**
MEZZY. JUST SO YOU KNOW...
I'M REALLY GLAD YOU LEFT.
YEAH. ME TOO.
They walked...heretofore unknown emotions swelling with each step...and for that moment it didn't matter where they were or what lay ahead.
For one blessed moment, it was as if they were the only people *left* in the whole wide world.
SO **NOW** CAN YOU TELL ME WHERE WE'RE GOING?
MACEO... DON'T FUCKING MOVE.

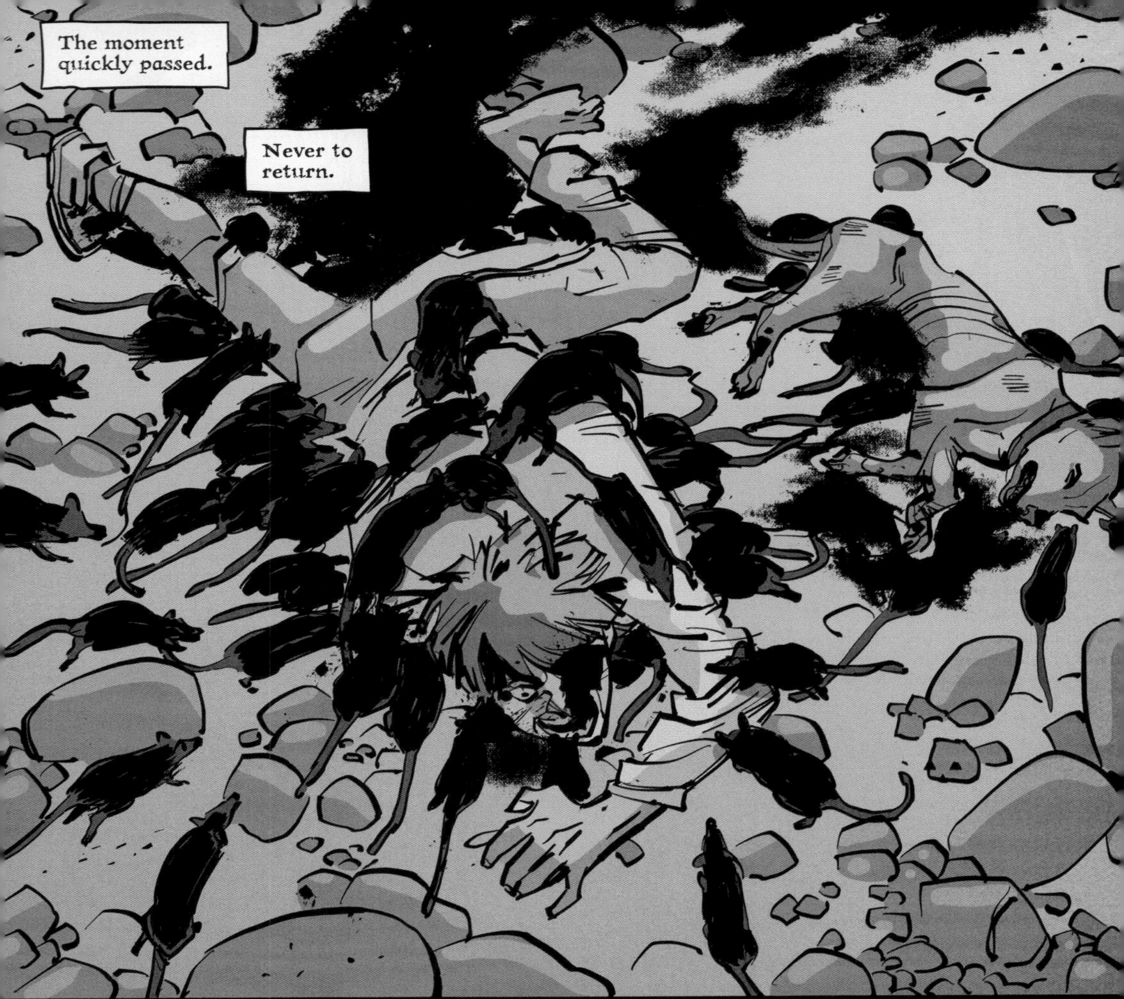
The moment quickly passed.
Never to return.

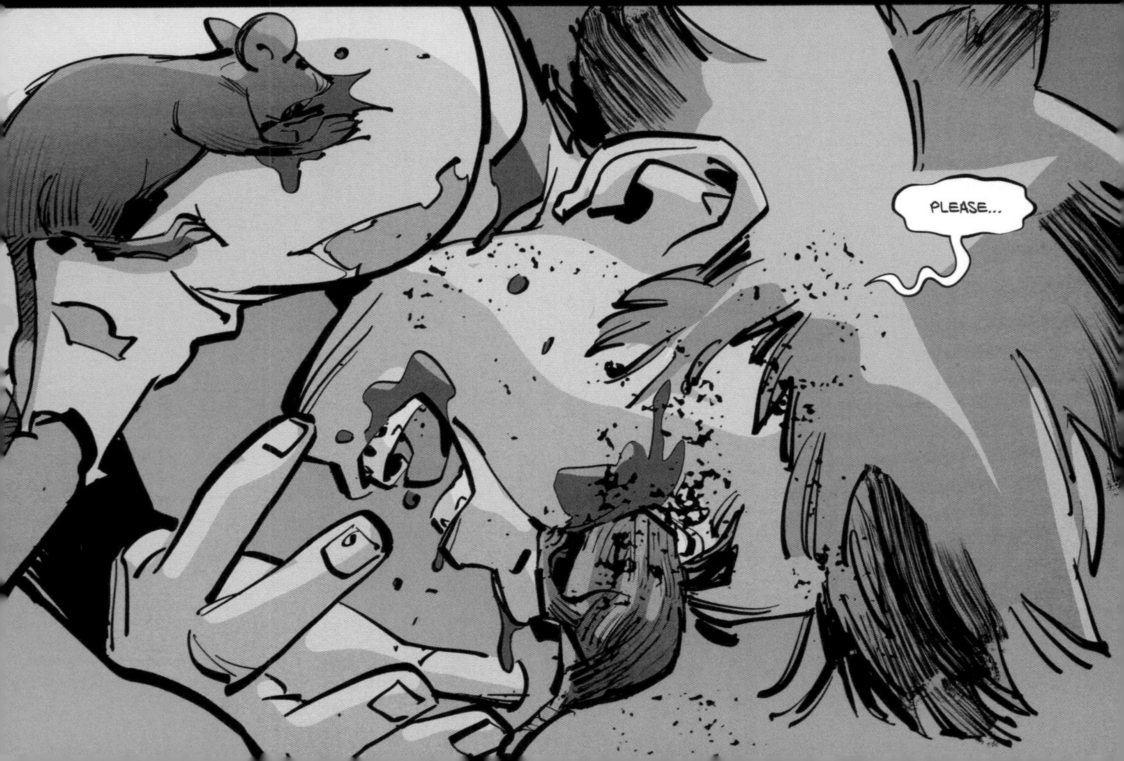
PLEASE...

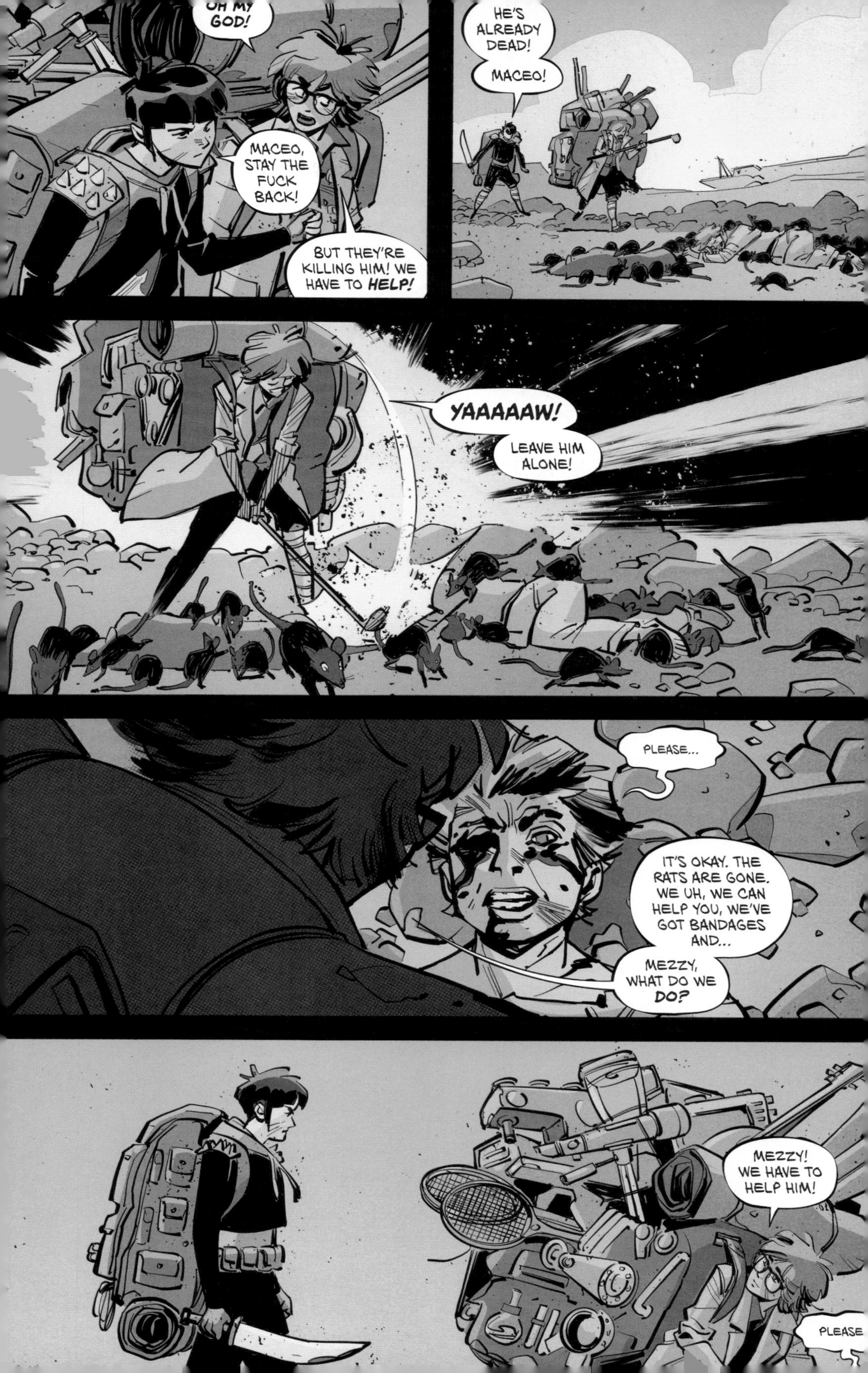
OH MY GOD!
MACEO, STAY THE FUCK BACK!
BUT THEY'RE KILLING HIM! WE HAVE TO HELP!
HE'S ALREADY DEAD!
MACEO!
YAAAAAW!
LEAVE HIM ALONE!
PLEASE...
IT'S OKAY. THE RATS ARE GONE. WE UH, WE CAN HELP YOU, WE'VE GOT BANDAGES AND...
MEZZY, WHAT DO WE DO?
MEZZY! WE HAVE TO HELP HIM!
PLEASE

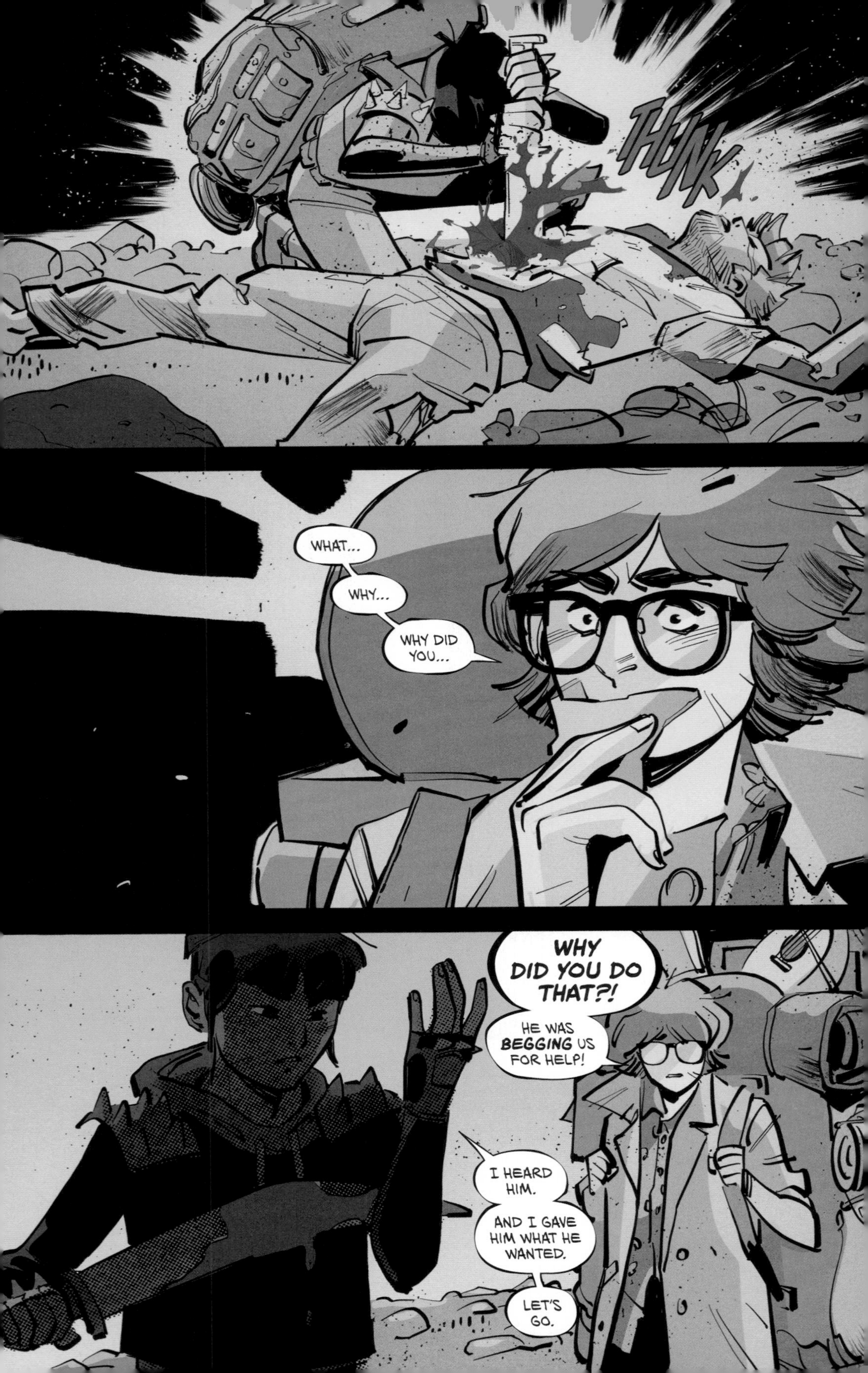
THUNK!
WHAT...
WHY...
WHY DID YOU...
WHY DID YOU DO THAT?!
HE WAS BEGGING US FOR HELP!
I HEARD HIM.
AND I GAVE HIM WHAT HE WANTED.
LET'S GO.

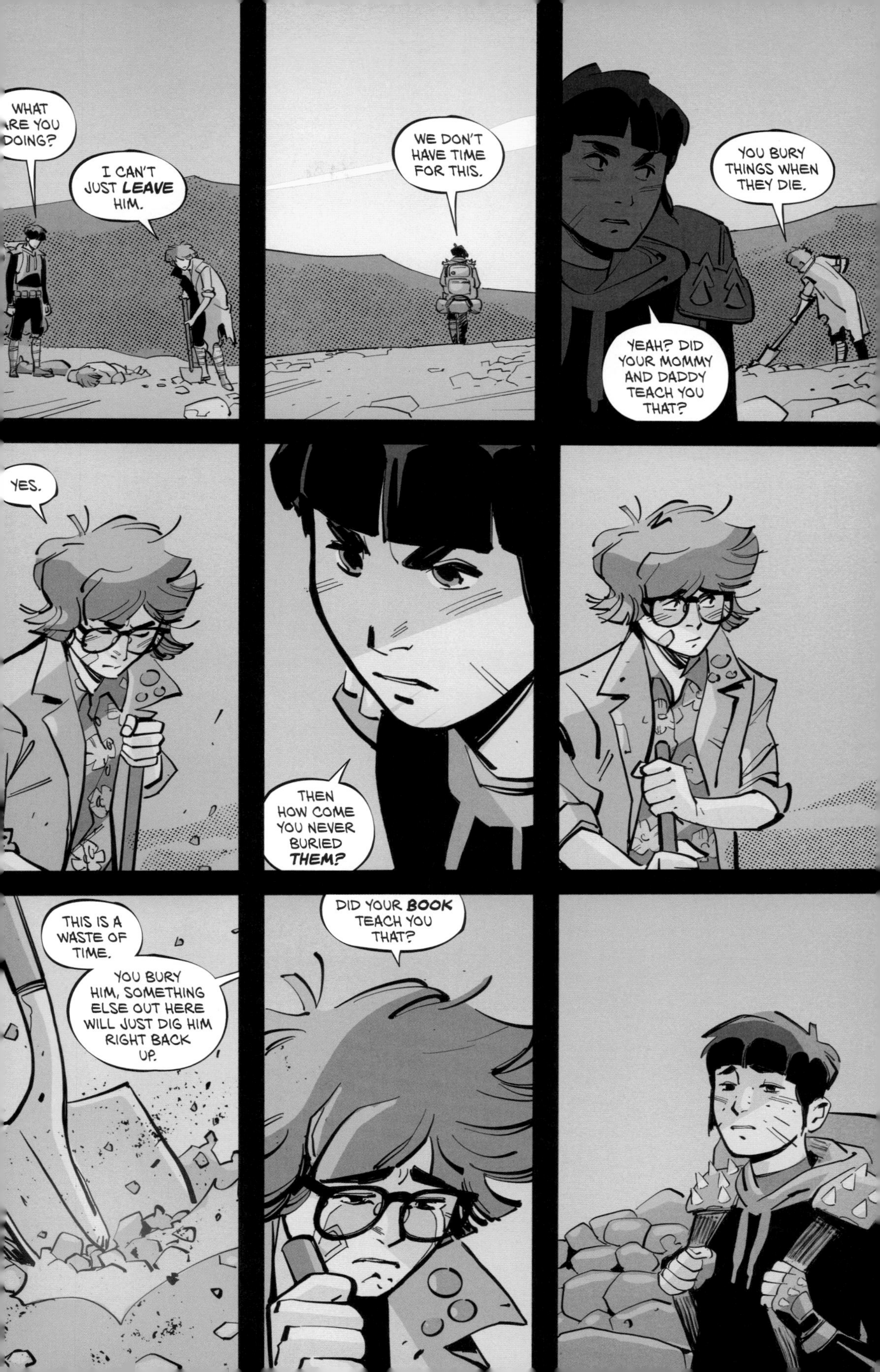
WHAT ARE YOU DOING?
I CAN'T JUST **LEAVE** HIM.
WE DON'T HAVE TIME FOR THIS.
YOU BURY THINGS WHEN THEY DIE.
YEAH? DID YOUR MOMMY AND DADDY TEACH YOU THAT?
YES.
THEN HOW COME YOU NEVER BURIED **THEM?**
THIS IS A WASTE OF TIME.
YOU BURY HIM, SOMETHING ELSE OUT HERE WILL JUST DIG HIM RIGHT BACK UP.
DID YOUR **BOOK** TEACH YOU THAT?

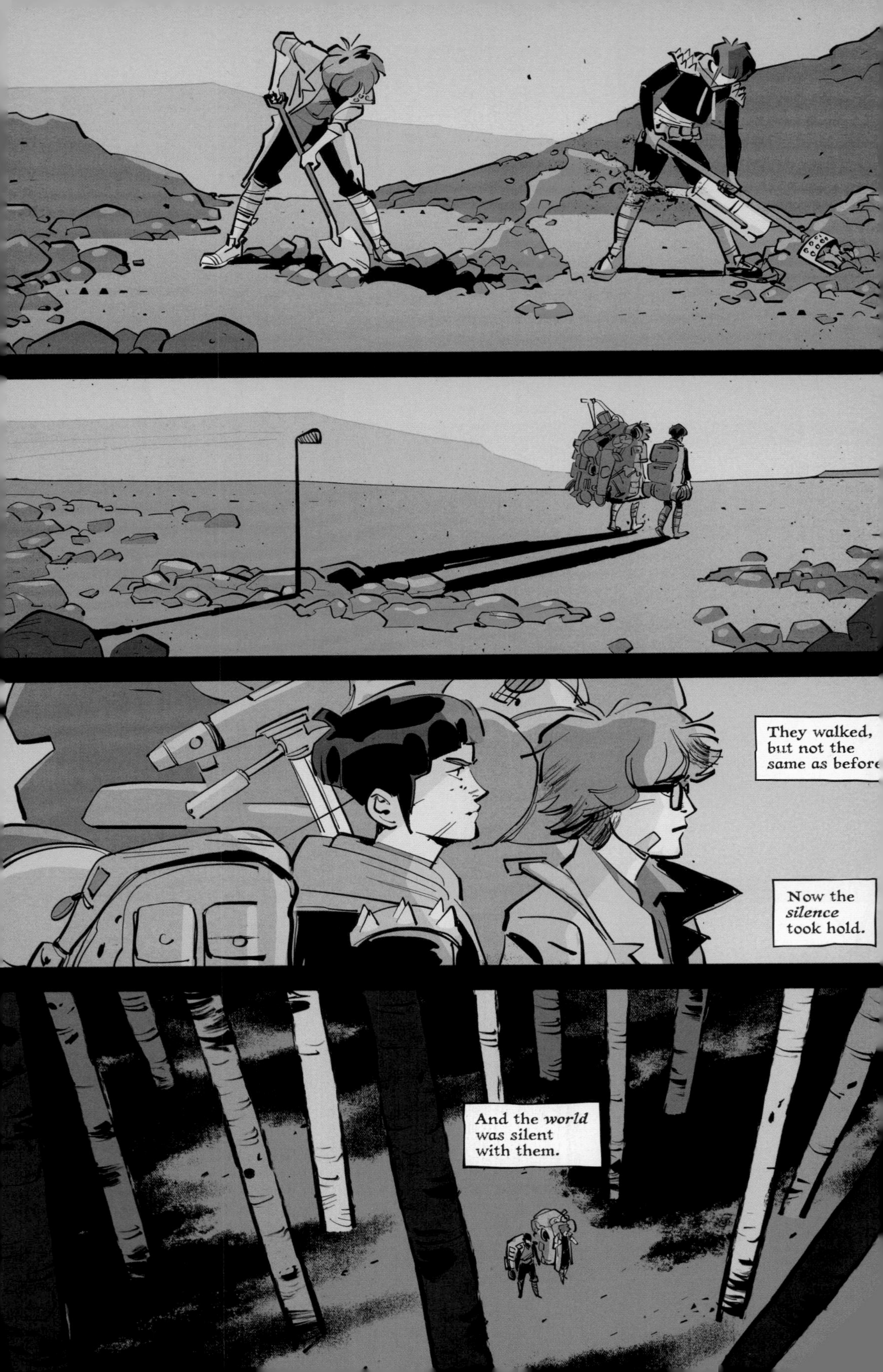

They walked, but not the same as before
Now the *silence* took hold.
And the *world* was silent with them.

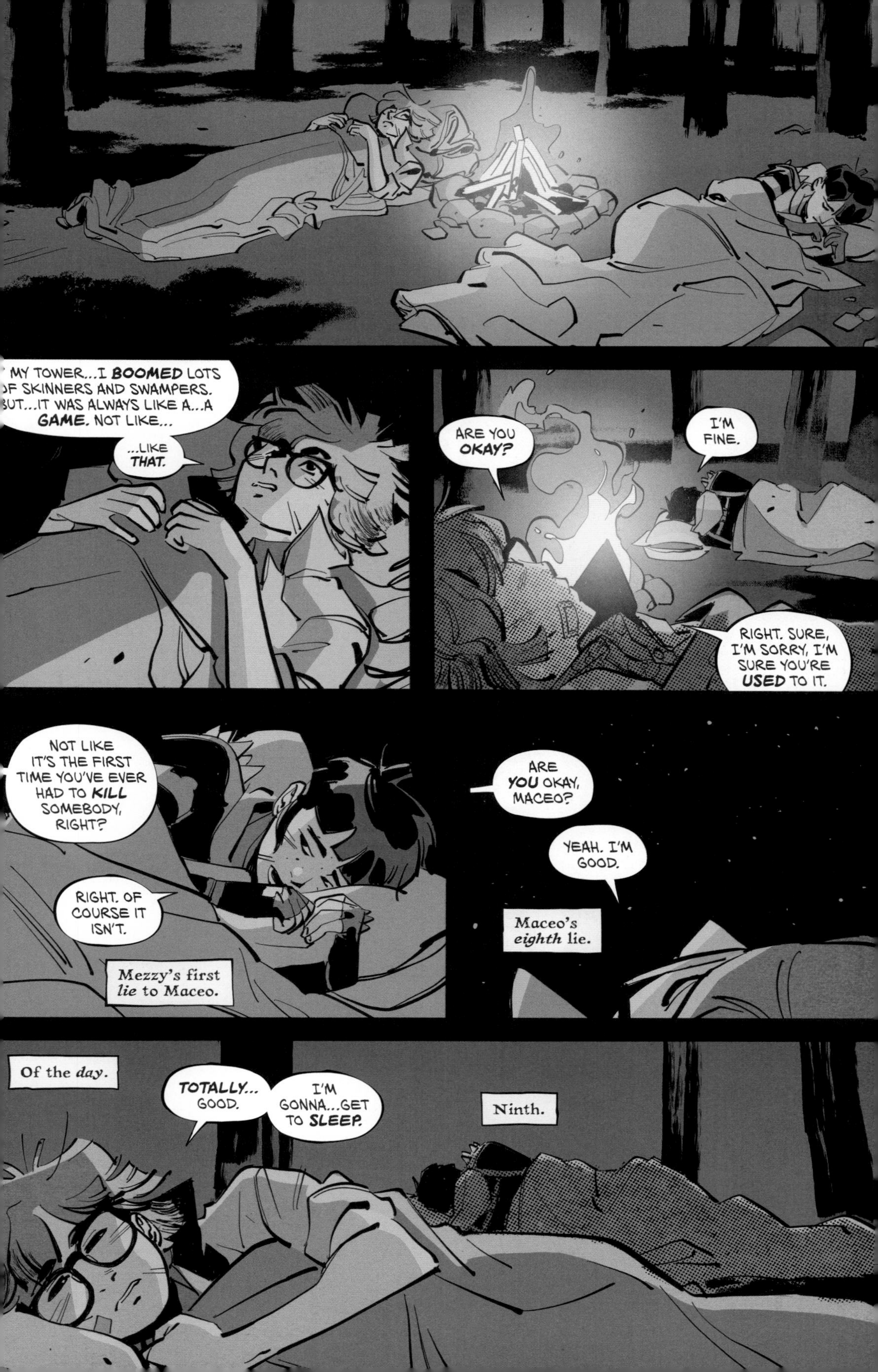

...MY TOWER...I BOOMED LOTS OF SKINNERS AND SWAMPERS. BUT...IT WAS ALWAYS LIKE A...A GAME. NOT LIKE...
...LIKE THAT.
ARE YOU OKAY?
I'M FINE.
RIGHT. SURE, I'M SORRY, I'M SURE YOU'RE USED TO IT.
NOT LIKE IT'S THE FIRST TIME YOU'VE EVER HAD TO KILL SOMEBODY, RIGHT?
RIGHT. OF COURSE IT ISN'T.
Mezzy's first lie to Maceo.
ARE YOU OKAY, MACEO?
YEAH. I'M GOOD.
Maceo's eighth lie.
Of the day.
TOTALLY... GOOD.
I'M GONNA...GET TO SLEEP.
Ninth.

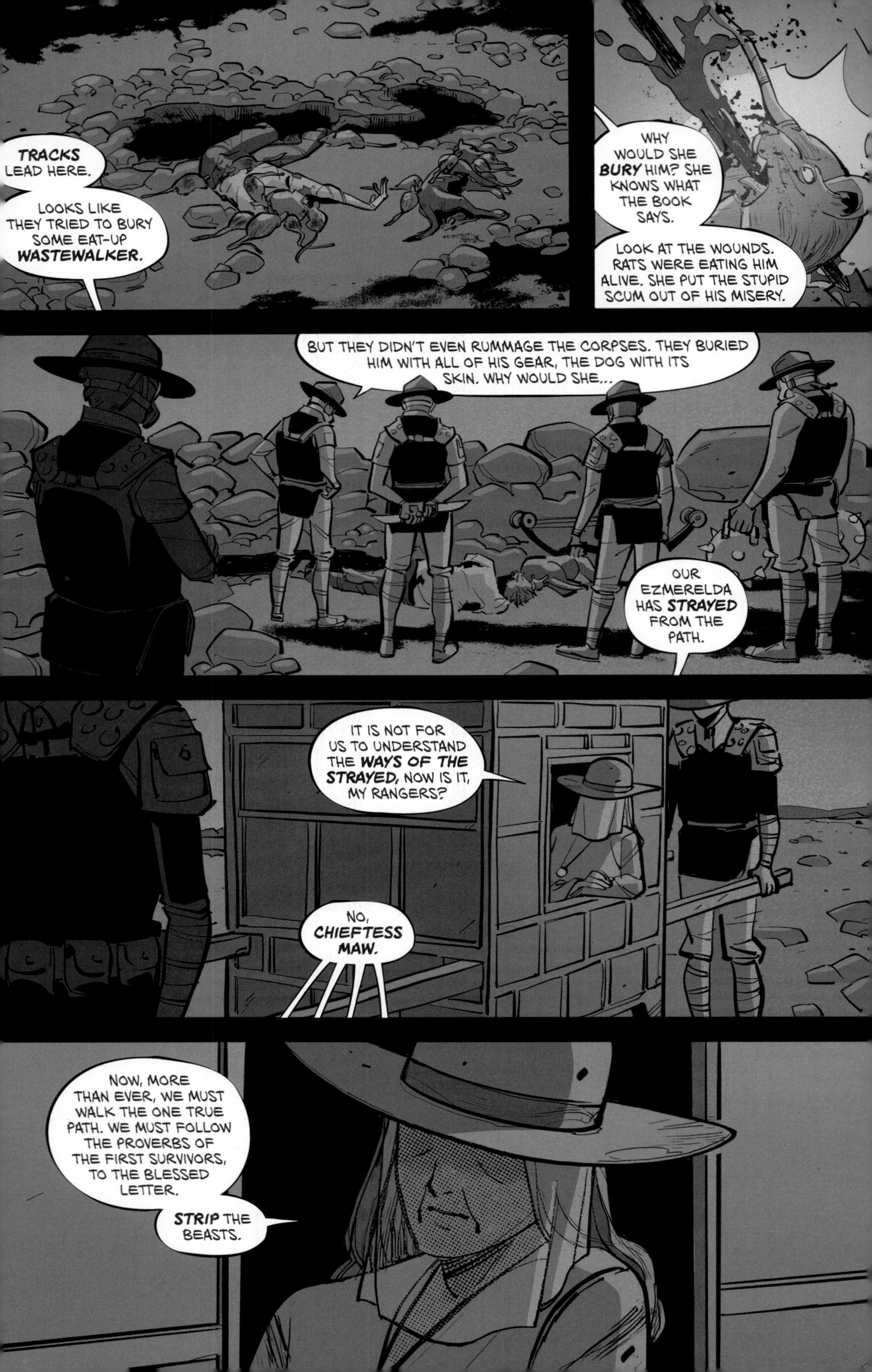
TRACKS LEAD HERE.
LOOKS LIKE THEY TRIED TO BURY SOME EAT-UP WASTEWALKER.
WHY WOULD SHE BURY HIM? SHE KNOWS WHAT THE BOOK SAYS.
LOOK AT THE WOUNDS. RATS WERE EATING HIM ALIVE. SHE PUT THE STUPID SCUM OUT OF HIS MISERY.
BUT THEY DIDN'T EVEN RUMMAGE THE CORPSES. THEY BURIED HIM WITH ALL OF HIS GEAR, THE DOG WITH ITS SKIN. WHY WOULD SHE...
OUR EZMERELDA HAS STRAYED FROM THE PATH.
IT IS NOT FOR US TO UNDERSTAND THE WAYS OF THE STRAYED, NOW IS IT, MY RANGERS?
NO, CHIEFTESS MAW.
NOW, MORE THAN EVER, WE MUST WALK THE ONE TRUE PATH. WE MUST FOLLOW THE PROVERBS OF THE FIRST SURVIVORS, TO THE BLESSED LETTER.
STRIP THE BEASTS.

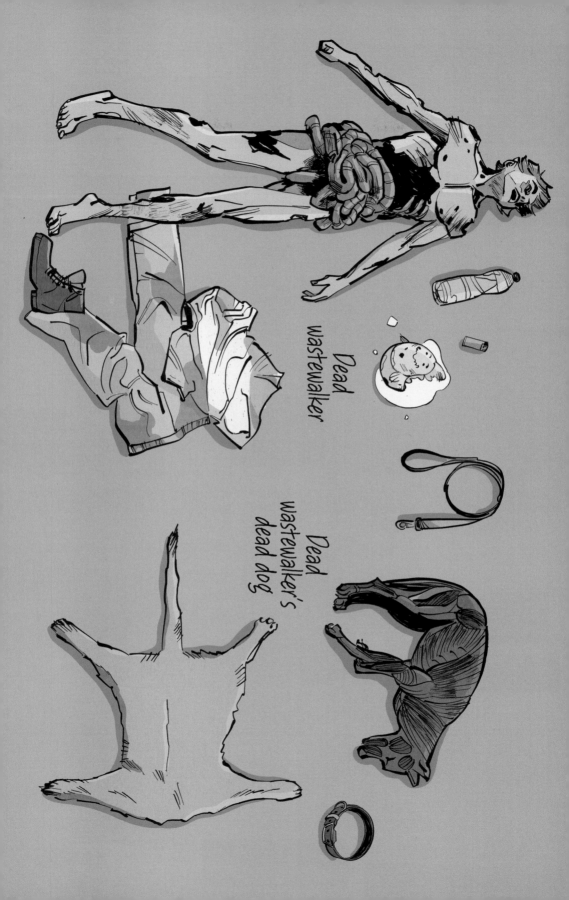

Dead
wastewalker

Dead
wastewalker's
dead dog

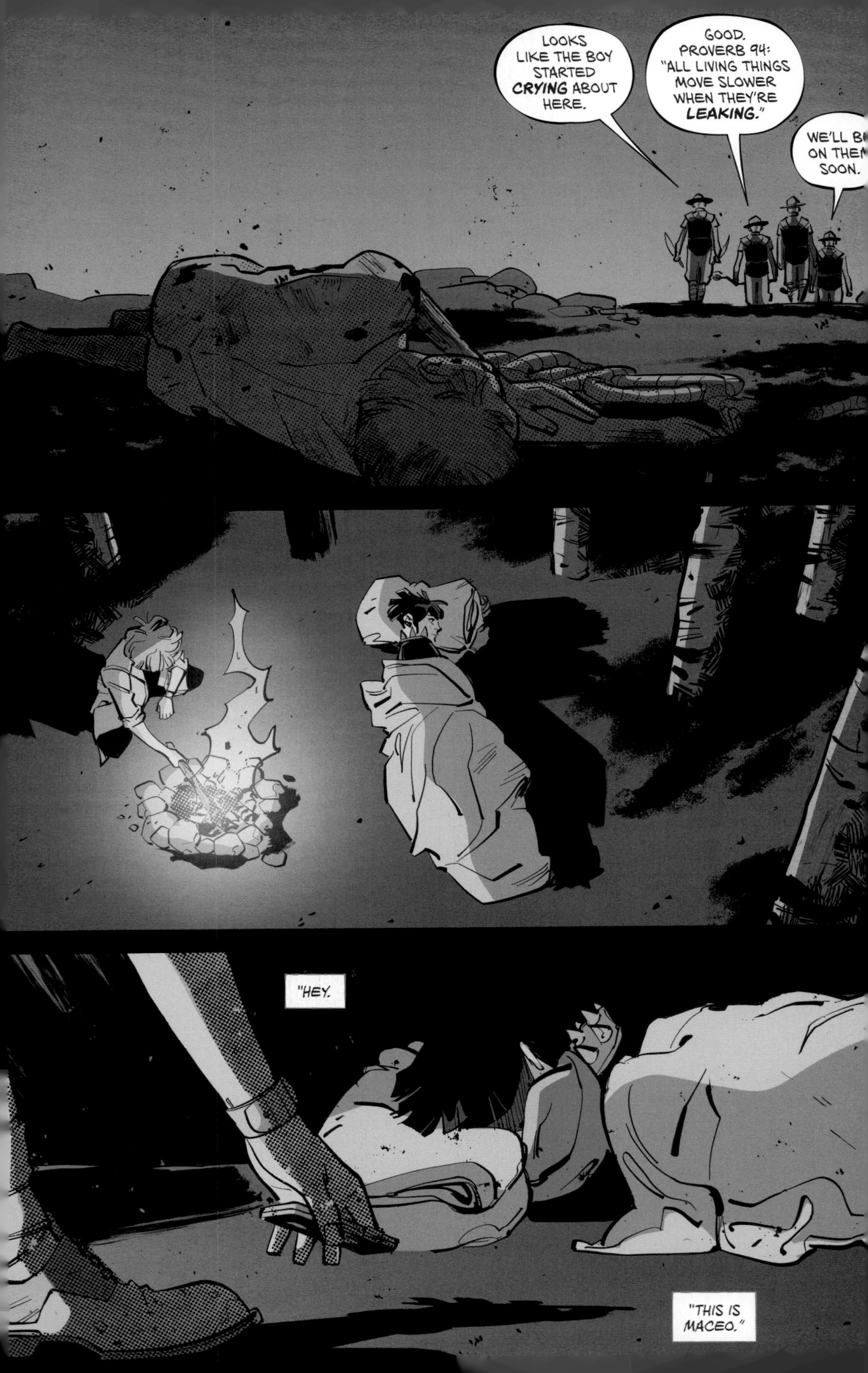
LOOKS LIKE THE BOY STARTED **CRYING** ABOUT HERE.
GOOD. PROVERB 94: "ALL LIVING THINGS MOVE SLOWER WHEN THEY'RE **LEAKING.**"
"HEY.
"THIS IS MACEO."

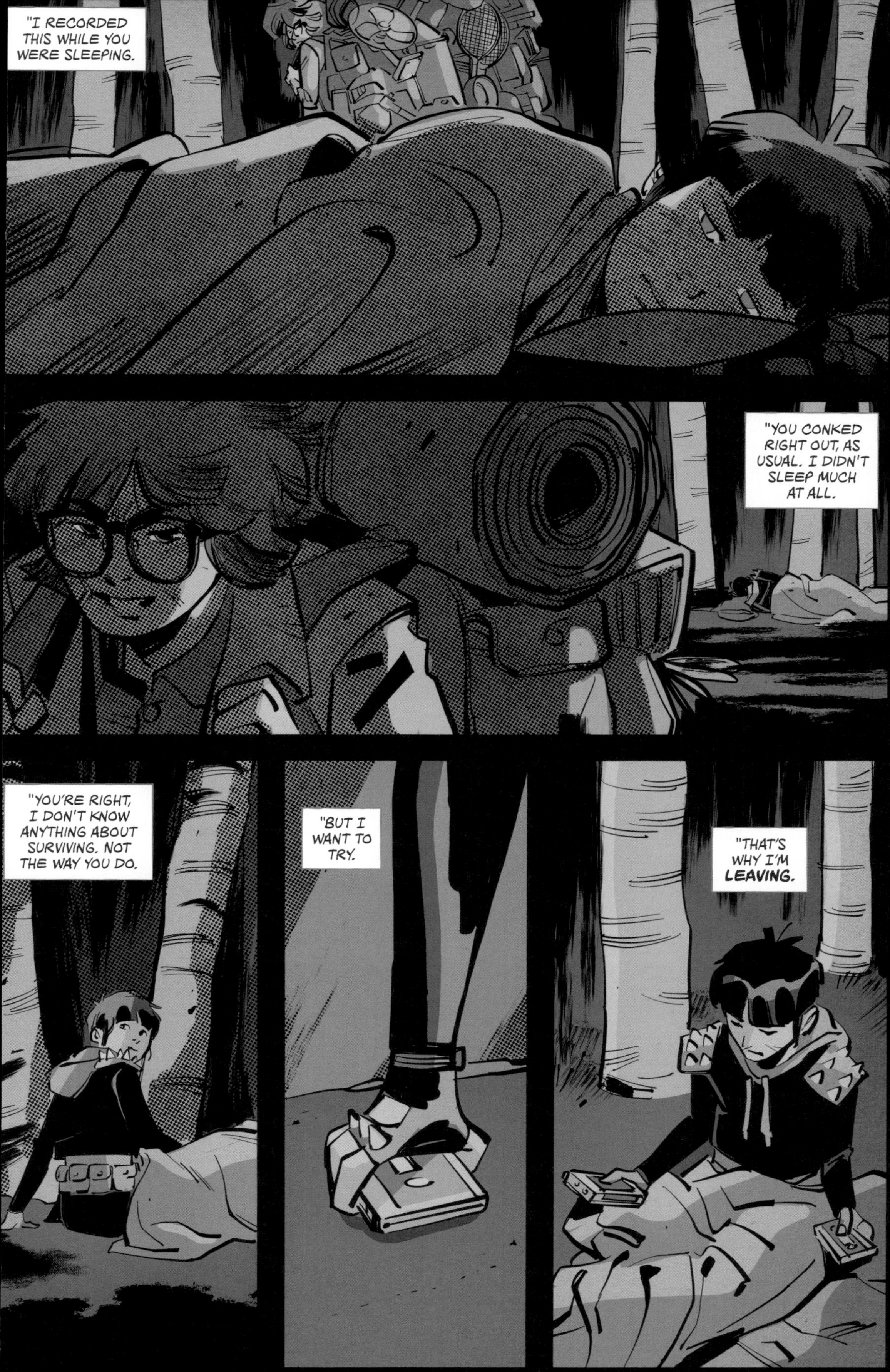
"I RECORDED THIS WHILE YOU WERE SLEEPING.
"YOU CONKED RIGHT OUT, AS USUAL. I DIDN'T SLEEP MUCH AT ALL.
"YOU'RE RIGHT, I DON'T KNOW ANYTHING ABOUT SURVIVING. NOT THE WAY YOU DO.
"BUT I WANT TO TRY.
"THAT'S WHY I'M **LEAVING**.

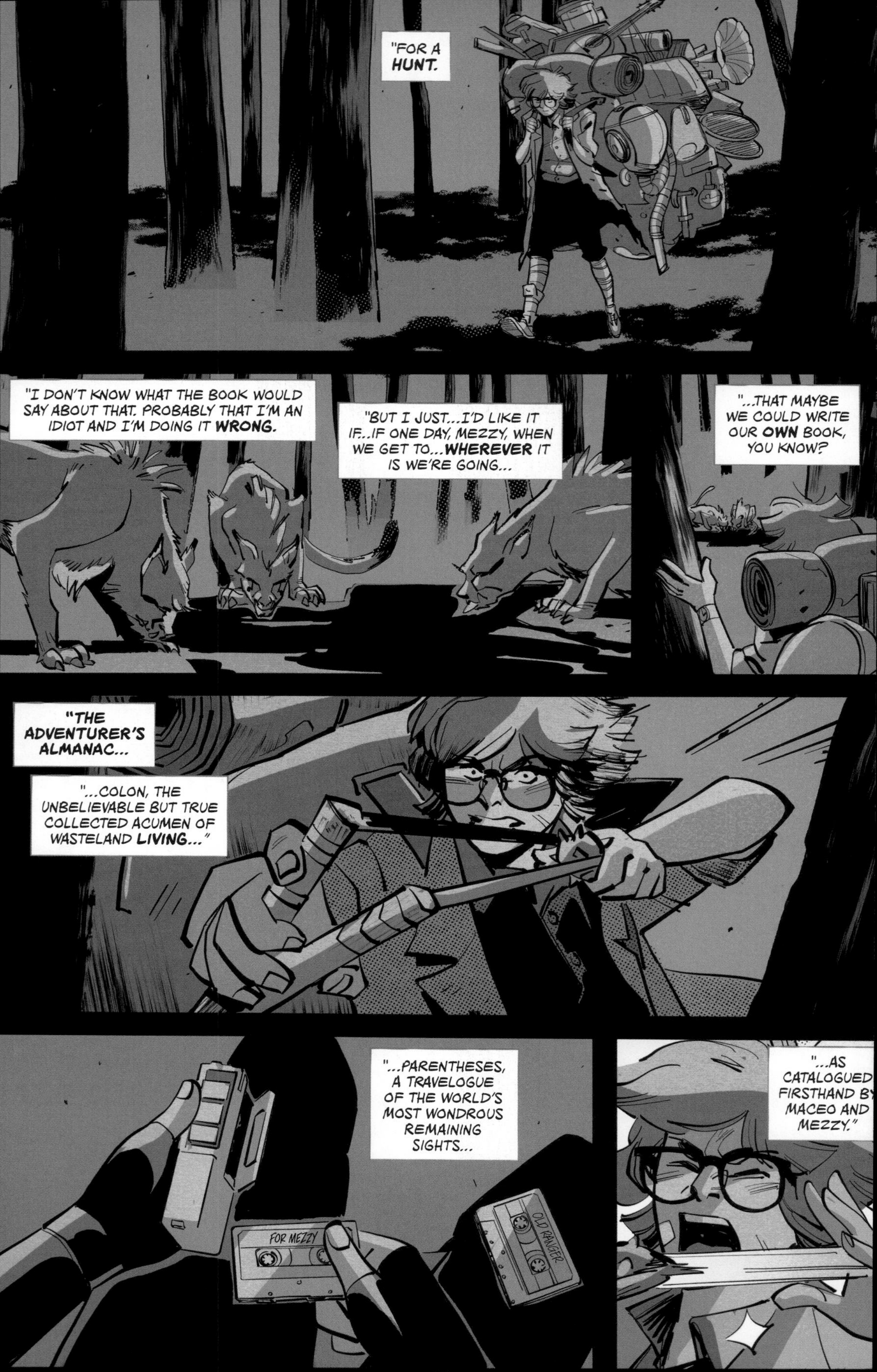
"FOR A HUNT.
"I DON'T KNOW WHAT THE BOOK WOULD SAY ABOUT THAT. PROBABLY THAT I'M AN IDIOT AND I'M DOING IT WRONG.
"BUT I JUST...I'D LIKE IT IF...IF ONE DAY, MEZZY, WHEN WE GET TO...WHEREVER IT IS WE'RE GOING...
"...THAT MAYBE WE COULD WRITE OUR OWN BOOK, YOU KNOW?
"THE ADVENTURER'S ALMANAC...
"...COLON, THE UNBELIEVABLE BUT TRUE COLLECTED ACUMEN OF WASTELAND LIVING..."
"...PARENTHESES, A TRAVELOGUE OF THE WORLD'S MOST WONDROUS REMAINING SIGHTS...
FOR MEZZY
OLD RANGER
"...AS CATALOGUED FIRSTHAND BY MACEO AND MEZZY."

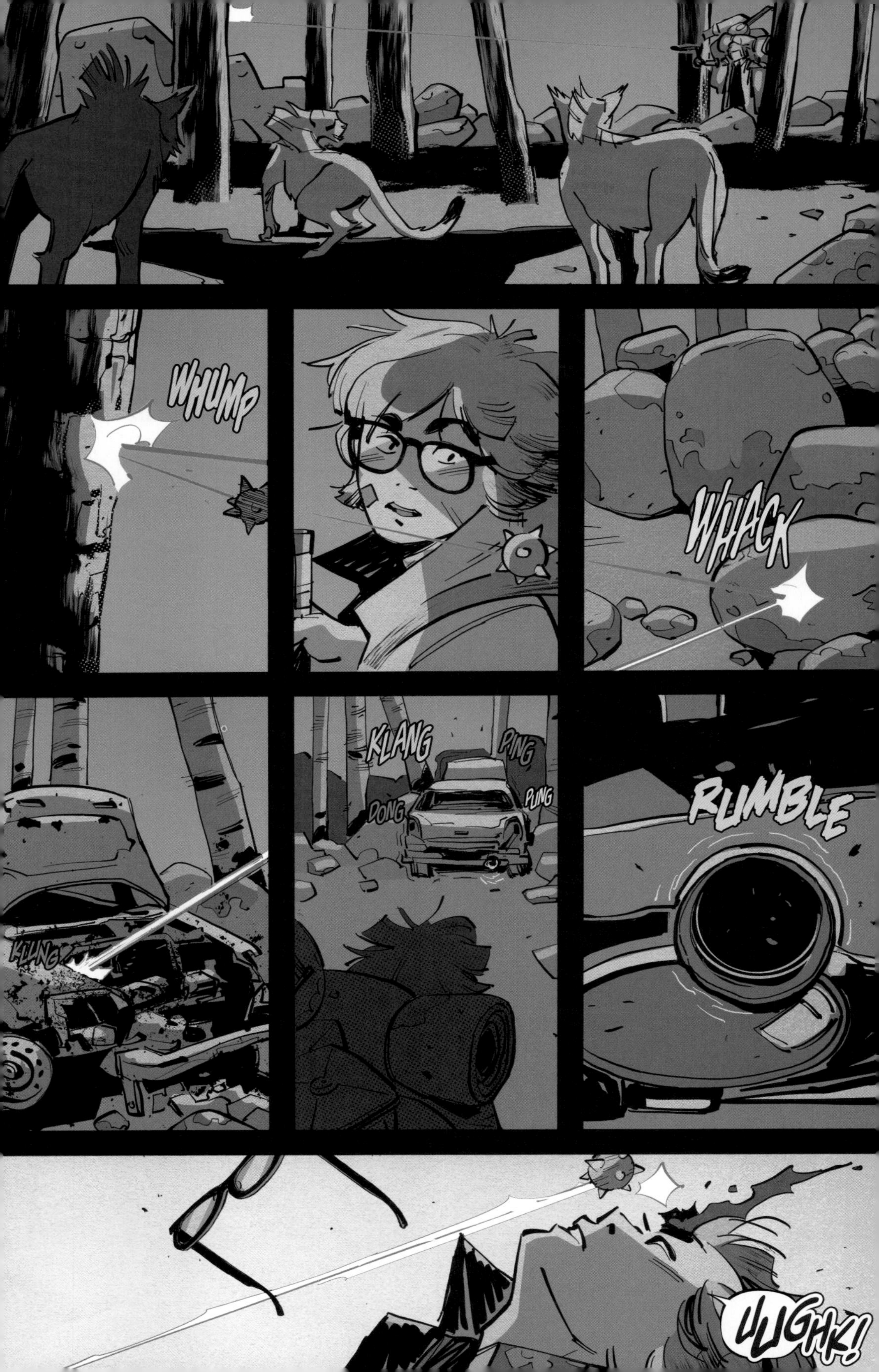
WHUMP
WHACK
KLANG
PING
DONG
PLING
KLUNG
RUMBLE
UUGHK!

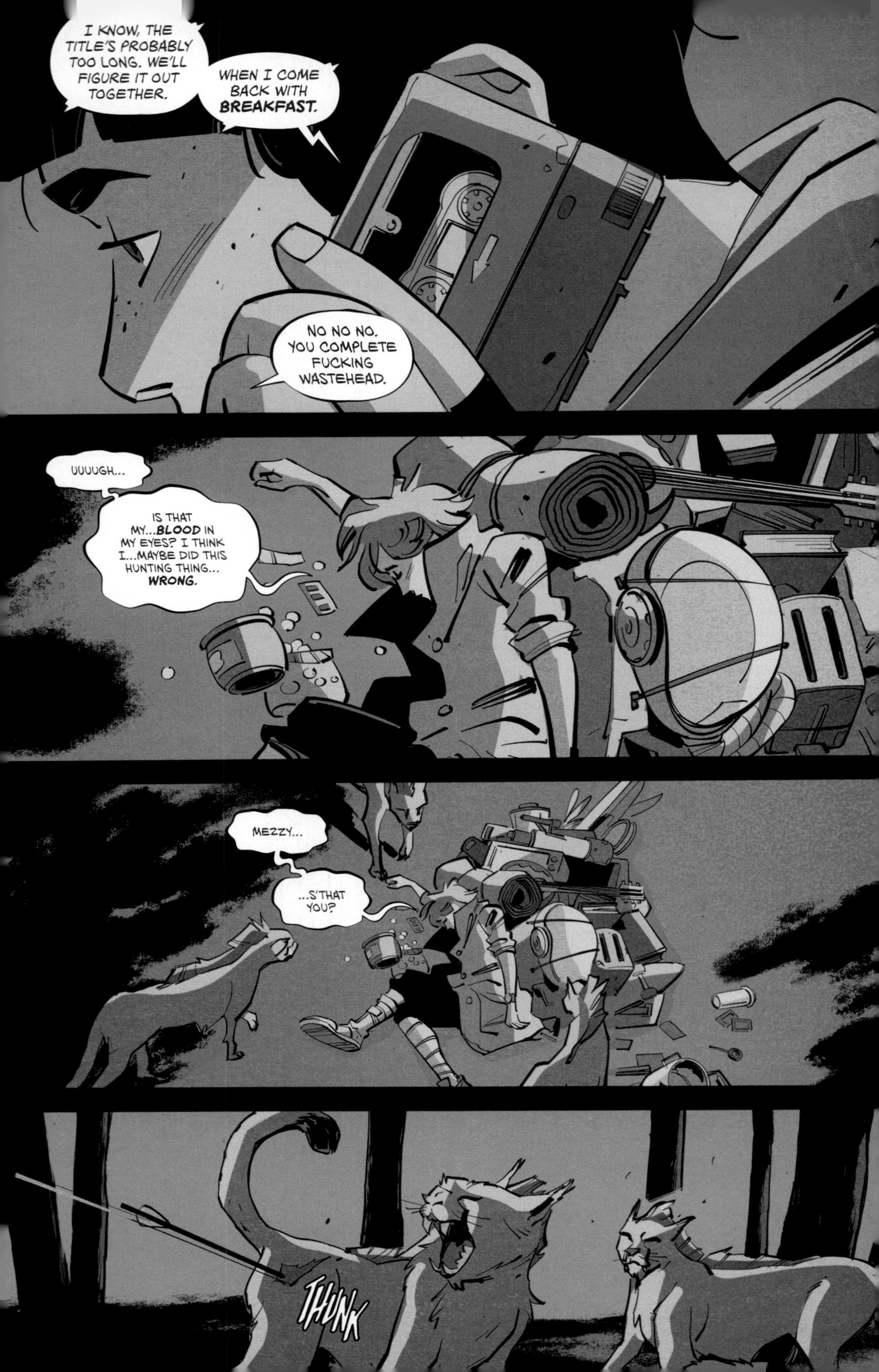
I KNOW, THE TITLE'S PROBABLY TOO LONG. WE'LL FIGURE IT OUT TOGETHER.
WHEN I COME BACK WITH **BREAKFAST.**
NO NO NO. YOU COMPLETE FUCKING WASTEHEAD.
UUUUGH...
IS THAT MY...**BLOOD** IN MY EYES? I THINK I...MAYBE DID THIS HUNTING THING... **WRONG.**
MEZZY...
...S'THAT YOU?
THUNK

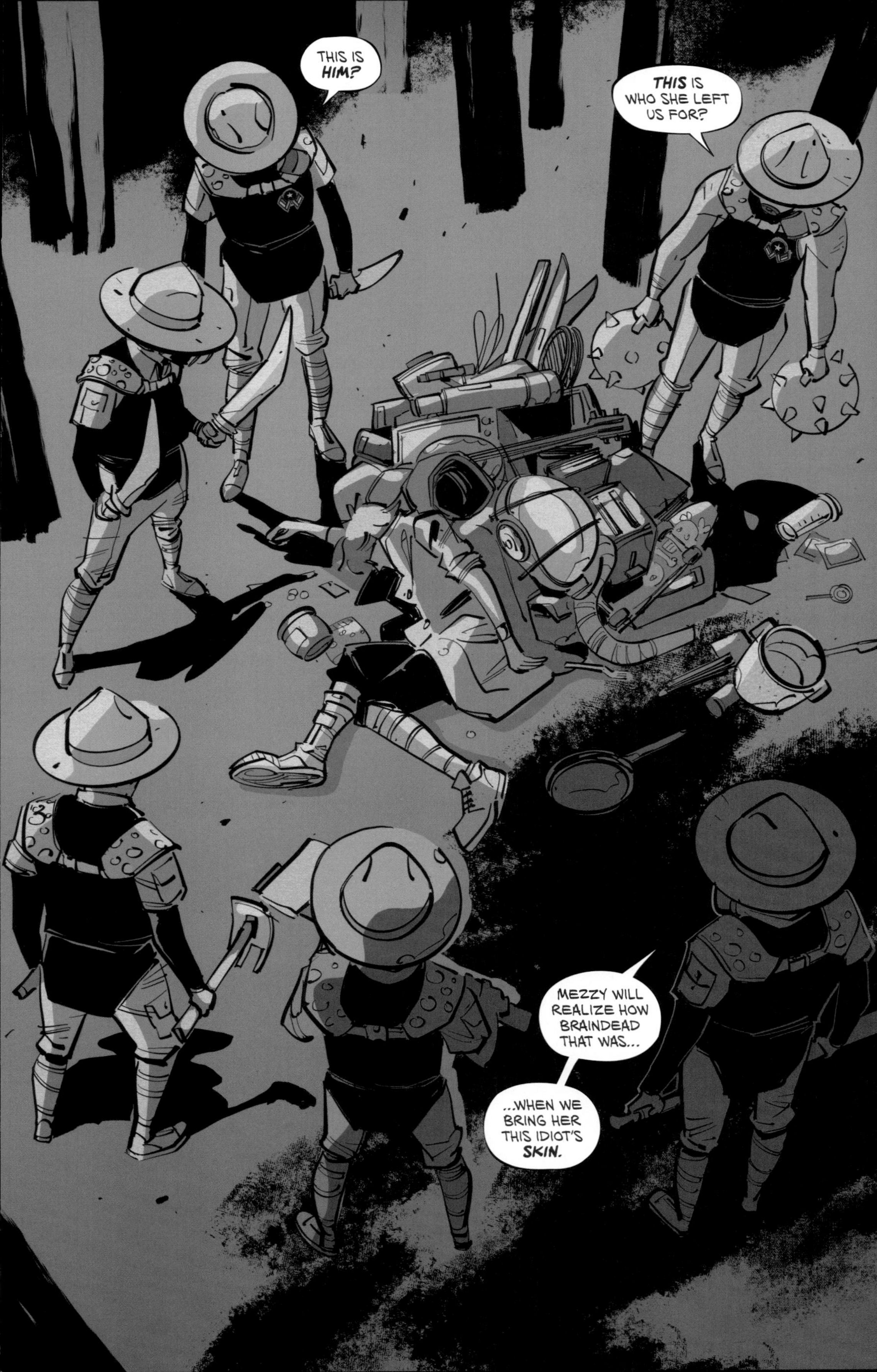
THIS IS **HIM?**
THIS IS WHO SHE LEFT US FOR?
MEZZY WILL REALIZE HOW BRAINDEAD THAT WAS...
...WHEN WE BRING HER THIS IDIOT'S **SKIN.**

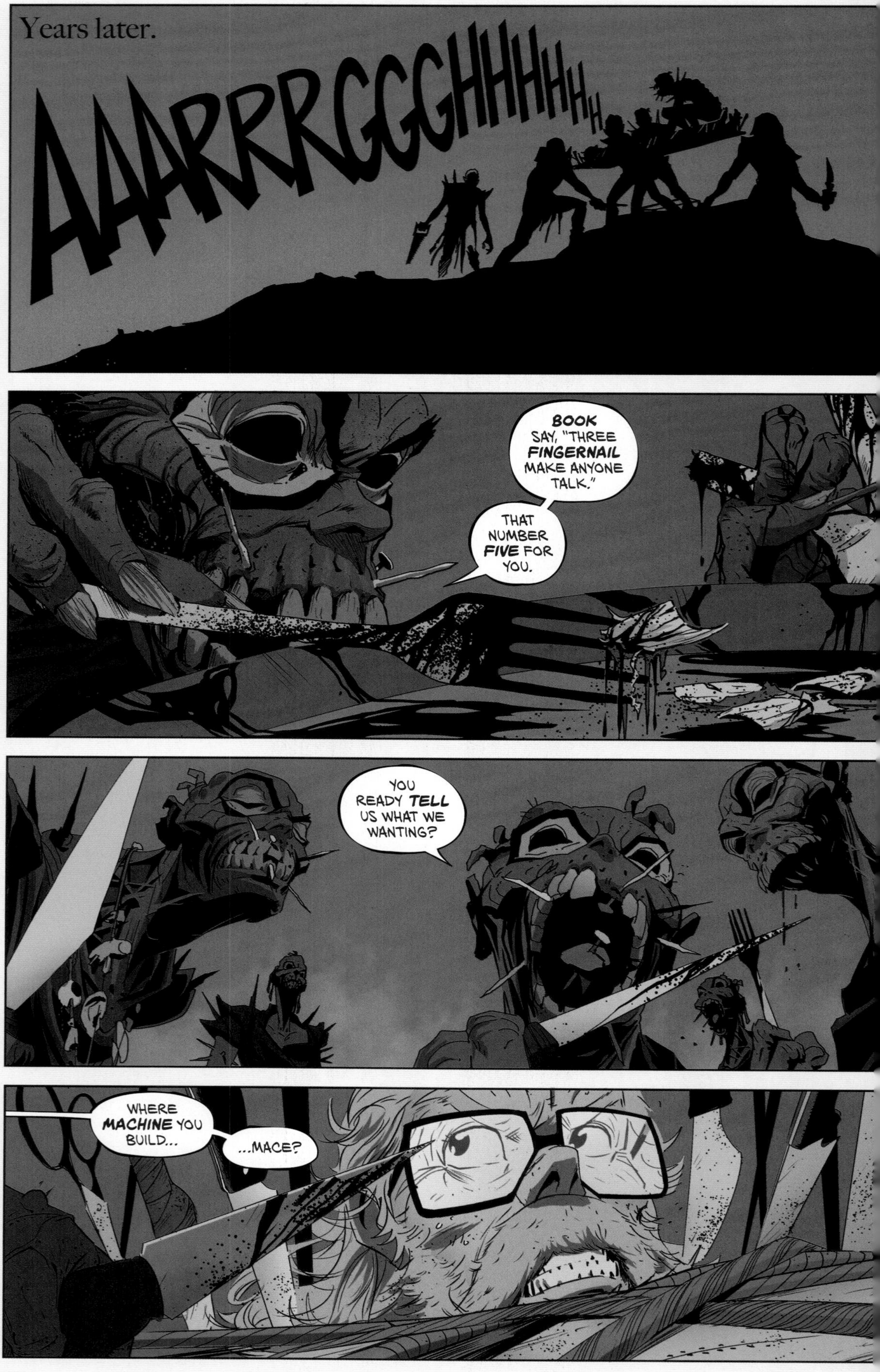
Years later.
AAARRRGGGHHHHHH
BOOK SAY, "THREE FINGERNAIL MAKE ANYONE TALK."
THAT NUMBER FIVE FOR YOU.
YOU READY TELL US WHAT WE WANTING?
WHERE MACHINE YOU BUILD...
...MACE?

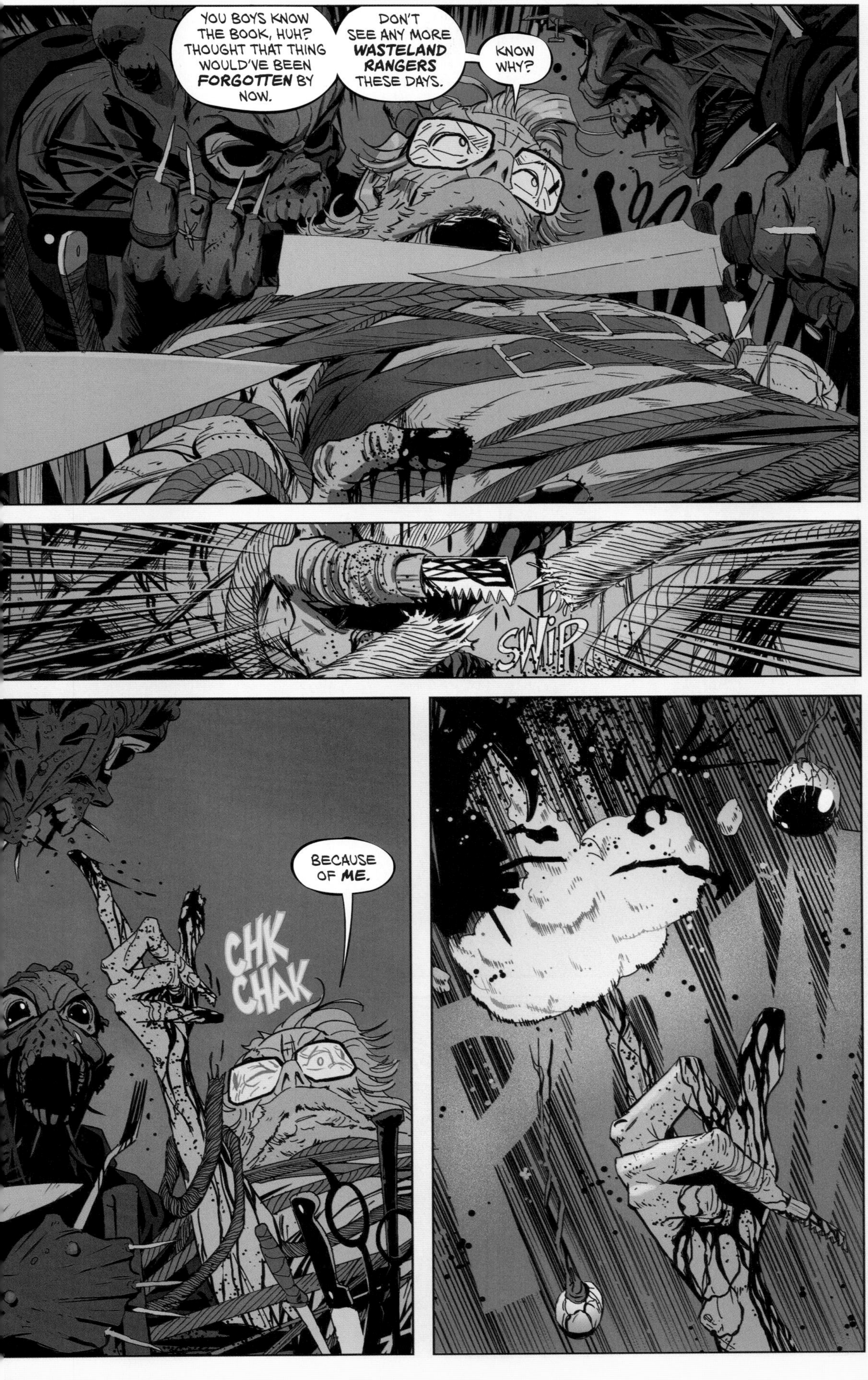
YOU BOYS KNOW THE BOOK, HUH? THOUGHT THAT THING WOULD'VE BEEN FORGOTTEN BY NOW.
DON'T SEE ANY MORE WASTELAND RANGERS THESE DAYS.
KNOW WHY?
SWIP
CHK CHAK
BECAUSE OF ME.

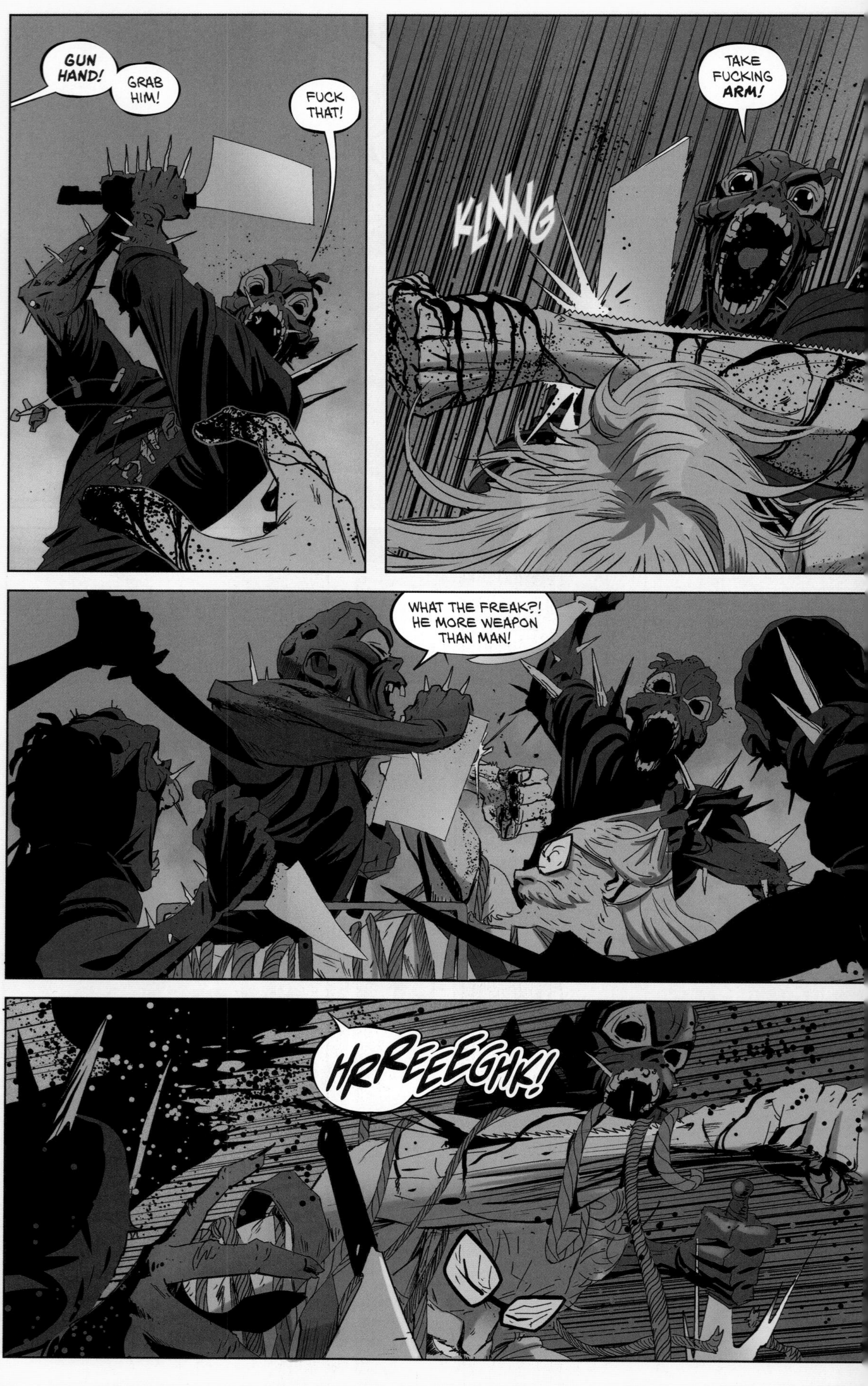
GUN HAND!
GRAB HIM!
FUCK THAT!
TAKE FUCKING ARM!
KLNNG
WHAT THE FREAK?! HE MORE WEAPON THAN MAN!
HRREEEEGHK!

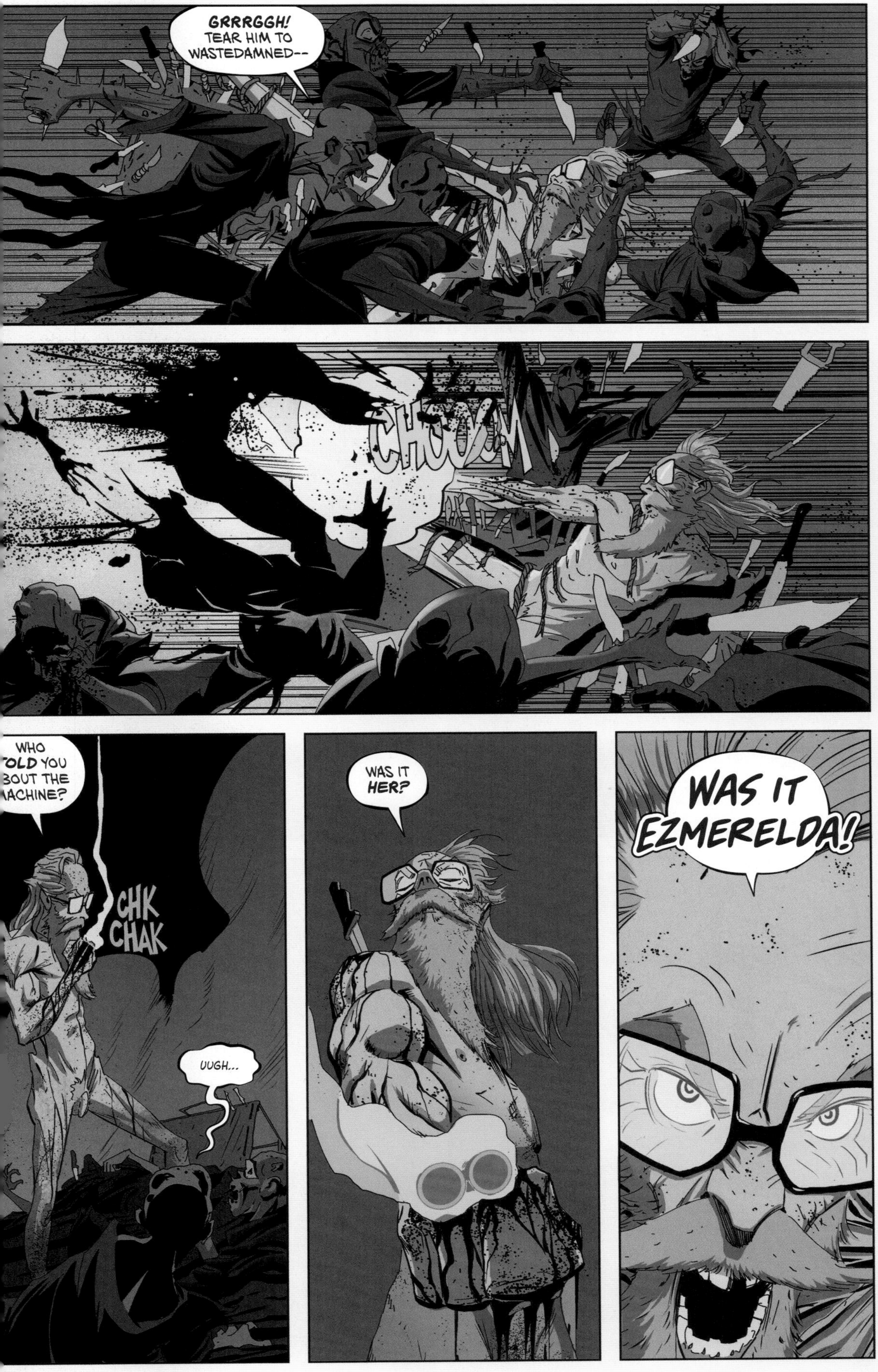
GRRRGGH! TEAR HIM TO WASTEDAMNED--
CHOOOM
WHO TOLD YOU ABOUT THE MACHINE?
CHK CHAK
UUGH...
WAS IT HER?
WAS IT EZMERELDA!

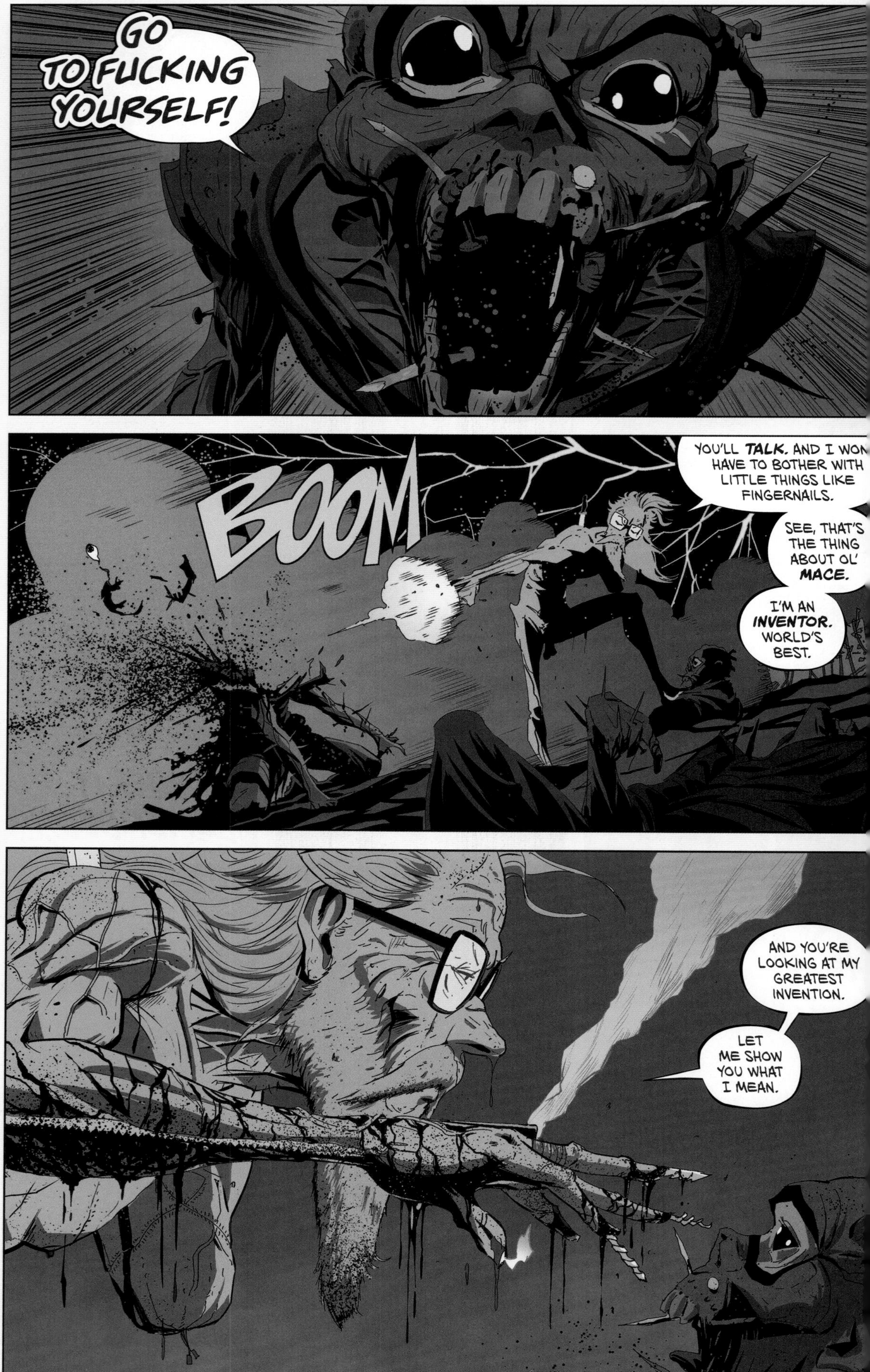
GO TO FUCKING YOURSELF!
BOOM
YOU'LL TALK. AND I WON HAVE TO BOTHER WITH LITTLE THINGS LIKE FINGERNAILS.
SEE, THAT'S THE THING ABOUT OL' MACE.
I'M AN INVENTOR. WORLD'S BEST.
AND YOU'RE LOOKING AT MY GREATEST INVENTION.
LET ME SHOW YOU WHAT I MEAN.

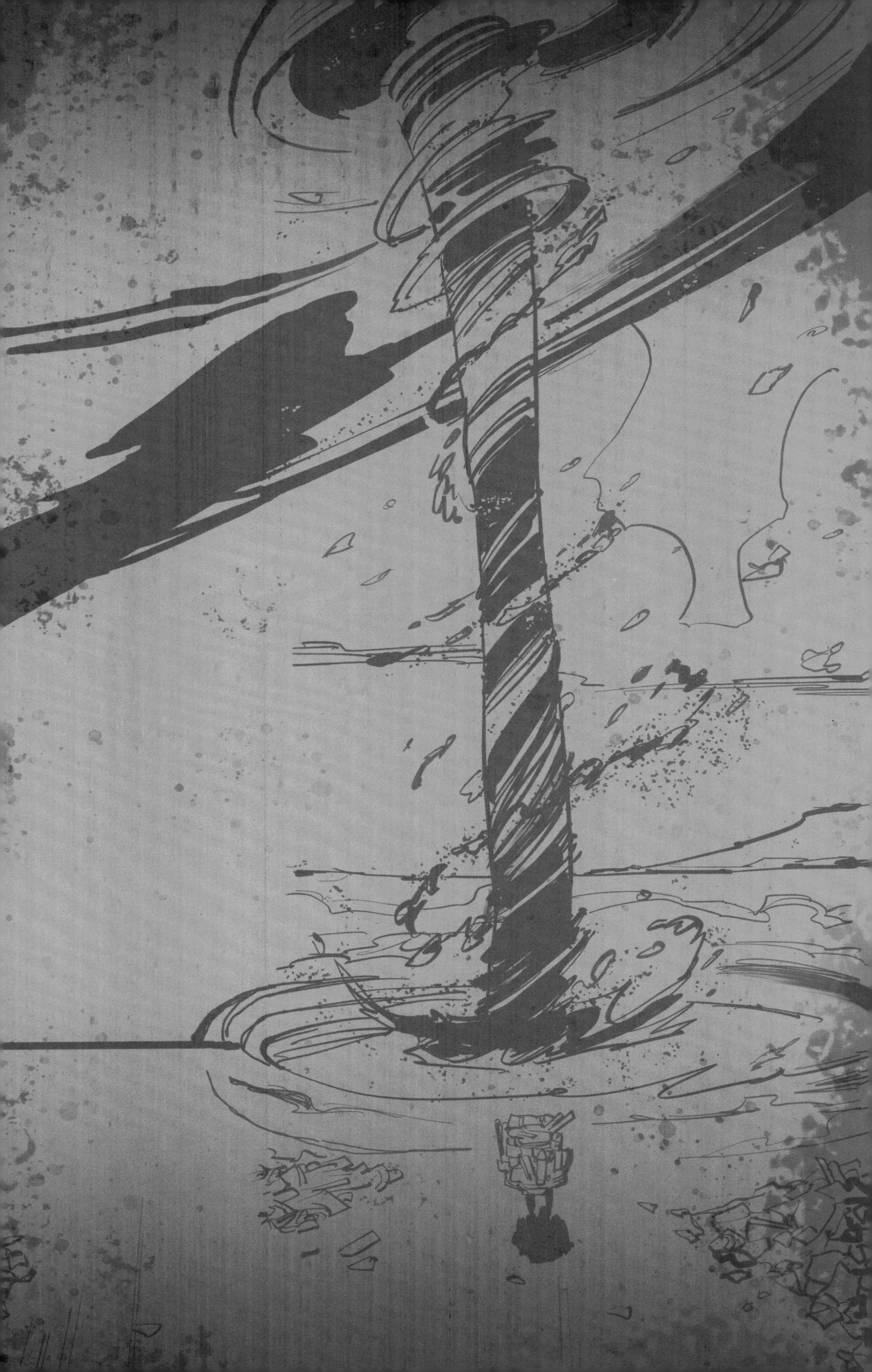

CHAPTER FOUR

THE WILD, THE WOKE, AND THE WASTELAND RANGERS

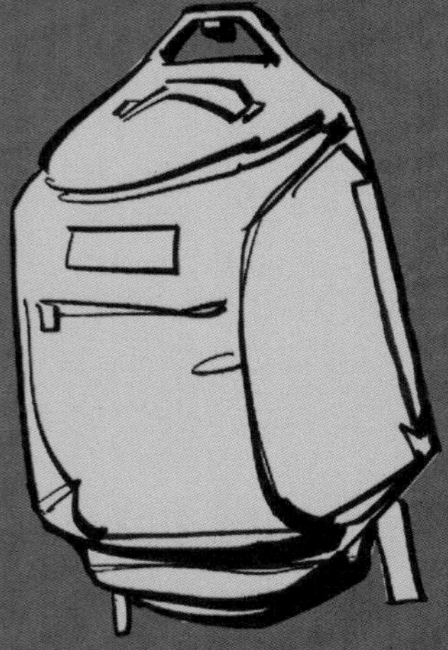

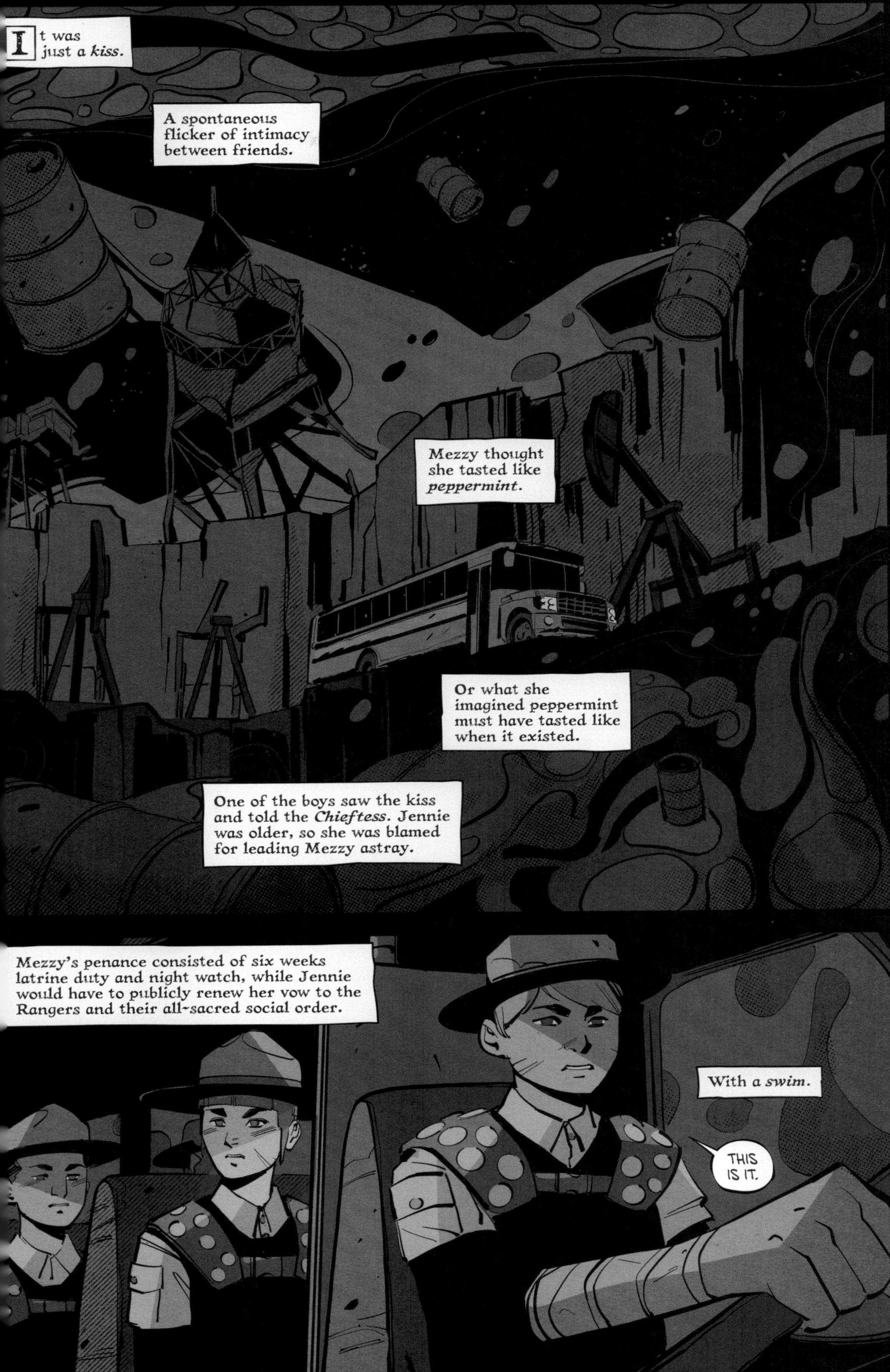
It was just a *kiss*.
A spontaneous flicker of intimacy between friends.
Mezzy thought she tasted like *peppermint*.
Or what she imagined peppermint must have tasted like when it existed.
One of the boys saw the kiss and told the *Chieftess*. Jennie was older, so she was blamed for leading Mezzy astray.
Mezzy's penance consisted of six weeks latrine duty and night watch, while Jennie would have to publicly renew her vow to the Rangers and their all-sacred social order.
With a *swim*.
THIS IS IT.

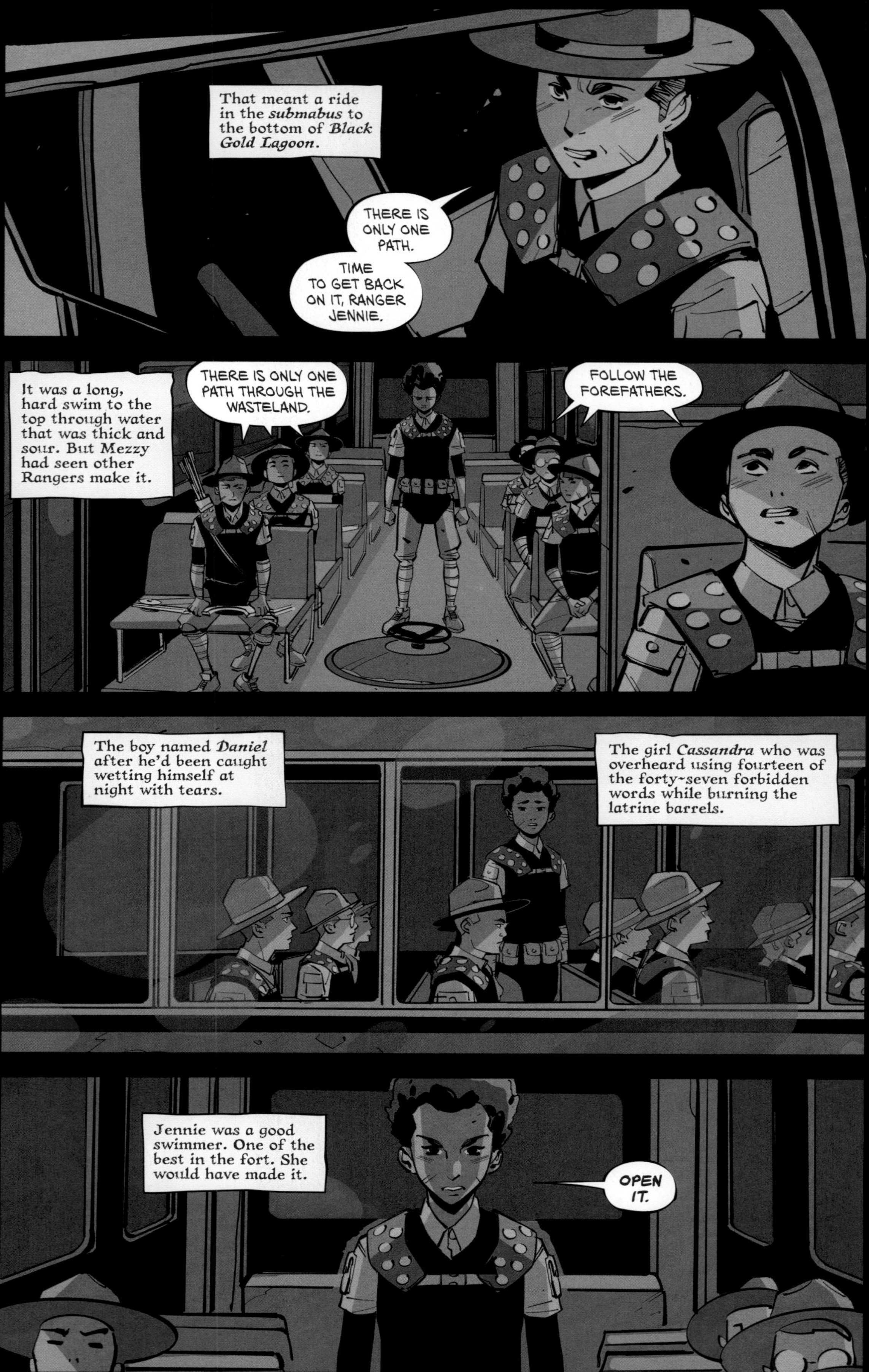
That meant a ride in the *submabus* to the bottom of *Black Gold Lagoon*.
THERE IS ONLY ONE PATH.
TIME TO GET BACK ON IT, RANGER JENNIE.
It was a long, hard swim to the top through water that was thick and sour. But Mezzy had seen other Rangers make it.
THERE IS ONLY ONE PATH THROUGH THE WASTELAND.
FOLLOW THE FOREFATHERS.
The boy named *Daniel* after he'd been caught wetting himself at night with tears.
The girl *Cassandra* who was overheard using fourteen of the forty~seven forbidden words while burning the latrine barrels.
Jennie was a good swimmer. One of the best in the fort. She would have made it.
OPEN IT.

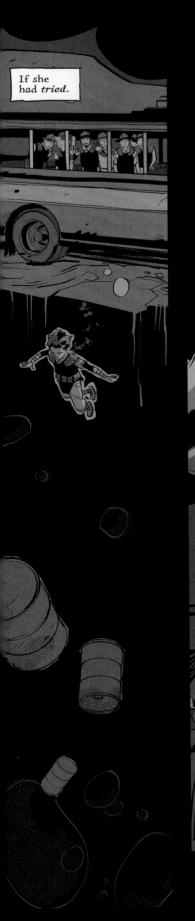

If she had *tried.*

WHAT'S SHE DOING? WHY ISN'T SHE SWIMMING?

WHY ISN'T YOUR *GIRLFRIEND* SWIMMING, MEZZY?

HEH. MEZZY THE LEZZY.

They used to *joke* about how they would do it.

At least, Mezzy thought they were jokes.

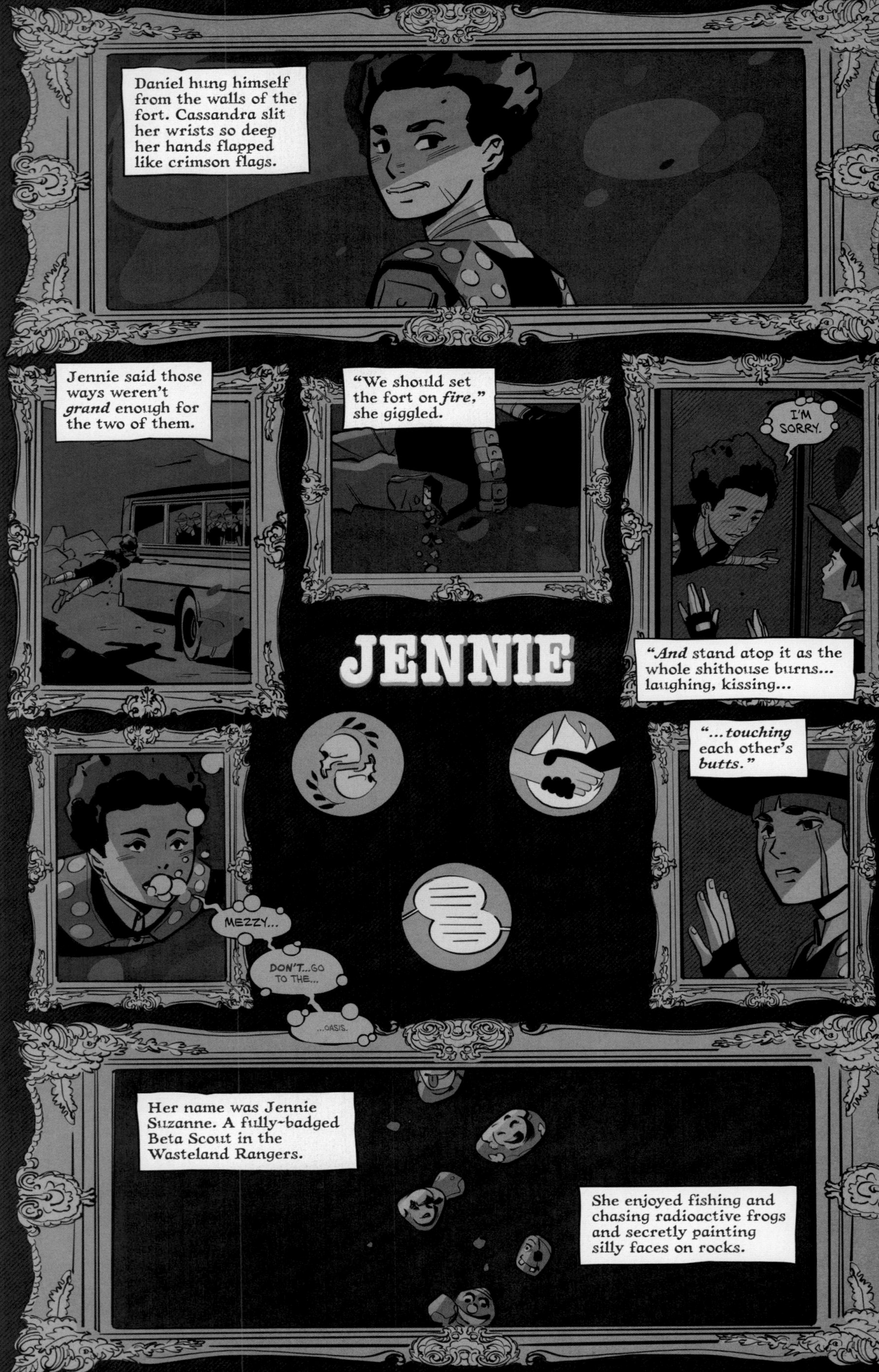
Daniel hung himself from the walls of the fort. Cassandra slit her wrists so deep her hands flapped like crimson flags.
Jennie said those ways weren't *grand* enough for the two of them.
"We should set the fort on *fire*," she giggled.
I'M SORRY.
"*And* stand atop it as the whole shithouse burns... laughing, kissing...
JENNIE
MEZZY...
DON'T...GO TO THE...
...OASIS.
"...*touching* each other's *butts.*"
Her name was Jennie Suzanne. A fully-badged Beta Scout in the Wasteland Rangers.
She enjoyed fishing and chasing radioactive frogs and secretly painting silly faces on rocks.

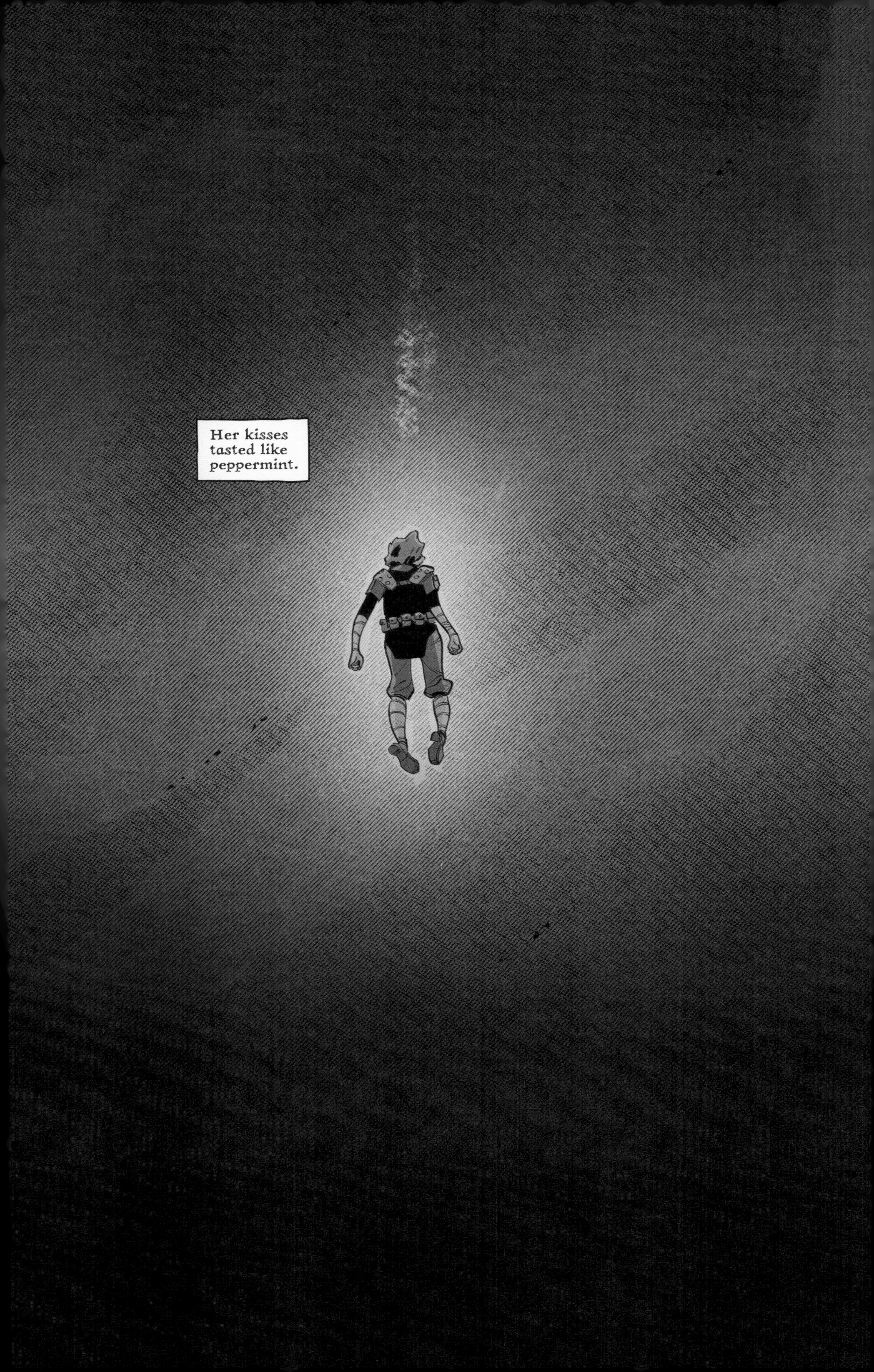
Her kisses tasted like peppermint.

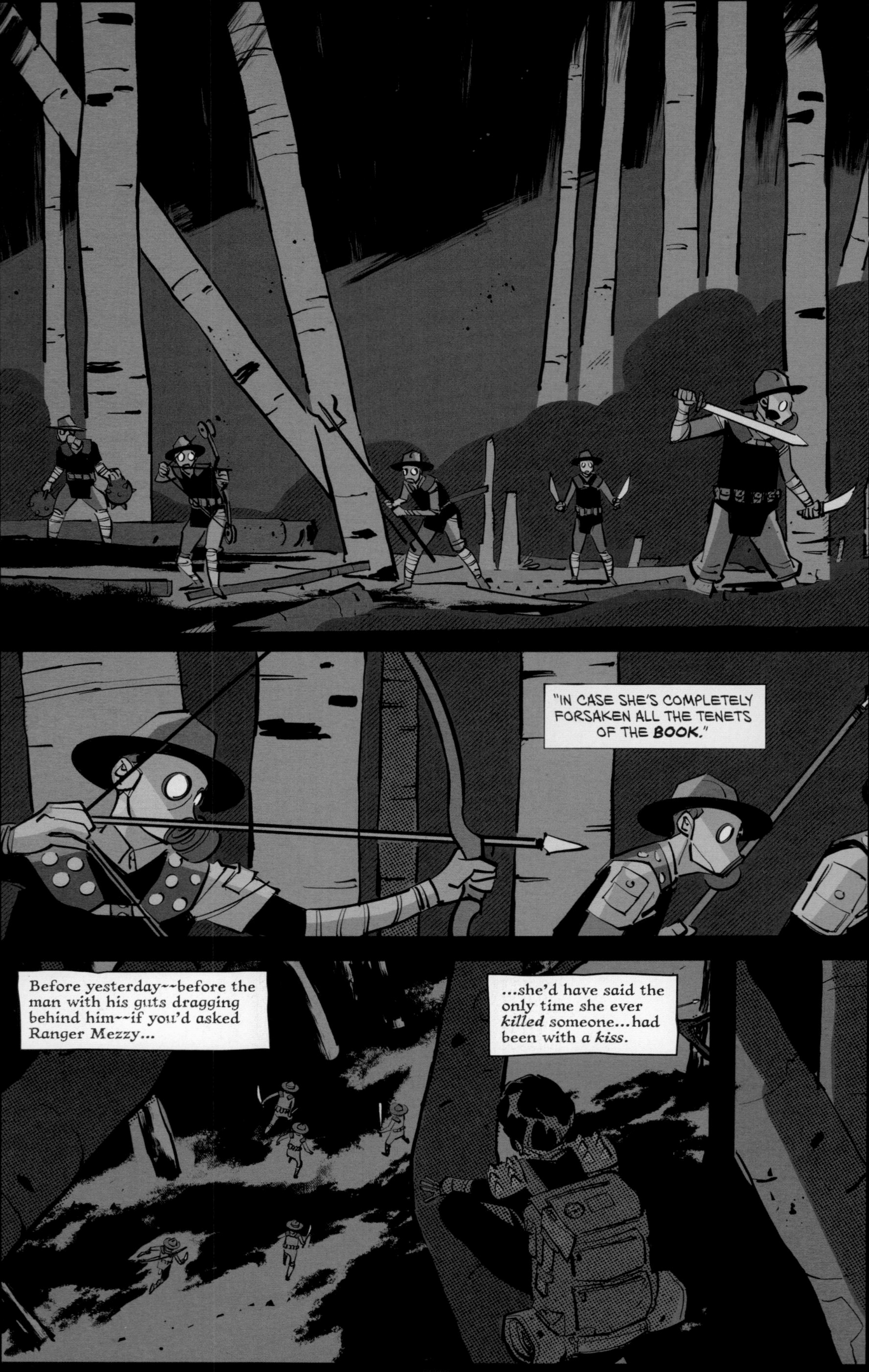
"IN CASE SHE'S COMPLETELY FORSAKEN ALL THE TENETS OF THE **BOOK.**"
Before yesterday--before the man with his guts dragging behind him--if you'd asked Ranger Mezzy...
...she'd have said the only time she ever *killed* someone...had been with a *kiss*.

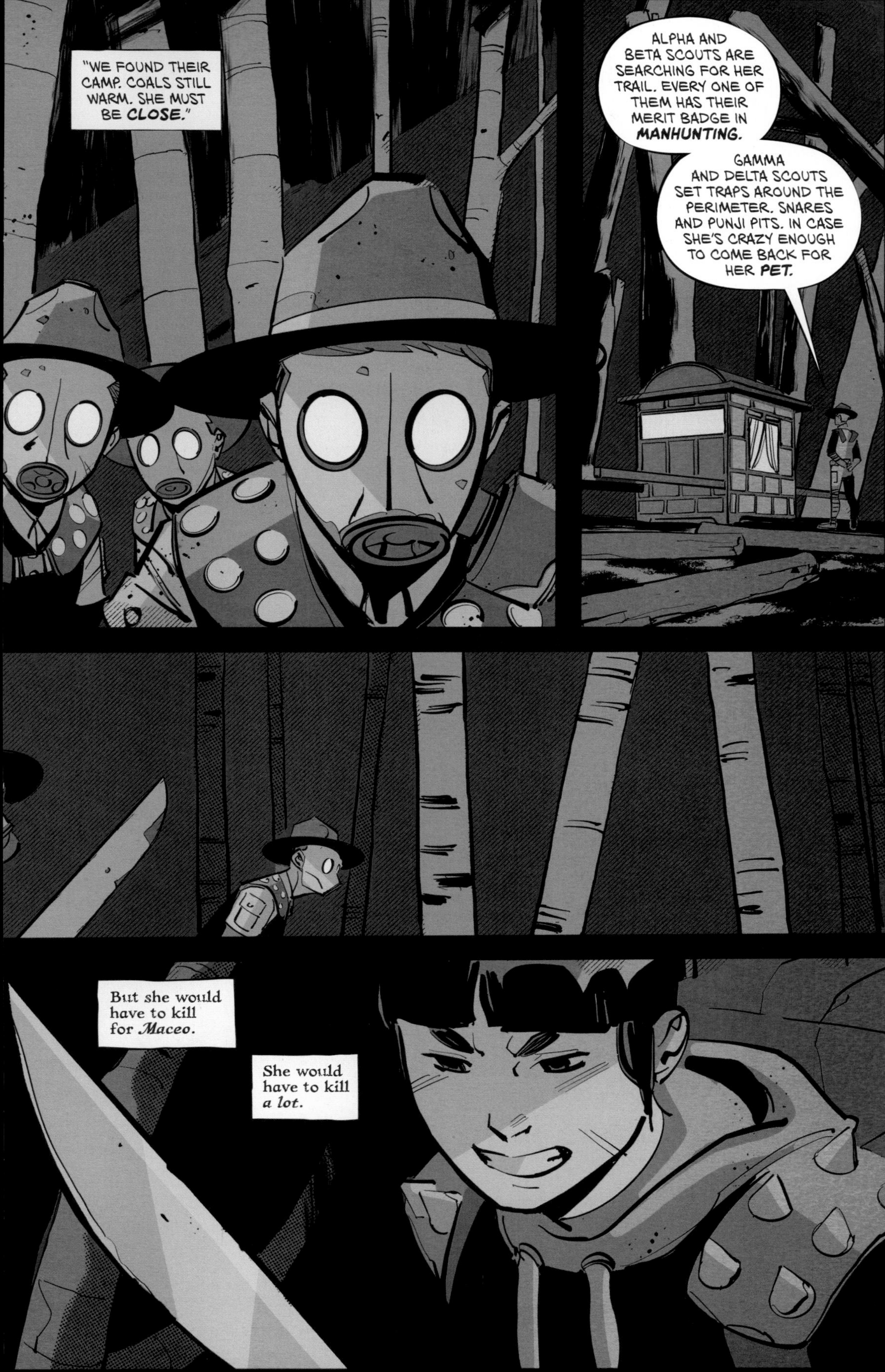
"WE FOUND THEIR CAMP. COALS STILL WARM. SHE MUST BE CLOSE."
ALPHA AND BETA SCOUTS ARE SEARCHING FOR HER TRAIL. EVERY ONE OF THEM HAS THEIR MERIT BADGE IN MANHUNTING.
GAMMA AND DELTA SCOUTS SET TRAPS AROUND THE PERIMETER. SNARES AND PUNJI PITS. IN CASE SHE'S CRAZY ENOUGH TO COME BACK FOR HER PET.
But she would have to kill for Maceo.
She would have to kill a lot.

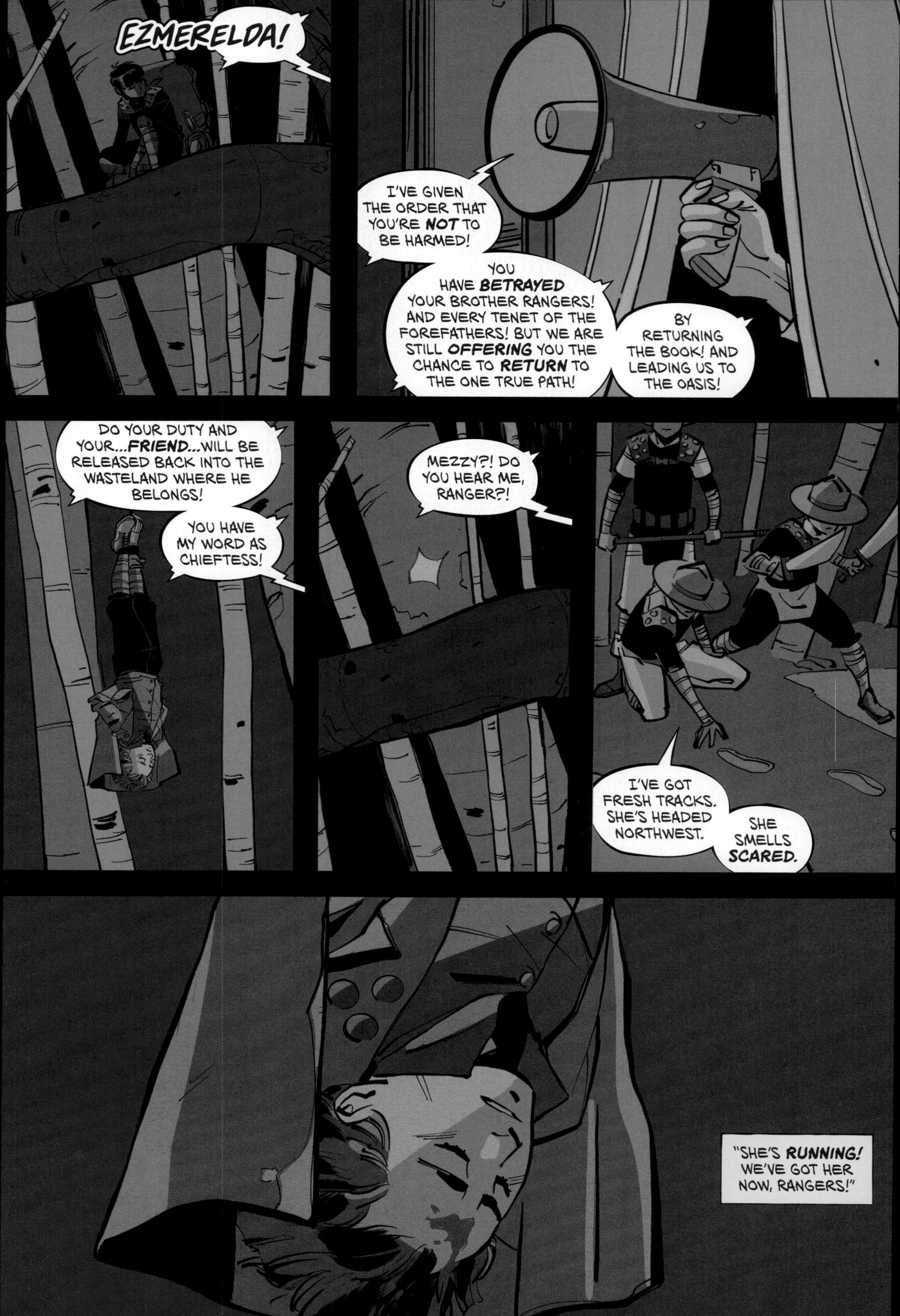
EZMERELDA!
I'VE GIVEN THE ORDER THAT YOU'RE **NOT** TO BE HARMED!
YOU HAVE **BETRAYED** YOUR BROTHER RANGERS! AND EVERY TENET OF THE FOREFATHERS! BUT WE ARE STILL **OFFERING** YOU THE CHANCE TO **RETURN** TO THE ONE TRUE PATH!
BY RETURNING THE BOOK! AND LEADING US TO THE OASIS!
DO YOUR DUTY AND YOUR...**FRIEND**...WILL BE RELEASED BACK INTO THE WASTELAND WHERE HE BELONGS!
YOU HAVE MY WORD AS CHIEFTESS!
MEZZY?! DO YOU HEAR ME, RANGER?!
I'VE GOT FRESH TRACKS. SHE'S HEADED NORTHWEST.
SHE SMELLS **SCARED.**
"SHE'S **RUNNING!** WE'VE GOT HER NOW, RANGERS!"

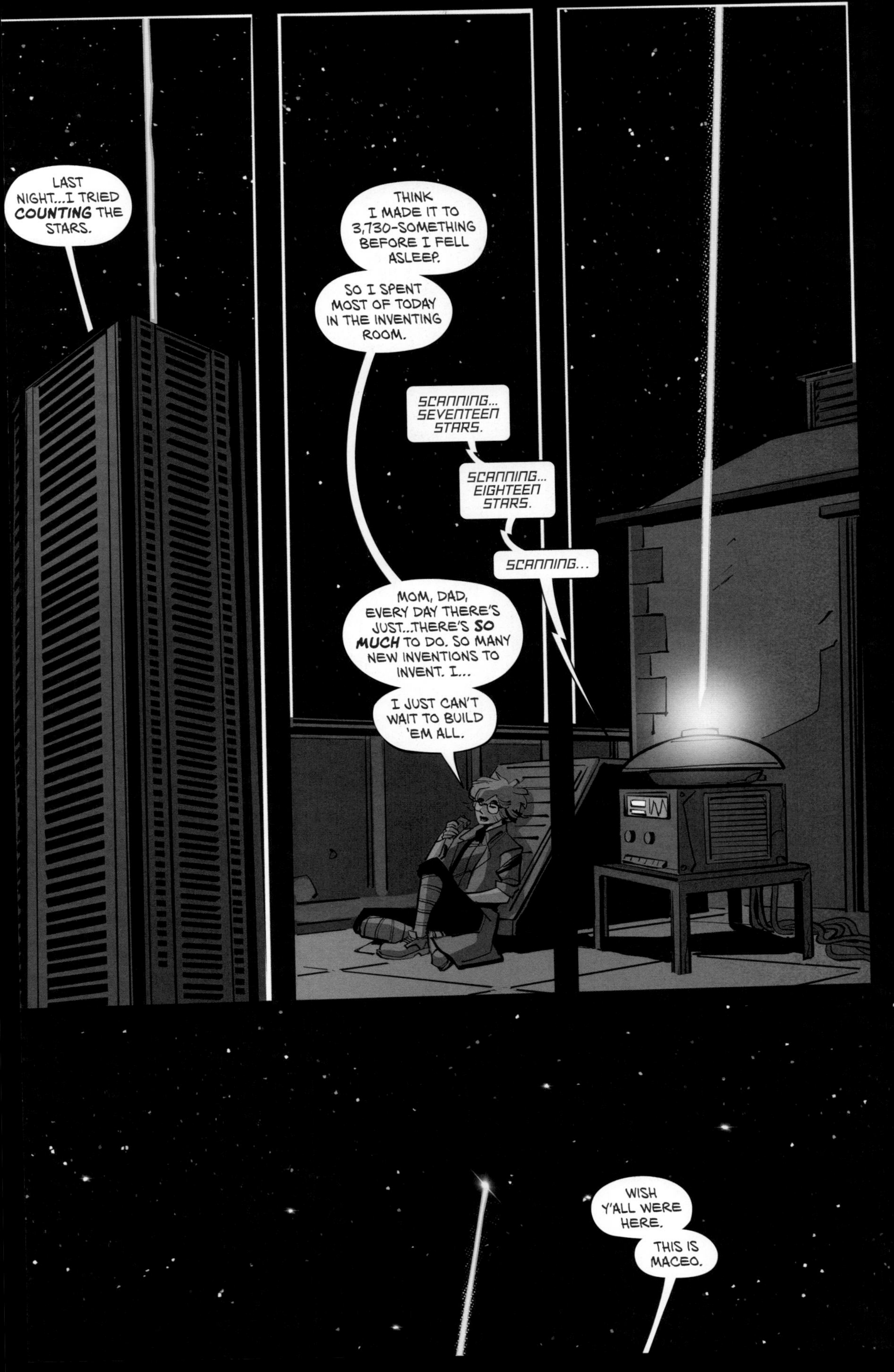
LAST NIGHT...I TRIED COUNTING THE STARS.
THINK I MADE IT TO 3,730-SOMETHING BEFORE I FELL ASLEEP.
SO I SPENT MOST OF TODAY IN THE INVENTING ROOM.
SCANNING... SEVENTEEN STARS.
SCANNING... EIGHTEEN STARS.
SCANNING...
MOM, DAD, EVERY DAY THERE'S JUST...THERE'S SO MUCH TO DO. SO MANY NEW INVENTIONS TO INVENT. I...
I JUST CAN'T WAIT TO BUILD 'EM ALL.
WISH Y'ALL WERE HERE.
THIS IS MACEO.

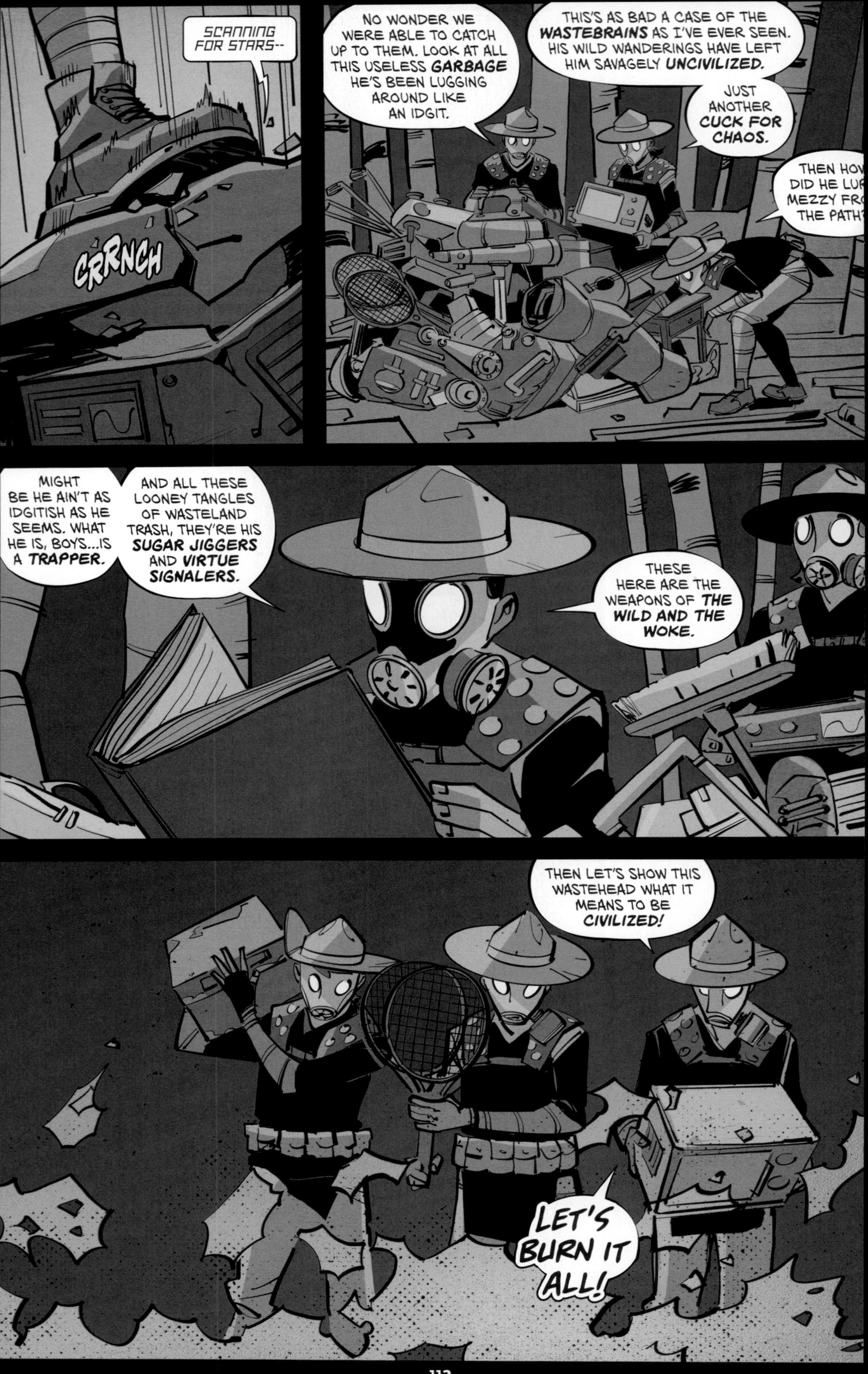

SCANNING FOR STARS--
CRRNCH
NO WONDER WE WERE ABLE TO CATCH UP TO THEM. LOOK AT ALL THIS USELESS GARBAGE HE'S BEEN LUGGING AROUND LIKE AN IDGIT.
THIS'S AS BAD A CASE OF THE WASTEBRAINS AS I'VE EVER SEEN. HIS WILD WANDERINGS HAVE LEFT HIM SAVAGELY UNCIVILIZED.
JUST ANOTHER CUCK FOR CHAOS.
THEN HOW DID HE LUR MEZZY FR THE PATH?
MIGHT BE HE AIN'T AS IDGITISH AS HE SEEMS. WHAT HE IS, BOYS...IS A TRAPPER.
AND ALL THESE LOONEY TANGLES OF WASTELAND TRASH, THEY'RE HIS SUGAR JIGGERS AND VIRTUE SIGNALERS.
THESE HERE ARE THE WEAPONS OF THE WILD AND THE WOKE.
THEN LET'S SHOW THIS WASTEHEAD WHAT IT MEANS TO BE CIVILIZED!
LET'S BURN IT ALL!

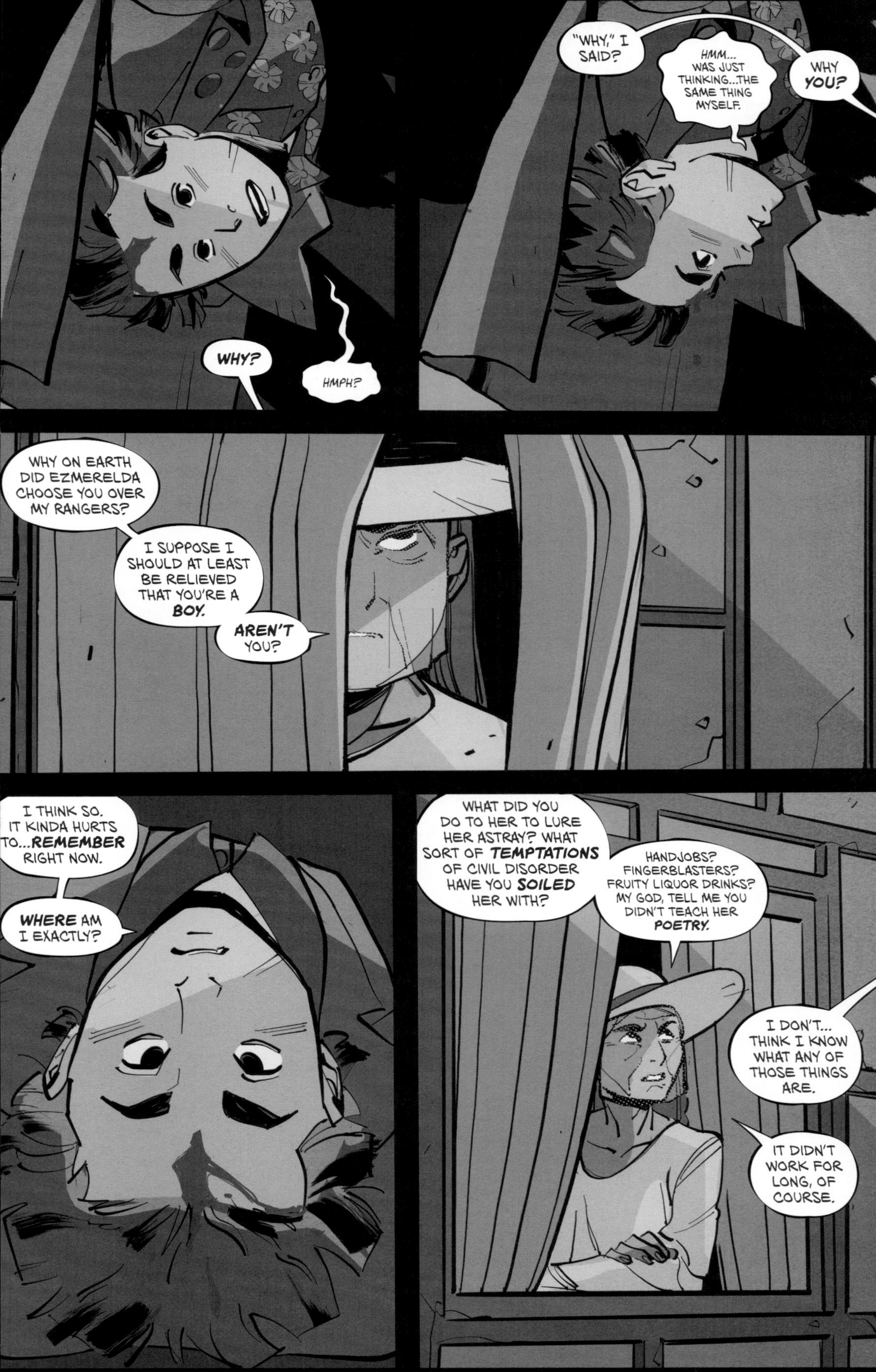
WHY?
HMPH?
"WHY," I SAID?
HMM... WAS JUST THINKING...THE SAME THING MYSELF.
WHY YOU?
WHY ON EARTH DID EZMERELDA CHOOSE YOU OVER MY RANGERS?
I SUPPOSE I SHOULD AT LEAST BE RELIEVED THAT YOU'RE A BOY.
AREN'T YOU?
I THINK SO. IT KINDA HURTS TO...REMEMBER RIGHT NOW.
WHERE AM I EXACTLY?
WHAT DID YOU DO TO HER TO LURE HER ASTRAY? WHAT SORT OF TEMPTATIONS OF CIVIL DISORDER HAVE YOU SOILED HER WITH?
HANDJOBS? FINGERBLASTERS? FRUITY LIQUOR DRINKS? MY GOD, TELL ME YOU DIDN'T TEACH HER POETRY.
I DON'T... THINK I KNOW WHAT ANY OF THOSE THINGS ARE.
IT DIDN'T WORK FOR LONG, OF COURSE.

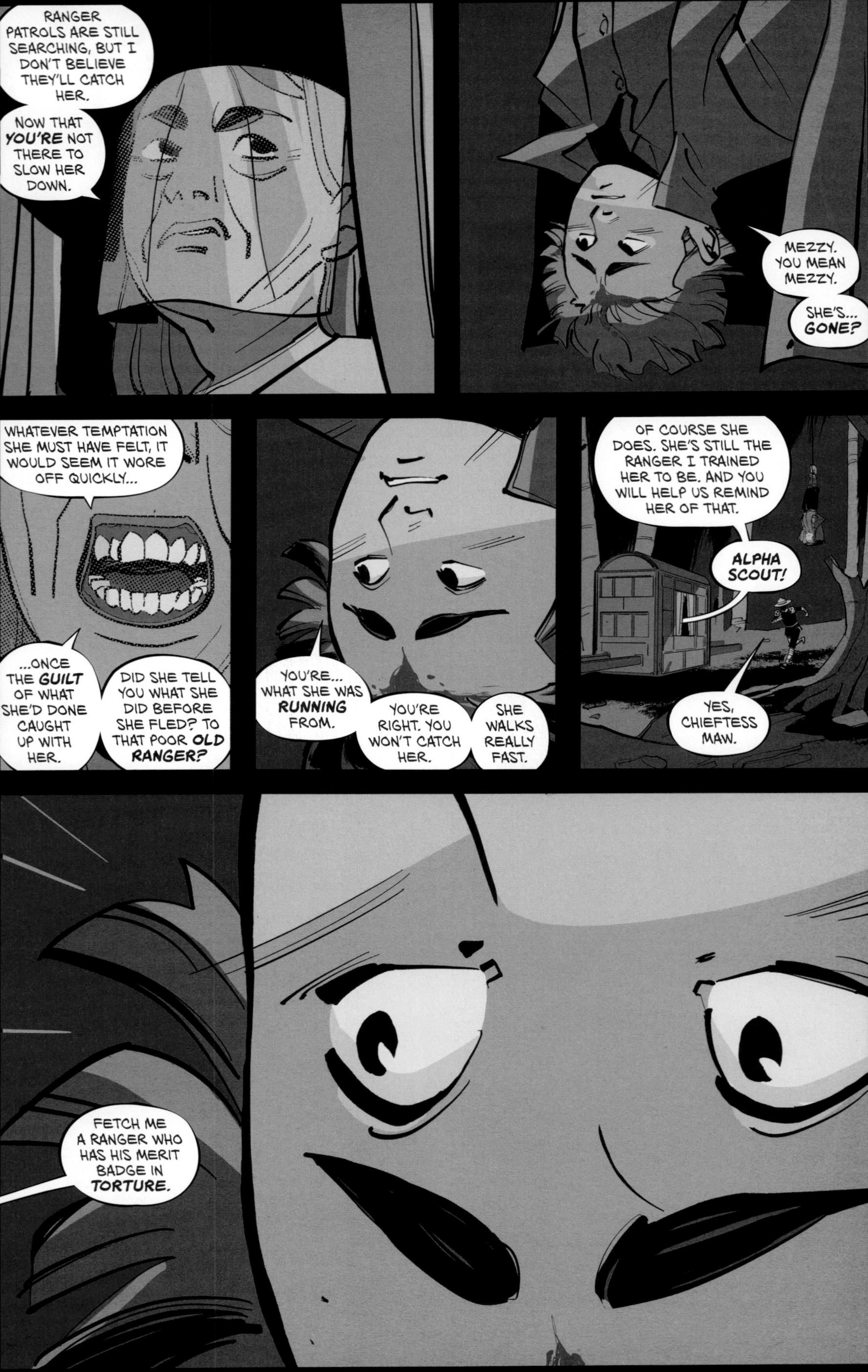
RANGER PATROLS ARE STILL SEARCHING, BUT I DON'T BELIEVE THEY'LL CATCH HER.
NOW THAT **YOU'RE** NOT THERE TO SLOW HER DOWN.
MEZZY. YOU MEAN MEZZY.
SHE'S... **GONE?**
WHATEVER TEMPTATION SHE MUST HAVE FELT, IT WOULD SEEM IT WORE OFF QUICKLY...
...ONCE THE **GUILT** OF WHAT SHE'D DONE CAUGHT UP WITH HER.
DID SHE TELL YOU WHAT SHE DID BEFORE SHE FLED? TO THAT POOR **OLD RANGER?**
YOU'RE... WHAT SHE WAS **RUNNING** FROM.
YOU'RE RIGHT. YOU WON'T CATCH HER.
SHE WALKS REALLY FAST.
OF COURSE SHE DOES. SHE'S STILL THE RANGER I TRAINED HER TO BE. AND YOU WILL HELP US REMIND HER OF THAT.
ALPHA SCOUT!
YES, CHIEFTESS MAW.
FETCH ME A RANGER WHO HAS HIS MERIT BADGE IN **TORTURE.**

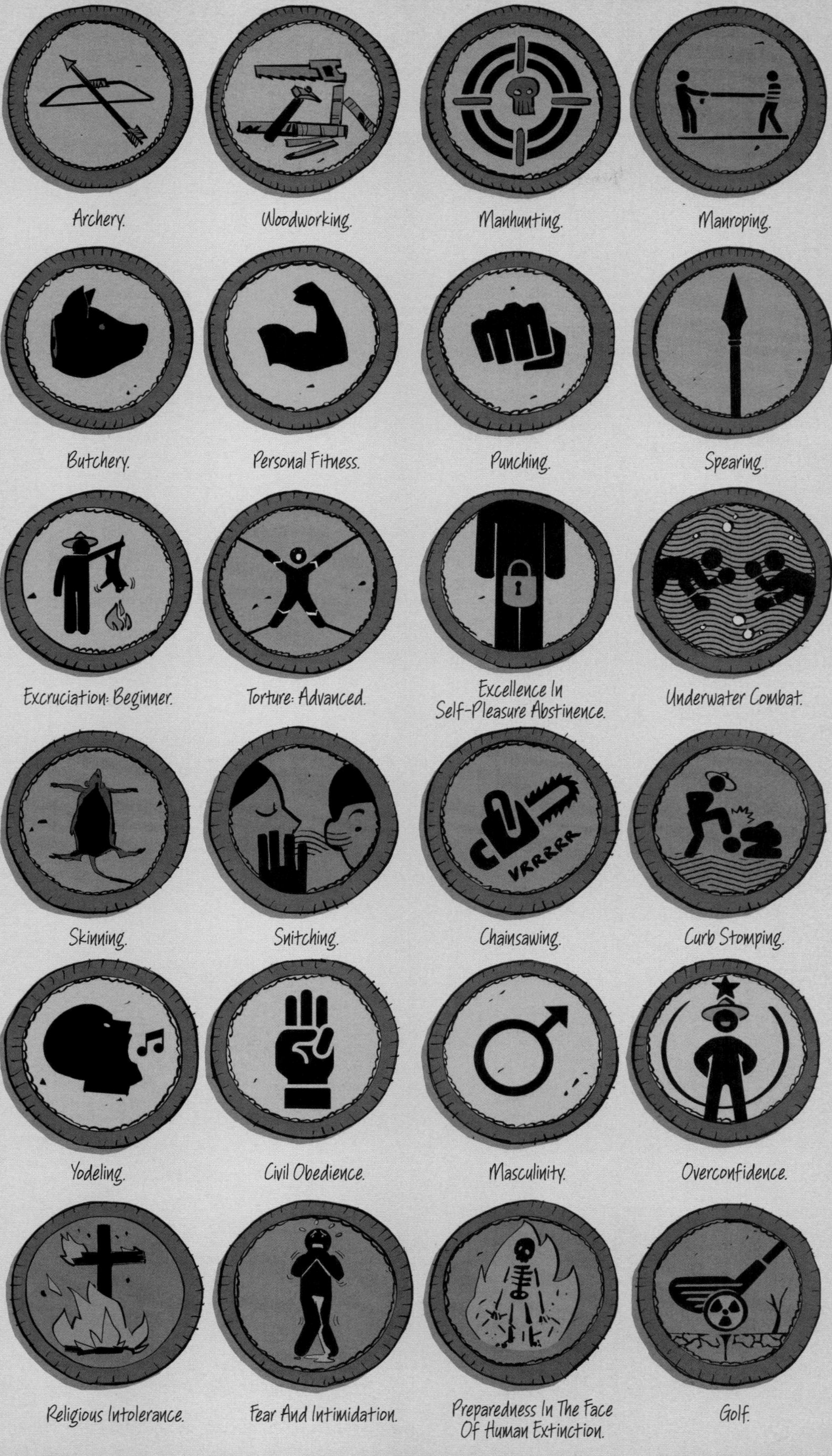
Archery.
Woodworking.
Manhunting.
Manroping.
Butchery.
Personal Fitness.
Punching.
Spearing.
Excruciation: Beginner.
Torture: Advanced.
Excellence In Self-Pleasure Abstinence.
Underwater Combat.
Skinning.
Snitching.
VRRRRR
Chainsawing.
Curb Stomping.
Yodeling.
Civil Obedience.
Masculinity.
Overconfidence.
Religious Intolerance.
Fear And Intimidation.
Preparedness In The Face Of Human Extinction.
Golf.

AT LEAST...

...THEY'LL KILL HIM *QUICKLY*.

SOMEONE WITH A BADGE IN BUTCHERY WILL DO IT.

HE'S... PROBABLY ALREADY DEAD.

AAAAAARRRRGGGHH!

EEEEIIRRGGGH!

OH, MACEO.

I'M SORRY...

HHHHRRRRREEEGGGHH!

I'M SORRY YOU EVER *MET* ME.

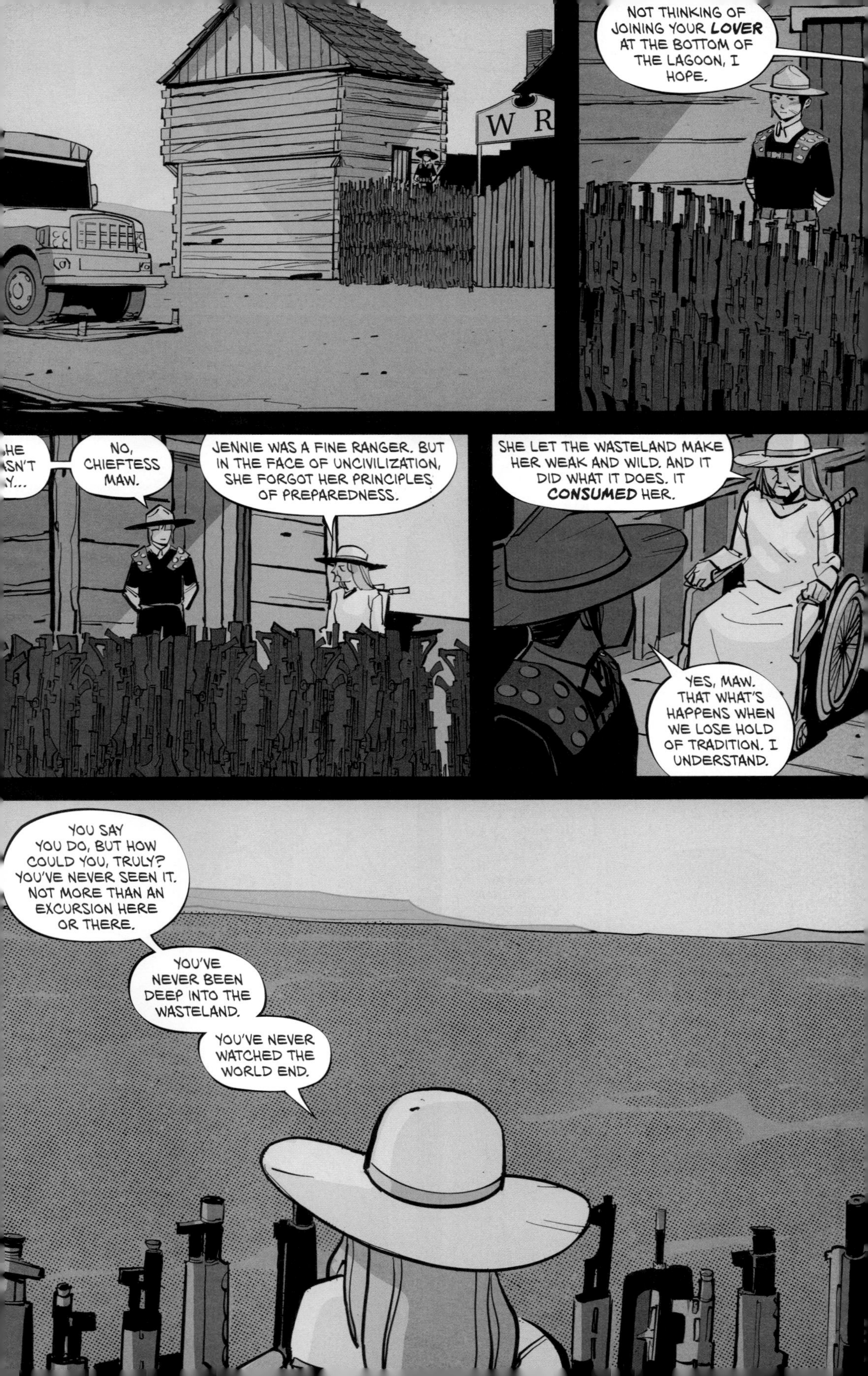
W R
NOT THINKING OF JOINING YOUR **LOVER** AT THE BOTTOM OF THE LAGOON, I HOPE.
HE ASN'T Y...
NO, CHIEFTESS MAW.
JENNIE WAS A FINE RANGER. BUT IN THE FACE OF UNCIVILIZATION, SHE FORGOT HER PRINCIPLES OF PREPAREDNESS.
SHE LET THE WASTELAND MAKE HER WEAK AND WILD. AND IT DID WHAT IT DOES. IT **CONSUMED** HER.
YES, MAW. THAT WHAT'S HAPPENS WHEN WE LOSE HOLD OF TRADITION. I UNDERSTAND.
YOU SAY YOU DO, BUT HOW COULD YOU, TRULY? YOU'VE NEVER SEEN IT. NOT MORE THAN AN EXCURSION HERE OR THERE.
YOU'VE NEVER BEEN DEEP INTO THE WASTELAND.
YOU'VE NEVER WATCHED THE WORLD END.

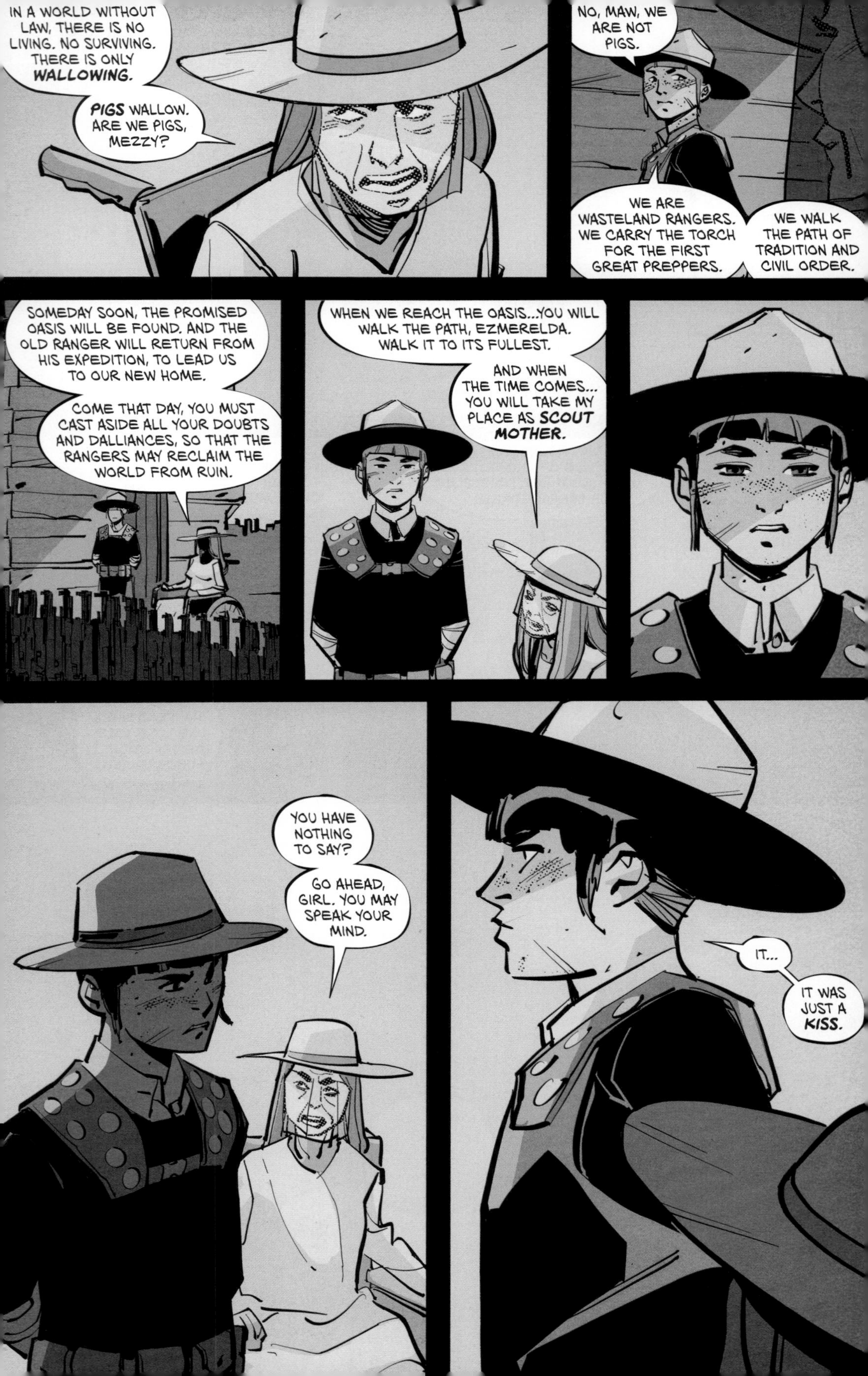
IN A WORLD WITHOUT LAW, THERE IS NO LIVING. NO SURVIVING. THERE IS ONLY WALLOWING.
PIGS WALLOW. ARE WE PIGS, MEZZY?
NO, MAW, WE ARE NOT PIGS.
WE ARE WASTELAND RANGERS. WE CARRY THE TORCH FOR THE FIRST GREAT PREPPERS.
WE WALK THE PATH OF TRADITION AND CIVIL ORDER.
SOMEDAY SOON, THE PROMISED OASIS WILL BE FOUND. AND THE OLD RANGER WILL RETURN FROM HIS EXPEDITION, TO LEAD US TO OUR NEW HOME.
COME THAT DAY, YOU MUST CAST ASIDE ALL YOUR DOUBTS AND DALLIANCES, SO THAT THE RANGERS MAY RECLAIM THE WORLD FROM RUIN.
WHEN WE REACH THE OASIS...YOU WILL WALK THE PATH, EZMERELDA. WALK IT TO ITS FULLEST.
AND WHEN THE TIME COMES... YOU WILL TAKE MY PLACE AS SCOUT MOTHER.
YOU HAVE NOTHING TO SAY?
GO AHEAD, GIRL. YOU MAY SPEAK YOUR MIND.
IT...
IT WAS JUST A KISS.

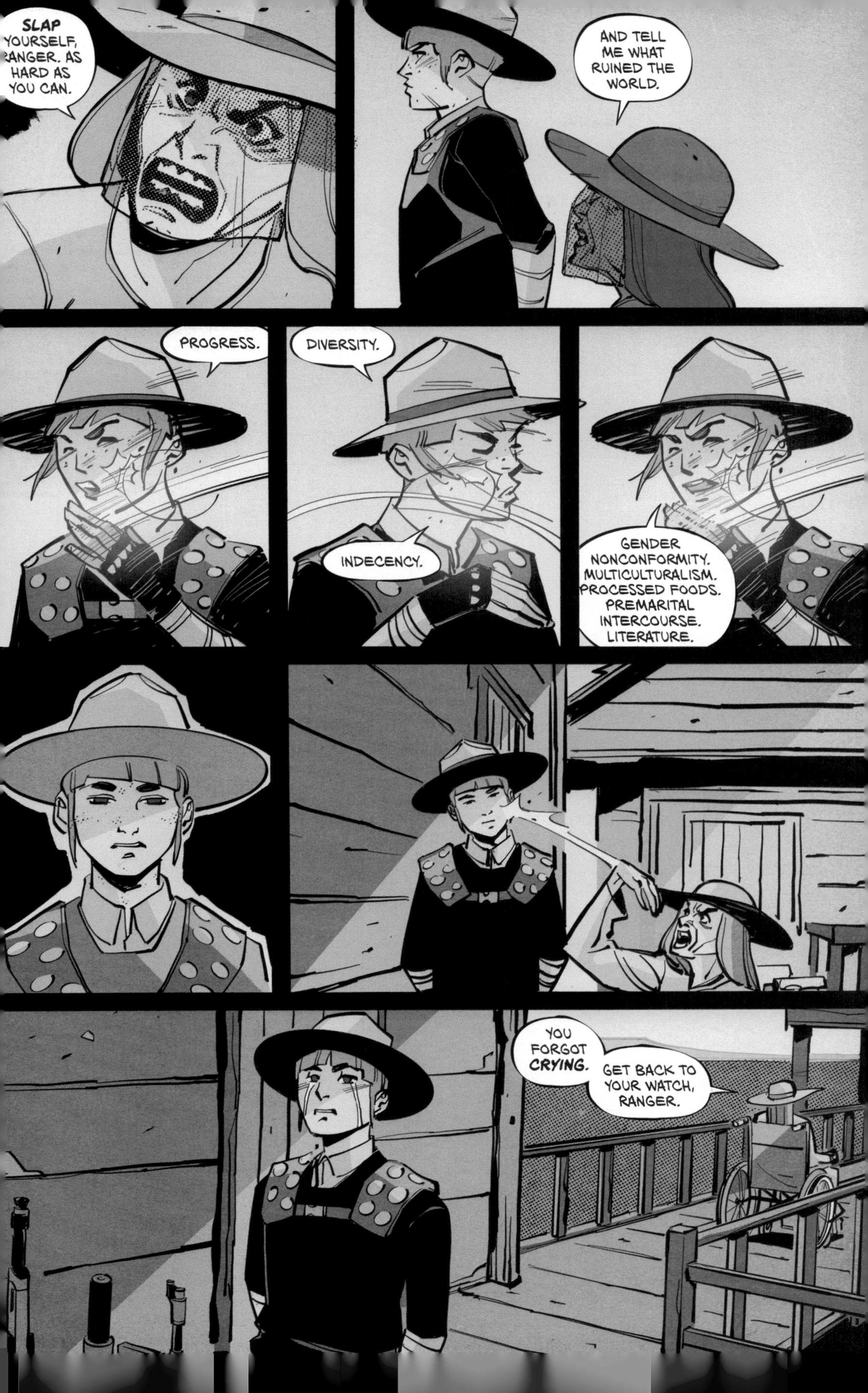
SLAP YOURSELF, RANGER. AS HARD AS YOU CAN.
AND TELL ME WHAT RUINED THE WORLD.
PROGRESS.
DIVERSITY.
INDECENCY.
GENDER NONCONFORMITY. MULTICULTURALISM. PROCESSED FOODS. PREMARITAL INTERCOURSE. LITERATURE.
YOU FORGOT CRYING.
GET BACK TO YOUR WATCH, RANGER.

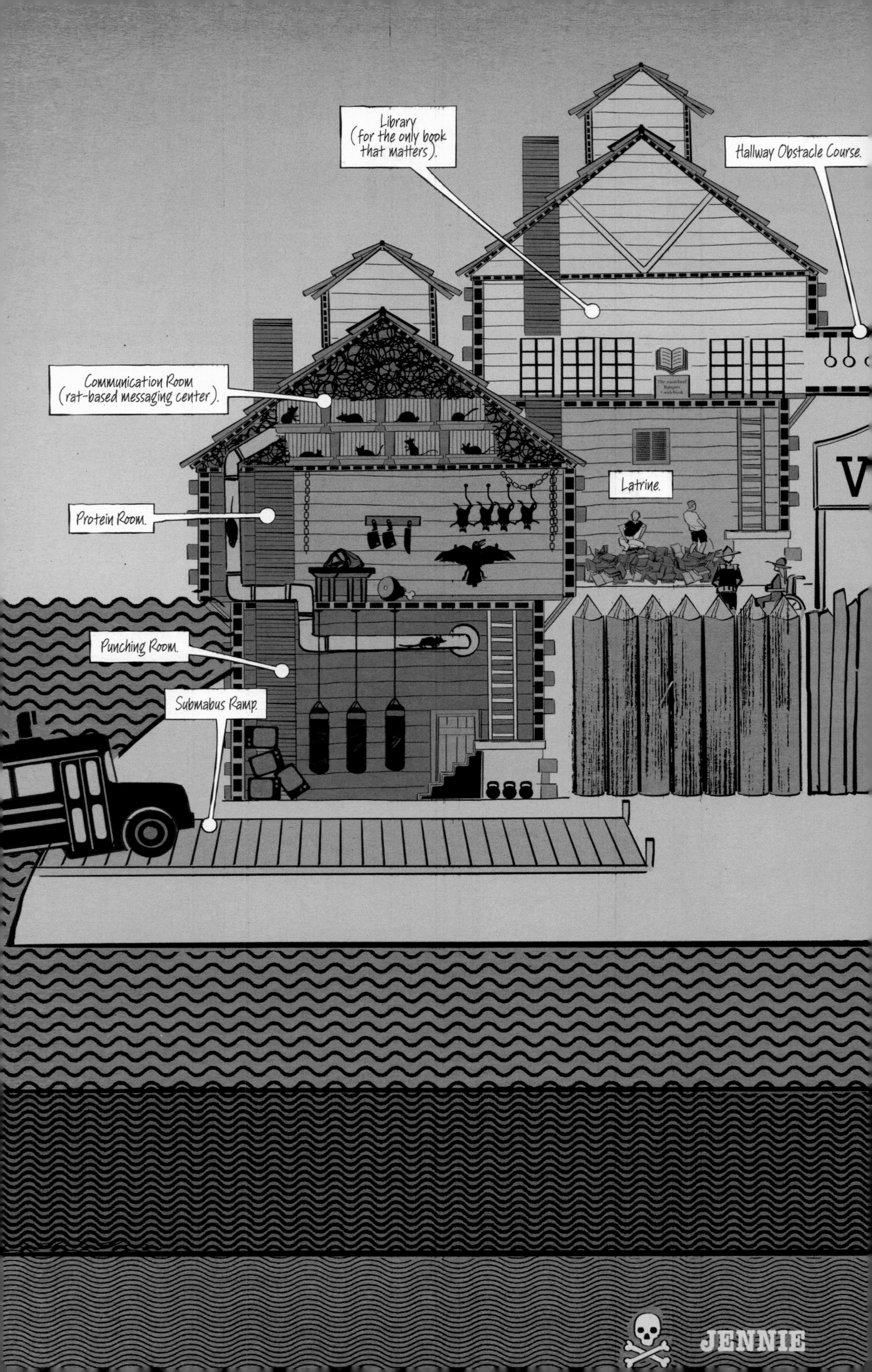
Library (for the only book that matters).
Hallway Obstacle Course.
Communication Room (rat-based messaging center).
Latrine.
Protein Room.
Punching Room.
Submabus Ramp.
JENNIE

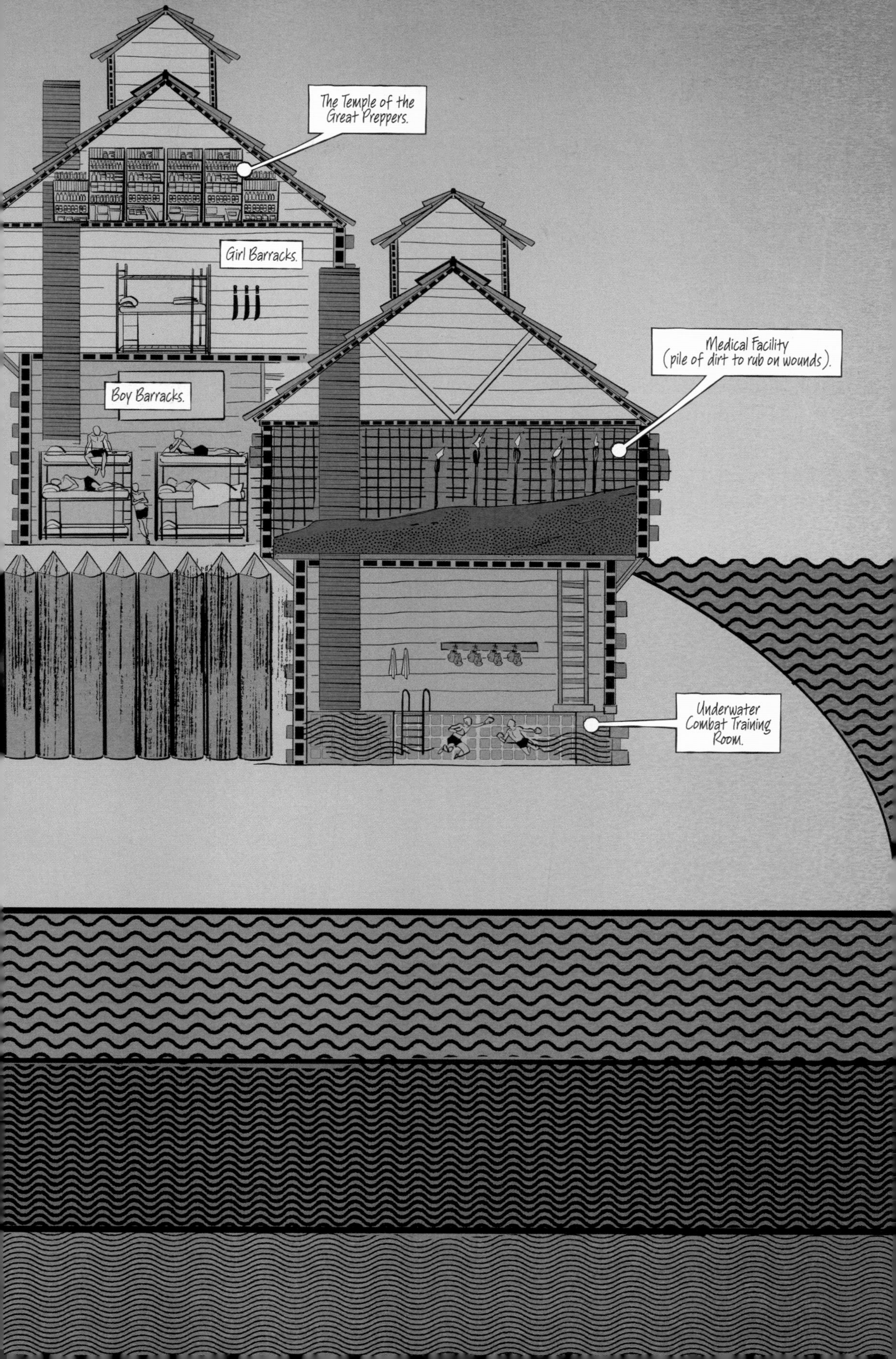
The Temple of the Great Preppers.
Girl Barracks.
Boy Barracks.
Medical Facility (pile of dirt to rub on wounds).
Underwater Combat Training Room.

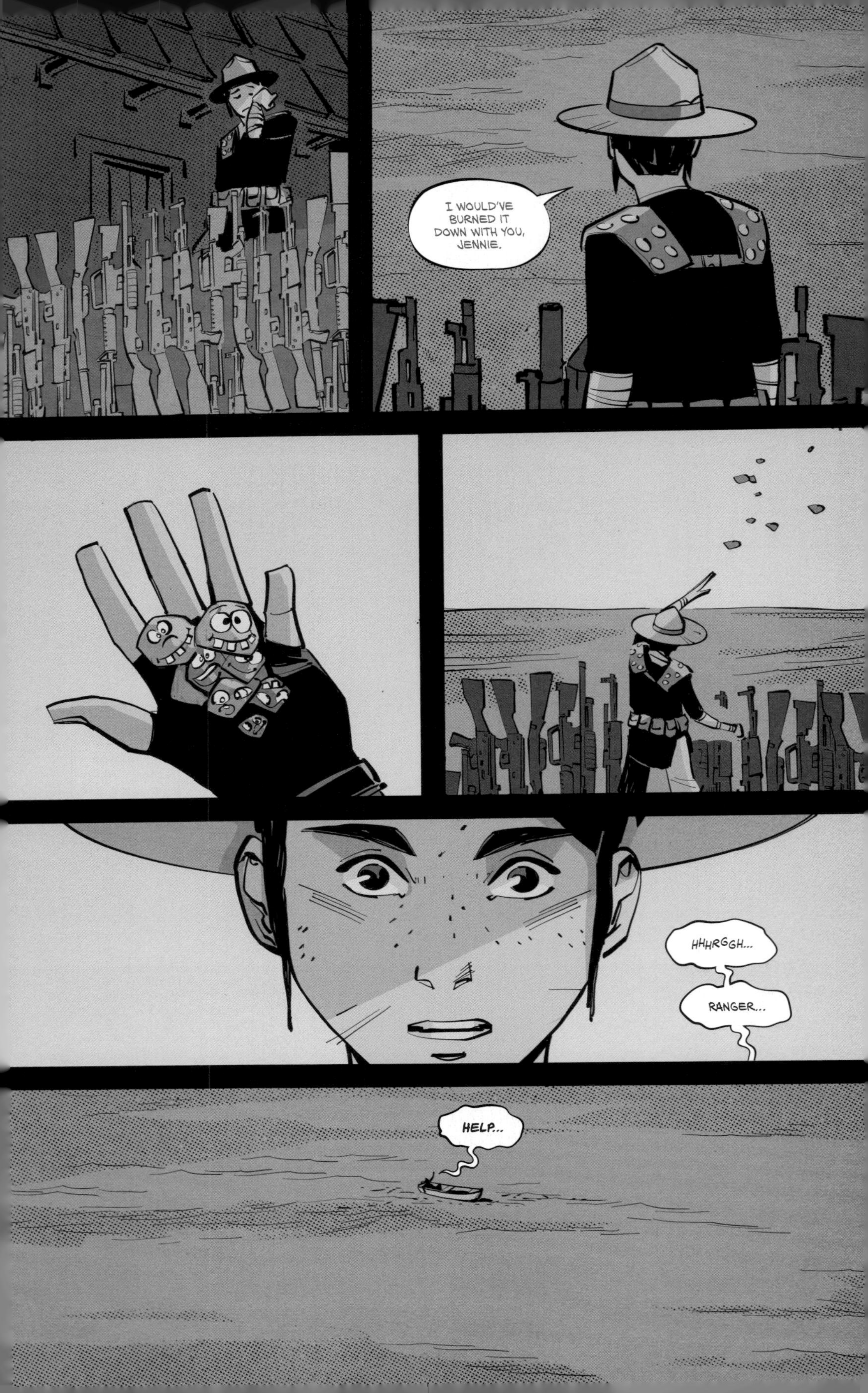
I WOULD'VE BURNED IT DOWN WITH YOU, JENNIE.
HHHRGGH...
RANGER...
HELP...

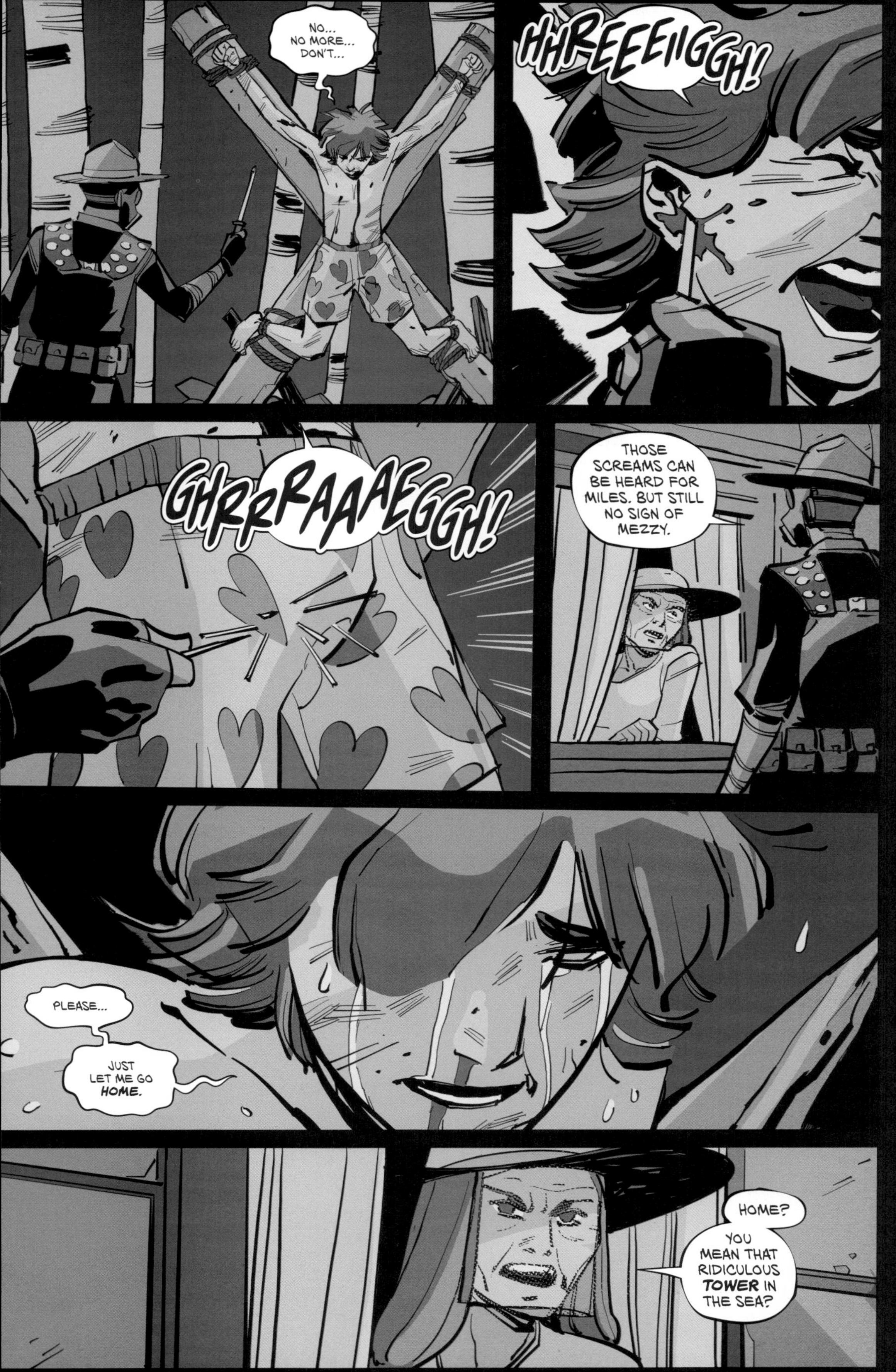
NO... NO MORE... DON'T...
HHREEEEIIGGH!
GHRRRAAAAEGGH!
THOSE SCREAMS CAN BE HEARD FOR MILES. BUT STILL NO SIGN OF MEZZY.
PLEASE...
JUST LET ME GO **HOME.**
HOME?
YOU MEAN THAT RIDICULOUS **TOWER** IN THE SEA?

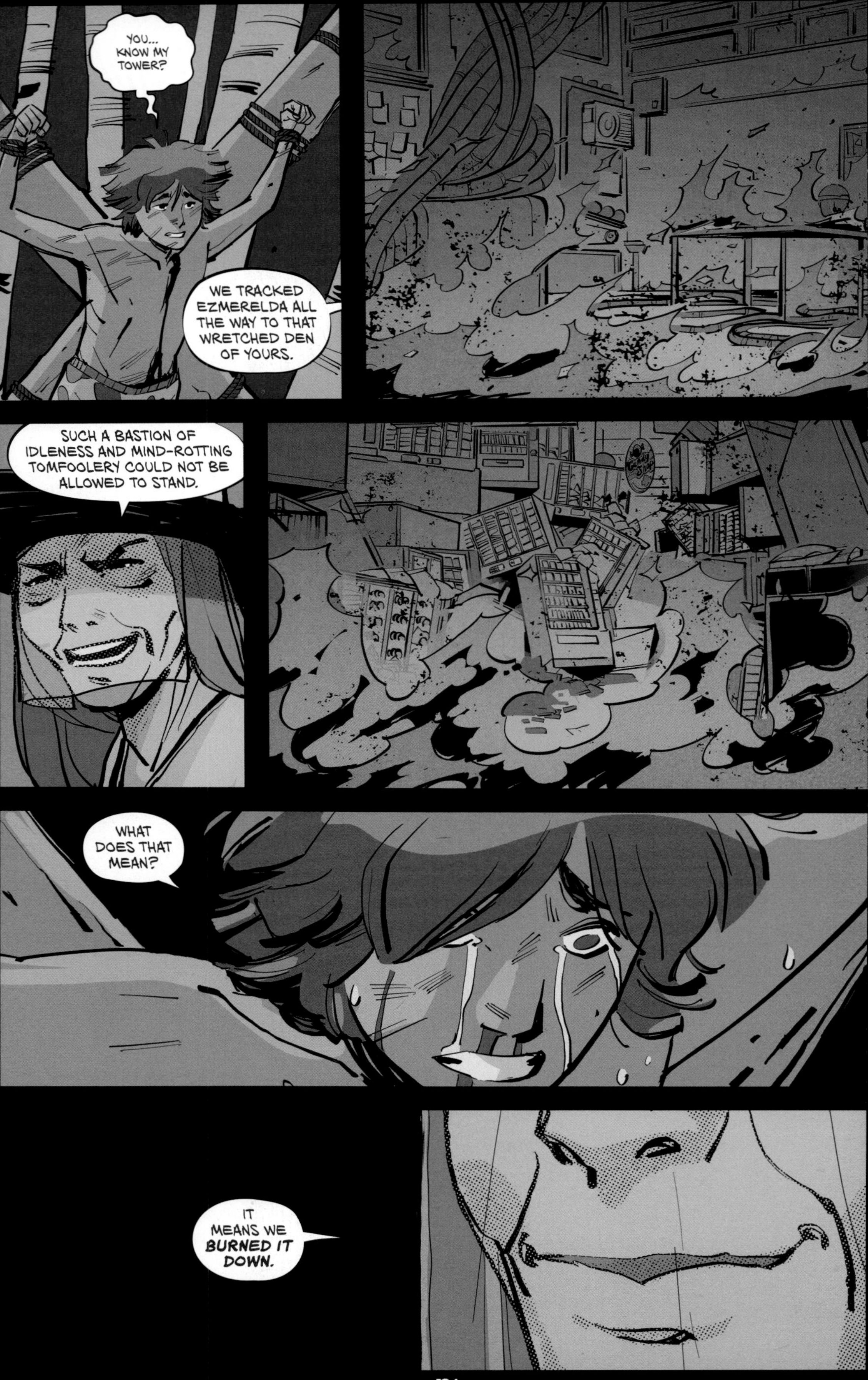

YOU... KNOW MY TOWER?
WE TRACKED EZMERELDA ALL THE WAY TO THAT WRETCHED DEN OF YOURS.
SUCH A BASTION OF IDLENESS AND MIND-ROTTING TOMFOOLERY COULD NOT BE ALLOWED TO STAND.
WHAT DOES THAT MEAN?
IT MEANS WE **BURNED IT DOWN.**

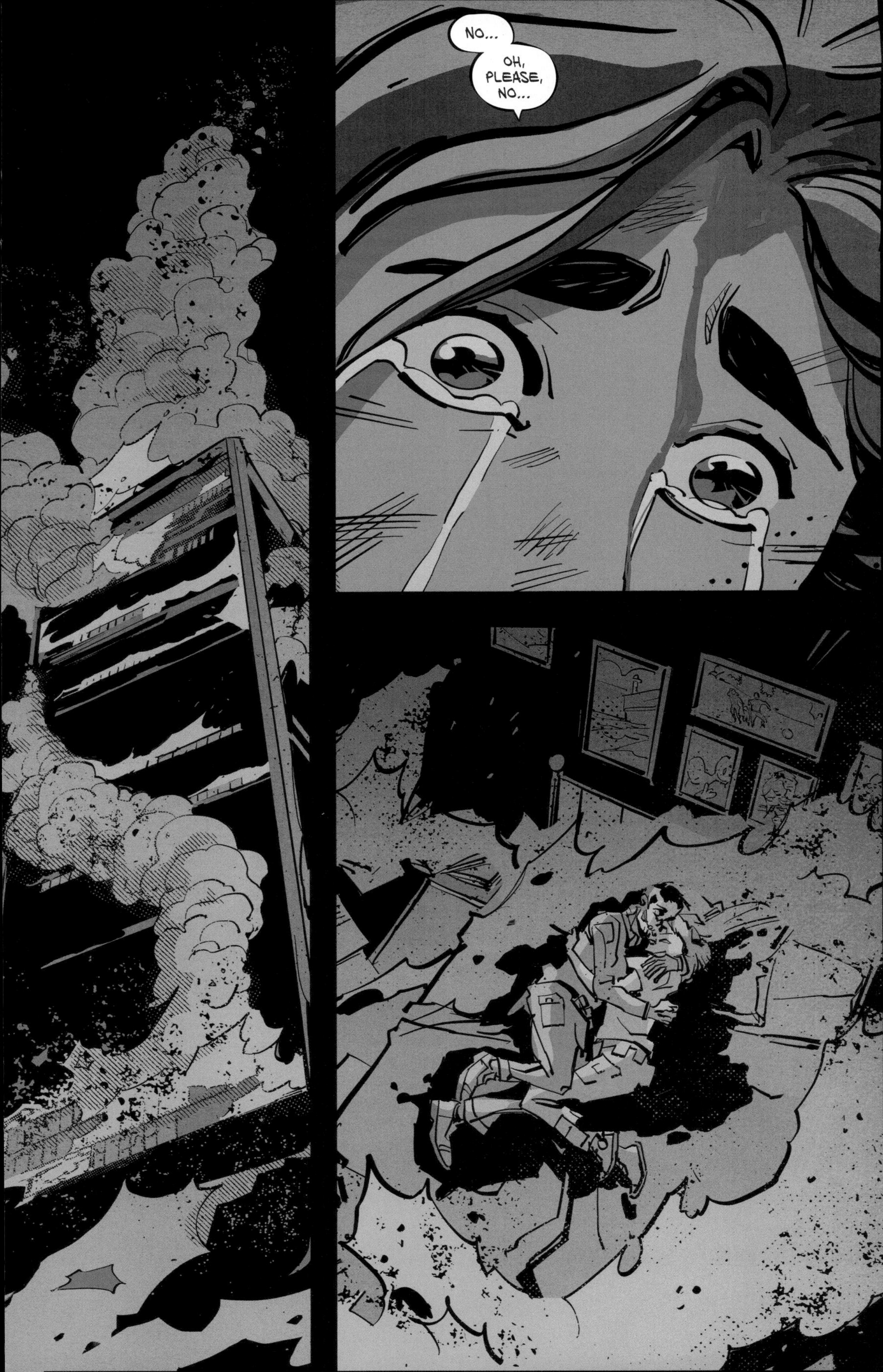
NO...
OH, PLEASE, NO...

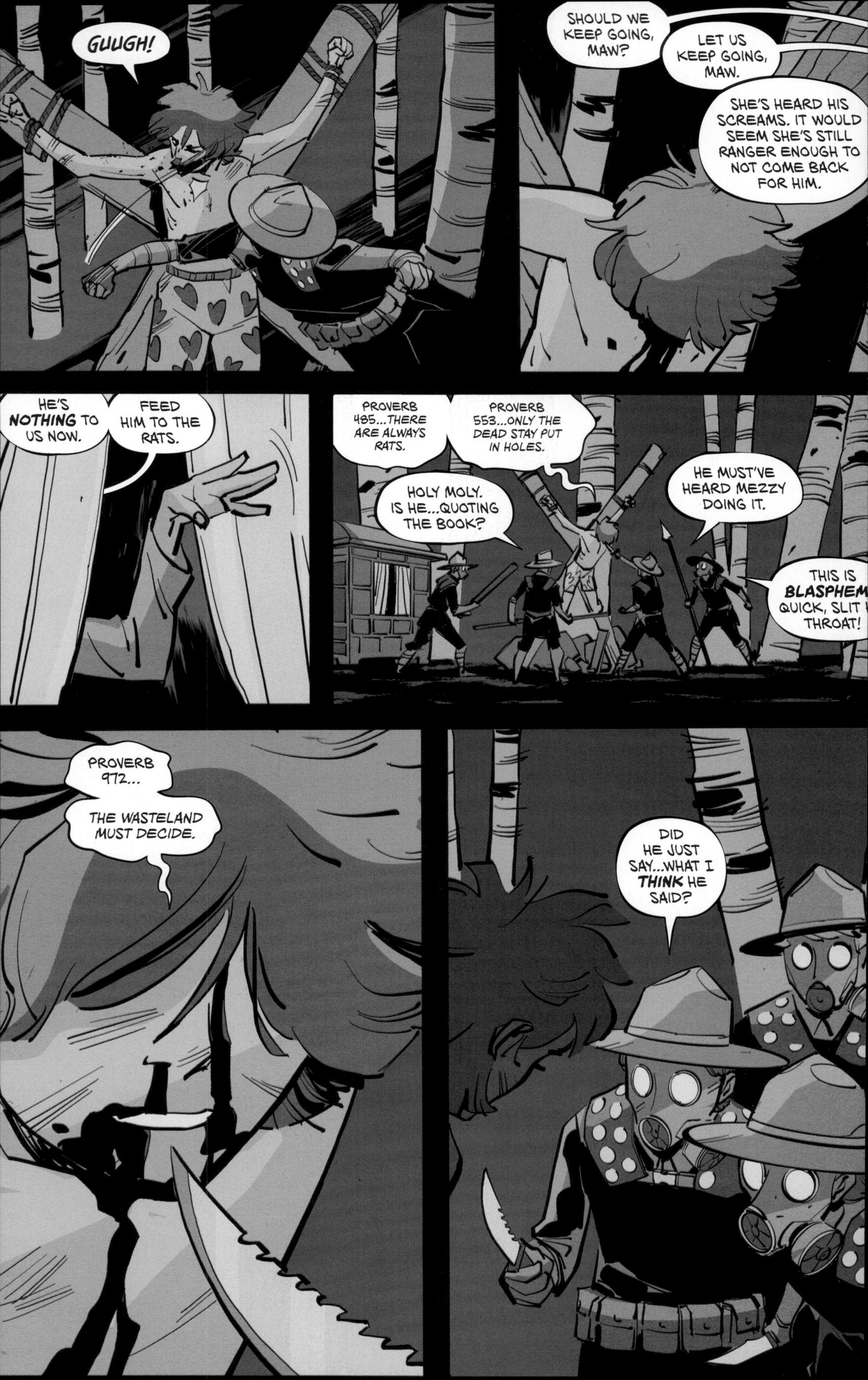
GUUGH!
SHOULD WE KEEP GOING, MAW?
LET US KEEP GOING, MAW.
SHE'S HEARD HIS SCREAMS. IT WOULD SEEM SHE'S STILL RANGER ENOUGH TO NOT COME BACK FOR HIM.
HE'S NOTHING TO US NOW.
FEED HIM TO THE RATS.
PROVERB 485...THERE ARE ALWAYS RATS.
PROVERB 553...ONLY THE DEAD STAY PUT IN HOLES.
HOLY MOLY. IS HE...QUOTING THE BOOK?
HE MUST'VE HEARD MEZZY DOING IT.
THIS IS BLASPHEM
QUICK, SLIT
THROAT!
PROVERB 972...
THE WASTELAND MUST DECIDE.
DID HE JUST SAY...WHAT I THINK HE SAID?

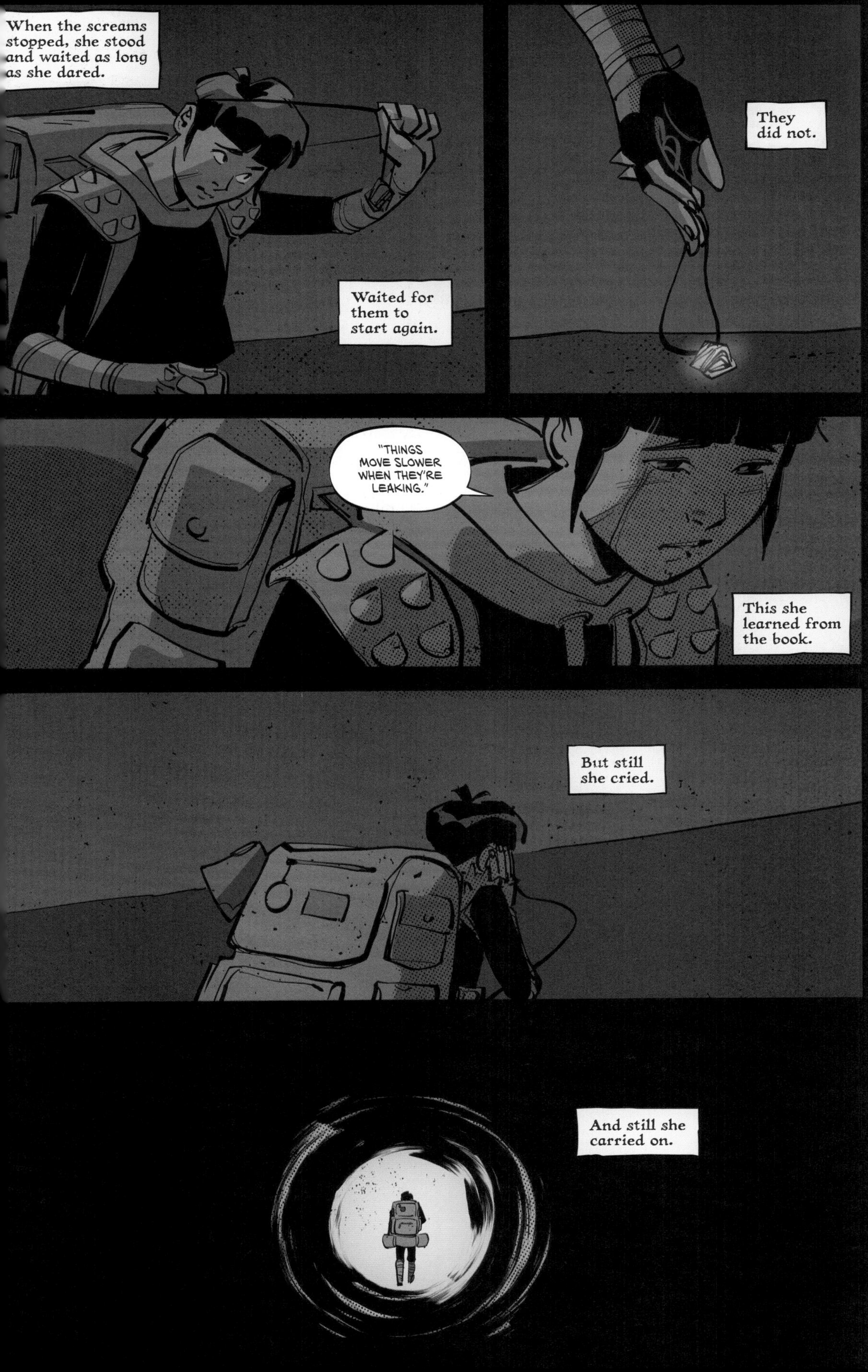

When the screams stopped, she stood and waited as long as she dared.
Waited for them to start again.
They did not.
"THINGS MOVE SLOWER WHEN THEY'RE LEAKING."
This she learned from the book.
But still she cried.
And still she carried on.

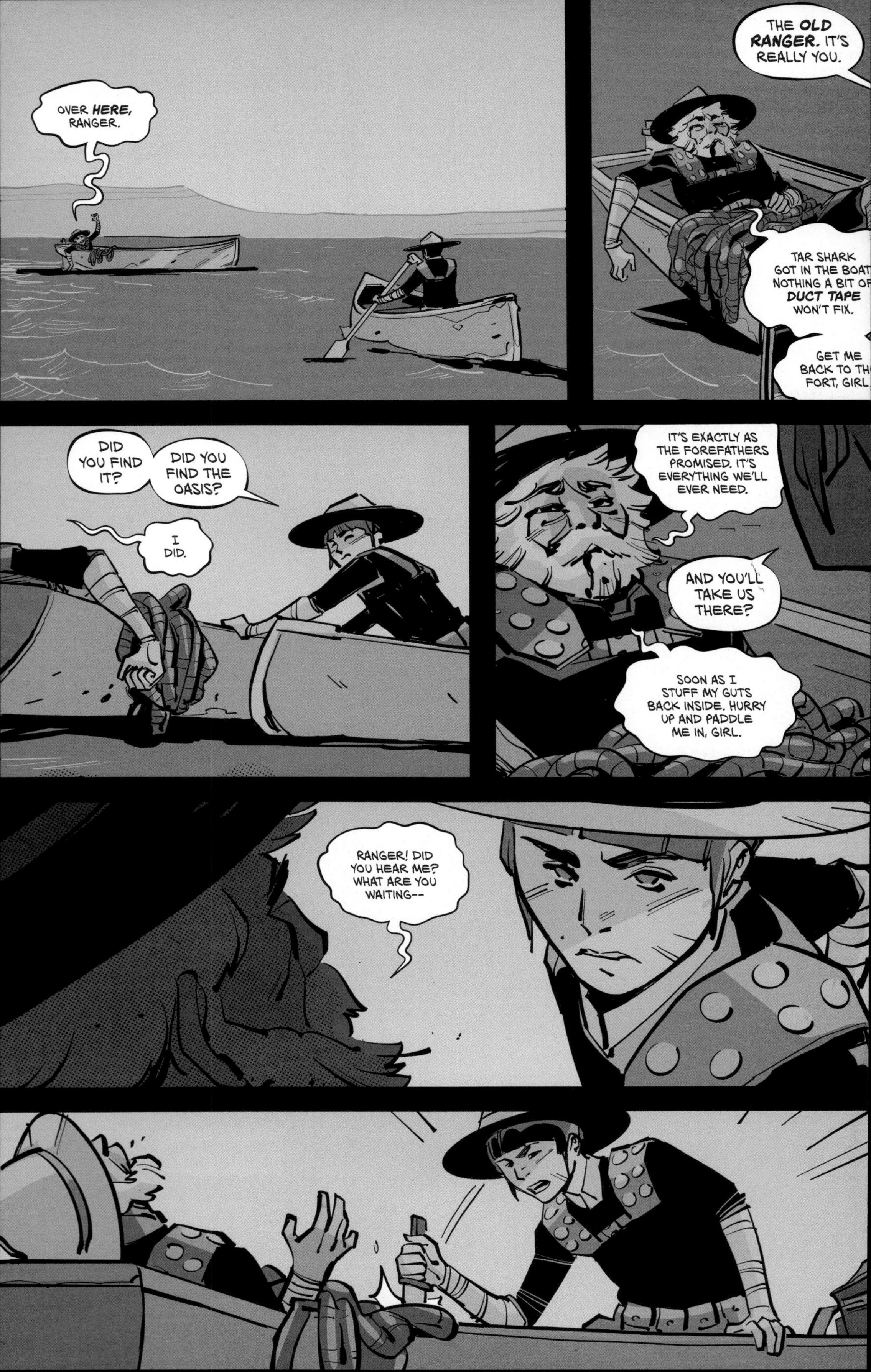
OVER HERE, RANGER.
THE OLD RANGER. IT'S REALLY YOU.
TAR SHARK GOT IN THE BOAT. NOTHING A BIT OF DUCT TAPE WON'T FIX.
GET ME BACK TO THE FORT, GIRL.
DID YOU FIND IT?
DID YOU FIND THE OASIS?
I DID.
IT'S EXACTLY AS THE FOREFATHERS PROMISED. IT'S EVERYTHING WE'LL EVER NEED.
AND YOU'LL TAKE US THERE?
SOON AS I STUFF MY GUTS BACK INSIDE. HURRY UP AND PADDLE ME IN, GIRL.
RANGER! DID YOU HEAR ME? WHAT ARE YOU WAITING--

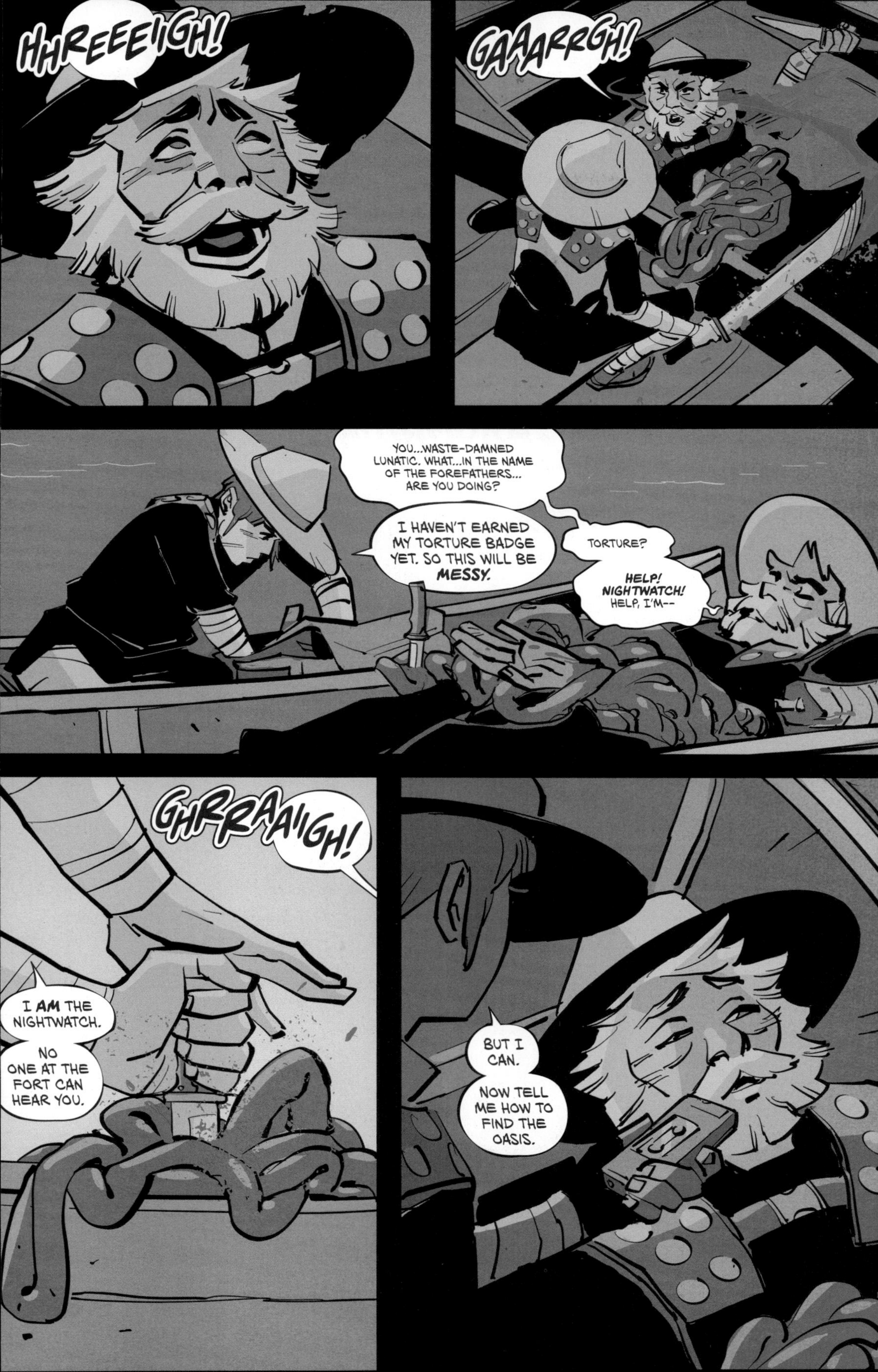
HHREEEIIGH!
GAAARRGH!
YOU...WASTE-DAMNED LUNATIC. WHAT...IN THE NAME OF THE FOREFATHERS... ARE YOU DOING?
I HAVEN'T EARNED MY TORTURE BADGE YET. SO THIS WILL BE MESSY.
TORTURE?
HELP! NIGHTWATCH! HELP, I'M--
GHRRAAIIGH!
I AM THE NIGHTWATCH.
NO ONE AT THE FORT CAN HEAR YOU.
BUT I CAN.
NOW TELL ME HOW TO FIND THE OASIS.

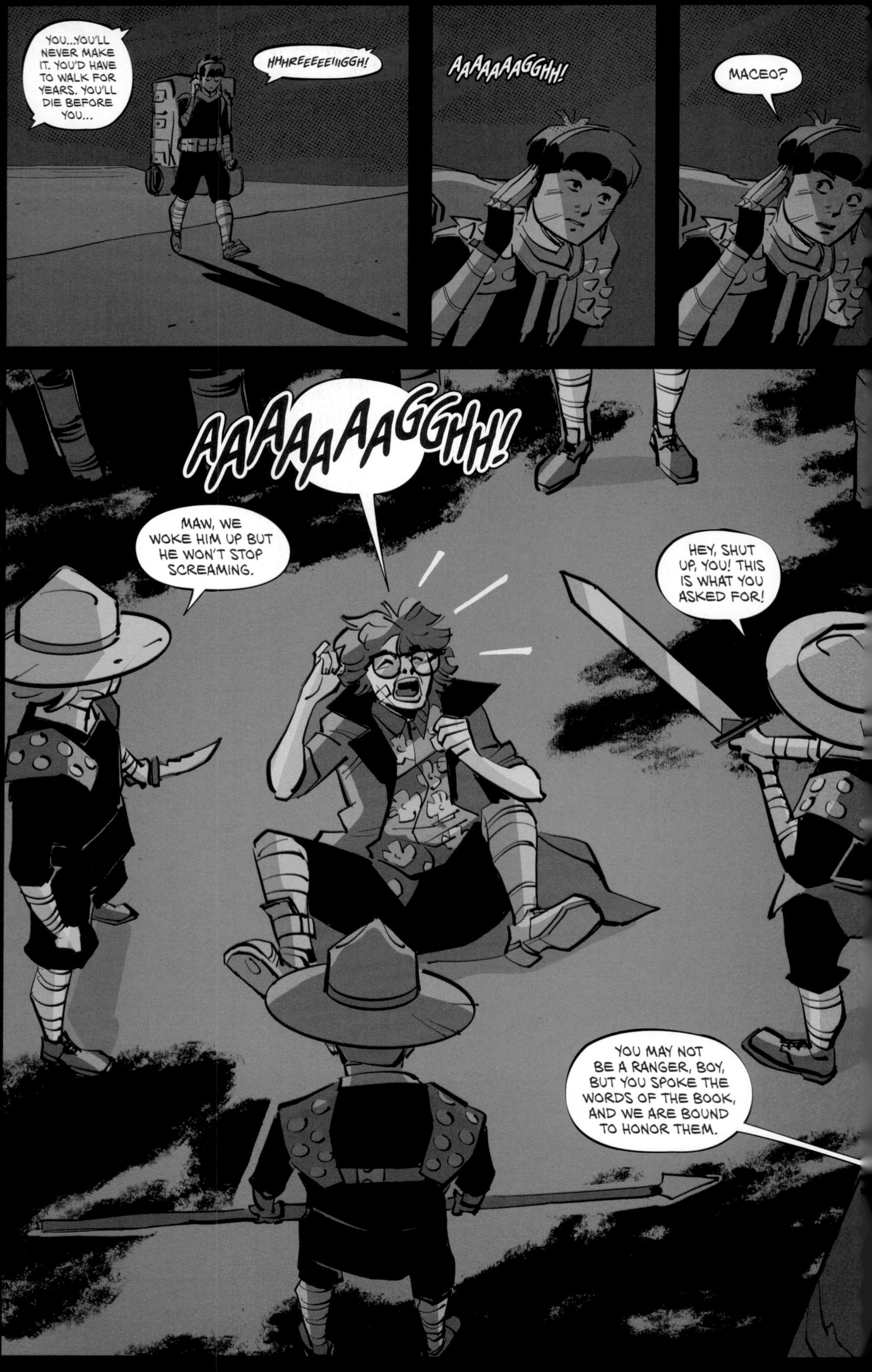

YOU...YOU'LL NEVER MAKE IT. YOU'D HAVE TO WALK FOR YEARS. YOU'LL DIE BEFORE YOU...
HHHREEEEEIIIGGH!
AAAAAAAGGHH!
MACEO?
AAAAAAAGGHH!
MAW, WE WOKE HIM UP BUT HE WON'T STOP SCREAMING.
HEY, SHUT UP, YOU! THIS IS WHAT YOU ASKED FOR!
YOU MAY NOT BE A RANGER, BOY, BUT YOU SPOKE THE WORDS OF THE BOOK, AND WE ARE BOUND TO HONOR THEM.

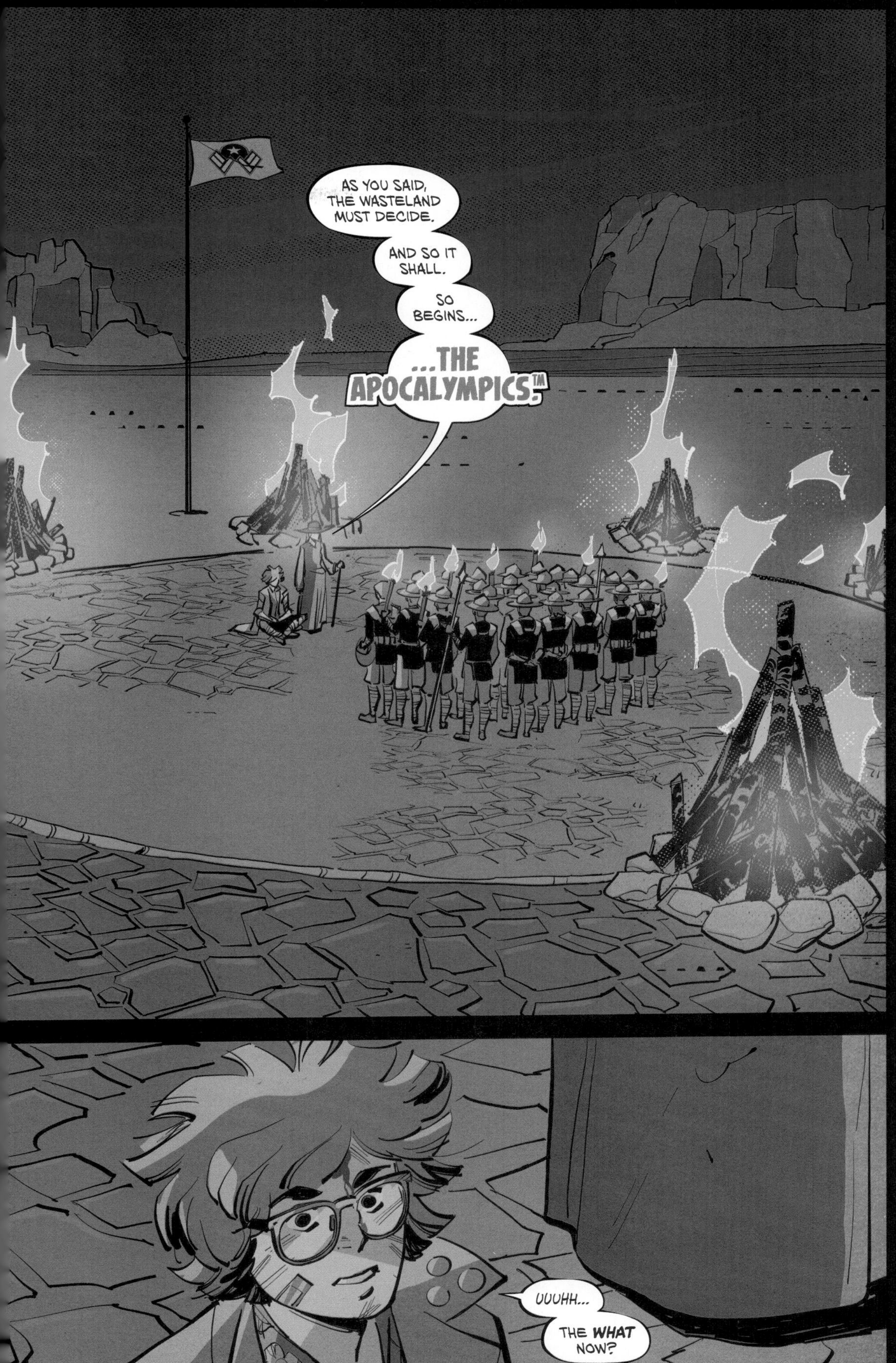
AS YOU SAID, THE WASTELAND MUST DECIDE.
AND SO IT SHALL.
SO BEGINS...
...THE APOCALYMPICS.™
UUUHH...
THE **WHAT** NOW?

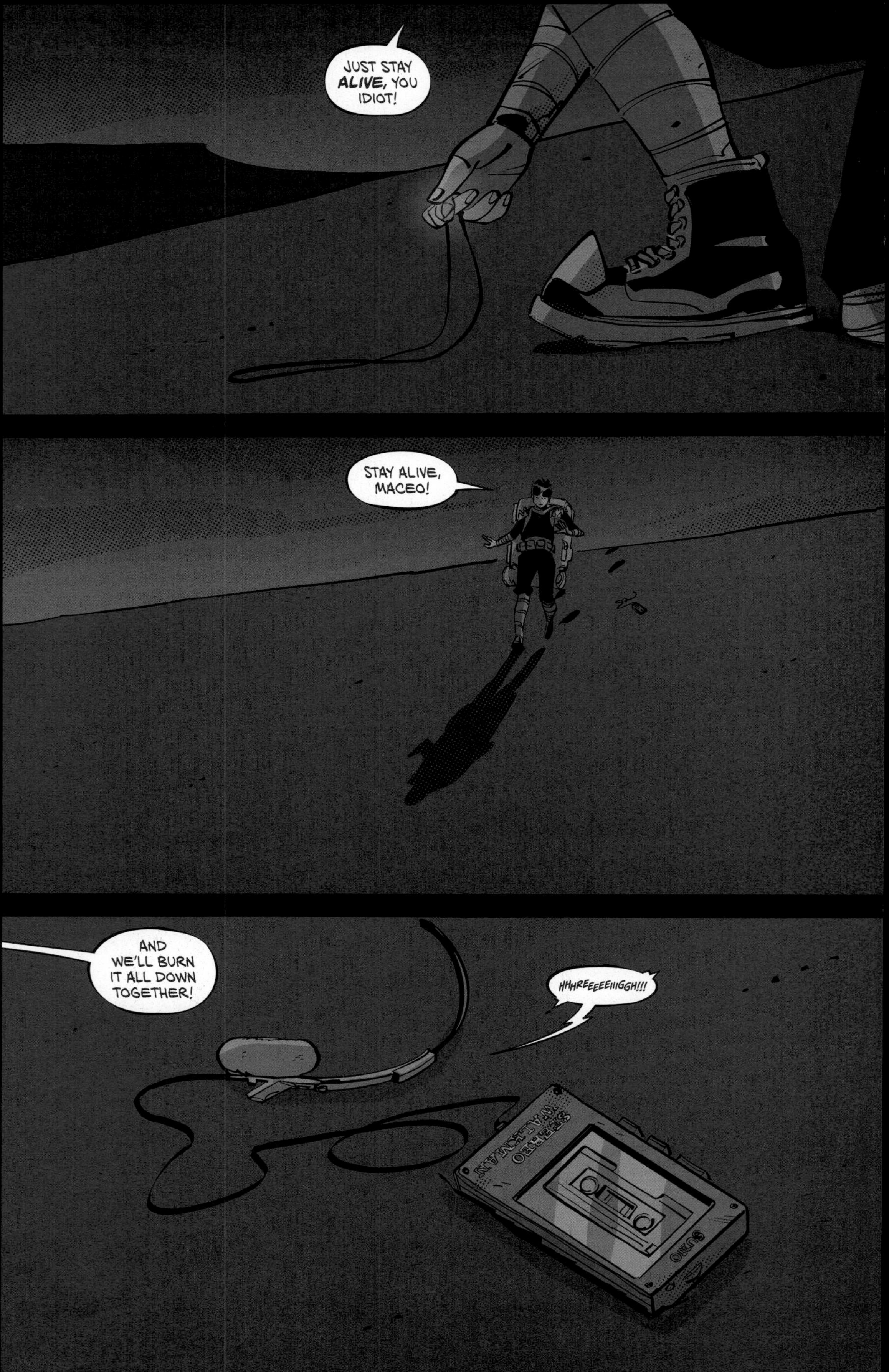
JUST STAY ALIVE, YOU IDIOT!
STAY ALIVE, MACEO!
AND WE'LL BURN IT ALL DOWN TOGETHER!
HHHREEEEEIIIGGH!!!

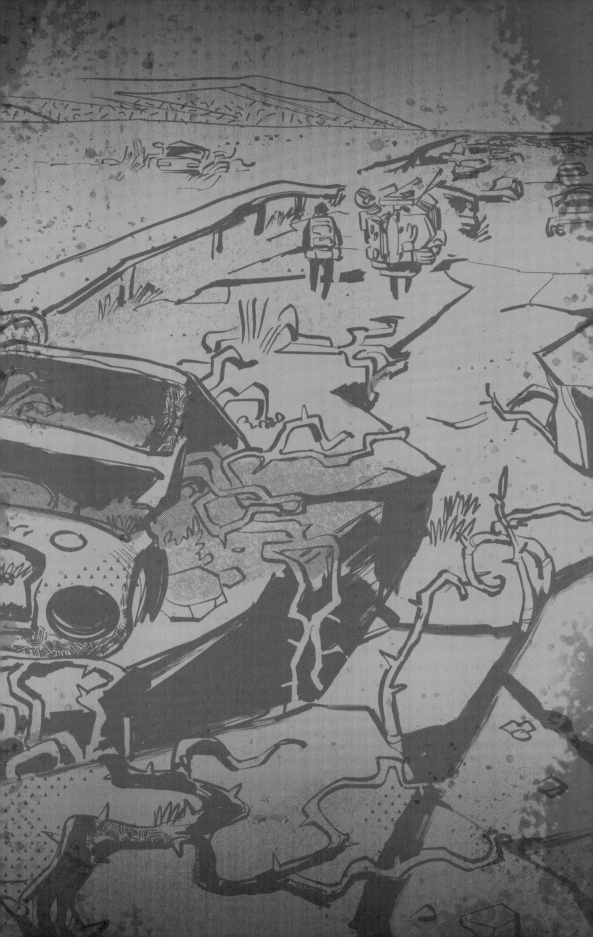

CHAPTER FIVE

THE APOCALYMPICS

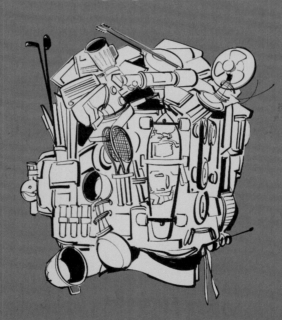

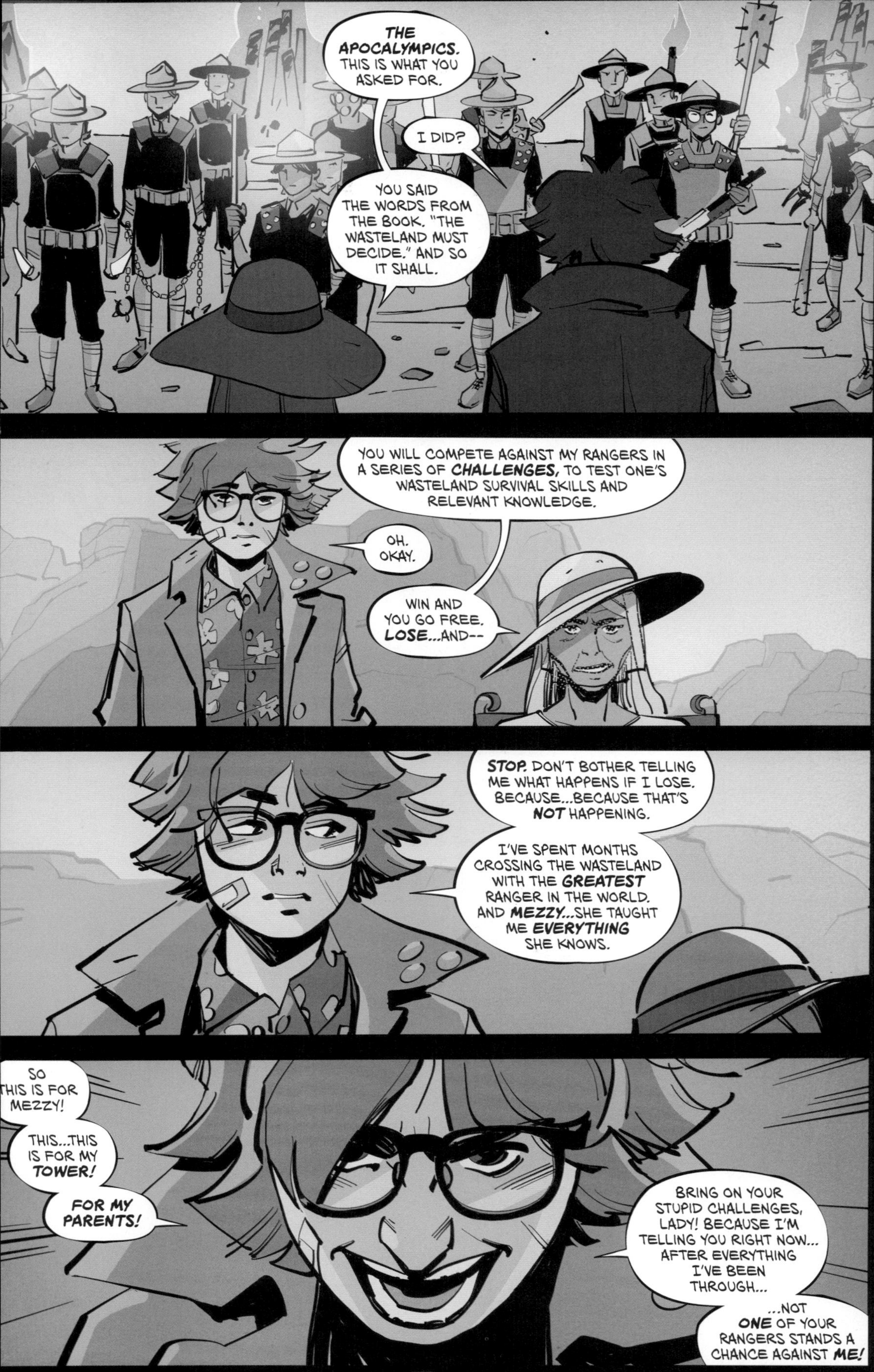
THE APOCALYMPICS. THIS IS WHAT YOU ASKED FOR.
I DID?
YOU SAID THE WORDS FROM THE BOOK. "THE WASTELAND MUST DECIDE." AND SO IT SHALL.
YOU WILL COMPETE AGAINST MY RANGERS IN A SERIES OF CHALLENGES, TO TEST ONE'S WASTELAND SURVIVAL SKILLS AND RELEVANT KNOWLEDGE.
OH. OKAY.
WIN AND YOU GO FREE. LOSE...AND--
STOP. DON'T BOTHER TELLING ME WHAT HAPPENS IF I LOSE. BECAUSE...BECAUSE THAT'S NOT HAPPENING.
I'VE SPENT MONTHS CROSSING THE WASTELAND WITH THE GREATEST RANGER IN THE WORLD. AND MEZZY...SHE TAUGHT ME EVERYTHING SHE KNOWS.
SO THIS IS FOR MEZZY!
THIS...THIS IS FOR MY TOWER!
FOR MY PARENTS!
BRING ON YOUR STUPID CHALLENGES, LADY! BECAUSE I'M TELLING YOU RIGHT NOW... AFTER EVERYTHING I'VE BEEN THROUGH...
...NOT ONE OF YOUR RANGERS STANDS A CHANCE AGAINST ME!

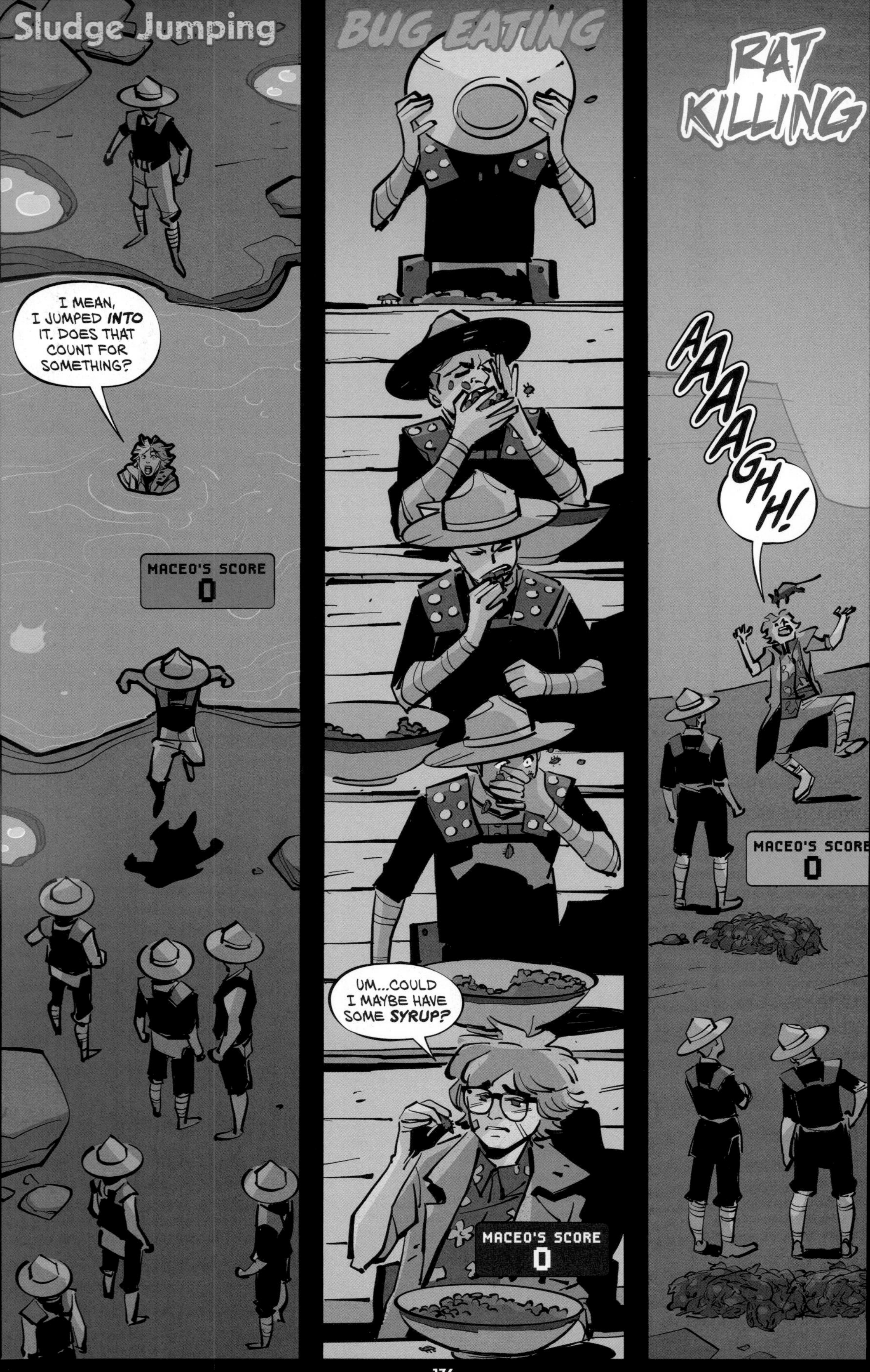

Sludge Jumping
I MEAN, I JUMPED INTO IT. DOES THAT COUNT FOR SOMETHING?
MACEO'S SCORE
0
BUG EATING
UM...COULD I MAYBE HAVE SOME SYRUP?
MACEO'S SCORE
0
RAT KILLING
AAAAAGHH!
MACEO'S SCORE
0

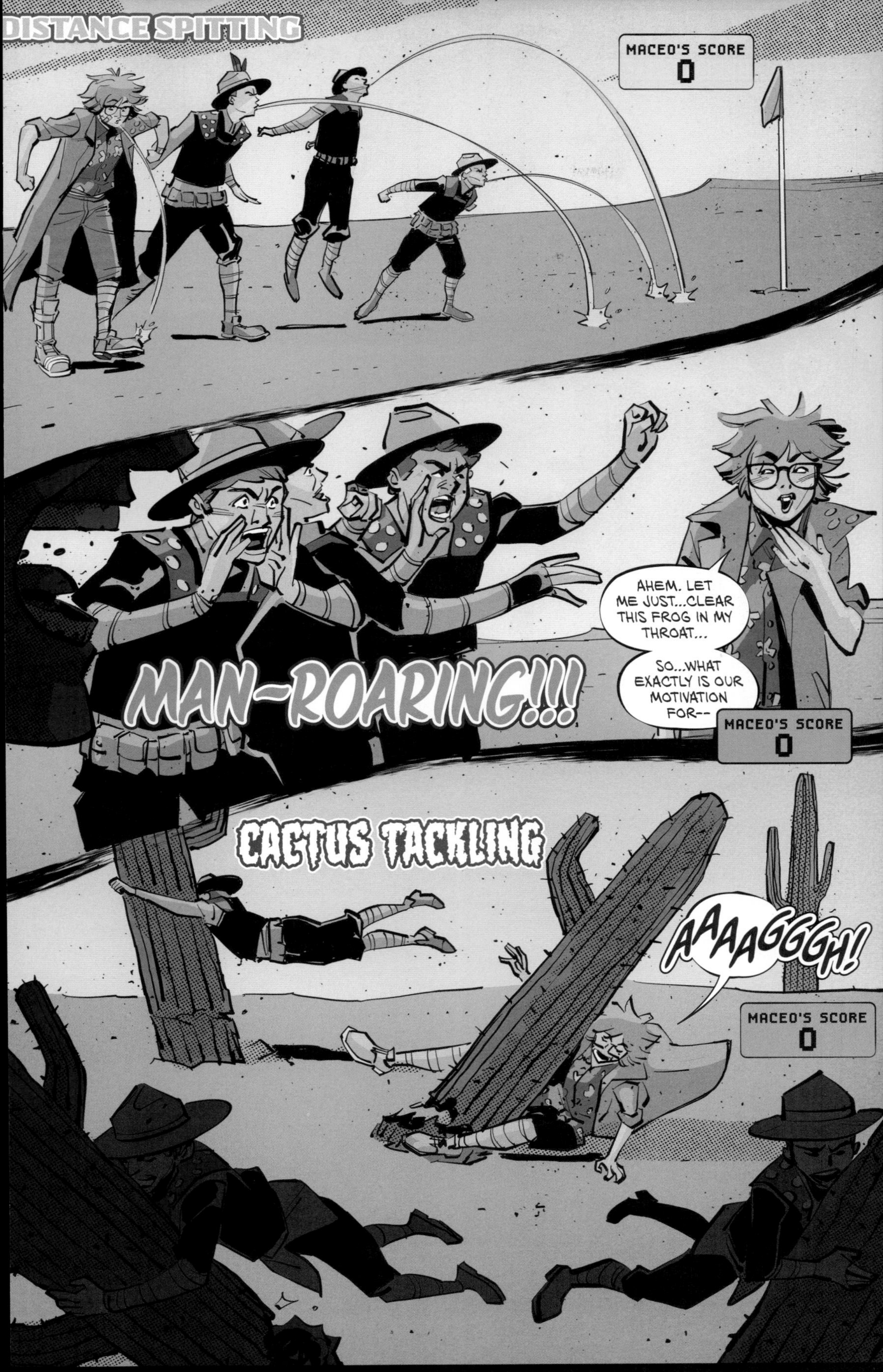
DISTANCE SPITTING
MACEO'S SCORE 0
MAN-ROARING!!!
AHEM. LET ME JUST...CLEAR THIS FROG IN MY THROAT...
SO...WHAT EXACTLY IS OUR MOTIVATION FOR--
MACEO'S SCORE 0
CACTUS TACKLING
AAAAGGGH!
MACEO'S SCORE 0

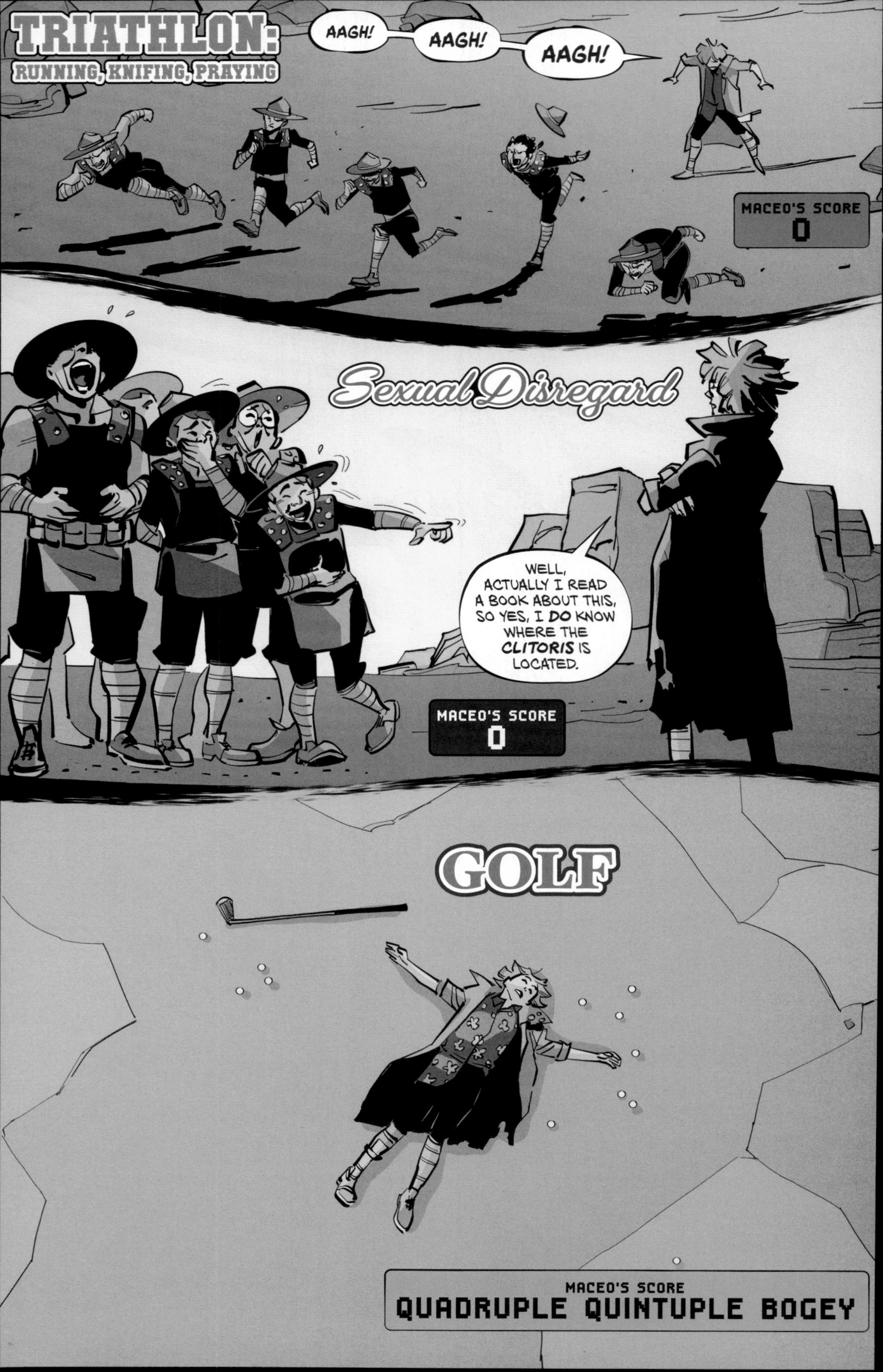
TRIATHLON:
RUNNING, KNIFING, PRAYING
AAGH!
AAGH!
AAGH!
MACEO'S SCORE
0
Sexual Disregard
WELL, ACTUALLY I READ A BOOK ABOUT THIS, SO YES, I DO KNOW WHERE THE CLITORIS IS LOCATED.
MACEO'S SCORE
0
GOLF
MACEO'S SCORE
QUADRUPLE QUINTUPLE BOGEY

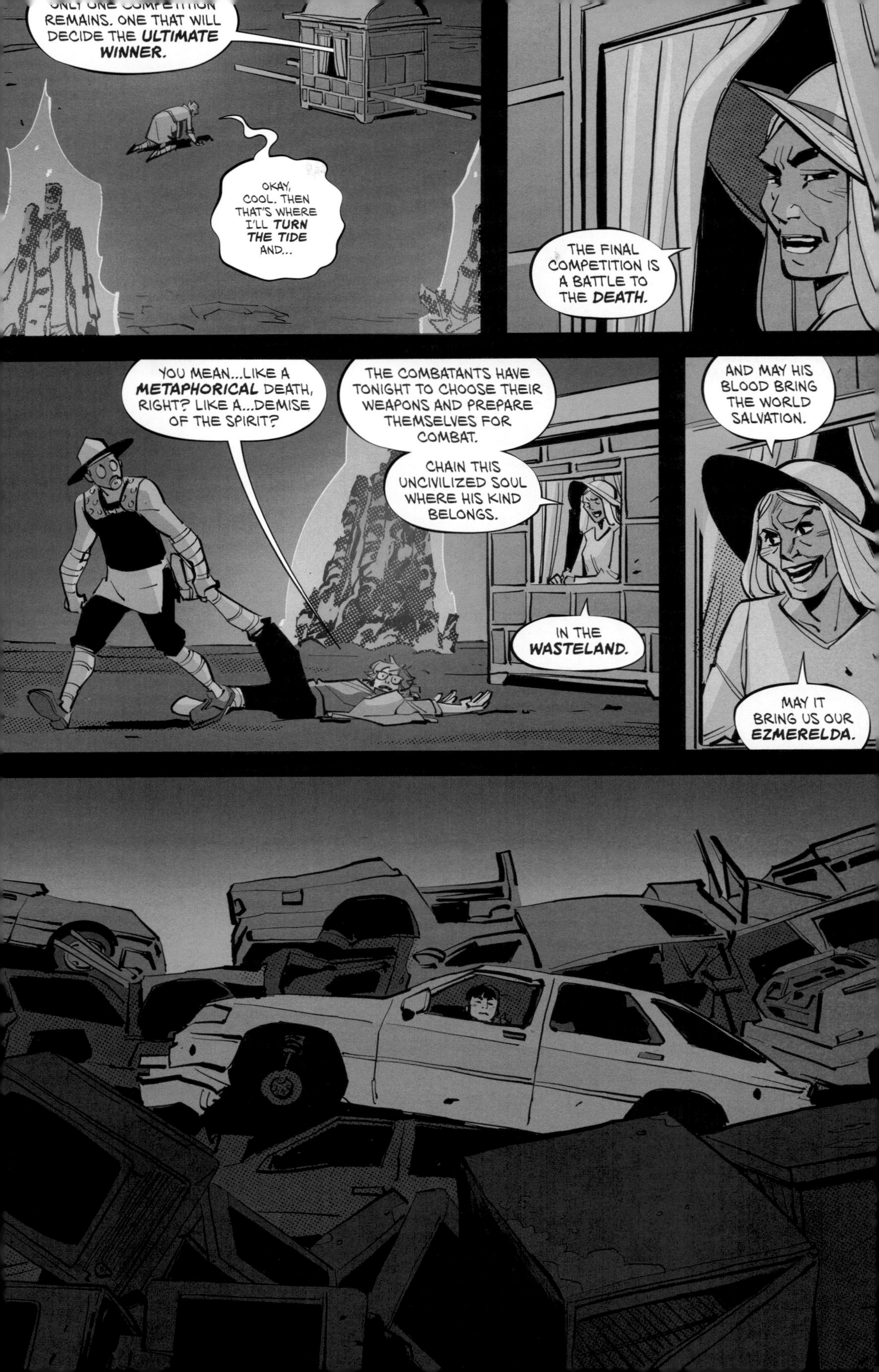
ONLY ONE COMPETITION REMAINS. ONE THAT WILL DECIDE THE **ULTIMATE WINNER.**
OKAY, COOL. THEN THAT'S WHERE I'LL **TURN THE TIDE** AND...
THE FINAL COMPETITION IS A BATTLE TO THE **DEATH.**
YOU MEAN...LIKE A **METAPHORICAL** DEATH, RIGHT? LIKE A...DEMISE OF THE SPIRIT?
THE COMBATANTS HAVE TONIGHT TO CHOOSE THEIR WEAPONS AND PREPARE THEMSELVES FOR COMBAT.
CHAIN THIS UNCIVILIZED SOUL WHERE HIS KIND BELONGS.
IN THE **WASTELAND.**
AND MAY HIS BLOOD BRING THE WORLD SALVATION.
MAY IT BRING US OUR **EZMERELDA.**

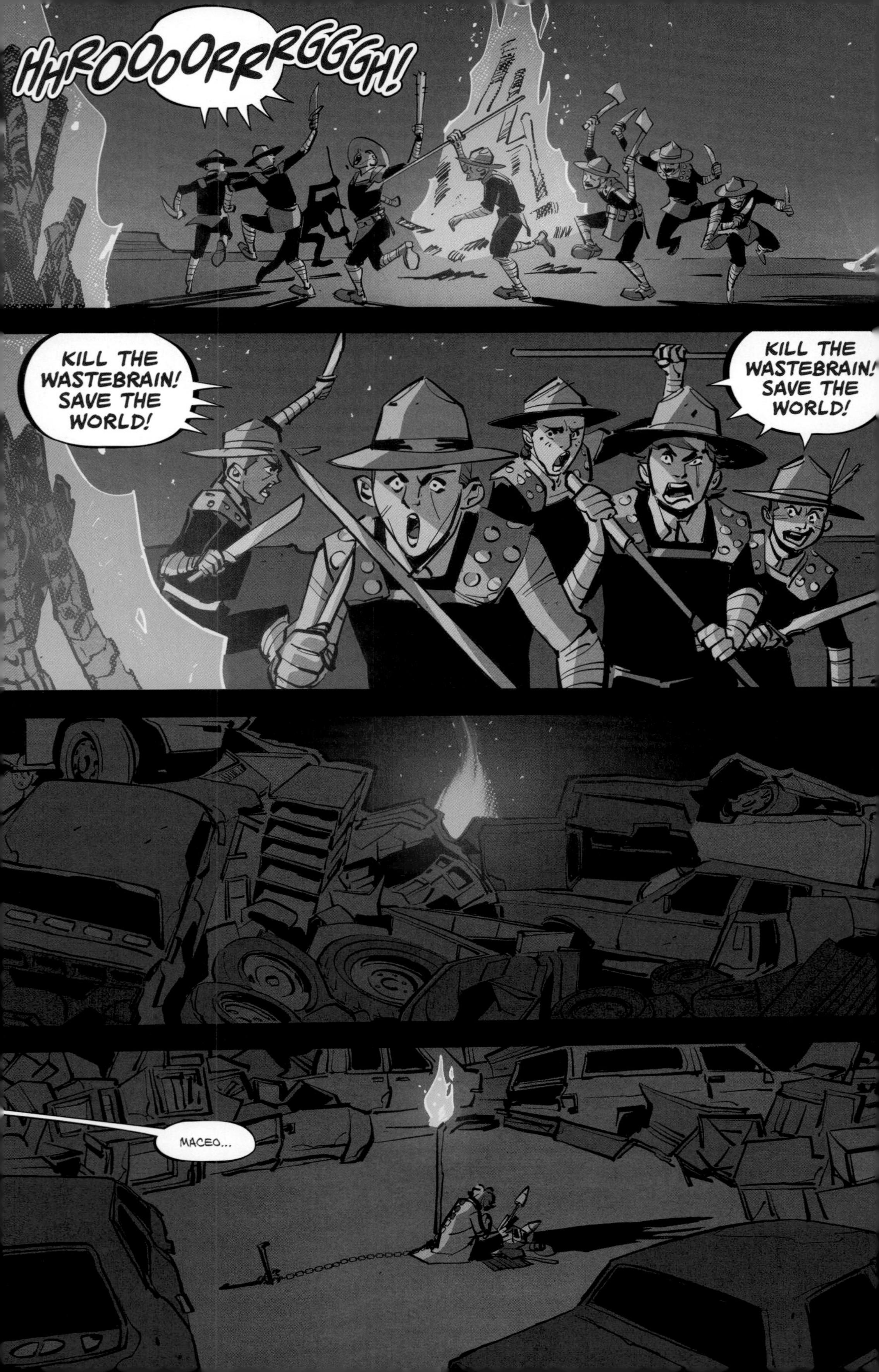
HHROOOOORRRRGGGGH!
KILL THE WASTEBRAIN! SAVE THE WORLD!
KILL THE WASTEBRAIN! SAVE THE WORLD!
MACEO...

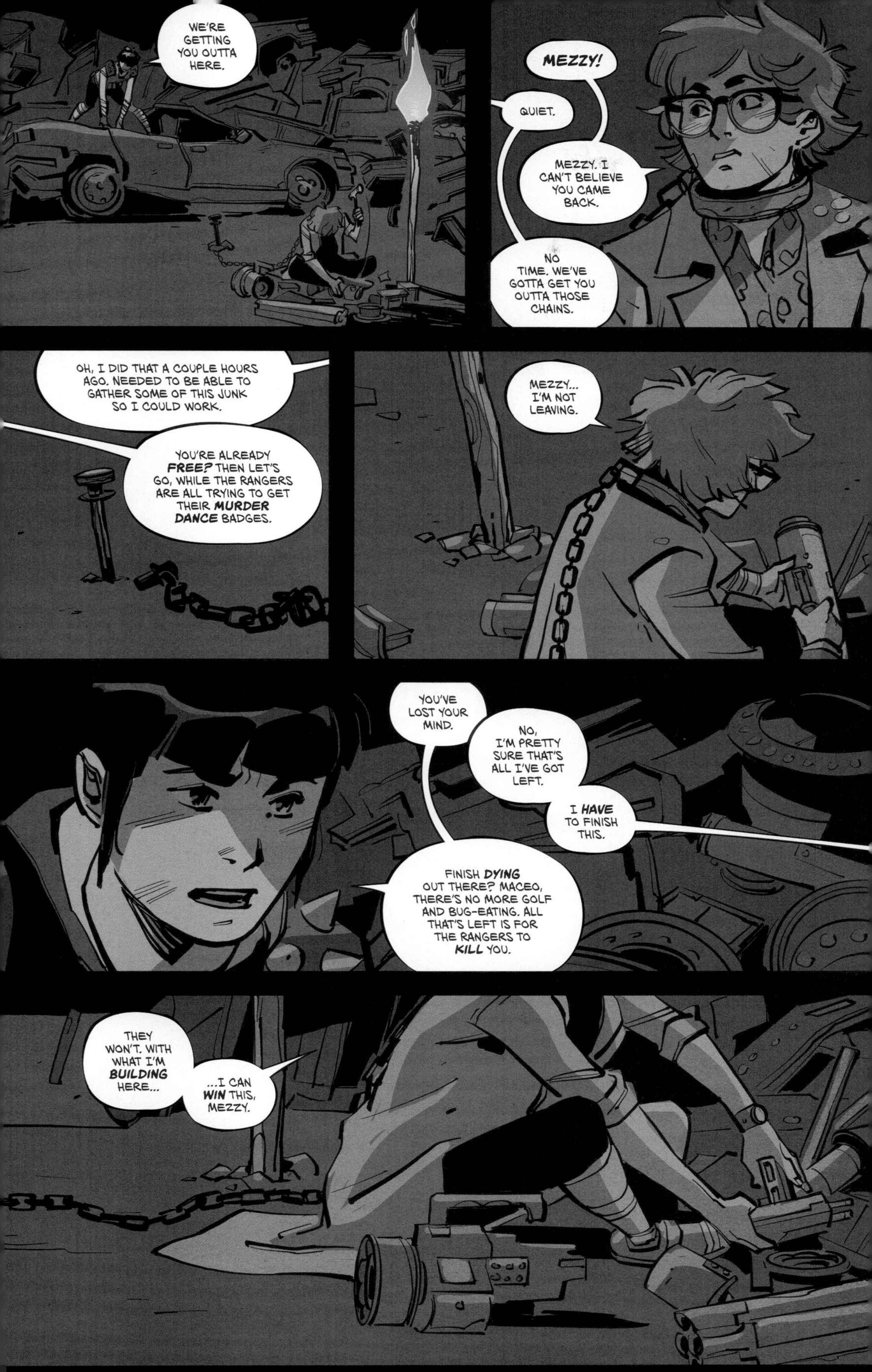
WE'RE GETTING YOU OUTTA HERE.
MEZZY!
QUIET.
MEZZY. I CAN'T BELIEVE YOU CAME BACK.
NO TIME. WE'VE GOTTA GET YOU OUTTA THOSE CHAINS.
OH, I DID THAT A COUPLE HOURS AGO. NEEDED TO BE ABLE TO GATHER SOME OF THIS JUNK SO I COULD WORK.
YOU'RE ALREADY FREE? THEN LET'S GO, WHILE THE RANGERS ARE ALL TRYING TO GET THEIR MURDER DANCE BADGES.
MEZZY... I'M NOT LEAVING.
YOU'VE LOST YOUR MIND.
NO, I'M PRETTY SURE THAT'S ALL I'VE GOT LEFT.
I HAVE TO FINISH THIS.
FINISH DYING OUT THERE? MACEO, THERE'S NO MORE GOLF AND BUG-EATING. ALL THAT'S LEFT IS FOR THE RANGERS TO KILL YOU.
THEY WON'T. WITH WHAT I'M BUILDING HERE...
...I CAN WIN THIS, MEZZY.

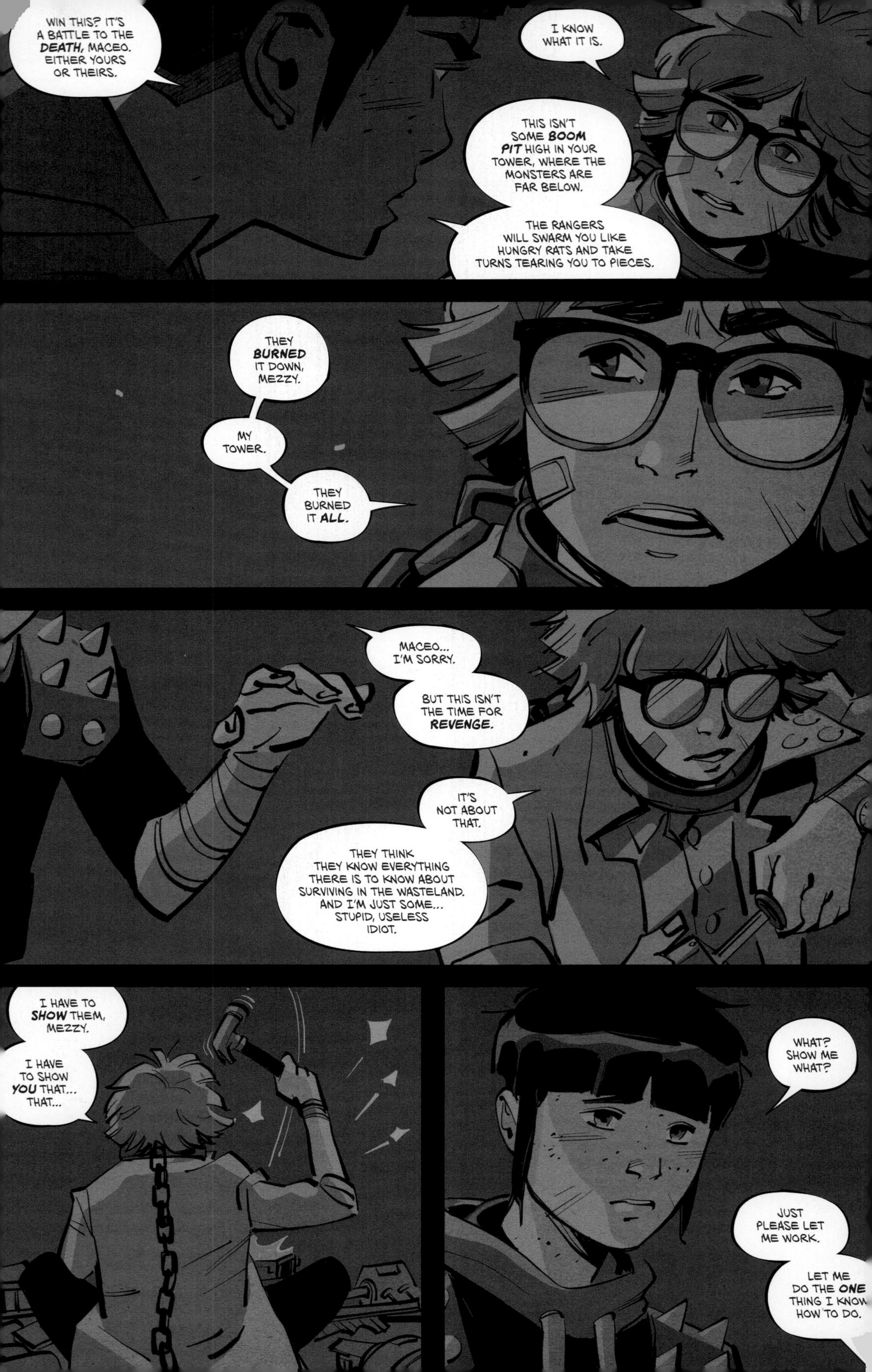
WIN THIS? IT'S A BATTLE TO THE **DEATH,** MACEO. EITHER YOURS OR THEIRS.
I KNOW WHAT IT IS.
THIS ISN'T SOME **BOOM PIT** HIGH IN YOUR TOWER, WHERE THE MONSTERS ARE FAR BELOW.
THE RANGERS WILL SWARM YOU LIKE HUNGRY RATS AND TAKE TURNS TEARING YOU TO PIECES.
THEY **BURNED** IT DOWN, MEZZY.
MY TOWER.
THEY BURNED IT **ALL.**
MACEO... I'M SORRY.
BUT THIS ISN'T THE TIME FOR **REVENGE.**
IT'S NOT ABOUT THAT.
THEY THINK THEY KNOW EVERYTHING THERE IS TO KNOW ABOUT SURVIVING IN THE WASTELAND. AND I'M JUST SOME... STUPID, USELESS IDIOT.
I HAVE TO **SHOW** THEM, MEZZY.
I HAVE TO SHOW **YOU** THAT... THAT...
WHAT? SHOW ME WHAT?
JUST PLEASE LET ME WORK.
LET ME DO THE **ONE** THING I KNOW HOW TO DO.

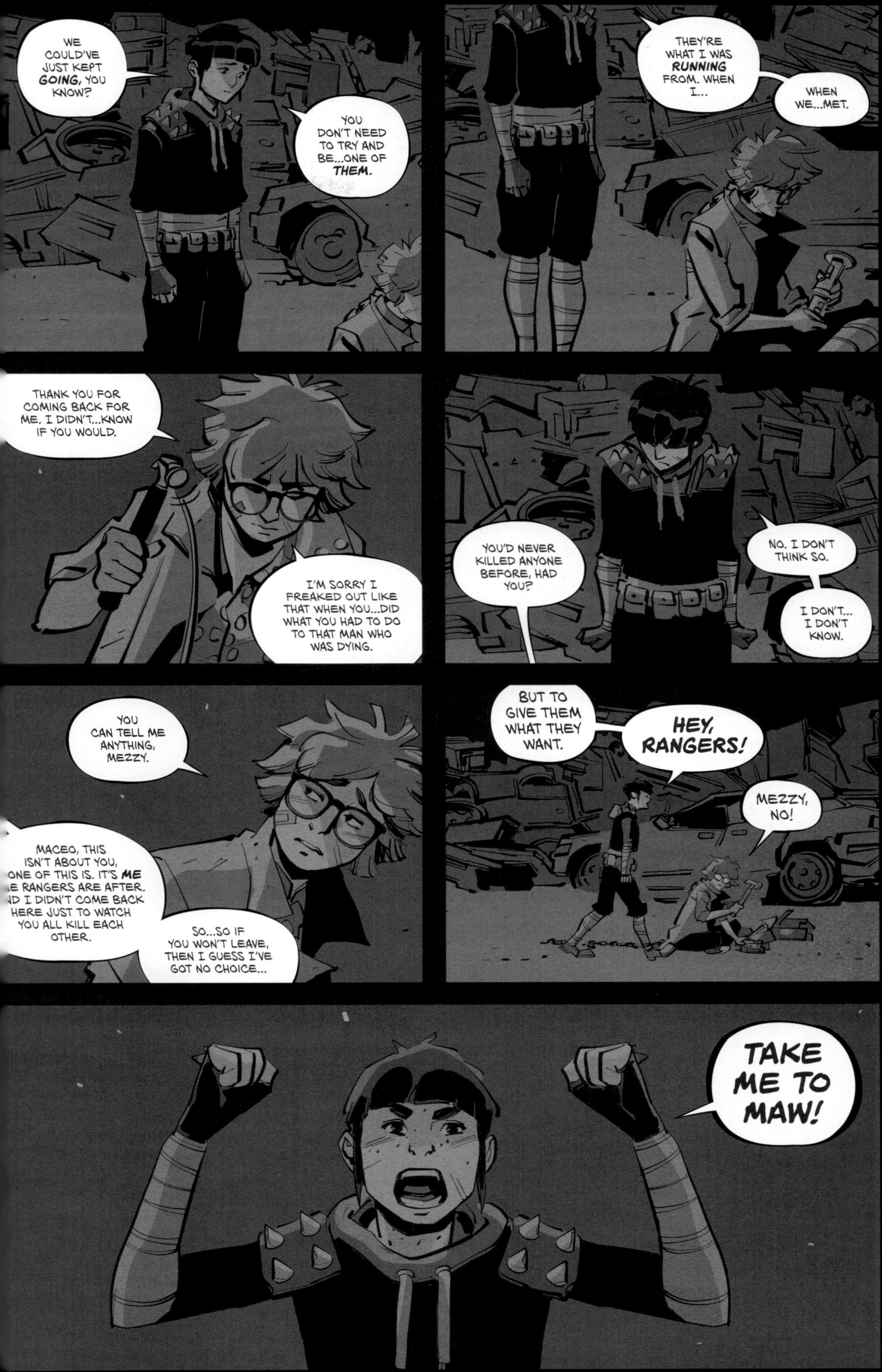
WE COULD'VE JUST KEPT **GOING,** YOU KNOW?
YOU DON'T NEED TO TRY AND BE...ONE OF ***THEM.***
THEY'RE WHAT I WAS **RUNNING** FROM. WHEN I...
WHEN WE...MET.
THANK YOU FOR COMING BACK FOR ME. I DIDN'T...KNOW IF YOU WOULD.
I'M SORRY I FREAKED OUT LIKE THAT WHEN YOU...DID WHAT YOU HAD TO DO TO THAT MAN WHO WAS DYING.
YOU'D NEVER KILLED ANYONE BEFORE, HAD YOU?
NO. I DON'T THINK SO.
I DON'T... I DON'T KNOW.
YOU CAN TELL ME ANYTHING, MEZZY.
MACEO, THIS ISN'T ABOUT YOU, ONE OF THIS IS. IT'S **ME** E RANGERS ARE AFTER. ND I DIDN'T COME BACK HERE JUST TO WATCH YOU ALL KILL EACH OTHER.
SO...SO IF YOU WON'T LEAVE, THEN I GUESS I'VE GOT NO CHOICE...
BUT TO GIVE THEM WHAT THEY WANT.
HEY, RANGERS!
MEZZY, NO!
TAKE ME TO MAW!

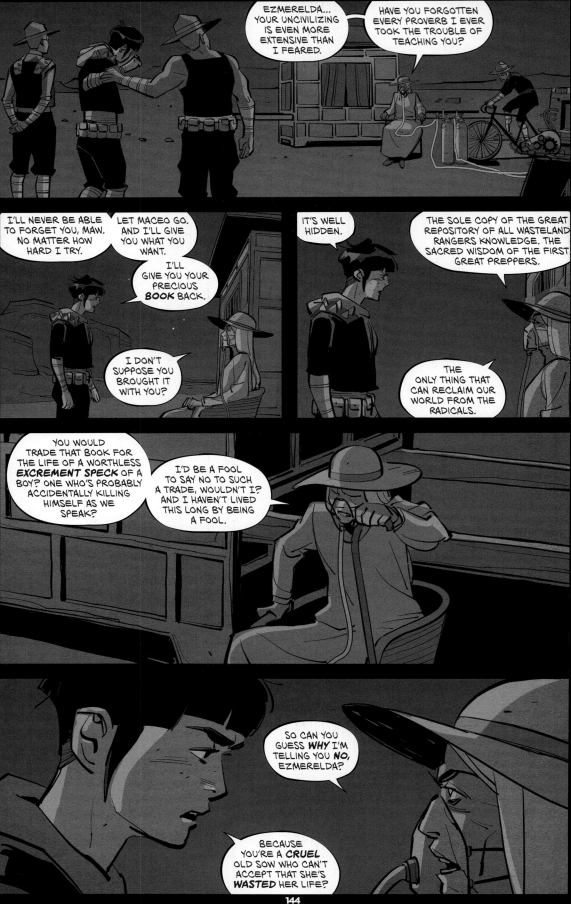

EZMERELDA... YOUR UNCIVILIZING IS EVEN MORE EXTENSIVE THAN I FEARED.

HAVE YOU FORGOTTEN EVERY PROVERB I EVER TOOK THE TROUBLE OF TEACHING YOU?

I'LL NEVER BE ABLE TO FORGET YOU, MAW. NO MATTER HOW HARD I TRY.

LET MACEO GO. AND I'LL GIVE YOU WHAT YOU WANT.

I'LL GIVE YOU YOUR PRECIOUS *BOOK* BACK.

I DON'T SUPPOSE YOU BROUGHT IT WITH YOU?

IT'S WELL HIDDEN.

THE SOLE COPY OF THE GREAT REPOSITORY OF ALL WASTELAND RANGERS KNOWLEDGE. THE SACRED WISDOM OF THE FIRST GREAT PREPPERS.

THE ONLY THING THAT CAN RECLAIM OUR WORLD FROM THE RADICALS.

YOU WOULD TRADE THAT BOOK FOR THE LIFE OF A WORTHLESS *EXCREMENT SPECK* OF A BOY? ONE WHO'S PROBABLY ACCIDENTALLY KILLING HIMSELF AS WE SPEAK?

I'D BE A FOOL TO SAY NO TO SUCH A TRADE, WOULDN'T I? AND I HAVEN'T LIVED THIS LONG BY BEING A FOOL.

SO CAN YOU GUESS *WHY* I'M TELLING YOU *NO*, EZMERELDA?

BECAUSE YOU'RE A *CRUEL* OLD SOW WHO CAN'T ACCEPT THAT SHE'S *WASTED* HER LIFE?

YOU'VE LAID YOUR HANDS ON ME FOR THE LAST TIME, MAW.

IT'S THE WASTELAND THAT IS CRUEL.

I DO WHAT I MUST TO PROTECT MY CHILDREN FROM A WORLD WHERE THE WEAK INFECT THE STRONG.

YOU ONCE UNDERSTOOD THAT, MEZZY. DESPITE YOUR STRAYING, PERHAPS YOU STILL DO. YOU'RE JUST AWED BY THE **RESPONSIBILITY** I'VE ASKED OF YOU.

YOU ARE RIGHT TO BE AWED. IT IS A WITHERING BURDEN. BUT WE WHO SURVIVE HAVE NO CHOICE. THERE IS ONLY ONE PATH.

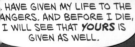

. HAVE GIVEN MY LIFE TO THE ANGERS. AND BEFORE I DIE, I WILL SEE THAT **YOURS** IS GIVEN AS WELL.

IF YOU TRULY WISH FOR UR FEEBLEMINDED COMPANION TO GO FREE...THEN I WANT MORE THAN THE BOOK.

I WANT THE LOCATION OF THE **OASIS**. AND MOST IMPORTANTLY...

I WANT **YOU**, EZMERELDA.

I WANT YOU TO TAKE MY PLACE. AS **CHIEFTESS** OF THE RANGERS.

AS **MOTHER** OF THE NEW WORLD.

NO FUCKING CHANCE IN SHITTING HELL.

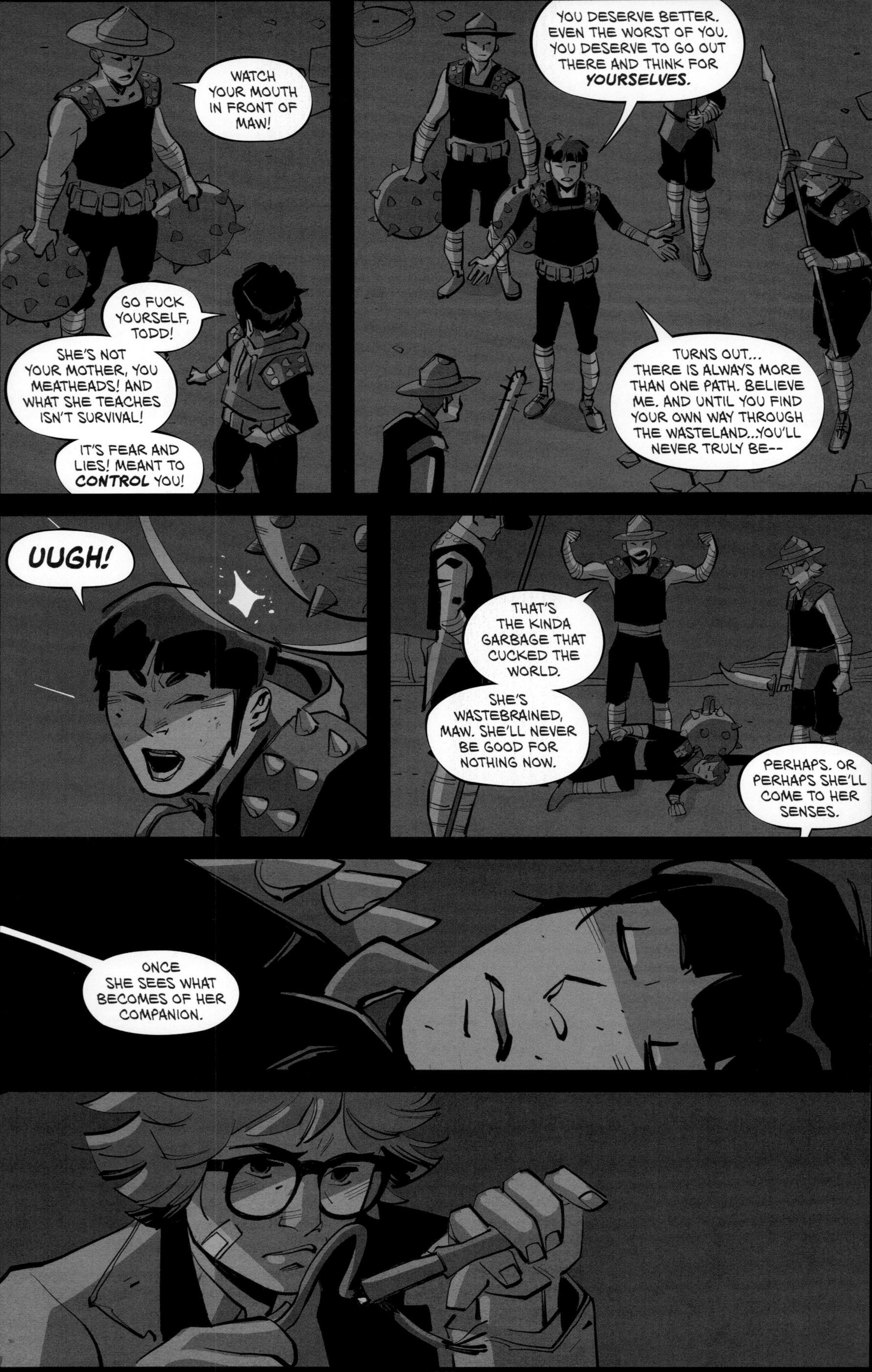
WATCH YOUR MOUTH IN FRONT OF MAW!
GO FUCK YOURSELF, TODD!
SHE'S NOT YOUR MOTHER, YOU MEATHEADS! AND WHAT SHE TEACHES ISN'T SURVIVAL!
IT'S FEAR AND LIES! MEANT TO CONTROL YOU!
YOU DESERVE BETTER. EVEN THE WORST OF YOU. YOU DESERVE TO GO OUT THERE AND THINK FOR YOURSELVES.
TURNS OUT... THERE IS ALWAYS MORE THAN ONE PATH. BELIEVE ME. AND UNTIL YOU FIND YOUR OWN WAY THROUGH THE WASTELAND...YOU'LL NEVER TRULY BE--
UUGH!
THAT'S THE KINDA GARBAGE THAT CUCKED THE WORLD.
SHE'S WASTEBRAINED, MAW. SHE'LL NEVER BE GOOD FOR NOTHING NOW.
PERHAPS. OR PERHAPS SHE'LL COME TO HER SENSES.
ONCE SHE SEES WHAT BECOMES OF HER COMPANION.

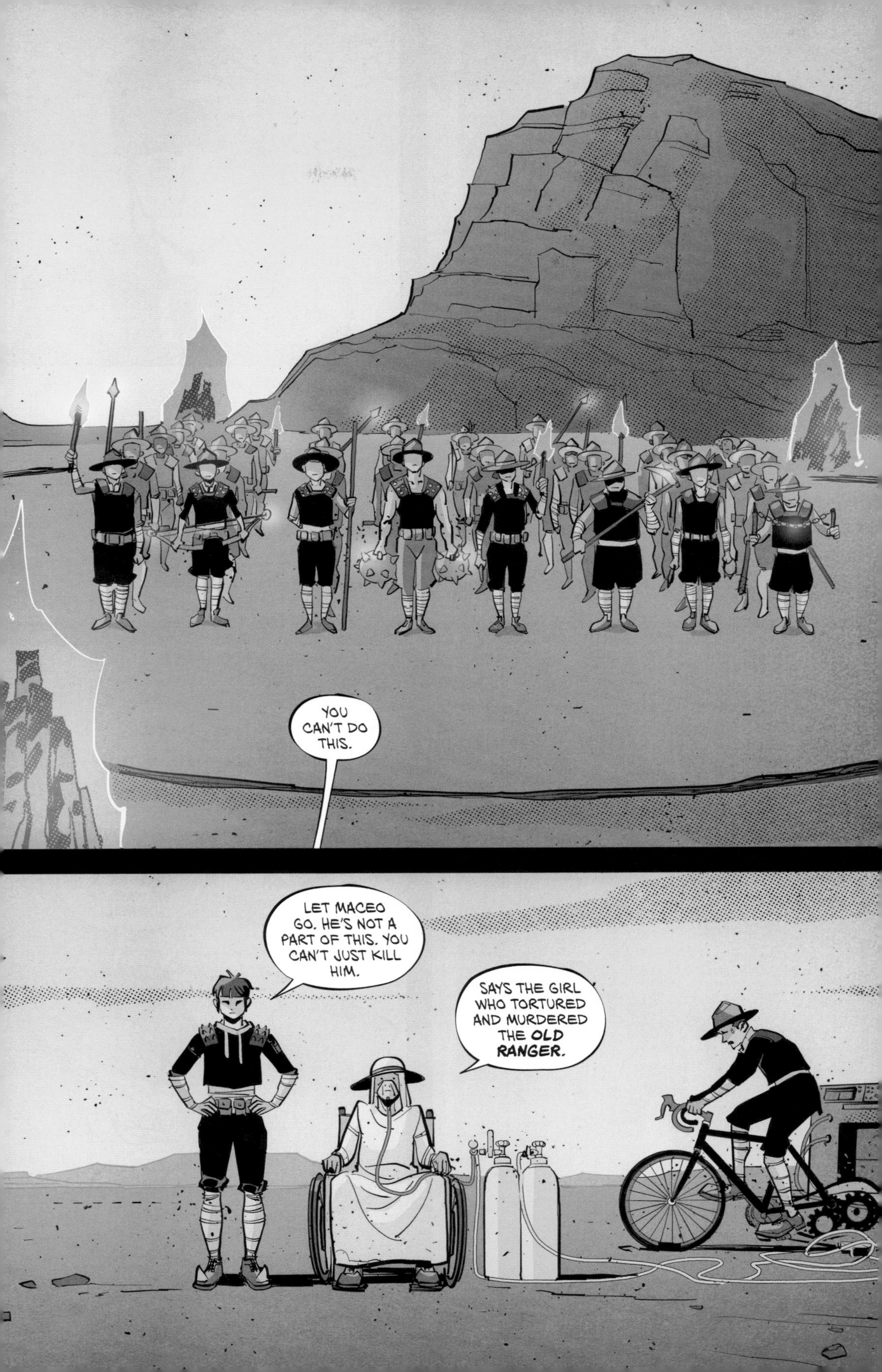
YOU CAN'T DO THIS.
LET MACEO GO. HE'S NOT A PART OF THIS. YOU CAN'T JUST KILL HIM.
SAYS THE GIRL WHO TORTURED AND MURDERED THE **OLD RANGER.**

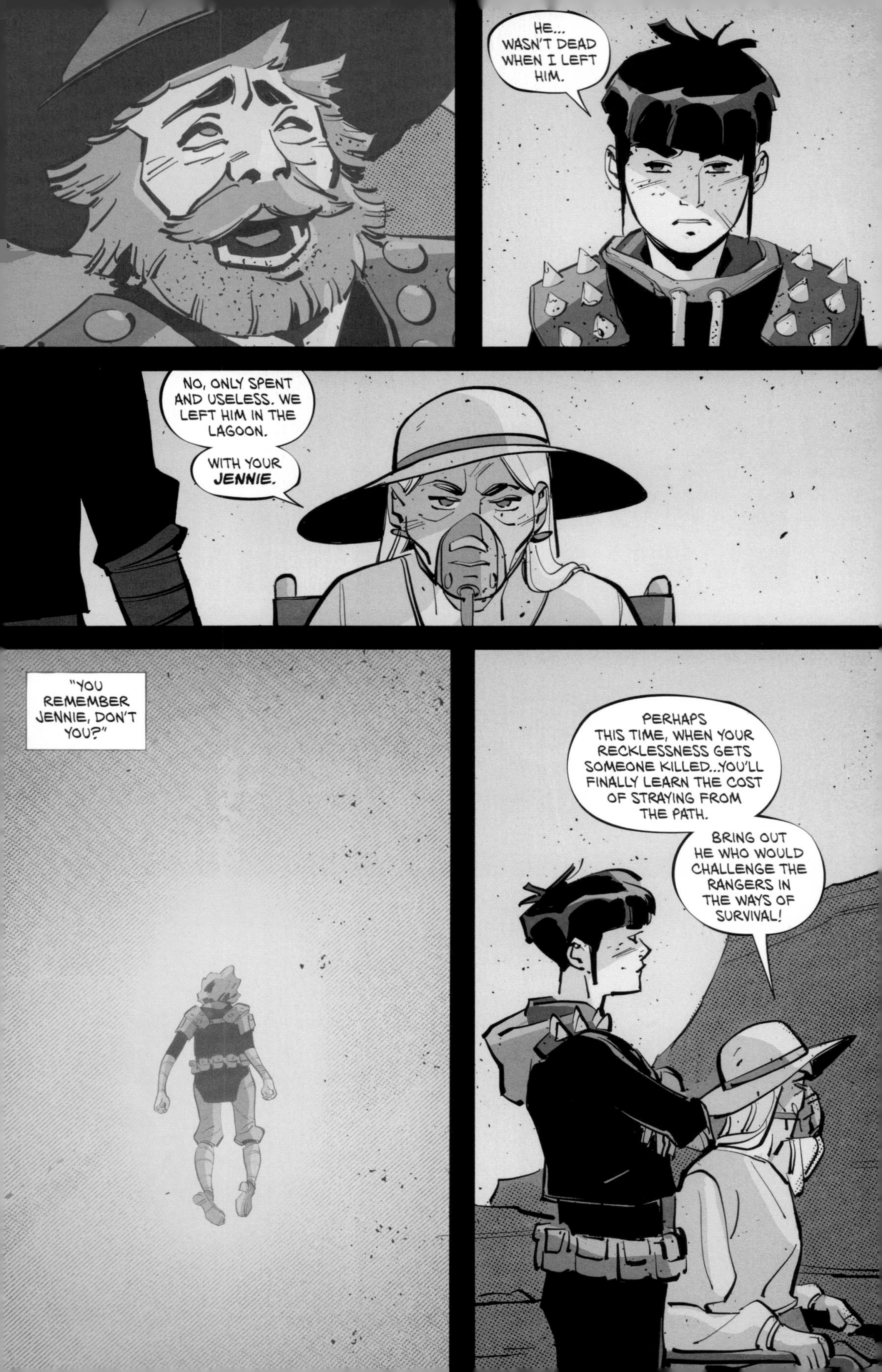
HE... WASN'T DEAD WHEN I LEFT HIM.
NO, ONLY SPENT AND USELESS. WE LEFT HIM IN THE LAGOON.
WITH YOUR JENNIE.
"YOU REMEMBER JENNIE, DON'T YOU?"
PERHAPS THIS TIME, WHEN YOUR RECKLESSNESS GETS SOMEONE KILLED...YOU'LL FINALLY LEARN THE COST OF STRAYING FROM THE PATH.
BRING OUT HE WHO WOULD CHALLENGE THE RANGERS IN THE WAYS OF SURVIVAL!

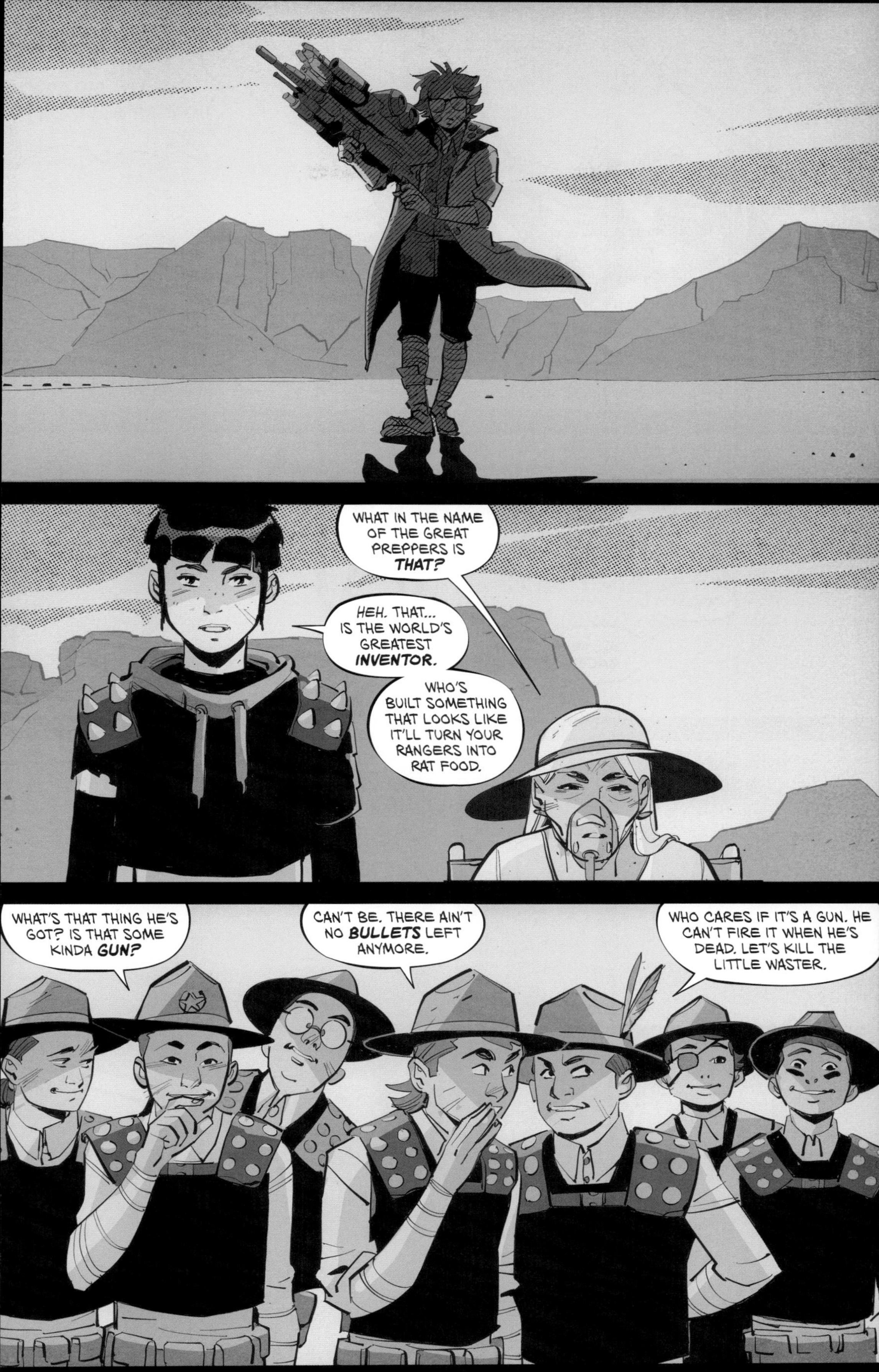
WHAT IN THE NAME OF THE GREAT PREPPERS IS **THAT?**
HEH. THAT... IS THE WORLD'S GREATEST **INVENTOR.**
WHO'S BUILT SOMETHING THAT LOOKS LIKE IT'LL TURN YOUR RANGERS INTO RAT FOOD.
WHAT'S THAT THING HE'S GOT? IS THAT SOME KINDA **GUN?**
CAN'T BE. THERE AIN'T NO **BULLETS** LEFT ANYMORE.
WHO CARES IF IT'S A GUN. HE CAN'T FIRE IT WHEN HE'S DEAD. LET'S KILL THE LITTLE WASTER.

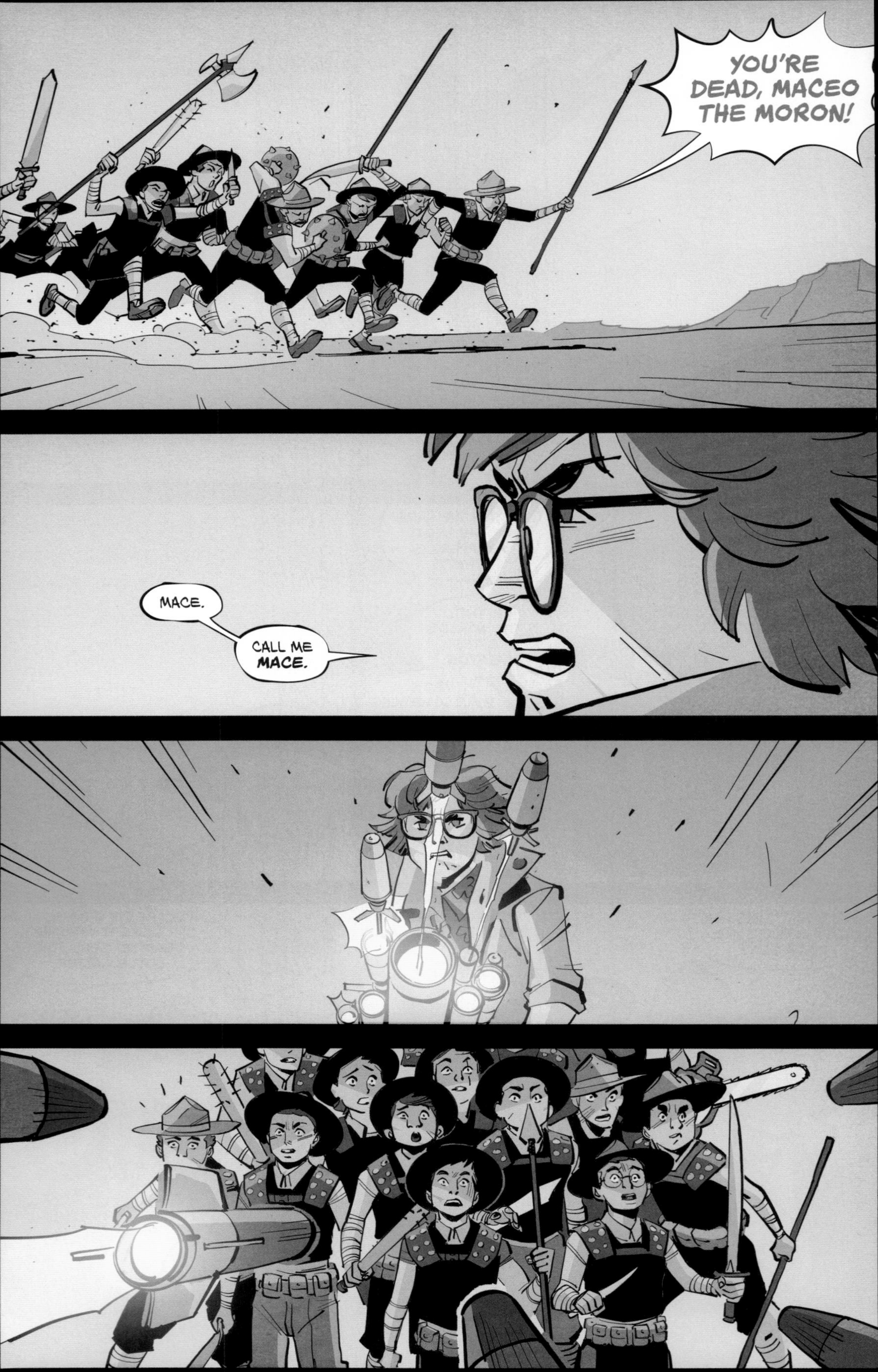
YOU'RE DEAD, MACEO THE MORON!
MACE.
CALL ME MACE.

HUH?

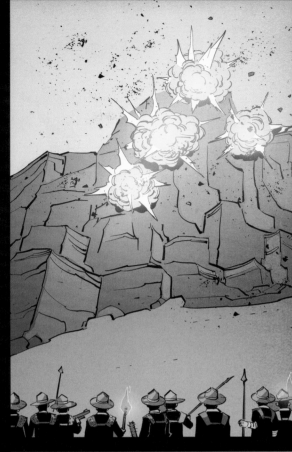

HA! YOU **MISSED** US!

NICE SHOT, FLAKEFACE!

YEAH.

IT WAS **PERFECT.**

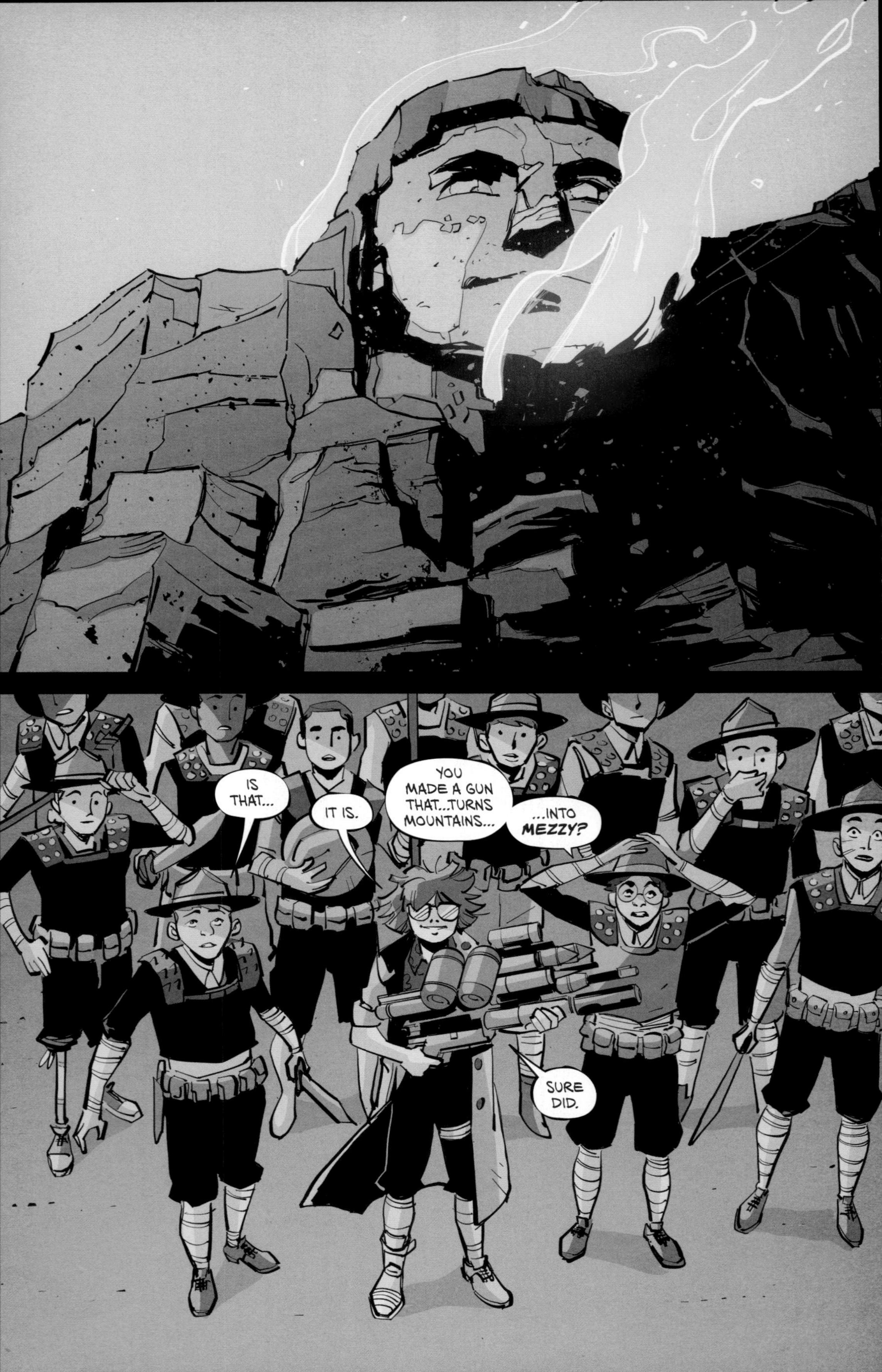
IS THAT...
IT IS.
YOU MADE A GUN THAT...TURNS MOUNTAINS...
...INTO MEZZY?
SURE DID.

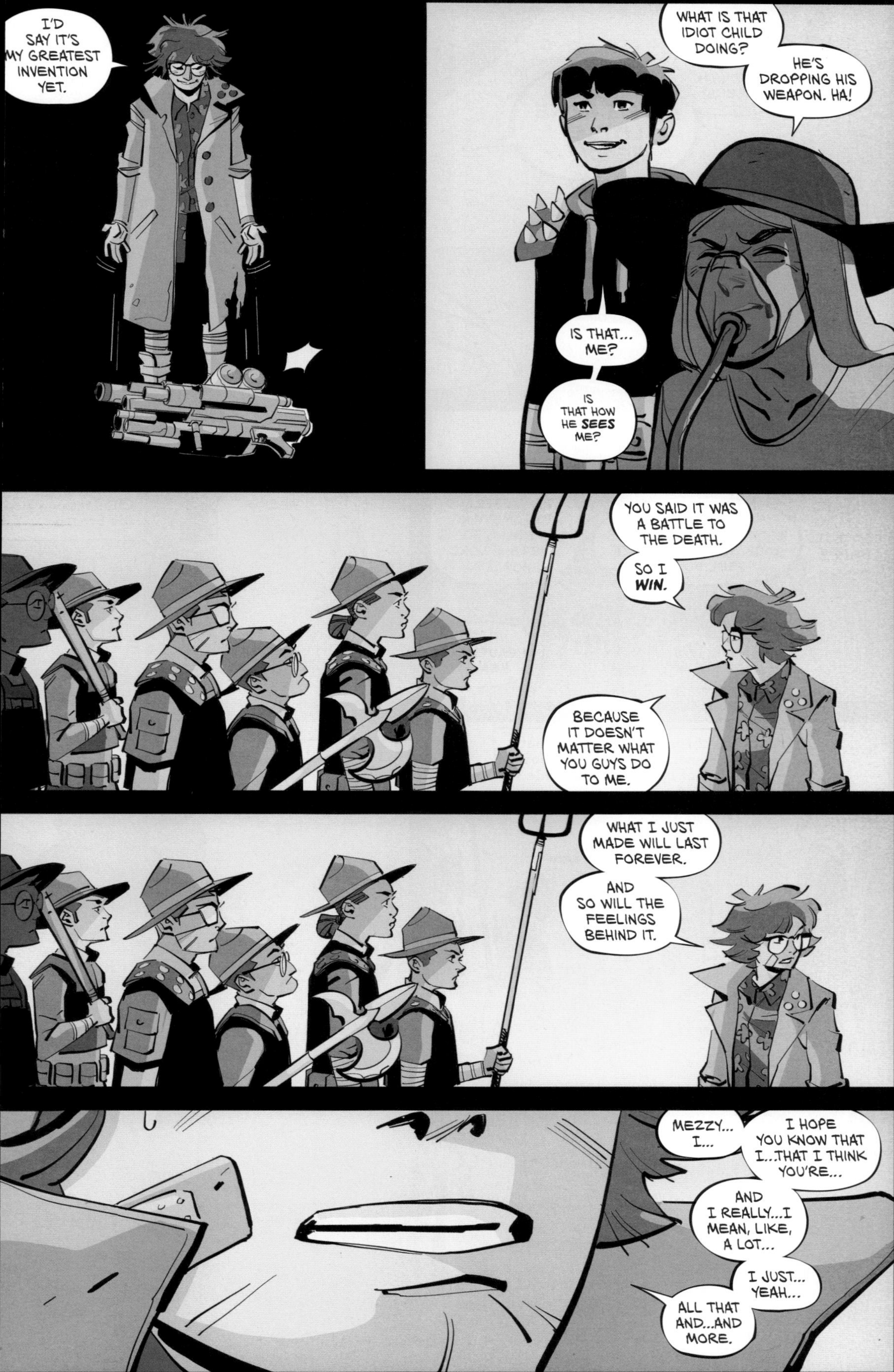

I'D SAY IT'S MY GREATEST INVENTION YET.
WHAT IS THAT IDIOT CHILD DOING?
HE'S DROPPING HIS WEAPON. HA!
IS THAT... ME?
IS THAT HOW HE **SEES** ME?
YOU SAID IT WAS A BATTLE TO THE DEATH.
SO I **WIN.**
BECAUSE IT DOESN'T MATTER WHAT YOU GUYS DO TO ME.
WHAT I JUST MADE WILL LAST FOREVER.
AND SO WILL THE FEELINGS BEHIND IT.
MEZZY... I...
I HOPE YOU KNOW THAT I...THAT I THINK YOU'RE...
AND I REALLY...I MEAN, LIKE, A LOT...
I JUST... YEAH...
ALL THAT AND...AND MORE.

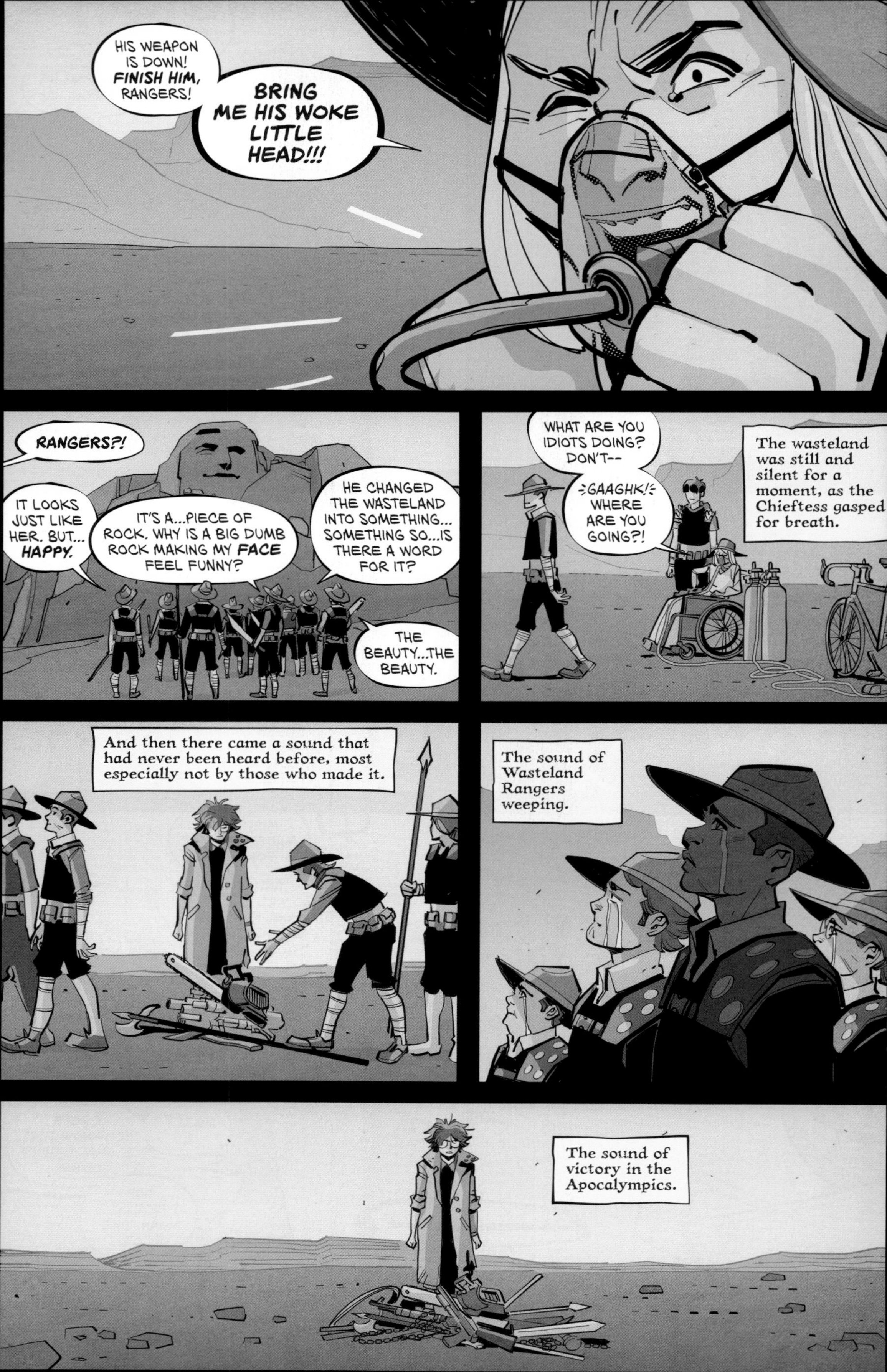

HIS WEAPON IS DOWN! FINISH HIM, RANGERS!
BRING ME HIS WOKE LITTLE HEAD!!!
RANGERS?!
IT LOOKS JUST LIKE HER. BUT... HAPPY.
IT'S A...PIECE OF ROCK. WHY IS A BIG DUMB ROCK MAKING MY FACE FEEL FUNNY?
HE CHANGED THE WASTELAND INTO SOMETHING... SOMETHING SO...IS THERE A WORD FOR IT?
THE BEAUTY...THE BEAUTY.
WHAT ARE YOU IDIOTS DOING? DON'T--
GAAGHK! WHERE ARE YOU GOING?!
The wasteland was still and silent for a moment, as the Chieftess gasped for breath.
And then there came a sound that had never been heard before, most especially not by those who made it.
The sound of Wasteland Rangers weeping.
The sound of victory in the Apocalympics.

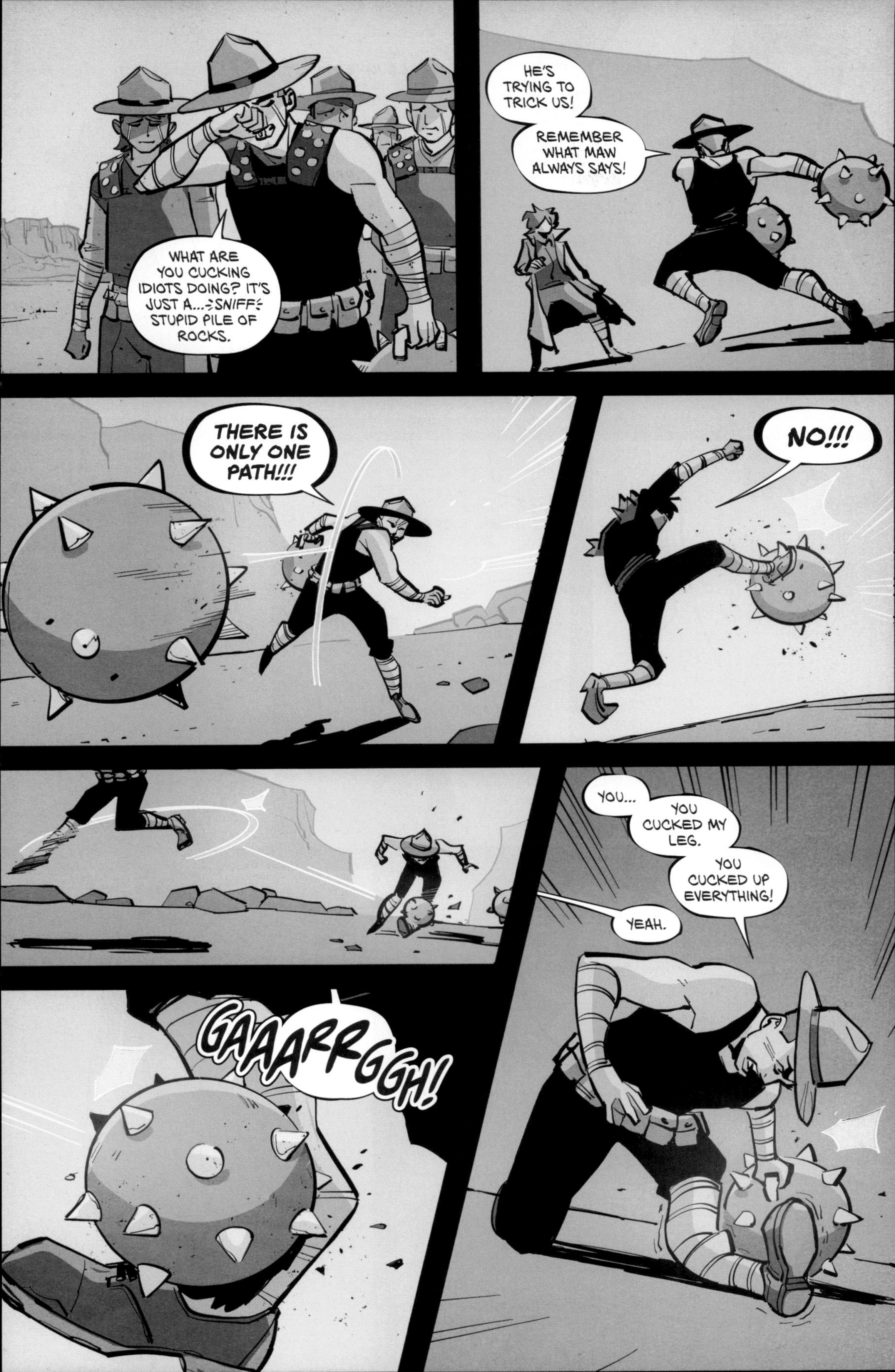
WHAT ARE YOU CUCKING IDIOTS DOING? IT'S JUST A...⊰SNIFF⊱ STUPID PILE OF ROCKS.
HE'S TRYING TO TRICK US!
REMEMBER WHAT MAW ALWAYS SAYS!
THERE IS ONLY ONE PATH!!!
NO!!!
YOU...
YOU CUCKED MY LEG.
YOU CUCKED UP EVERYTHING!
YEAH.
GAAARRGGH!

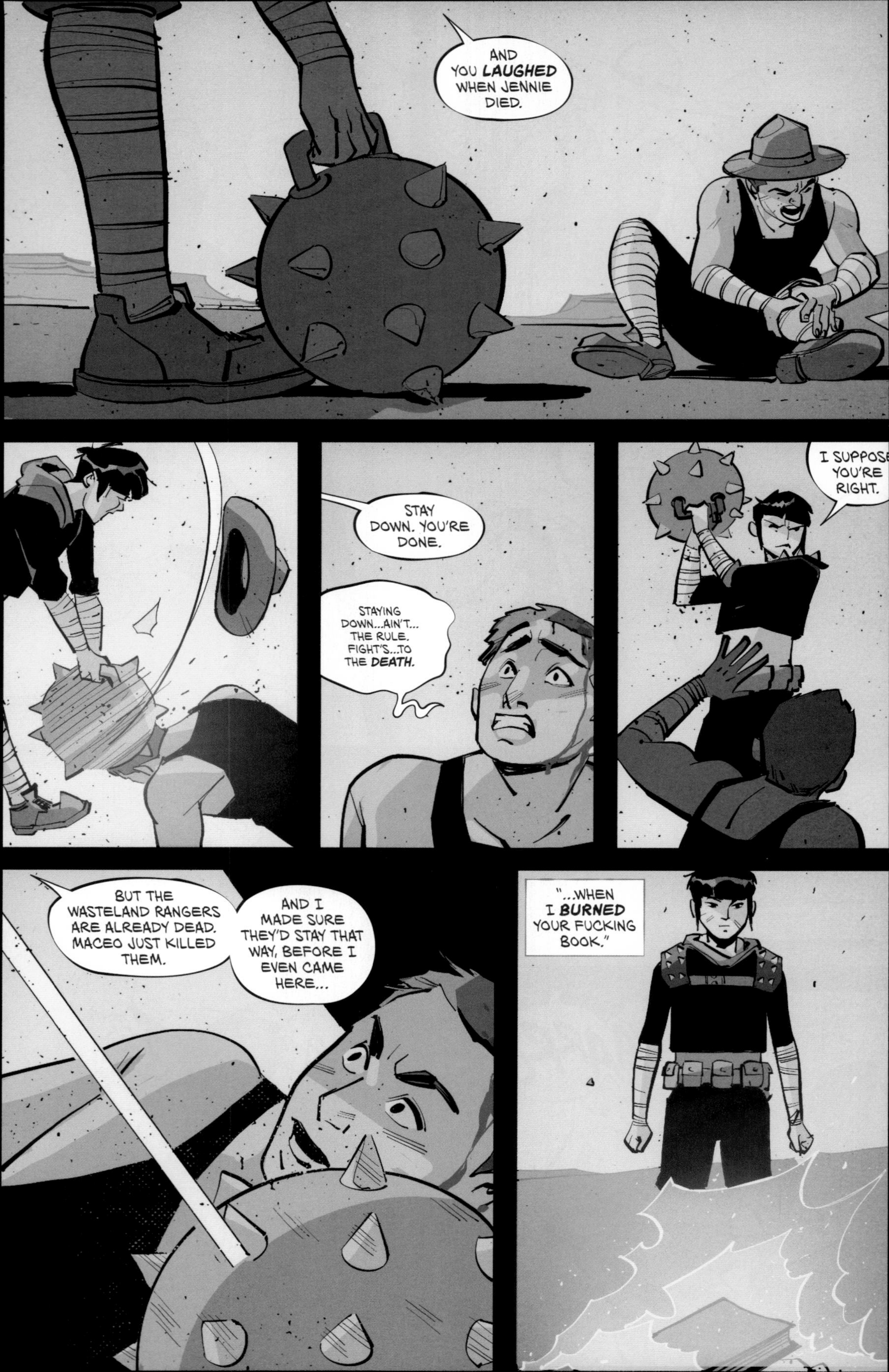
AND YOU **LAUGHED** WHEN JENNIE DIED.
STAY DOWN. YOU'RE DONE.
STAYING DOWN...AIN'T... THE RULE. FIGHT'S...TO THE **DEATH.**
I SUPPOSE YOU'RE RIGHT.
BUT THE WASTELAND RANGERS ARE ALREADY DEAD. MACEO JUST KILLED THEM.
AND I MADE SURE THEY'D STAY THAT WAY, BEFORE I EVEN CAME HERE...
"...WHEN I **BURNED** YOUR FUCKING BOOK."

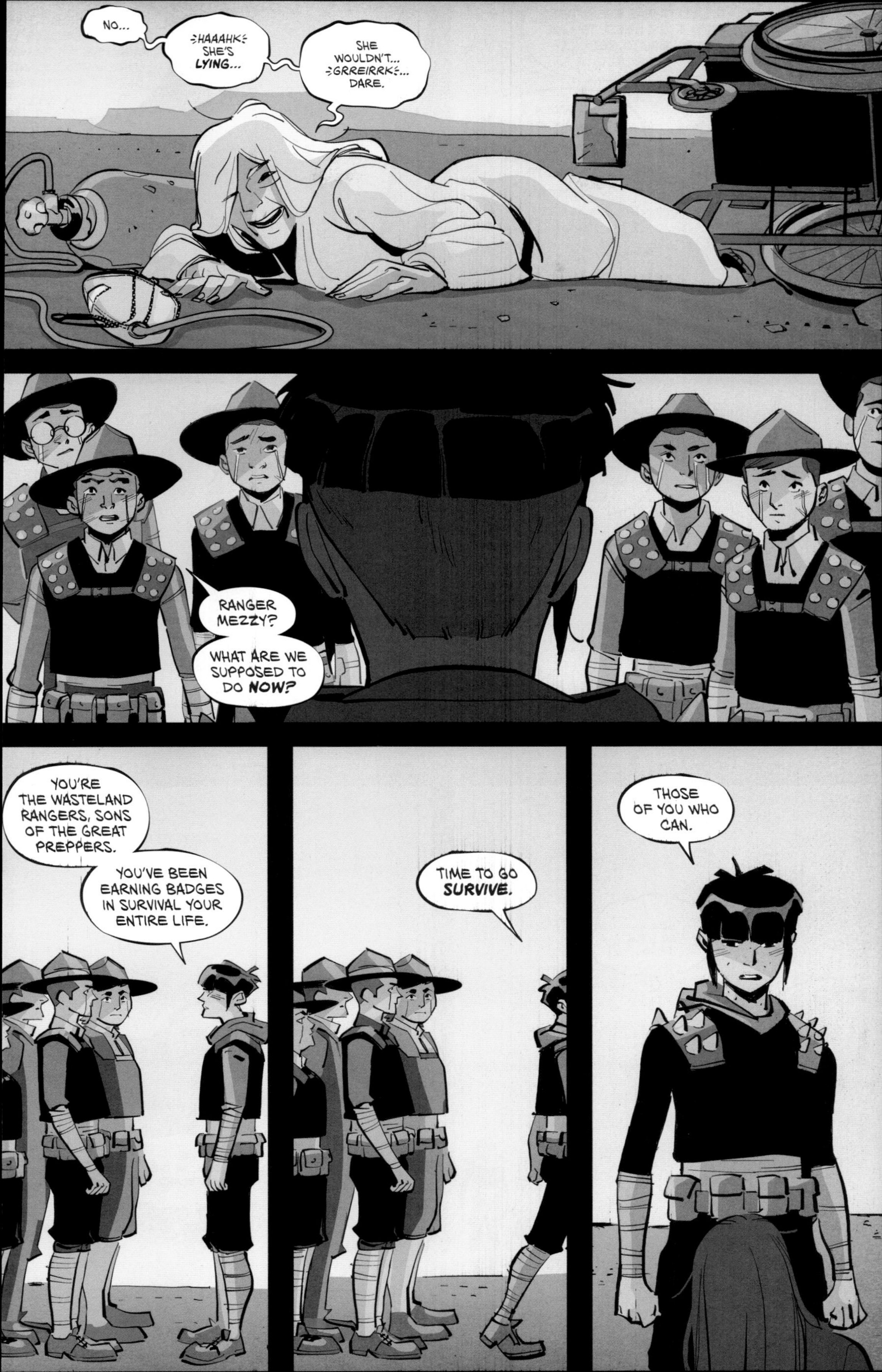
NO...
≶HAAAHK≶ SHE'S LYING...
SHE WOULDN'T... ≶GRREIRRK≶... DARE.
RANGER MEZZY?
WHAT ARE WE SUPPOSED TO DO NOW?
YOU'RE THE WASTELAND RANGERS, SONS OF THE GREAT PREPPERS.
YOU'VE BEEN EARNING BADGES IN SURVIVAL YOUR ENTIRE LIFE.
TIME TO GO SURVIVE.
THOSE OF YOU WHO CAN.

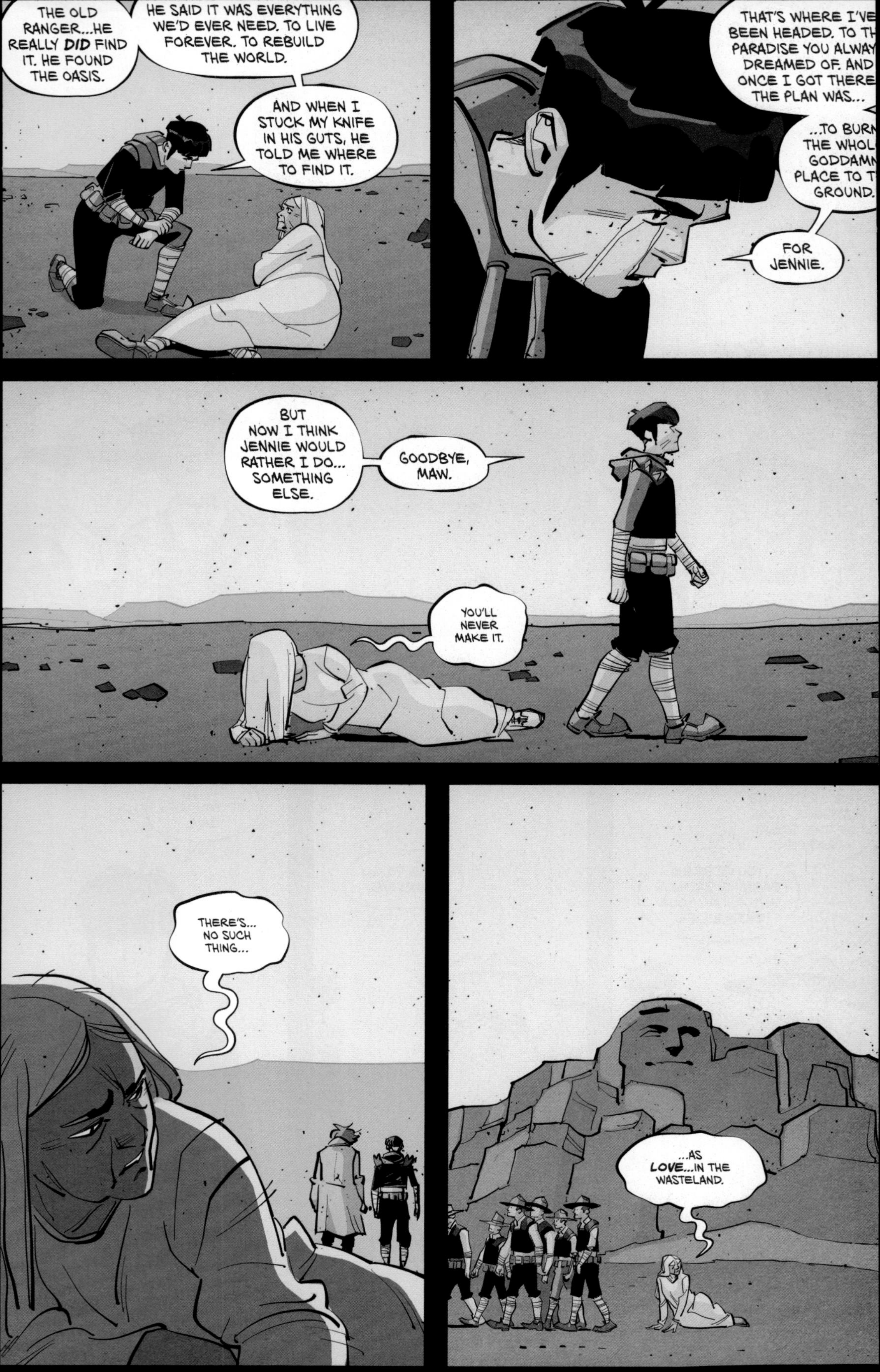
THE OLD RANGER...HE REALLY **DID** FIND IT. HE FOUND THE OASIS.
HE SAID IT WAS EVERYTHING WE'D EVER NEED. TO LIVE FOREVER. TO REBUILD THE WORLD.
AND WHEN I STUCK MY KNIFE IN HIS GUTS, HE TOLD ME WHERE TO FIND IT.
THAT'S WHERE I'VE BEEN HEADED. TO TH PARADISE YOU ALWAY DREAMED OF. AND ONCE I GOT THERE THE PLAN WAS...
...TO BURN THE WHOL GODDAMN PLACE TO T GROUND.
FOR JENNIE.
BUT NOW I THINK JENNIE WOULD RATHER I DO... SOMETHING ELSE.
GOODBYE, MAW.
YOU'LL NEVER MAKE IT.
THERE'S... NO SUCH THING...
...AS **LOVE**...IN THE WASTELAND.

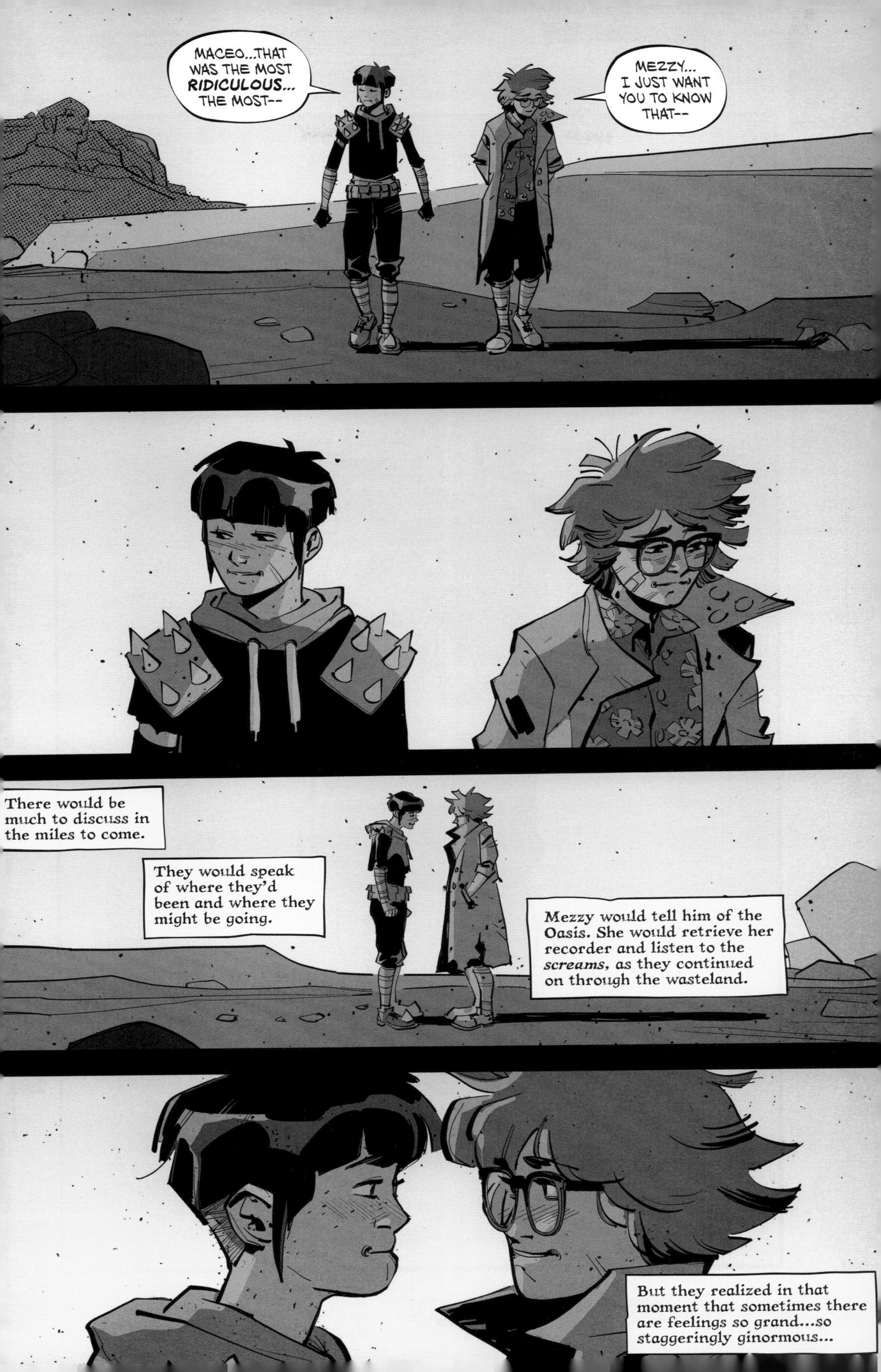
MACEO...THAT WAS THE MOST **RIDICULOUS...** THE MOST--
MEZZY... I JUST WANT YOU TO KNOW THAT--
There would be much to discuss in the miles to come.
They would speak of where they'd been and where they might be going.
Mezzy would tell him of the Oasis. She would retrieve her recorder and listen to the *screams,* as they continued on through the wasteland.
But they realized in that moment that sometimes there are feelings so grand...so staggeringly ginormous...

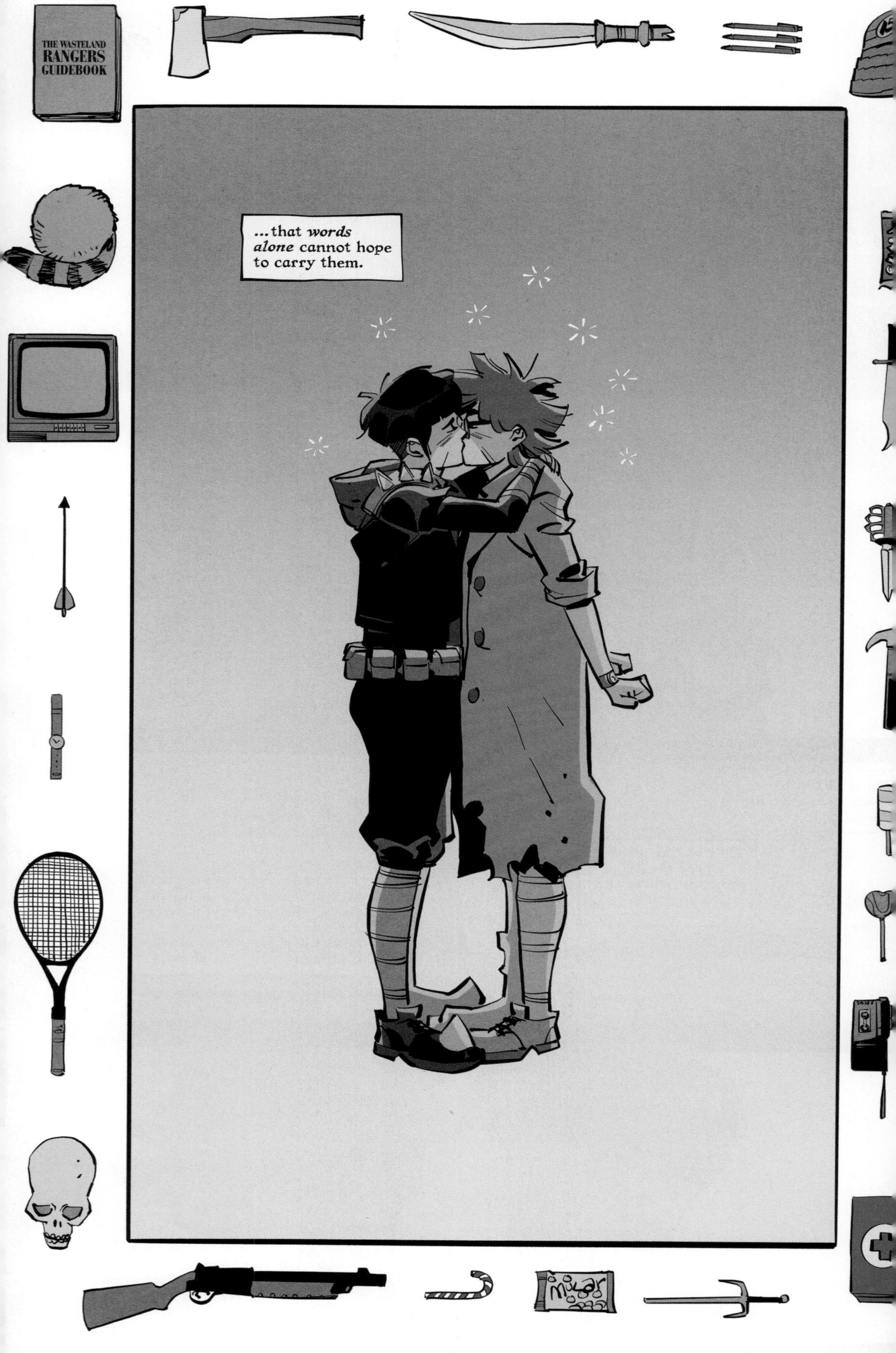
THE WASTELAND RANGERS GUIDEBOOK
...that *words alone* cannot hope to carry them.

AAEEEIIRRGGH!

MY *MACHINE*... WHO TOLD YOU ABOUT IT?

EIRRRGGH!

AND WHAT IS IT YOU THINK YOU'RE GONNA *DO* WITH IT?

HEH! WE KNOW ALL ABOUT MACEO, DESTROYER OF RANGERS!

BUILDER OF *GOLGONOOZA*, CITY OF MANY LOVE!

QVRT

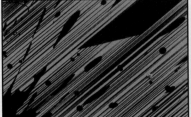

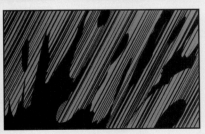

YOUR *MACHINE*...

YOUR *ENGINE*...

...WILL BE USE FOR MOST GREATEST PURPOSE.

HA HA

HA HA HA

KILLING.

KILLING WHOLE FUCKED *WORLD*.

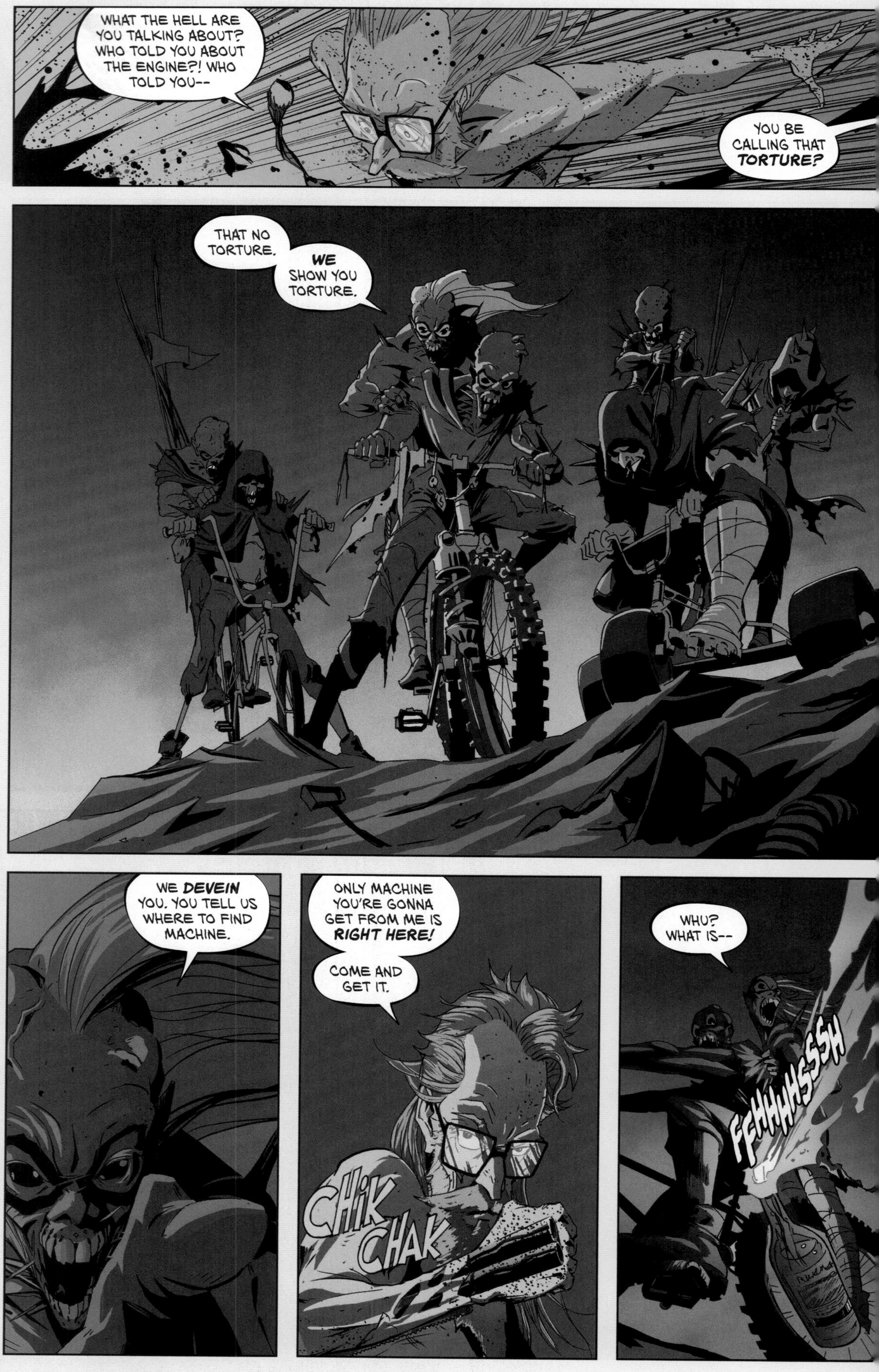

WHAT THE HELL ARE YOU TALKING ABOUT? WHO TOLD YOU ABOUT THE ENGINE?! WHO TOLD YOU--
YOU BE CALLING THAT TORTURE?
THAT NO TORTURE.
WE SHOW YOU TORTURE.
WE DEVEIN YOU. YOU TELL US WHERE TO FIND MACHINE.
ONLY MACHINE YOU'RE GONNA GET FROM ME IS RIGHT HERE!
COME AND GET IT.
CHIK CHAK
WHU? WHAT IS--
FFHHWHSSSH

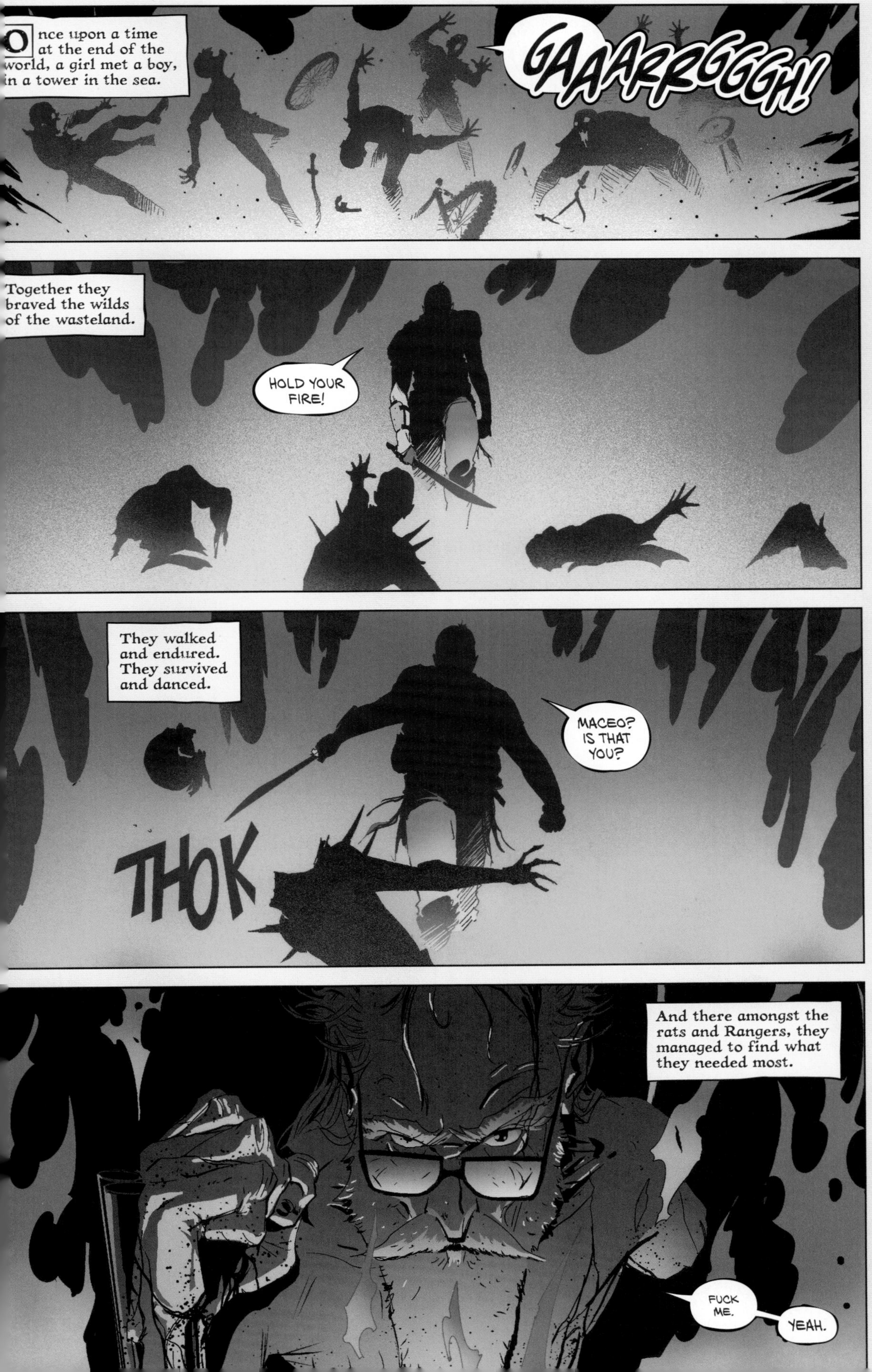
Once upon a time at the end of the world, a girl met a boy, in a tower in the sea.
GAAARRGGGH!
Together they braved the wilds of the wasteland.
HOLD YOUR FIRE!
They walked and endured. They survived and danced.
MACEO? IS THAT YOU?
THOK
And there amongst the rats and Rangers, they managed to find what they needed most.
FUCK ME.
YEAH.

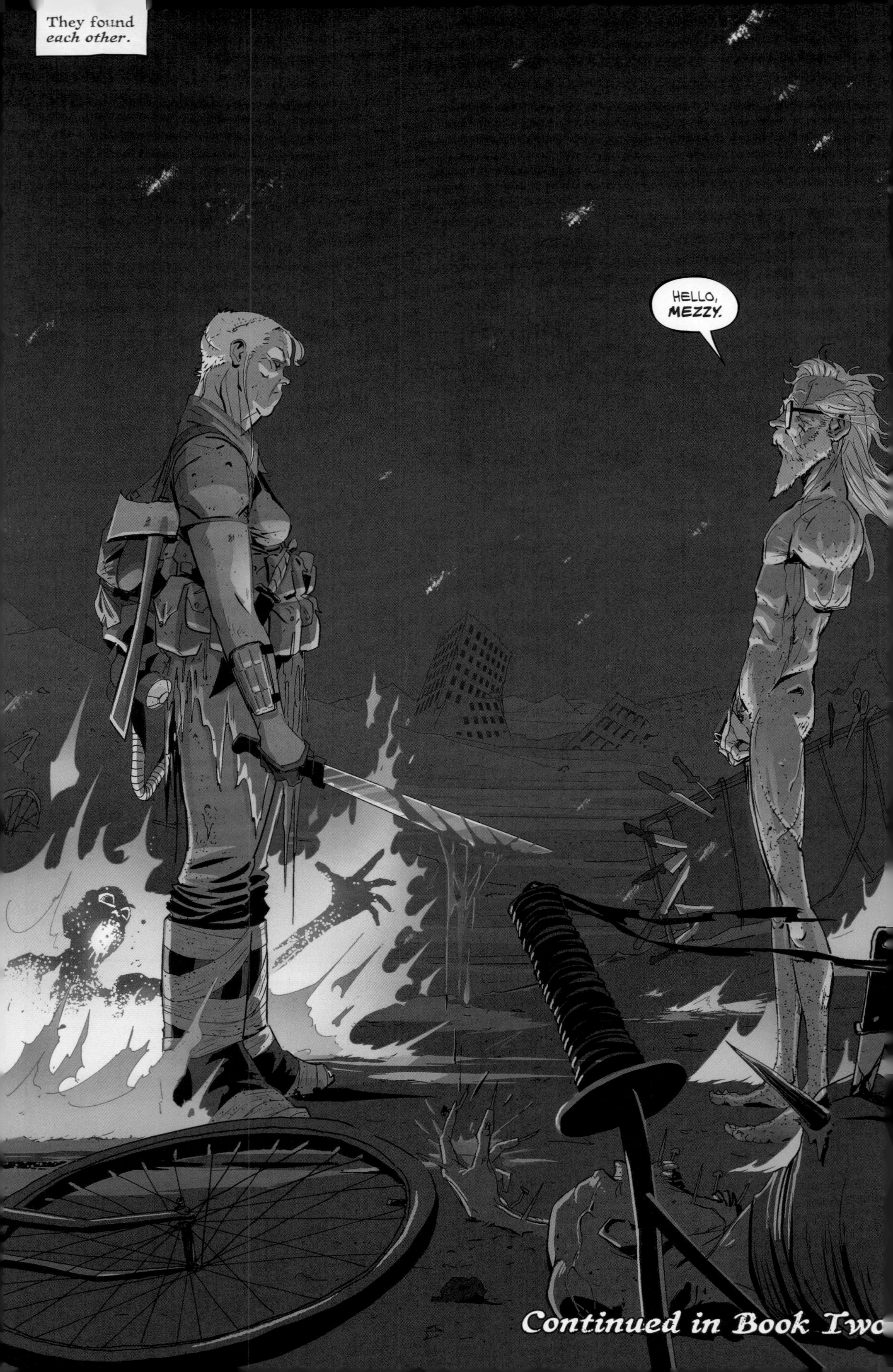
They found each other.
HELLO, MEZZY.
Continued in Book Two

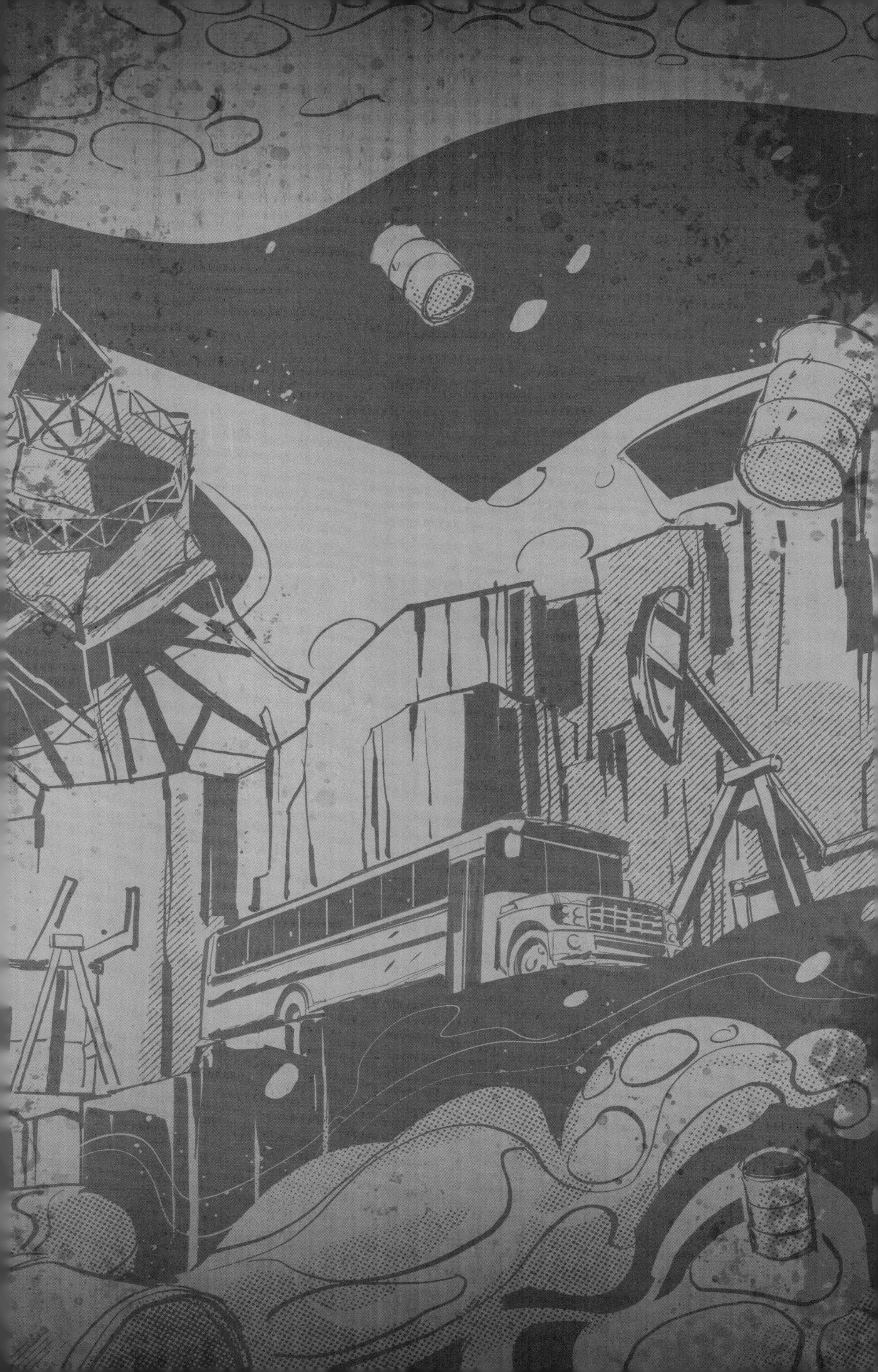

SCRIPT TO PAGE *Chapter Three, pages 2 -3*

TWO PAGE SPLASH:

2.1   Later, in another location. Maceo and Mezzy are small figures walking through a ruined landscape. This was once a stretch of road. But we can't see the roadway anymore. The ground is covered with thorns and briars. But we still see the rusted remains of cars scattered here and there, a trail of them, leading toward the horizon. Their tires are all gone, long since disintegrated or stolen for firewood. Their glass is long since smashed and crumbled away as well. They're just empty metal husks now. Like giant insect exoskeletons that have been molted away and left behind.

NARRATION:	They slept in ditches and dead trees.
NARRATION:	Upon snow and smoldering embers.
NARRATION:	In the rusted cars that covered the landscape like the leavings of some great, forgotten insect swarm…
NARRATION:	…husks sloughed off when they grew wings and took flight…
NARRATION:	…headed for better worlds.
NARRATION:	They slept in fits and starts. Ate whatever they could find that wouldn't leave them too sick to stand upright.
NARRATION:	And then they walked some more.

SCRIPT TO PAGE *Chapter Three, pages 4-5*

WO PAGE SPREAD, FOUR PANELS:

.1   Later, in another location. Maceo and Mezzy are looking out at a stretch of ground before them
hat has sprung leaks. The land is spewing hot oil into the air in huge gushing geysers. Steaming hot.
nough to melt their flesh right off their bones.

EZZY: We'll have to go around.

.2   Maceo is using a big wonky looking glass to peer into the distance along the sides of this stretch
f seemingly uncrossable hot-death-oil-field. Mezzy is already turning away, knowing they'll find another
ay.

MACEO: I mean, we could I guess, but it looks like it's all a buncha big rocks on either side.
MACEO: And I don't know, I don't think we really have to. I mean, I've got balloons.
MEZZY: Maceo, I thought I told you to stop being an idiot.
MEZZY: Those geysers are boiling hot. How would some balloons possibly keep us from dying horribly?

.3   Moments later, they're crossing through the geysers together. Maceo has blown up a bunch of
alloons, holding their strings in his hand. On top of the balloons are umbrellas, blocking the hot oil.
t's still burning through and dripping in places. But it's enough to keep them safe long enough to get
cross. Mezzy is looking up at this mess of balloons and umbrellas, begrudgingly impressed by it.

MEZZY: Huh. I'll be damned.
MACEO: Right? Not bad, right?
MEZZY: Yeah, Maceo.

.4   They walk on together, under their ridiculous cover of balloons and umbrellas, enjoying a lovely
troll together, despite the black rain of hot death all around them.

MEZZY: Not bad.
NARRATION: A lovely stroll on a rainy day.

SCRIPT TO PAGE *Chapter Three, pages 6-7*

TWO PAGE SPREAD, FIVE PANELS:

6.1   Later, in another location. The land is all low, rolling hills, without a single tree or bush to be seen, and it seems to go on and on forever. Anything that was once there has been long since burned away. The ground is scorched and blackened. Black smoke burps from holes in the land here and there, holes that glow with red embers, of fires still churning deep below. It's night. Maceo and Mezzy are sitting atop one of these low hills, in the midst of this sea of ruin, with light coming from their TV as they're watching cartoons together.

NARRATION: In the burnt plains that went on and on, past the limits of man's sight and sanity…
NARRATION: …they watched cartoons.

6.2   Tighter on them, watching cartoons. This is the same TV set Maceo used last issue. And the same cartoon. Now the TV is hooked to a cage and a hamster wheel, being powered by some rats that are running frantically. The kids are lost in the cartoon, seemingly oblivious to their surroundings, to their circumstances, lost in a moment of joy.

NARRATION: On a rat-powered television.
NARRATION: It was the 17th time they'd seen this cartoon together. But the one time they would never forget.
MEZZY: Heh.

6.3   Tight on Mezzy, suddenly and unexpectedly erupting with laughter.
MEZZY: Ha haa ha!

6.4   Mezzy touches her face, in shock and fear. What the hell was that? She's never laughed before and never heard it done. She's worried there's something wrong with her.
MEZZY: What was that?
MEZZY: That noise I just made?
MEZZY: Something's fucking wrong with me.

6.5   Tight on Maceo, beaming proudly, happy as can be, falling for her more and more with every passing day.

SCRIPT TO PAGE *Chapter Three, pages 8-9*

TWO PAGE SPREAD, FOUR PANELS:

3.1   Later, in another location. Maceo and Mezzy are walking through a long dark tunnel. She carries a burning torch. He holds a flashlight. Something drips from above them. The ground is covered with bones and rotting bodies and all sorts of bugs, things we only glimpse in the shadowy darkness. Our kids move forward cautiously.

NARRATION: Inside a two-mile tunnel where the ceiling dripped blood for some reason they did not linger long enough to decipher…
NARRATION: …she taught him how to listen for holes, how to smell exposed fangs… how to see a tick waiting in deepest shadow.

3.2   Later, in another location. They're camping for the night atop a wrecked train. Derailed, toppled onto its side, coiled like an old dead snake. And Maceo is showing Mezzy his dance moves. She watches, laughing even more. Maceo is no doubt a terrible dancer. But he dances with such enthusiasm and profound joy that you'd think he was the greatest dancer alive. And who knows, at this point, maybe he is.

NARRATION: He showed her how to dance.

3.3   Later, in another location. They're walking through the remains of an old battlefield. Trenches, barbed wire, unexploded bombs sticking out of the dirt, a tank half-buried in the mud, a downed fighter jet. Rain is falling. The ground is wet and muddy, pockmarked with puddles, some of them glowing green with radiation. Of course Maceo loves to splash in rainy puddles, like a kid would do, but she's warning him to stay away from the puddles that glow.

NARRATION: The more they walked, the more Mezzy showed Maceo how to survive.
MEZZY: Don't splash in the puddles that are glowing.
MACEO: Okay, Mezzy.

3.4   Later, in another location. They're crossing a dry riverbed, of what was once a massive river. There's a tugboat stuck in the dirt.

CHARACTER DESIGNS BY
ALEXANDRE TEFENKG

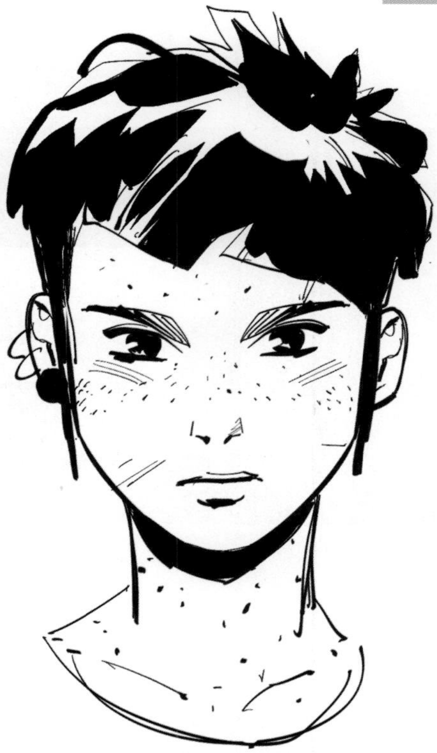

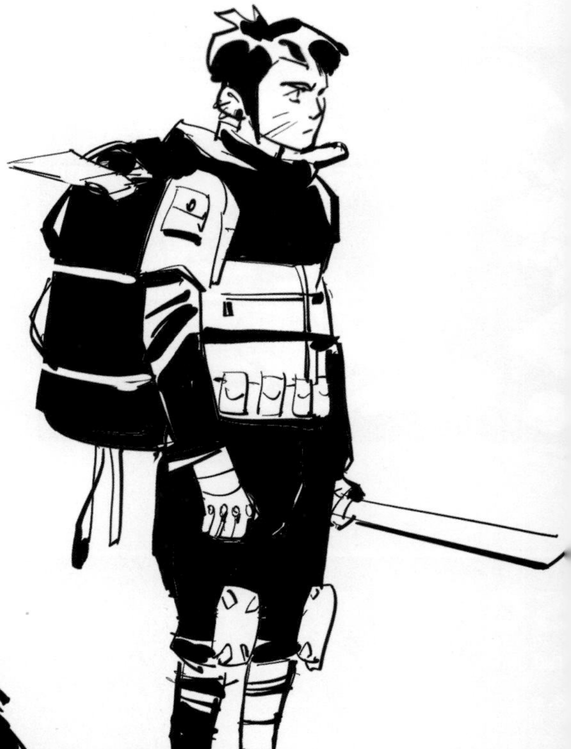

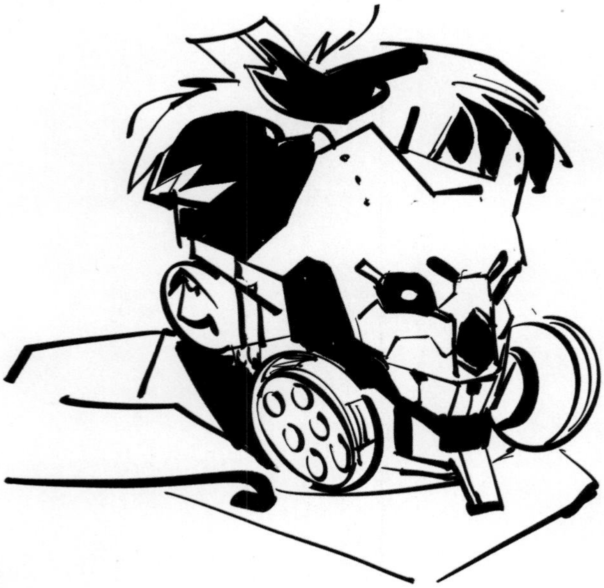

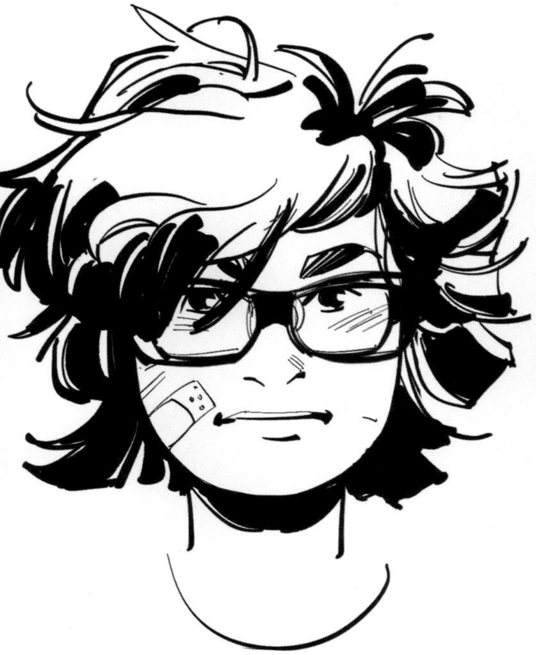
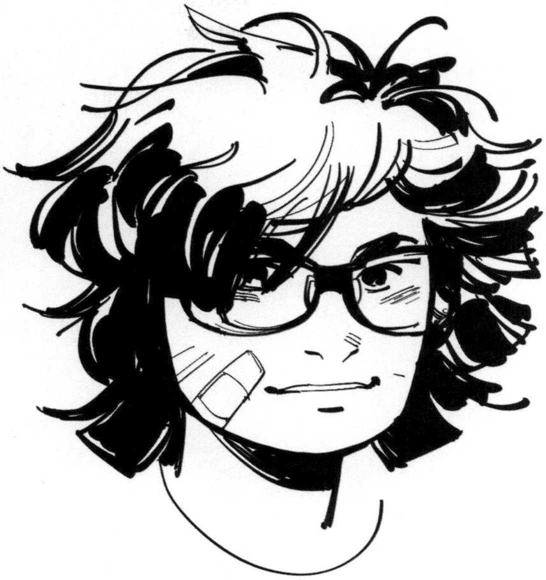
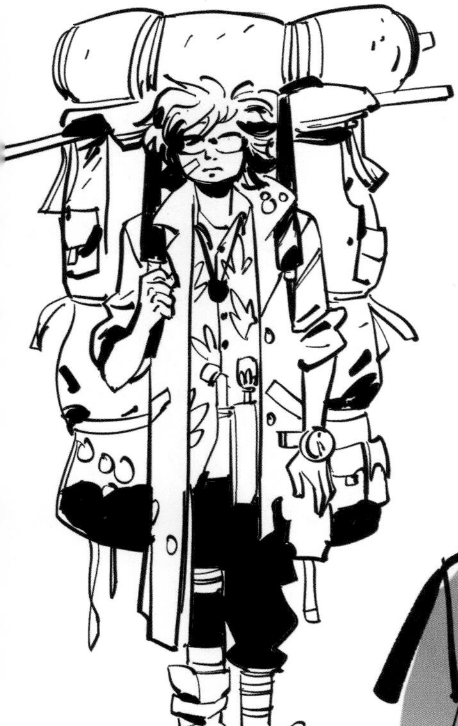
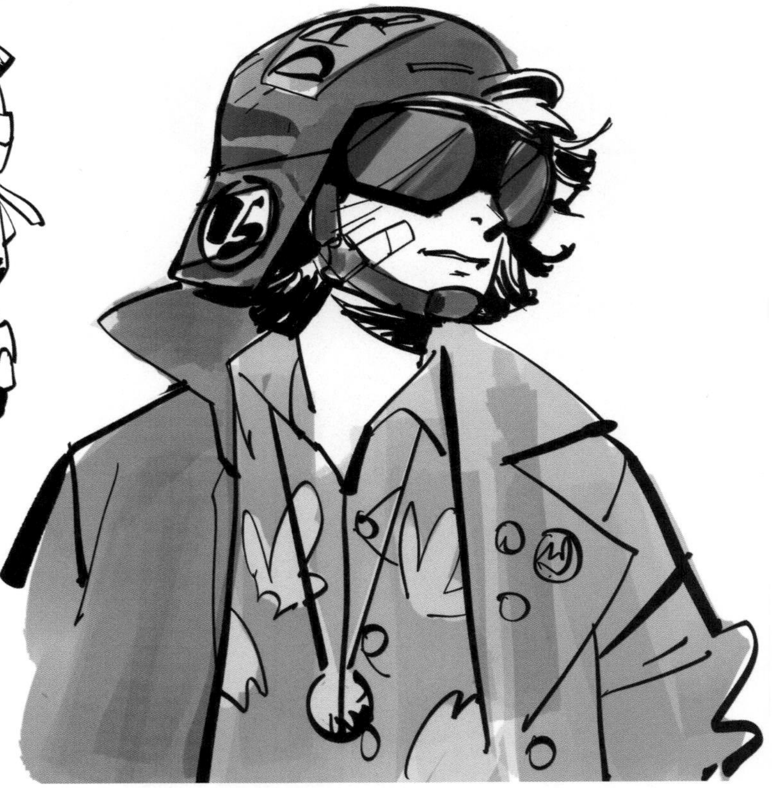

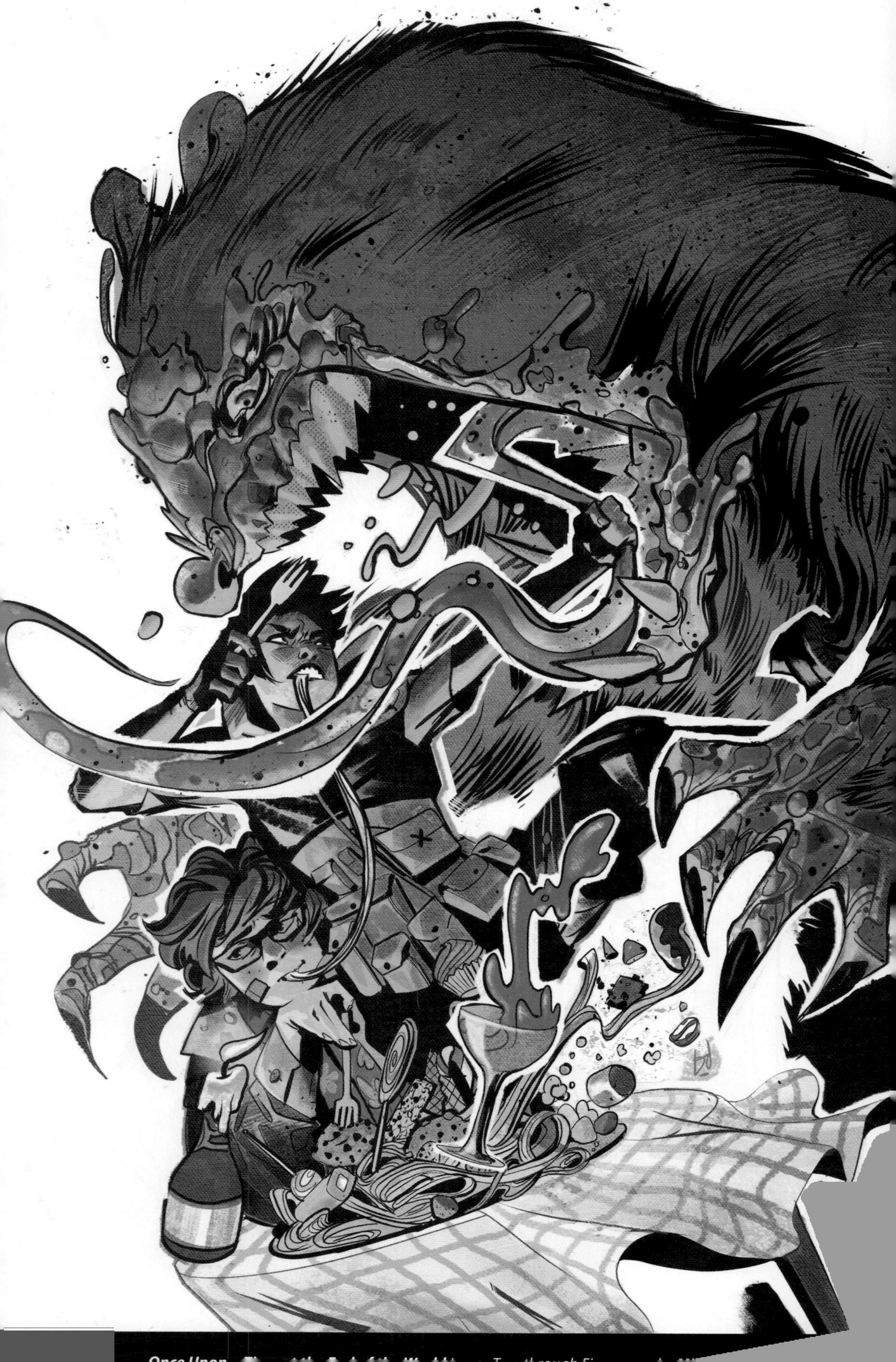

Once Upon

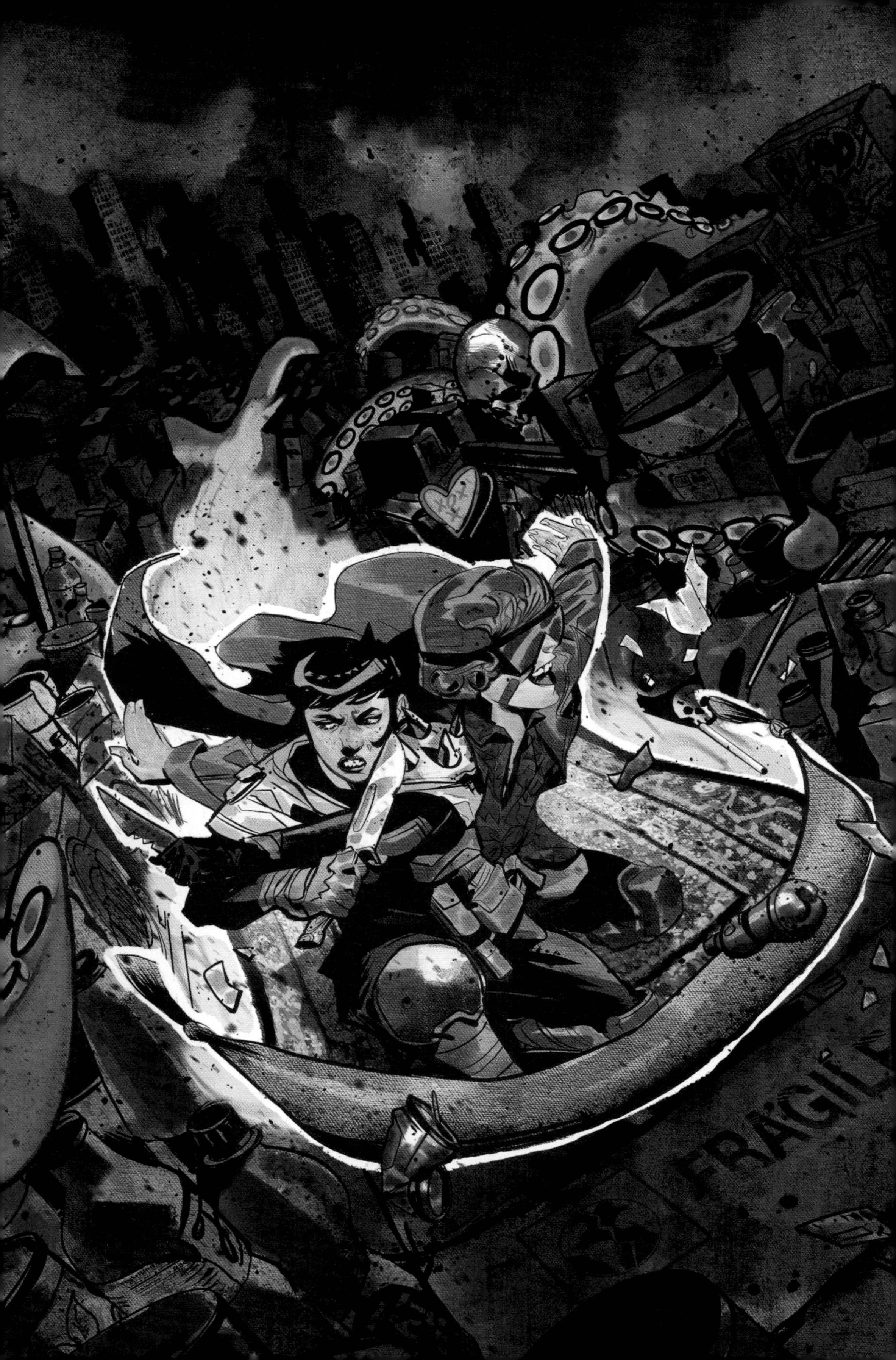
FRAGIL

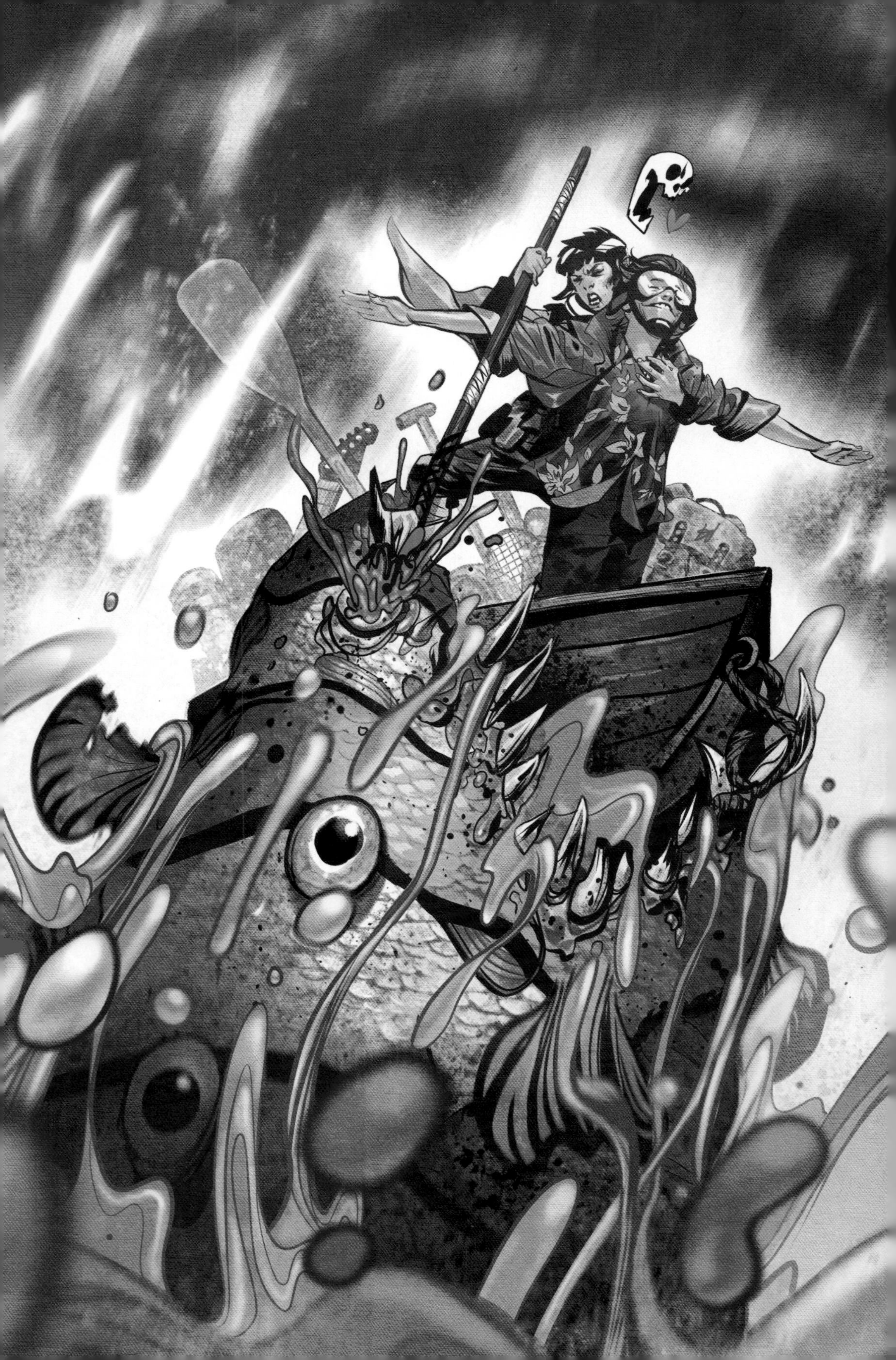

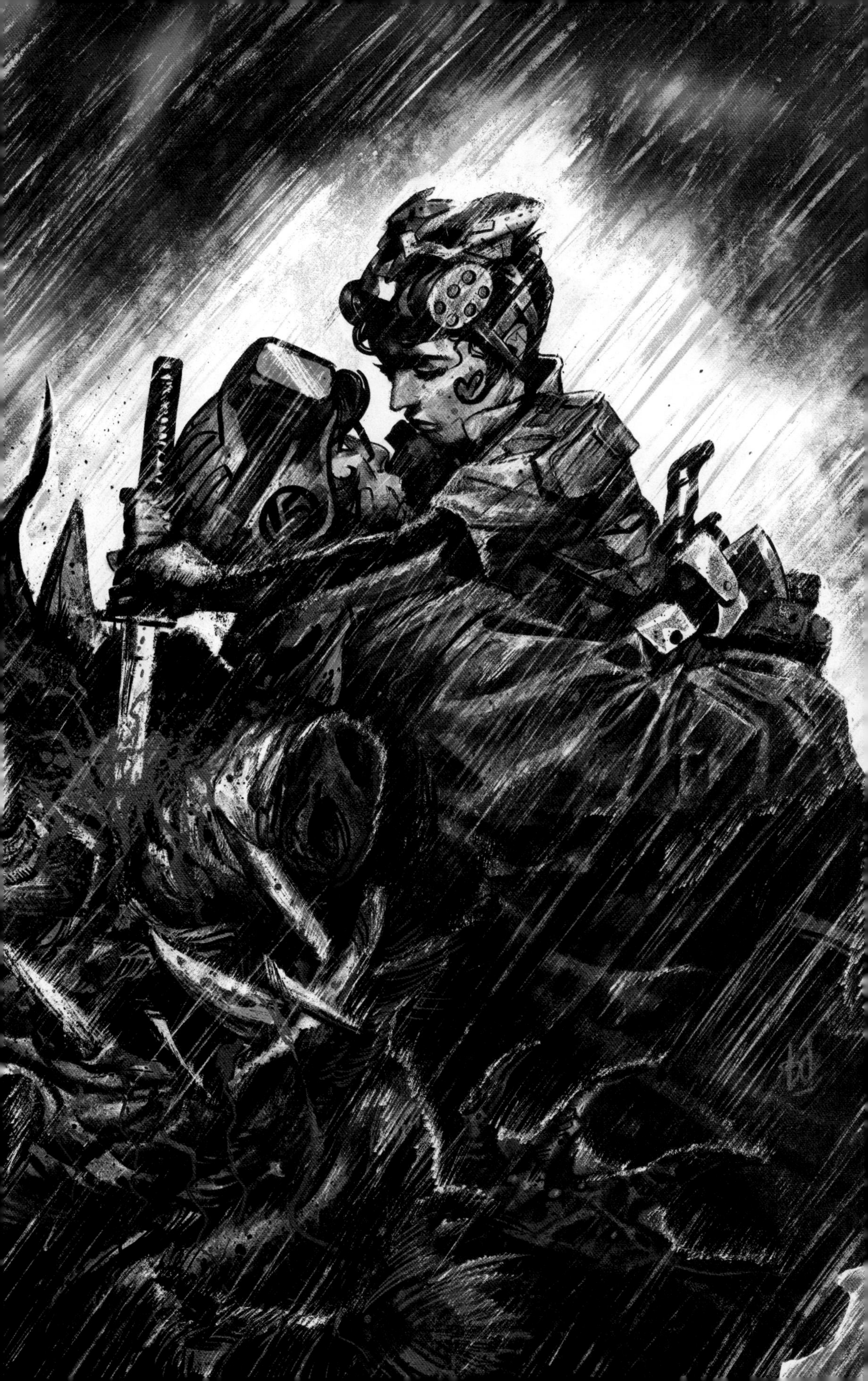

ABOUT THE CREATORS

Jason Aaron is an award-winning comic book writer best known for his work with Marvel Comics, including a landmark seven-year run on *Thor* that introduced Jane Foster as the hammer-wielding Mighty Thor. He's also had celebrated stints writing *Wolverine, Doctor Strange, Ghost Rider, Conan* and the 2015 Marvel relaunch of *Star Wars* that was the best-selling American comic book in more than 20 years. Aaron is the current writer on Marvel's flagship *Avengers* book and its spinoff, *Avengers Forever*, along with a brand-new, character-defining *Punisher* series. His critically acclaimed creator-owned work includes the Eisner and Harvey Award-winning *Southern Bastards* from Image Comics and the *New York Times* bestselling crime series *Scalped* from Vertigo Comics. Aaron was born and raised in Alabama and currently resides in Kansas City.

Alexandre Tefenkgi is an award-winning comic book artist and the visual creator of *The Good Asian* and *Outpost Zero*. Since his first book in 2009 in France, his work has been published and awarded in multiple countries. He specializes in character-driven stories and emotional poetry. His craft is devoted to expressing the complexity of human relationships.

Lee Loughridge is a human man who has been working primarily in the comics industry for well over 20 years. He has worked on hundreds of titles for virtually every company in the business. You can check out a list of his works at comics.org.

Nick Dragotta is a writer and artist. Dragotta co-created the Eisner Award-nominated series *East of West* with Jonathan Hickman at Image Comics after working together on highly acclaimed runs of *The Fantastic Four* at Marvel Entertainment. Dragotta also worked on various iconic Marvel and DC characters such as *Captain America, Spider-Man, the X-Men, X-Statix, Batman,* and *Superman*. His latest book is *Ghost Cage,* which he co-wrote and illustrated for Image Comics.

Rico Renzi is an artist, colorist, and designer from Washington, DC. His work has appeared in the Academy Award-winning *Spider-Man: Into The Spider-Verse* and Marvel Comics series like *Spider-Gwen, She-Hulk, Unbeatable Squirrel Girl* and many more. He currently resides in Charlotte, North Carolina with his wife and daughter, who tolerate his foolishness.

AndWorld Design is the design and production studio founded by veteran letterer Deron Bennett. The comic-based company's extensive list of clients includes BOOM!, Z2, Image, Dark Horse, Vault, IDW, Oni Press, AHOY, and DC Comics. They also produce typesetting, cover design, and illustration for Amazon Publishing. You can see their work on such acclaimed titles as *Something is Killing the Children, The Many Deaths of Laila Starr,* and *The Nice House on the Lake.* AndWorld's team of artists have garnered multiple Harvey, Ringo, and Eisner nominations.